THE COMPLETE GUIDE TO
MEDIATION
HOW TO EFFECTIVELY REPRESENT YOUR CLIENTS AND EXPAND YOUR FAMILY LAW PRACTICE
SECOND EDITION

THE COMPLETE GUIDE TO MEDIATION

HOW TO EFFECTIVELY REPRESENT YOUR CLIENTS AND EXPAND YOUR FAMILY LAW PRACTICE

SECOND EDITION

FORREST S. MOSTEN
ELIZABETH POTTER SCULLY

Cover design by Tamara Kowalski/ABA Publishing.

The materials contained herein represent the opinions of the authors and/or the editors, and should not be construed to be the views or opinions of the law firms or companies with whom such persons are in partnership with, associated with, or employed by, nor of the American Bar Association or the Family Law Section unless adopted pursuant to the bylaws of the Association.

Nothing contained in this book is to be considered as the rendering of legal advice for specific cases, and readers are responsible for obtaining such advice from their own legal counsel. This book is intended for educational and informational purposes only.

© 2015 American Bar Association. All rights reserved.

No part of this publication may be reproduced, stored in a retrieval system, or transmitted in any form or by any means, electronic, mechanical, photocopying, recording, or otherwise, without the prior written permission of the publisher. For permission contact the ABA Copyrights & Contracts Department, copyright@americanbar.org, or complete the online form at http://www.americanbar.org/utility/reprint.html.

Printed in the United States of America.

19 18 17 16 15   5 4 3 2 1

Library of Congress Cataloging-in-Publication Data

Mosten, Forrest S., 1947-
  The complete guide to mediation : how to effectively represent your client and expand your family law practice / Forrest S. Mosten and Elizabeth Potter Scully. -- 2nd edition.
       pages cm
  Includes bibliographical references and index.
  ISBN 978-1-63425-010-8 (softcover : alk. paper) -- ISBN 978-1-63425-011-5 (e-book)
 1. Family mediation--United States. 2. Domestic relations--United States. 3. Attorney and client--United States. I. Scully, Elizabeth Potter, author. II. Title.
  KF505.5.M675 2015
  346.7301'5--dc23   2015011904

Discounts are available for books ordered in bulk. Special consideration is given to state bars, CLE programs, and other bar-related organizations. Inquire at Book Publishing, ABA Publishing, American Bar Association, 321 N. Clark Street, Chicago, Illinois 60654-7598.

www.ShopABA.org

This book is dedicated to the memory of my younger sister, Margo Hudson Parker (1950–2014), who was the true peacemaker in our family. And to the memory of Louis M. Brown (1909–1996), Father of Preventive Law, who was my mentor, colleague, and close friend and whose care for the people we serve has inspired and enriched our profession.

—Forrest (Woody) Mosten

For my son, Benjamin Tilden Scully, who is my pride and joy, and for my grandmother, Hadassah Wagman Heins, who never loses hope.

—Elizabeth Potter Scully

Section of Family Law Publications Development Board

Hon. Gail D. Baker and Steven N. Peskind, Co-Chairs
Allen M. Bailey
Joseph Booth
Alan Boudreau
Sara Busche
Hon. Edward H. Newman
Linda Ravdin
Lynne A. Ustach

Contents

About the Authors   xvi

Foreword   xvii

Acknowledgments   xix

Eleven Questions Most Commonly Asked About Representing Clients in Mediation   xxiii

Chapter 1	**Expanding Your Practice by Representing Clients in Mediation**	1
	Consumerism	2
	Growth of the Pro Se Movement	5
	Nonlawyer Providers	7
	Fear of Discontented Clients	7
	Lawyer Bashing, Stress of Law Practice, Resultant Lawyer Malaise	8
	Economic Pressures of Operating a Family Law Practice	9
	Lawyer Benefits of Mediation	11
	Family Lawyers Retain or Increase Their Share of the Divorce Market	11
	Mediation Increases Profits	12
	Higher Collection Rates and Lower Malpractice Exposure	13
	Control	13
	Better Lives for Lawyers	15
	Notes	16
Chapter 2	**Family Lawyer as Dispute Resolution Manager**	19
	Dispute Resolution Manager as Lawyer of Record	20

	Ethical Duty to Advise About ADR	20
	Rules of Professional Responsibility	20
	Voluntary ADR Pledges	24
	Malpractice Exposure	25
	How to Advise Clients Properly About Alternatives to Litigation	27
	1. Explain to Client the Purpose of This Portion of the Consultation (Learn Options to Litigation to Have Full Information Before Making a Decision and Certainly Before Filing a Lawsuit)	28
	2. Explain Litigation—Benefits and Mythology	28
	3. Explain the Existence of Options (Within and Outside Courthouse)	29
	4. Explain Options—Benefits and Downsides	30
	5. Compare and Contrast Options with Litigation and with Each Other Using the Following Factors	31
	ADR Pledge of the Beverly Hills Bar Association	33
	Practice Tips	33
	Notes	33
Chapter 3	**Mediation Confidentiality**	35
	A Core Principle	35
	Confidentiality: A Key Benefit	36
	Sources of Confidentiality Rules	38
	Conflicting Public Policies	39
	Exceptions to Mediation Confidentiality	40
	Settlement Agreements	40
	Practice Tips	41
	Notes	43
Chapter 4	**Representing Clients in Court-Ordered Mediation**	47
	Court-Annexed Mediation	48
	Are Mandatory Mediation Proceedings Confidential?	48
	When Does Court-Annexed Mediation Take Place?	49
	Who Participates in Court-Annexed Mediation?	49
	Do the Parties Meet Individually or Together?	50
	How Are Mediated Agreements Finalized?	50
	What Happens If a Party Refuses to Participate?	51
	What Issues Are Covered by Court-Annexed Mediation?	52

	Mediation by Court Referral	52
	Malpractice Protection for Court Mediators	53
	The Role of Lawyers in Court Mediation	54
	Mandatory Settlement Conferences	55
	Is the MSC Judge the Trial Judge?	56
	Mediation Versus Mandatory Settlement Conferences	57
	Practice Tips	58
	Notes	59
Chapter 5	**Using a Limited Scope Approach (Unbundling) to Represent Clients Outside and Inside the Mediation Room**	**61**
	Unbundling: Rethinking How to Package and Deliver Legal Services	62
	The Traditional Full-Service Package	62
	Unbundling Defined	63
	Attorney Coach: Educator and Adviser	64
	General Conflict Management Client Coaching	67
	Coach or First Class?	68
	Negotiation Coach	69
	Court Coach	72
	Fear of Malpractice as a Barrier to Unbundling	72
	Notice of Limited Scope Role	73
	Using an Unbundled Approach Outside the Mediation Room	74
	Using an Unbundled Approach in the Mediation Room	76
	Practice Tips	78
	Notes	78
Chapter 6	**Representing Clients in Mediation with a Collaborative Lawyering Approach**	**81**
	Collaborative Lawyering	81
	Why You Will Get More Work by Offering a Collaborative Approach	83
	How to Use a Disqualification Agreement in Your Mediation Representation Work	83
	Mediation Disqualification Agreement	88
	Use of Other Collaborative Professionals in Mediation	89
	Practice Tips	94
	Notes	95

Chapter 7	**Setting Up the Mediation**	97
	Selecting the Mediator	97
	Letting the Other Spouse/Counsel Nominate a Mediator	99
	The Mediator Nominating Process	100
	Designing the Process	101
	Preliminary Private Planning (PPP) Sessions	106
	Mediation Briefs	108
	Costs of the Mediation	109
	Who Pays the Mediator?	109
	Methods of Payment	110
	The Site of the Mediation	111
	Food and Drink: Agents of Collaboration	112
	Practice Tips	113
	Notes	114
Chapter 8	**Building an Agreement Your Client Can Live With**	115
	Adviser and Coach	116
	Educating and Advising on the Client's Legal Position	117
	Compiling the Client's Financial Information and Assessing Needs	117
	Obtaining the Documents Needed to Make an Informed Decision	118
	Monitoring the Progress of the Mediation	121
	Lawyers at the Mediation Table	123
	When Lawyers Should Be Present	123
	The Role of Lawyers at the Session	123
	Use of Experts	125
	The Lawyer as Negotiation Coach	126
	Practice Tips	127
	Notes	128
Chapter 9	**Reaching Agreement**	129
	Typical Divorce Agenda	129
	Agreement Readiness	130
	Identify and Acknowledge Initial Positions of the Parties	131
	Encourage Ground Rules	132
	Interest-Based Negotiations	134
	Normalcy and Solvability	137

        Use Professional Articles and Research to Offer
           Commonality 138
    Experiment and Test Solutions 138
    Involvement of Children 138
    Starter Toolbox for Reaching Agreements 139
        Emotional Reframing 140
        Bifurcate Divorce Issues: Salvage Agreements, Plan for
           Contained Litigation 140
    Negotiating with the Mediator 140
    Working with Mediator Proposals 141

Chapter 10 Reviewing and Drafting Mediated Agreements 145
    Review Summary Letters and Have Your Client Prepare a
        Memorandum 147
        Will There Be a Writing? What Is the Product of
           Successful Mediation? 148
        Is the Mediator a Lawyer? 150
    The Level of Review 151
    Drafting the Agreement 153
        Sharing Boilerplate Early 155
        Don't Forget Aspirations 155
        To Sign or Not to Sign? 156
    Practice Tips 158
    Notes 159

Chapter 11 Preventing Future Conflict 163
    Drafting Future Dispute Resolution Clauses 163
        Written Notice of Dispute 164
        Parties Meet and Confer 164
        Required Mediation 165
        Confidential Mini-Evaluation (CME) 166
        Formal Evaluation Report 168
        Binding Adjudication 168
        Preventive Mediation 171
        Preventive Legal Wellness Checkups 173
    Practice Tips 176
    Notes 177

Chapter 12	**Be a Peacemaker**	**179**
	What Is a Peacemaker?	179
	Foster Mindfulness	180
	Identify Your Core Values	181
	Actively Prevent Future Conflict	184
	Apply Peacemaking to Your Daily Lawyering Work	184
	Get Training in Mediation and Collaborative Law	184
	Collaborate with Peacemaking Lawyers, Mediators, and Other Professionals	185
	Honor Your Colleagues	185
	Contribute to Family Law Organizations	186
	Your Next Steps in Using Peacemaking to Improve and Expand Your Practice	186
	Notes	187
Glossary		**189**
Appendix A	**Model Standards of Practice for Family and Divorce Mediation (2000)**	**197**
	Convening Organizations	197
	Overview and Definitions	197
	Standard I	198
	Standard II	199
	Standard III	199
	Standard IV	200
	Standard V	201
	Standard VI	202
	Standard VII	202
	Standard VIII	203
	Standard IX	204
	Standard X	204
	Standard XI	205
	Standard XII	206
	Standard XIII	206
	Appendix: Special Policy Considerations for State Regulation of Family Mediators and Court Affiliated Programs	206

Appendix B	**Highlights in Divorce Mediation Research**	209
	Who Chooses to Mediate?	209
	The Mediation Process	210
	Outcome and Satisfaction	211
	Effect of Intimate Partner Violence	213
	Impact of the Timing of Mediation	213
	Impact of a Limited Number of Mediation Sessions	213
	Use of Directive Strategies in Session or Outside	214
	Assumptions About Goals of Divorce Lawyers	214
	Long-Range Impact of Mediation and Process Used	214
	Pattern of Couple Interaction After Divorce	214
	Impact on Fee Based Mediation on Relationships of Divorced Spouses	214
	Use of Therapeutic Mediation Model and Couple Relationships	215
	Relationship Between Informality and Supportive Nature of Mediators and Views of Neutrality	215
	Disparity of Attachment Between Spouses and Problem-Solving Behavior	215
	Sources	215
Appendix C	**Key California Mediation Confidentiality Cases**	217
Appendix D	**Phrases for Active Listening and to Prevent Miscommunication**	221
	Phrases for Miscommunication	221
	Phrases for Active Listening	221
Appendix E	**Divorce Mission Statement**	223
Appendix F	**Sample Agreement for Consulting Attorney Services**	227
Appendix G	**Sample Estimate of Consulting Lawyer Fee**	231
Appendix H	**Notice of Limited Scope Representation**	233
Appendix I	**Factors Affecting Appropriateness of Mediation, CollaborativeLaw, and Cooperative Law Procedures**	237
Appendix J	**Client Information About Collaborative Representation**	241

Appendix K	Sample Letter to Client Discussing Risks of Going into Mediation	245
Appendix L	Sample Mediator's Contract	247
Appendix M	Sample Estimate of Mediation Expenses	257
Appendix N	Sample Agenda for Divorce Mediation	261
Appendix O	Sample Client Handout: My Role as Your Collaborative Lawyer	265
Appendix P	Sample Agreement for Attorney Disqualification in Mediation	271
Appendix Q	Sample Dispute Resolution Protocol and Mediation Clause	275
	Mediation Clause	275
	Mediation Clause (Short)	275
	Mediation Clause (Long)	275
Appendix R	Personal Legal Wellness Checkup and Protocol	277
	Sample Personal Legal Checkup Protocol	279
	General Steps Individuals Can Take to Help Keep Their Legal Health in Order	280
	General Steps	281
	Checklists	282
Appendix S	Required Statutory Forms for Financial Disclosure (California)	285
Appendix T	Court Endorsement of ADR (San Mateo County)	297
Appendix U	Letter from Presiding Judge of Family Law Division Endorsing Mediation (English and Spanish)	301
Appendix V	Making Your Office a Classroom for Client Education	305
	Establish a Client Library in Your Office	305
	Show Videos to Clients	306
	Lending Books to Clients	306
Appendix W	Books and Articles	309
	Representing Clients in Mediation	309
	Mediator Concepts and Strategies	310

Mediation Confidentiality	310
Negotiation Concepts and Strategies	310
Limited Scope Representation	311
Collaborative Law	311
Preventive Law	312
Peacemaking	312
Expanding Your Practice with a Client-Centered Consumer Approach	312
Divorce Books for Clients	313
Divorce Books for Children	314

Index 315

About the Authors

Forrest "Woody" Mosten has been in private mediation practice since 1979, is an international master trainer in mediation and collaborative practice, and is recognized as "The Father of Unbundling." Woody is certified as a Specialist in Family Law by the California State Bar Board of Legal Specialization and handles family law matters involving substantial assets and high-conflict parenting matters both as a lawyer representing clients and as a neutral mediator—and he never goes to court! Woody is the author of three other books, *Collaborative Divorce Handbook* (2009), *Mediation Career Guide* (2001), and *Unbundling Legal Services* (2000) and numerous articles. Since 1989, he has been Chair of the International Client Consultation Competition that bears his name (www.brown-mosten.com). Woody is the recipient of the ABA Lawyer as Problem Solver Award, the ABA Lifetime Award for Legal Access, the New York State Council on Divorce Mediation Lifetime Service Award, and the Los Angeles County Bar Conflict Prevention Award, and he was named Peacemaker of the Year by the Southern California Mediation Association. Since 2002, Woody has been an Adjunct Professor of UCLA School of Law where he teaches Mediation, Lawyer as Peacemaker, and Family Law Practice: A Non-Litigation Approach. Woody can be reached at Mosten@MostenMediation.com.

Elizabeth Potter Scully is a founding partner at Jacobson Scully Shebby LLP. Her practice is devoted to family law and includes mediation, collaborative law, litigation, drafting pre- and post-marital agreements, and court-appointed minor's counsel work. She is certified as a Specialist in Family Law by the California State Bar Board of Legal Specialization. She received her AB in Classics (Latin) magna cum laude from Harvard in 1993 and her JD from the University of California Hastings College of the Law in 1996. She teaches clinical courses in mediation at UCLA School of Law. Ms. Scully frequently lectures on family law and dispute resolution issues. She serves on the Family Law Executive Committee of the Beverly Hills Bar Association and on the Board of Levitt & Quinn Family Law Center, a nonprofit law firm serving the working poor.

Foreword

Barbara A. Stark

Twenty years since the first edition of *Complete Guide to Mediation*!

The last 20 years have sped by, characterized by growing acceptance and use of mediation within the family law field—in no small part due to this book written in 1994–1995 and published by the ABA Family Law Section in 1997.

Many of Woody Mosten's cutting-edge ideas in the first edition—unbundling, mediation in the courts, and the lawyer's role in representing clients—were groundbreaking foundations for establishing statutory and judicial reforms and changing family law practices nationally and internationally.

In 1994, I was serving on the ABA Section of Family Law's Publication Board when one of our members, Frieda Gordon, told us about the innovations and robust mediation practice of a Los Angeles Family Lawyer, Forrest (Woody) Mosten. Many of us on the Pub Board were familiar with Woody's articles and teachings, but he had never before authored a book. After approaching Woody, Frieda reported that he was willing to take on this project within our time frame.

Woody's book surpassed all of our expectations. As the Pub Board member who was responsible for the manuscript, I was impressed by Woody's comprehensive, forward-looking approach presented in an accessible, friendly style. The quality of the book was so good that the immediate past ABA President, Rita Cooper Ramo, put her prestige on the line by writing the Preface and endorsing it on the book cover. The list of other leaders in both family law and mediation who endorsed the book paved the way for its success.

I'm pleased to now have the honor of writing this preface to the second edition, and I must say that this is not really a second edition at all. It is a brand new book with fresh ideas and complete updates for 2015. Due to mediation's development since 1994, Woody and his co-author, Elizabeth Potter Scully, have chosen to focus the book exclusively on the role and practice of family lawyers. This makes sense for two reasons. First, since 1994, there have been a plethora of superb books on mediation, many of them building on the first edition. Second, although there are good books for the role of commercial lawyers in mediation, Woody and Liz's second edition addresses the use of mediation in the context of family law. They provide a multitude of strategies and resources for family lawyers to put to immediate use in their practices.

The book also benefits from Woody's growth in the last 20 years as a national leader in family law and Liz's fresh look at the subject. Since the first edition, Woody has received two ABA prestigious awards—Lawyer as Problem Solver and Lifetime Legal Access Award— and has published three additional books in the field. In addition to teaching mediation at UCLA School of Law, his reputation as an international trainer and conference keynote speaker to lawyers and mediators has been unparalleled in our field. Most importantly, he has an additional 20 years of practical experience as a mediator and peacemaking lawyer who never goes to court. Woody generously shares this experience on every page.

Liz's full involvement in this book offers to the profession's next generation her perspective and insight about the lawyer's role in mediation. A magna cum laude Classics graduate of Harvard, Liz adds her clarity and nuance of writing with a keen wit that makes the book even more readable and useful for professionals. It is one of life's evolutionary coincidences that Liz's law partner, Jeffrey Jacobson, was acknowledged in the First Edition for research contributions he made while still a law student prior to establishing himself in his own right as a major presence in our field.

The Family Law Section has every reason to be proud of this publication. I am— and I look forward to Section programs and conferences that will apply the lessons and wisdom of this book, adding to the competence of our profession and enhanced consumer confidence in the divorce mediation process.

Acknowledgments

An essential underpinning of mediation is the creative use of collaboration. Throughout my career and in writing this book, I have been blessed and helped by so many people who have given generously of their talent, time, and caring.

Forrest S. Mosten

Just when I was drowning in the drafting stage of the first edition, Jeff Jacobson appeared deus ex machina and volunteered to help. A promising law student at UCLA with a proven passion and commitment to peace and people, Jeff sacrificed countless hours researching, writing, and editing the ever-moving manuscript. Jeff is now a leading family lawyer in Los Angeles recognized for his peacemaking. Andrea Kushner, then a law student from cross-town rival University of Southern California (by way of Birmingham, Alabama), devoted countless hours in competently researching newest developments and providing source material for the notes and bibliography. Andrea has become an accomplished estate planner.

My professional associations in family law, mediation, collaborative law, and legal access have provided inspiration and friendship, which have contributed to this book. I am indebted to the members of my Family Law and Mediation Study Groups with whom I have developed ideas over the years. The countless professionalswho contribute to many listserves have provided comments and sources that have found their way into the book. My friends at the Beverly Hills Bar, Los Angeles County Bar, Association of Family and Conciliation Courts, Association of Family Law Specialists, International Academy of Collaborative Professionals, Los Angeles Collaborative Family Law Association, Resolution, and the American Bar Association have supported and contributed to my work. Will Hornsby of the ABA deserves special mention as the walking sourcebook on legal access policy and research.

In preparing the final manuscript, I turned to my closest colleagues to read and offer well-needed criticism in a way that would not cause me to become paralytic in despair. My heartfelt appreciation for adding this chore to already overcommitted lives goes to Professor Larry Teply of Creighton Law School, who is the U.S. Representative to the Louis M. Brown/Forrest S. Mosten International Client Consultation Competition (www.brownmosten.com). Frank Garfield and Jeff Krivis, both esteemed lawyers and mediators in Los Angeles, took time from their overloaded practices to offer their insights. Nancy

Manning, a family lawyer and mediator from Rapid City, South Dakota, took particular care in reading the manuscript and offering helpful suggestions.

My special gratitude goes to Professor Emeritus John Wade of Bond University in Australia. One of the world's finest mediators, scholars, and trainers, John has been my professional alter ego and is a source of continuous inspiration and friendship.

My appreciation to Frieda Gordon for conceiving of this project and working as my liaison with the ABA Family Law Publications Development Board. My thanks to Barbara Kahn Stark, Lynne Ustach, and other members of the board for making sure that the final product in both editions reflects the needs of the ABA Section of Family Law. I will always appreciate Don Gecewicz, my editor of the first edition and godfather at the ABA and Jeffrey Salyards, editor of the second edition, who were always available, candid, and helpful.

I am fortunate to have learned from some of the world's authorities in client counseling and mediation. Professor David Binder of UCLA, Professor Thomas Shaffer of Notre Dame, and the late psychologist/lawyer Dr. Robert Redmount all taught me client-centered counseling. Dr. Constance Ahrons and Dr. Mary Lund have given me expanded views of family systems and therapeutic interventions through our joint teaching and co-mediation. I also wish to thank all my faculty colleagues at UCLA School of Law, particularly Professor Russell Korobkin and Luz Herrear, Assistant Dean for Clinical Education, Experiential Learning, and Public Service for their constant flow of ideas and personal support. My students in both Mediation Clinic and Lawyer as Peacemaker update my thinking, and the students whom I supervise in their independent research papers stimulate an evolving agenda of scholarship.

My colleagues throughout the country and internationally provide me with ideas and projects. David Hoffman from Boston and I speak at least weekly, sharing approaches to practice and teaching, and he always provides a peacemaking and creative perspective. John Lande from the University of Missouri is the consummate collegial presenter and co-author, and I marvel how we are always able to reconcile different perspectives. Ron Ousky, former IACP President from Minneapolis, is always sharing cutting-edge ideas that shape my thinking. Professor Andrew Schepard, longtime editor of the Family Court Review, has provided me inspiration with his contributions to both mediation and collaborative law as well as has afforded me the opportunity to test out my own scholarship and "not yet ready for prime time ideas" by publishing my articles and special issues. Finally, my 35-year friendship with Sir Geoffrey Bindman of London, England, provides me with a never-ending stream of approaches from his lifelong commitment to human rights and legal access.

My career and my life have been inspired by Louis M. Brown, to whom the first edition of this book was dedicated. Until his death at age 87 on September 19, 1996, Louis was my teacher, role model, and friend for more than 25 years—and with whom I enjoyed discussing and debating most of the issues and trends featured in this book. Louis's legendary body of work and ambitious agenda for the 21st century offer a challenge that will take our profession several decades to even partially fulfill.

One of the great fortunes of my professional life is my teaching and writing partnership with Elizabeth Potter Scully. Liz's brilliance and hard work are demonstrated on the pages of this second edition. As I am now past Medicare age, I feel comfortable that many future editions of this book will be in Liz's most capable stewardship. Until then, we will continue laughing together about our writing, teaching, and ourselves.

On the home front, during the first edition, my daughter, Jordana, and my stepson, Derek, deserved major kudos for having me unavailable way too often. "He's still up in the study!" was the mantra imprinted on their psyches and hopefully will not impair their future development. Twenty years later, they seem to have turned out fine. Jordana is now a lawyer herself and Derek is a successful business person who has given me a wonderful daughter in law, Juli, and a grandson, Daniel.

From my first breath, my mother, Shelia Mosten, offered me a model of flexibility, empathy, and gentle resolve. During her welcomed visits from Missouri as the manuscript evolved, my mother displayed her lifelong patience and acceptance when I was absorbed in this project. She and my dear sister, Margo, are very much missed but have left me a full family of nieces and grandnieces and nephews.

Finally, I wish to thank my in-home editor and consultant, Jody Mosten, for her tireless patience and unfailing support and encouragement during both editions. Jody, a far better writer and certainly more organized, agrees that our personal collaboration on this project has taken over our lives—fortunately, we continue to have so much fun together in the process.

Elizabeth Potter Scully

Like Woody, I have been fortunate enough to enjoy a career marked by warm and sustaining relationships with talented teachers and colleagues. Professor Melissa L. Nelken at U.C. Hastings College of the Law introduced me to mediation, igniting that first spark of interest, which I have carried with me since. Susanne Stanford, Patty Kushner, and Suzanne Mascarena, our stellar family law team at Luce Forward Hamilton & Scripps LLP in San Diego, California, taught me about teamwork, pursuit of excellence, and a client-focused practice. When Susanne, at the top of her profession, first took me to court with her, she had us sit in the gallery with our client while all of the other attorneys sat bantering together in the well. Her public and unconventional choice to prioritize client comfort over assertion of her own professional status was eye-opening and unforgettable. I am grateful as well to my talented and settlement-oriented colleagues at Kaufman Young Spiegel Robinson and Kenerson LLP.

Judith C. Nesburn, Michelle "Micki" Katz, and David Kuroda have been unfailingly gracious, both personally and professionally, and I treasure their support and insight. I am grateful to Hon. Mitchell Beckloff of the Los Angeles Superior Court, who first gave me the opportunity to represent children in contested guardianship cases; this work renewed my passion for family law and gave me the opportunity to implement my mediation skills effectively in an unexpected new context. I am also grateful for the wisdom and good humor of Hon. Cindy D. Davis of the San Diego Superior Court. Their humility, kindness, hard work, and unfailing respect for self-represented litigants are unparalleled.

Also like Woody, I deeply appreciate the clinical faculty at UCLA Law School, including Prof. Korobkin, Assistant Dean Herrera, David Babbe, and Associate Dean for Curriculum and Academic Affairs Eileen A. Scallen, who is as generous a colleague as she was a Civil Procedure professor lo these many years ago. The students in our mediation clinical courses challenge and delight us on a regular basis and give us great hope for the future of mediation and peacemaking in the legal profession.

I am forever indebted to my brilliant law partners, Jeffery S. Jacobson and David P. Shebby, whose commitment to excellence and integrity is as boundless as their patience with my frequent absences from the office for teaching and writing and my penchant for taking my heels off at work. Jeff, a creative, problem-solving, and passionate mediator and collaborative attorney, encouraged me to start my own practice—only the first of many instances in which following his advice has transformed my life for the better. Dave's perspective as a trial attorney is invaluable to my thinking about tradition and innovation in the world of Family Law, and his commitment to furthering the needs of the poor and vulnerable is an inspiration. Randi Akasaki and Kristen Hirashima, our hard-working associate attorneys, make us all proud, as does our world-class team. Deborah Uhtof in particular, who can make any document beautiful, contributed a great deal of time and skill to this project, and we simply could not have done it without her.

I count myself beyond lucky in my friends, old and new, and my family, whose support cannot be measured. I especially acknowledge Tom Scully, co-parent extraordinaire, for his flexibility, reliability, and devotion to our bright, soulful, and loving little fellow, Benjamin Tilden Scully.

Last but not least, I acknowledge my co-author Woody Mosten—gifted teacher, mediation visionary, and tireless advocate for sanity and innovation in our field. The teaching, writing, and speaking opportunities our collaboration have opened for me have been among the most transformative and satisfying of my career, and I am so grateful to count him and Jody among my most valued friends.

Eleven Questions Most Commonly Asked About Representing Clients in Mediation

Most lists contain numbers of items that have a traditional context—7, 10, or 20. A list of 12 even has a ring to it. But 11? In mediation, people can customize their process and their agreements. They don't have to be controlled by a system designed for one size to fit all. We tried to fit the questions into a series of 10, but 11 seemed to work better.

1. If both lawyers are settlement-minded, why should we spend money for yet another professional and hire a mediator?

If the lawyers can work together and settle the case quickly, amicably, and inexpensively, perhaps mediation is not needed. Quite often, their role as adversary professional causes the other lawyer or party to respond aggressively or to initiate preemptive strikes that the other party finds threatening. It is difficult for you to take care of a client and to play a mediative role at the same time. If lawyers do most if not all of the negotiating, their parties do not experience direct communication with the other party to make their own agreement—which may also improve their future interaction. Using a mediator might be similar to taking out an insurance policy to maintain an amicable situation between all parties and counsel. It also affords the family the benefit of a trained innovative problem solver. Finally, as Baruch Bush and Folger (*The Promise of Mediation*, 1994), Daniel Bowling and David Hoffman (*Bringing Peace into the Room*, 2003), and others have argued, the use of mediation can be a transformative experience that may improve the interaction and lives of the family members instead of just putting a settlement Band-Aid on family dysfunction.

2. Isn't mediation just another form of one attorney having dual representation of two parties with all of the limitations that such conflict situations bring with them?

It is true that in preventive mediations involved in premarital agreements, adoptions, and putting together a family business, the mediator's role of putting together and building harmonious relationships seems very much like dual representation. In representing two clients, a single lawyer must withdraw if conflicts appear irreconcilable unless there is a written waiver from all parties. Conflicts, real or apparent, are generally present in virtually all dual representational situations.

As a third-party neutral, the mediator represents *neither* party. This may be clearer in the mediator's role of dispute resolver and case manager than it is in preventive mediation. Most mediators and all recognized standards in the field encourage parties in a mediation to consult independent counsel. In many mediations, counsel attend sessions with their clients and participate at the mediation table.

3. Do I have legal malpractice exposure if I sign off on an agreement that is worked out in mediation when I'm not there?

There is malpractice exposure for a lawyer who gives wrong advice or recommends settlement based on inadequate information. It is also true that lawyers who are doing their job to promote settlement never have all of the necessary information. We cut corners all the time. If we didn't, fewer cases would settle. Transaction costs and litigated conflict can destroy a family—to say nothing of overrunning the courts! The issue isn't whether corners are cut, but which ones are cut and how important they are. Successful mediation depends on adequate information being disclosed, and an attorney can take numerous strategies in mediation to ensure adequate financial disclosure. Finally, clients who mediate have higher satisfaction with and are more involved in their own divorces, so they are less likely to sue their lawyers.

4. I have spent years learning the law and craft of representing clients. I have seen gross unfairness as a result of untrained and inexperienced mediators, many of whom probably never read a reported decision. Why should I refer another case to mediation? Could I be sued for giving a negligent referral?

If the client is referred to an unqualified mediator, there is an unjust result or process, and the client blames the lawyer for a negligent referral, the lawyer can be sued for professional negligence. However, a failure to disclose appropriate options to litigation can also bring on malpractice and disciplinary exposure. There is a growing movement to assess and certify mediator competency and to expand mediation training programs. However, the lawyer's obligation is to play a constructive and knowledgeable role in selecting the mediator and to play a proactive role during the process. Turning away clients who want mediation may mean turning down an increasingly growing source of revenue.

5. With all of the economic pressures on my practice, will the growth of mediation cut into my income?

Actually, representing clients in mediation and offering mediation-related services can add new clients and help you improve collections on fees earned. Most family law attorneys do not get paid for approximately 30 percent of the work they perform in litigated matters. Lawyers who use mediation to settle their cases collect over 90 percent of their fees.

6. I have been successfully negotiating settlements for many years and have been to hundreds of settlement conferences. Can I start being a mediator and charge my customary hourly rate?

You can. Currently there is no state regulation of mediation and no requirement for training. However, you might find that you can enrich your mediation craft by taking some training as it is very different from traditional law school education and continuing legal education seminars. You are required to role-play in simulated settings and to participate in other active training that is a far cry from a panel of experts giving lectures. Although there is certainly a demand for lawyer-mediators with substantive knowledge and law practice experience, other effective styles of mediation are being used. Also, there are significant differences in the settlement process between court mandatory settlement conferences and mediation.

7. I can understand sending amicable couples to mediation. But it seems that my entire case roster consists of high-conflict career cases in which I spend so much time in court that I should rent a cot in the courthouse. How can mediation help in these disasters?

Because over 90 percent of cases settle in private mediations, the issue isn't whether a case will settle, but when, how, and with what transaction costs the settlement will occur. Many jurisdictions now have mandatory mediation on both parenting and economic issues. In litigation horror stories, lawyers are often the victims because of lost stomach lining, unsatisfied clients, and unpaid receivables. A major but less known function of mediators is to provide consensual case management that can put some structure onto such runaway chaos and still give lawyers the freedom of traditional advocacy that judicial case management can take away.

8. I've heard that some mediators are charging fees that are higher than mine. There is not enough money in the case to hire yet another lawyer. Can mediators justify their fees when two competent lawyers are already working toward settlement?

Some mediators may overcharge, and others may not produce a process or a result that is worth the expenditure of scarce client resources. However, even with the use of a mediator and independent consulting attorneys, the cost of a mediated divorce is not higher—and may be far lower—than a case directly negotiated between two lawyers. Certainly it is generally lower than litigated divorces. Even co-mediated divorces do not increase fees compared with negotiated divorces. In addition, parties may have the benefits of an interdisciplinary (lawyer-therapist or lawyer-CPA), intergender co-mediation team that often brings settlement faster and more comprehensively compared with working with a sole mediator.

9. I know that mediators should not give legal advice. How can parties make a meaningful agreement if they don't know the law?

You are correct that a neutral mediator should not give advice—that is, tell the client what to do or what decisions to make. However, mediators differ in the amount of legal information that they provide. Even if a mediator does give legal information (e.g., cases, statutes, tax laws, procedure, support guideline calculations), most clients benefit from individual legal advice and negotiation coaching from an independent family lawyer.

10. I have heard that representing clients who use mediation requires a very different office setup than I currently have. How do I set up a mediation-friendly practice?

First, take the pressure off yourself. Many lawyers who represent parties in mediation do so as a part-time supplement to their law practice. Other lawyers who want to make a career change focusing on mediation do so over a long period of time working from their law office space. A number of tips to setting up a mediation-friendly office can be implemented whether you choose to mediate (full- or part-time) or want to become more active in representing clients in mediation. Marketing in these emerging areas requires a different emphasis and orientation that can also help your existing law practice.

11. I just got my first case to represent a client in a mediation. What do I do?

Assuming that you have had sufficient training, take a deep breath and look forward to a stimulating and satisfying experience. You might want to review some of the resources at the end of this book. Good luck. And remember: it's probably not as frightening as your first case as a lawyer, and it is the parties' mediation, not yours. They will probably help you out.

CHAPTER 1

Expanding Your Practice by Representing Clients in Mediation

On December 4, 2013, in Coffee County, Tennessee, a bitter divorce turned violent when Brenda Bartee shot her husband just before 1 p.m. near the Manchester town square immediately following a divorce mediation session at a nearby law firm. According to authorities, Brenda Bartee fired seven shots with a .40-caliber pistol and hit her husband at least four times. "It appears to have been a serious domestic issue," said Manchester Police Department Assistant Chief Adam Floied. "They had been meeting with attorneys at [Rogers, Duncan and North] about a divorce. The mediation broke down and Mrs. Bartee left the office and went outside and got the pistol. When the man left the law office, the woman fired . . . ." Dr. Harry Bartee was transported to a Chattanooga hospital in critical condition. Brenda Bartee has been charged with attempted murder. They have four children.[1]

Emotional tension, intense conflict, tight deadlines, high overhead, unpaid bills, and fear of malpractice—these are only *some* of the pressures that family lawyers encounter every day. It is no wonder that they often become burned out, cynical, or testy. The lawyer "locker room" banter is filled with malaise and dissatisfaction. Instead of waking up eager to get to the office and meet clients, many lawyers live for their vacations—then for their retirement. Fallout from this career dissatisfaction impacts colleagues, office staff, and family members.

Instead of feeling that our efforts contribute meaningfully to our clients' lives and to society, we often feel like guns hired to play out family pathology, ultimately trying to protect ourselves from the very clients who hired us. We may begin to view our career as one more set of written pleadings, one more court hearing, one more hostile interaction with opposing counsel, one more haggle over the bedroom set or an alternating Wednesday overnight visit. Instead of maintaining an energetic, positive commitment to our vocation, many of us see our offices as prison cells and clients and courts as our perpetual jailers.

Yet, most of us are not ready to take down our shingles. How did we get here? And where are we going?

We enter family law practice for a variety of reasons. For some, a job with a family lawyer may be our first (or only) job offer. Other family lawyers are drawn to the human interest aspect of this work, the emotional intensity, or the ability to gain courtroom experience.

Some of us enjoy the breadth of the substantive issues family law cases pose (we are known, after all, as the last true generalists of the legal world) and the challenge of cutting-edge legal issues such as interstate and federal rights of same-sex marriage. Others are attracted by the varied and complex procedural issues, ranging from jurisdictional disputes to sanctions for discovery abuse. Many of us are interested in the family as a system and the role of the lawyer in the healthy development of children and the emotional recovery of their parents. Others find meaning in helping people in crisis. Still others are drawn to the public policy and political issues, such as family violence, cultural competence, gender power imbalances, and societal responses to evolving concepts of family.

Whatever our motivations were when we first embarked, we are at this moment being challenged by forces inside and outside the legal profession. Most family lawyers are infatuated, albeit unconsciously, with the English solicitor-barrister model of law practice. In that model, solicitors handle client concerns, collect the fees, and pay the barristers to provide the quality courtroom advocacy for which they are recognized worldwide. In the American integrated system, most lawyers perform both the solicitor and barrister roles. We file court documents, examine witnesses, present evidence, and make legal arguments in court. American family lawyers are also responsible for interviewing and advising the client "up close and personal." In addition to client care responsibilities, we face practice development chores like office design, updating firm blogs and websites, fee collection, and paying suppliers of staples, exhibit tabs, and letterhead. In addition to operating a profitable business, we must make time to attend CLE seminars and read advance copies of court opinions as well as practice development books (such as this one) to deliver a high-quality product to an ever more demanding client population.

Instead of yearning for the good old days, we need to recognize that the days of just practicing traditional family law are gone for good (if they were ever here in the first place) and concentrate on coping with the societal forces that are transforming family law practice in the 21st century.

Consumerism

We are a nation of consumers. People clip coupons (or print Groupons) for groceries or concert tickets, bargain with the car dealer in person or online, choose the credit cards that offer free airline miles, and access the Internet routinely to learn about products and services. Potential clients do not stop being consumers when they shop for legal services to solve their family problems.

In the good old days (circa 1970), before there was a glut of lawyers, before lawyer advertising and the rise (and fall) of legal clinics, it was harder for people to find lawyers. Clients rarely attempted to negotiate the price, terms, or extent of legal services. Most clients did not know they could negotiate the financial terms of their business relationship with their lawyer—they were so insecure and needy that discussing fees with their lawyer was the last thing on their minds. Lawyers typically rejected clients' infrequent attempts at fee negotiation. It was a seller's market. "If you want my talent, time, and stomach lining, you'll pay my fee" was the message we sent out. To be fair, it was a kinder, gentler world. Lawyers were more ready and able to work on a handshake, would carry unpaid fees for months and years, and rarely sued clients (or each other).

Today, clients have access to all kinds of information about attorneys before they even pick up the phone for an initial consultation. The prevalence of social media makes it easy to confer at the touch of a button with a wide range of friends and acquaintances about attorney referrals. Websites such as LinkedIn and Google searches help clients instantly identify attorneys with whom they believe they will share a personal connection or who have been publicly endorsed by another professional whom the client already knows and trusts. Online attorney evaluation websites such as Avvo, Super Lawyers, and Best Lawyers put ratings, reviews, profiles, and disciplinary records at clients' fingertips, making the search for an attorney as easy as figuring out where to go for frozen yogurt.

Moreover, clients often comparison shop and "kick the tires" in various law offices before plunking down a retainer. Good faith comparison shopping is an accepted consumer practice (in contrast to the outrageous behavior of some people who contact every top lawyer in town for the sole purpose of creating a conflict of interest which will preclude that lawyer from representing their spouse.)

Clients want a friendly, accessible office space. They want professional, complete websites that describe the background of the service providers and the range of services offered by the firm. They want clear explanations of the fees, payment options (e.g., credit cards) and any available financing terms. Just as on a car lot, clients often expect to negotiate the terms of their contracts. Savvy clients want to know about lawyer availability for office visits and telephone conversations when it is convenient for the client, not just the lawyer. Many clients want to know when and how associates and staff members will participate and under what circumstances will the attorney delegate tasks. Clients are vitally interested in reducing their legal costs and retaining control.

Lawyers compete fiercely in the divorce marketplace with one another and with a burgeoning number of nonlawyer providers, including paralegal and document preparation services. Consumers have learned (and are continuing to learn) purchasing techniques and ways to improve their leverage in the lawyer-client relationship. Clients expect lawyers to understand, react positively, and accommodate these consumer-oriented trends. Consumers have expressed their unequivocal preference for user-friendly, price-sensitive products and services outside the legal services arena. Why should shopping for legal services be any different?

Family law mediation got its jump start from consumers who believed that the family lawyer's main service product (husband and wife each being represented by adversarial lawyers operating in or around the courthouse) was not sensitive to their financial or personal needs. Clients did not see resolution through imposed court decision (or coerced by the imminence of a trial) as meeting their consumer concerns of cost; privacy; client control; speed; and self-generated, creative solutions.

Since the birth of modern family law mediation, which is often credited to the 1978 publication of *Structured Mediation in Divorce Settlement* by O. J. Coogler, an Atlanta attorney, the prevailing view has been that mediation has grown and succeeded in spite of, not because of, family lawyers.[2]

The following quote from Nathan Davidovich from an article on www.mediate.com sums up this view:

> Unfortunately, the lawyer sometimes gets caught up in the client's insistence that the lawyer be his/her "mouthpiece," including mimicking the emotions of the client. There then develops a point in the litigation process in which the process becomes self sustaining (a goal in and of itself), leaving little hope for early peaceful resolution.[3]

A premise of this book is that family lawyers who are mediation-friendly in their representational work or serve as neutral mediators will find consumer reception positive and profitable. Mediation is a growth industry. Lawyers who embrace it are on the cutting edge and will be less vulnerable to the pro se movement, growth of nonlawyer providers, malpractice, and other economic forces.

Giving Up Litigation Was the Most Profitable Decision of My Career[4]

Well over a decade ago, Woody decided to focus totally on peacemaking and to refuse any further litigation. He reflects:

"While I was afraid that I would eat tuna casserole four times a week, with the support of my wife, I turned down large retainers and referred all potential court clients to competent litigators in my community. Much like Canadian peacemaker Nancy Cameron, I felt that I was a rider of two horses:

> I have often thought of this dual role of conflict resolver and courtroom advocate as akin to being asked to ride two horses. . . . At some point to remain riding it will be necessary to commit to one horse or the other. The difference between the skills I bring as a collaborative practitioner and those I used settling within a litigation template is the difference between riding one horse rather than two. NANCY CAMERON, COLLABORATIVE PRACTICE: DEEPENING THE DIALOGUE 66, 97 (2004).
>
> "My practice is now divided roughly into two equal parts. I serve as a neutral mediator 50 percent of the time, and the other half is composed of four representative roles: client representative during mediations presided by other neutrals (often with a litigator co-counsel); collaborative lawyer; unbundled lawyer for self-represented parties; and transaction lawyer building relationship agreements such as premarital, post marital, cohabitation, and other matters involving long-range relationships such as business partnerships, probate disputes, and adoption and surrogacy agreements. Rather than being a financial disaster, my decision to be a non-court family lawyer resulted in rapid growth of my practice beyond my most optimistic expectations. My gross receipts increased by over 33 percent during my first year of practice and uncollectible fees went down from 30 percent of gross billables to 2 percent."

Growth of the Pro Se Movement

The ultimate consumer reaction today is "No thanks, I will do it myself." The do-it-yourself movement has been felt by contractors, plumbers, and carpenters in the construction industry. Home Depot, Plummers, and other havens for the home do-it-yourselfer have flourished at the expense of licensed service providers. Instead of being looked down on or stigmatized, it has become almost glamorous to make things from scratch and rely on oneself instead of professional service providers. The same has been true across industries, including real estate, the securities industry, and medicine.

The legal profession has already experienced this phenomenon in the field of real estate closings. Not too many years ago, the transfer of title and negotiation of contract terms were seen as so complex and important that the common practice was to go to a lawyer for a home sale. Consumers saw the lawyer's fees (a customary 1 percent of the sales price) for these services as necessary, nonnegotiable, and appropriate. Today, primarily in the western United States, the title insurance and escrow industries have virtually replaced lawyers in residential home closings.

The same trend is influencing traditional adversarial representation in divorce cases, and the transition has been rough. Litigants are voting with their feet and demonstrating their consumer preference by using paralegal document services or online services at a fraction of the cost or self-representing with the assistance of commercial self-help books and materials (LegalZoom and Nolo are major self-help providers.) The rate of pro se representation is at least 50 percent of all litigants in many jurisdictions. Some judges and court staff treat self-represented litigants with resignation at best and callous hostility at worst. Because self-represented litigants are not familiar faces, do not wear the right uniforms, and generally do not know what to do or how to do it correctly, they get little help and can be made to feel like unwelcome intruders in the courthouse. Court clerks are generally forbidden by statute or court rules from providing help in filling out court forms (It is not atypical to encounter posted signs in courtrooms reading "Clerk Cannot Give Legal Advice" or words to that effect.)[5] Judges often caution struggling self-represented litigants by telling them that they are hurting themselves and that they will be held to the same standards as lawyer-represented parties. Such lectures are rarely followed by any assistance that helps solve the litigant's problems. Judges who are former family lawyers may view self-represented litigants as taking income away from their friends and colleagues. These litigants often have unsophisticated or abrasive communication styles that only make matters worse. It is little wonder that unrepresented litigants feel abused by the court system that is ironically supported by their tax dollars.[6]

Litigants without lawyers are, however, effecting changes in the court system. In Maricopa County, Arizona, an American Bar Association report (1993)[7] found that 88 percent of divorce cases were filed with only one party represented by a lawyer and 62 percent of the cases progressed through the court system with no lawyers at all. Reacting to consumer demand and going further due to bold and innovative court leadership supported by state and local government, Maricopa initiated consumer-oriented reforms that include less complex procedures, uniform support guidelines, model pleadings, and courthouse assistance, which includes paid facilitators to help people fill out forms. Unlike most jurisdictions, Maricopa offers night court, child care, client libraries in the courthouse and in community public libraries, and a large court referral list of lawyers trained in unbundled services (see Chapter 5) who are willing to help self-represented litigants.

Now, approximately 20 years later, many jurisdictions have picked up the gauntlet thrown by Maricopa County and have gone to great lengths to accommodate self-represented parties by providing a wide range of support and resources. In August 2014, the American Bar Association Standing Committee on the Delivery of Legal Services published "The Self-Help Center Census: A National Survey." The ABA identified approximately 500 self-help centers around the country, 222 of which responded to an online survey. The Census, based on the results of that survey, sheds light on the structure and operation of self-help centers around the country, including details on staffing, funding, consumers, and types of services provided. It illustrates the extent to which self-help centers are a vibrant and effective resource nationwide.[8]

Nonlawyer Providers

Despite the plethora of books, online information, and available forms, some litigants still want the help and advice of a human being. Many of them, however, are not going to lawyers. A major 1994 Legal Needs Study conducted by the ABA[9] found that 12 percent of identified legal needs were handled by nonlegal helpers. Combined with 23 percent of needs that were handled on a citizen's own initiative and 26 percent of legal needs that were not remedied at all, 61 percent of identified legal needs never reached a lawyer's office.

With the loosening of restrictions on unauthorized practice, the proliferation of independent paralegal and document preparation services is staggering. In 1995, the ABA Commission on Nonlawyer Practice recognized this consumer preference and recommended that the legal profession take an open-access approach—rather than punish paralegals through prosecution for unauthorized practice. This report, in addition to a long line of U.S. Supreme Court decisions opening up legal service access and competition, sends a strong message to us: develop new competitive service products or continue to lose a share of the divorce market.[10]

Fear of Discontented Clients

Ironically, the growing protection for clients against lawyer professional negligence has caused an increase in legal fees. We are increasingly afraid of our own clients. The more we operate out of fear of clients, the less motivation we have to give our clients options for saving costs. Many lawyers believe it poses less risk to get an adverse judicial decision than to be blamed by the client for the compromise inherent in any settlement. Malpractice is harder to prove in second-guessing a lawyer's litigation strategy, especially when the case is over-lawyered to protect against later client claims that the lawyer did not do enough. This type of defensive lawyering causes lawyer bills to go up—with a concurrent downward slide of the public's view of our profession. The recent buzz around the 2014 film exposé *Divorce Corp* demonstrates just some of the discontent with the family law profession.

Instead of synergy and collaboration, clients and family lawyers seem to be in a no-win war against each other. Citizens' groups, the plaintiff bar, and state legislatures are engaged in efforts to increase the protections for clients by beefing up lawyer discipline, expanding rights to sue for malpractice, cutting back or eliminating malpractice immunity, and increasing client rights in the attorney-client relationship. We are faced with requirements of written agreements, disclosure to clients of the existence of malpractice insurance, limitations on use of arbitration in malpractice claims, and one-way mandatory use of arbitration by clients in fee disputes.

As availability of malpractice coverage is reduced and rates for coverage increase (as well as the ever-growing deductibles), we feel unprotected from and fearful of our own clients. With increased flexibility of courts to extend statutes of limitations for client claims of professional negligence, in addition to an increasing anti-lawyer sentiment in civil juries, family lawyers are motivated to withdraw as counsel of record quickly to start the statute of limitations period running and to limit their advice and representation to the matter presented by the client.[11] Fearful of being sued for wrong advice or failure to investigate or engage experts properly, many family lawyers are increasingly recommending (or insisting) that their clients engage a growing stable of experts (e.g., CPAs, real estate and business appraisers, tax lawyers, financial planners), who may improve client information but whose primary function may be to protect the lawyer.

The result of this unfortunate trend is to increase the transaction costs of getting a divorce. Lawyers are charging higher initial deposits, and the overall bills claim a larger and larger percentage of the average marital estate. Even when the case is over, a second piece of litigation is often commenced against the client for the collection of unpaid fees or against the lawyer for client claims of professional negligence, ethical violations, or other transgressions. We become more selective in taking on clients, particularly those with difficult legal and financial issues or troublesome personal dynamics, when these are often the clients who need us the most. One basis for client selection is the ability or willingness of the client to pay higher fees, which is seen by many of us as a fair trade-off for taking on increased risk and client hassle. The result is that fewer potential clients can afford us to provide needed legal services. People who can't or won't pay higher fees still have problems involving custody, support, or property division. They still want to adopt children or terminate parental rights. If lawyers are not economically available, consumers will be forced to make other choices to meet their needs.

Lawyer Bashing, Stress of Law Practice, Resultant Lawyer Malaise

In a preemptive (and some would say overtly political) strike against a marked increase in lawyer jokes and client violence against lawyers, a former California State Bar president received national press by calling for lawyer jokes to be banned as hate speech. Following the despicable carnage, death, and destruction at the San Francisco law firm of Petit and Martin by a disgruntled client, that bar leader chose to appeal to the basest self-interested motives in lawyers to attack societal antipathy by self-protective (and perhaps constitutionally deficient) lawyer-sponsored legislation and an intensification of the us-versus-them mentality on the part of the nearly 1 million U.S. lawyers. To our profession's credit, the hate-speech trial balloon burst—but the underlying safety concerns about disgruntled clients remain.

We family lawyers fear the public's wrath at the highest level. With the rise in domestic violence being reported and handled in the courts, security has become a major concern. Office security is a frequent topic at family law conferences. Some police forces have developed special units for judges' protection against litigants. Such a unit was involved recently when a lawyer in our community, as well as the judge and the other family lawyer, was threatened by a former client.

Lawyer stress is also a major problem. Lawyers are 3.6 times more likely to suffer from the effects of stress and depression than are members of other professions.[12] This stress is aggravated by conflict generated within families, between lawyers, and by an unwelcoming and underbudgeted court system. The most intense pressure comes from our clients; it also comes from the clients' parents, children, employees, accountants, and therapists. We may expect hassles from a client's estranged spouse, opposing counsel, court-appointed experts, or creditors or even from the clerks and judges at the courthouse. However, when pressure, threats, neediness, and emotion come at us from the client's new spouse, significant other, or parents, our stress can reach crisis levels.

It is amazing that, despite these pressures, virtually every Comprehensive Legal Needs Study reports high levels of client satisfaction with and trust in lawyers' problem resolution. This satisfaction drops off considerably when we steer our clients into the adversarial court system. In fact, much less satisfaction was experienced with the courts than with lawyers.[13] Clients report high satisfaction with lawyers' honesty and explanation of the process, with their keeping clients informed of the progress of the case, and with their promptness in carrying out document work and returning phone calls. The lesson for us is that the public can maintain high confidence in and satisfaction with our professional services if we help them solve their problems by minimizing their contact with the court system.

Economic Pressures of Operating a Family Law Practice

Family law offices traditionally have been operated and managed like litigation firms. Most of us generally require a deposit or retainer to be applied against fees earned and make arrangements to have additional fees paid on a monthly basis, upon certain events (e.g., income tax refund or house sale), or at the end of the case. The deposit is calibrated to balance two competing goals: it should be high enough to cover anticipated costs of service but low enough not to scare away the client and to compete successfully with other service providers bidding for the client's work. However, unlike large corporate or personal injury defense offices, which also bill by the hour (often at lower rates and generally with more secure sources of payment), we often represent clients with limited resources (even more limited at the time of divorce). The financial "hit" for our clients is even greater when they are supporting two households on one income. There are also other nonrecurring divorce-related expenses, such as child custody evaluators, vocational counselors, and start-up expenses for new residences.

Several other factors exacerbate the limited ability of family law clients to pay legal fees. First, it is difficult to estimate the amount of work needed in any litigation, particularly in family law matters. Assessments of the degree of conflict or complexity of the issues involved are often distorted. Clients invariably hope for a quick and simple resolution and often color their initial presentations with that hope. Even when both spouses start high in their desire to be amicable and conciliatory, the role, style, and chemistry of the lawyers affect the time, cost, and manner of resolution. Fees can escalate because of a personality conflict between lawyers or between a spouse and the other spouse's new significant other. These variables may not be anticipated at the outset, and fees often end up much higher than originally anticipated.

In addition to resource limitations and unexpected developments, the nature of divorce litigation makes fee payment problematic. Satisfied clients pay their bills faster and more fully. Family law clients finishing litigation are rarely satisfied. In the rare instance when a client "wins" in court, the fees expended and/or problems with compliance or modification often nullify the victory in the client's mind. The result is that the client is faced with a large outstanding bill with little or no money to pay it. Monday morning quarterbacking, remorse, and general dissatisfaction further reduce otherwise low motivation to pay the bill. Add in any lawyer mistake or poor communication and even a winning client may be resistant to the idea of full payment. We are considered the last in line for payment—long after rent, food, car maintenance, child and spousal support, credit card payments, and even an occasional vacation.

These problems intensify when a client has been on the short end of a court result or feels unfairly treated in a negotiated settlement. A look at the economics of a family law litigation practice might be helpful. Assuming that you currently have an uncollectible rate in the 30 percent range, it means that you are working 30 percent of the time for free. From another perspective, you must work about 130 percent of your normal schedule to be paid for every hour you are currently billing.

Therefore, if providing litigation services is not fulfilling some of your financial goals, you might consider offering other family law service products with higher rates of collection. Because you either write off unpaid bills with attendant loss of income or try collecting and risk being sued for malpractice, alternative income of sources, such as representing clients in mediation and unbundled legal services, may be attractive.

Despite the pressures discussed in this chapter, think about why you choose to devote so much of your life dealing with family conflict. Also think about what it is like to be a client going through a family crisis. Many of these consumers are choosing a different way—the path of mediation.

Lawyer Benefits of Mediation

Higher consumer satisfaction with mediation over court litigation (or even lawyer-lawyer negotiation) has been found in study after study. This doesn't mean that it is necessary to close your law office and open a mediation practice, although that is an option to consider. Just as bypass surgery might motivate a person to follow a low-fat diet, we must accept the fact that many clients who face catastrophic family law conflict prefer mediation. With this acceptance, family lawyers have a few options:

1. Assess the current market and service offerings and continue to offer traditional representational services with the hope that demand for such current service offerings holds steady.
2. Modify existing service products (adversarial representation) to meet consumer demand.
3. Offer new service products (mediation, client coaching, collaborative law, preventive checkups) to supplement the current full-service product.

The first step in the market assessment process is to understand that clients prefer mediation for working out family problems and seek family lawyers who are mediation-friendly. Also, if we understand that embracing mediation is in our own best interests as a profession, acceptance of mediation will be accelerated. Benefits to attorneys include:

- Retaining or increasing your share of the divorce market.
- Increasing profits.
- Achieving higher rates of payment.
- Reducing malpractice exposure.
- Increasing control.
- Having a better quality of life.

Family Lawyers Retain or Increase Their Share of the Divorce Market

Just as they go to the dentist or pay 6 percent to a real estate broker to sell the family home, divorce clients pay for lawyers because they believe they have no other choice. Apparently, however, clients now believe that they do have other choices. Clients are doing the work themselves; turning to nonlawyer providers; or, when they do use lawyers, trying to unbundle and limit the lawyer's work and attendant costs. See Chapter 5 for discussion on unbundling, also called *limited scope representation*. Family law consumers are also demanding mediation, so lawyers should represent parties in mediation for no other reason than to stay in business. As Woody told a *Wall Street Journal* reporter long ago: "Lawyers may see the difference as being between a $10,000 fee for full-service representation and a $1,000 fee for serving as an unbundled lawyer consultant during a mediation.

Actually, the true difference may be between the $1,000 fee as mediation consultant or receiving no fee at all."[14]

In the areas of commercial and business litigation, corporate counsel are more closely monitoring the activities and billings of outside law firms conducting the litigation. More law firms are being selected on the strength of their alternative dispute resolution (ADR) orientation, their conduct, and the training of their lawyers. Companies are fed up with receiving high bills for legal work that doesn't solve their problems, is protracted, and is costly to them in terms of their reputation in the industry. The same consumer revolution is taking place in family law. The high attendance of family lawyers in mediation training courses indicates that we are truly hearing this message.

Mediation Increases Profits

While maintaining a steady flow of clients is the lifeblood of any professional practice, being paid for work performed does not hurt either.

Performing professional services and not getting paid causes defensive and self-destructive business practices by family lawyers that only worsen our standing in the marketplace. Due to sad experiences of client nonpayment, lawyer locker-room banter includes wisdom such as "If you don't get it up front, you'll never get it!" Yet, the practice of demanding retainers reduces consumer access to qualified family lawyers, and clients go elsewhere—or do without lawyers altogether.

A second consequence of client nonpayment is self-destructive retaliation toward family lawyers by lawyers in other fields who charge less. For example, insurance defense lawyers often charge less than 50 percent the rate of family lawyers due to the dependability of payment and the expectation of repeat business (perhaps also due to the economic bargaining leverage and sophistication of insurance companies). Commercial litigators also generally charge less than their family law colleagues. We justify our rates in part by invoking uncollectibility and the increased emotional burdens that we face. It is also true that we have increased leverage in fee setting due to our clients' vulnerability. Our clients who have used lawyers in other fields of law may find the family lawyer rates confusing and off-putting.

Higher retainers and hourly rates may also turn off referral sources that have been traditional feeders for the family law bar. Hardworking estate planners and civil litigators may refer clients to family lawyers even if their hourly fees are higher than their own. But just as escrow companies and title companies became replacement referrals for real estate lawyers in residential home closings, lawyers in other fields have fiduciary duties to their clients to help them make informed decisions regarding cost.

Given a choice between a family lawyer who is limited to full-package adversarial representation and a second lawyer who supplements the adversarial model with a meditative approach, many nonlawyers such as therapists and accountants may recommend the more client-friendly alternative.

In sum, family lawyers who represent parties in mediation enjoy greater profitability in their practices in a few ways:

- Clients are increasingly selecting family lawyers who support mediation and are skilled in guiding them through the mediation process.
- Referral sources, lawyers, related professionals (e.g., accountants and therapists), and the general public are also preferring lawyers who supplement trial orientation with an emphasis on dispute resolution.
- Because overall fees incurred during a mediated divorce are lower, family lawyers using mediation can reduce the amount of upfront retainer, making their services more affordable and less of an economic barrier for prospective clients.

Clients selecting mediation and unbundled use of lawyers' discrete services do not incur such runaway bills, pay more timely and in full, and have lower uncollectible fees at the end of the attorney-client relationship. Satisfied clients are the best marketing tool available to help lawyers reduce future client acquisition costs, thereby increasing profits.

Higher Collection Rates and Lower Malpractice Exposure

Many malpractice claims are filed in the form of cross-complaints for malpractice in response to lawyers' lawsuits for nonpayment of fees. To protect ourselves, many family lawyers make a management practice never to sue clients for unpaid fees. We simply eat the loss. This approach does reduce malpractice actions, but it costs both us and future clients, who may pay higher fees, set as a response to uncollectibility.

If you represent clients in mediation, you can decrease your malpractice exposure in several ways. Satisfied clients more often pay their bills. Smaller bills are more often paid or are less costly to write off. Decreased motivation to sue for fees reduces malpractice exposure. Many clients are willing to "let sleeping dogs lie," provided they are not sued to pay up. When those dogs awake, malpractice cross-complaints are not far behind.

Control

Just like our clients, we want greater empowerment and predictability in our lives. Just as for Alice in her journey through Wonderland, our long-held beliefs about the levers of control may not hold true. Let's look at trial work. Young lawyers fantasize about the ability to hold a courtroom spellbound with their silver-tongued eloquence. The truth is that regardless of how heady it might feel to deliver a well-planned cross-examination or final argument, we lose total control when the matter is submitted. When the judge renders a decision, even the best courtroom advocate is rendered virtually powerless.

True, there are appellate courts. However, if the cost, time, and odds against success are not daunting enough, the best result possible after an appeal is a decision to reverse that obliges the parties to pay for yet another trial. Most experienced family lawyers know that although the appellate process is a safeguard against naked abuse, it is rarely used and even more rarely successful.

Seasoned litigators often say that a bad settlement is generally better than a good court verdict. This wisdom is based on sad experience with how clients view the litigation process. If the case is won, it's because the client deserved the win. If the case is lost, it's the lawyer's fault. In addition to client retaliation of nonpayment, bad-mouthing to referral sources, or worse, losing often makes the lawyer feel empty and worthless. All the work, late nights, and emotional investment didn't pay off. In fact, the client may be hostile, vindictive, or even dangerous. In those situations, an estate-planning practice or even barista work may seem like a better career option.

Judicial decisions that are too one-sided, even in your client's favor, can intensify and perpetuate family conflict. When the losing client feels disenfranchised (and as though he or she has nothing further to lose), any incentive to modify behavior or comply with court edicts may drop away. All experienced litigators have encountered situations in which they won the battle triumphantly, only to watch their client lose the war.

Clients like mediation because it empowers them and restores their control. The same advantages inure to us when we advance the client's position through creative proposals and persuade the opposing party and counsel. This is quality lawyering at its best—not subject to being stymied by the start of a hearing or a judge's order. Lawyers who represent mediation parties report a high level of satisfaction by clients and control for lawyers in this process.

Following Your Heart Pays Off in the Long Run

A highly respected peacemaking lawyer learned the long and hard way to follow her heart.

Betty[15] was a university professor who yearned for more. She heard about mediation-centered lawyering and gave up her tenured position to attend a well-ranked law school. Her sole motivation was to be a family mediator and lawyer coach for mediation upon graduation.

Betty's talent and success got in her way. First, there was the invitation to law review and then to be a law review editor. Upon graduation, she was offered a highly paid job in a large corporate firm in a city where she did not want to live. While she was seduced by the money, she was even more drawn by the fact that such a prestigious firm had made her an offer.

Two horrible years passed and Betty landed in the hospital with a permanent disability due to the stress and competition of the firm. On the advice of her doctor, she quit

> the firm, took a year off from work, and moved to a small town in a bucolic setting. She opened a bakery and spent five years blissfully baking and hiking.
>
> Throughout this hiatus in her active legal career, Betty maintained her law license by attending Continuing Legal Education programs. During a program on legal ethics, Betty learned that mediation was taking off. With her apron still on, Betty started attending local bar association meetings and met a renegade lawyer who was offering unbundled and mediation services to the unrepresented. Betty teamed up with her and quickly had so many clients that she sold her bakery (for a handsome profit).
>
> Betty is now the happiest lawyer we know. She is doing fulfilling work, can support herself, and has control over her life such that her stress is reduced and her culinary creativity has expanded—but as an avocation for her friends and family!

Better Lives for Lawyers

Representing clients in mediation also gives us flexibility in our careers and personal time. Litigators are subject to time pressures (many artificially self-created) imposed by opposing counsel, court rules, and the presiding judicial officer. While any job has time constraints, few can expose you to lockup or monetary sanctions for coming 30 minutes late or turning papers in late. It is true that bosses yell and there are hurtful political intrigues in academia and business, but few careers rival the abuse lawyers absorb. Hurtful, public *ad hominem* comments by opposing counsel and humiliation at the hands of impatient judges are not uncommon. We must develop thick hides, but even with that armor, it is difficult to accept the cancellation of a family vacation or the inability to attend a child's piano recital dictated by the mood of a judge or the petty vindictiveness of opposing counsel. It is true that professional codes of courtesy and civility are emerging, as is the use of punitive sanctions for outrageously discourteous conduct. However, such sanctions are rarely imposed so as not to deter lawyers from being zealous advocates. Adding mediation representation to the mix of professional activities may ameliorate some of this pressure. Mediation scheduling does require some personal compromise on the lawyer's part to meet the demands of the client, the opposing counsel and party, and the mediator. However, neither of us can recall a lawyer ever canceling a vacation to attend a mediation session. Also, if lawyers have family responsibilities, medical appointments, car repairs, or personal exercise or enrichment, consensual appointments give more flexibility than does an 8:30 a.m. court calendar call.

Those of us who regularly represent mediation parties appreciate the reduced stress in our lives stemming from more control and less naked conflict. Client demands are every bit as rigorous when mediation is utilized; some would say demands even increase because the responsibility for results remains with us rather than being relinquished to the judge. However, as client empowerment and informed decision making become the shared values of both the lawyer and client, we become less a shaman and more a coach. It is true that coaches in professional sports get blamed and fired with steady regularity. Still, the player who misses the free throw rarely blames the coach. In contrast, family law litigators are often blamed by ungrateful clients for the disappointments of a judge's decision. The occasional thank-you card or even fully paid bill is often not enough to compensate for the frustrations and unhappiness of handling family conflict in the courtroom. Burnout is common, and even the most lauded litigators lament, "The practice of law would be great if it wasn't for the clients. They are a pain in the foot."[16]

Part of lawyer stress is having to live up to the white knight image that we ourselves have cultivated. By surrendering this omniscient role and becoming more of a partner in the lawyer-client team, we get the monkey partly off our backs. Most lawyers know that it is the clients who created their own problems long before we were called to the rescue. Instead of taking on the mission of "making everything better," mediation helps us concentrate on giving the client the tools and resources for making the best decisions themselves. The distinction may not be apparent at first glance, but it is meaningful in the attempt to be a helper, not a principal, in the conflict.

Mediation is not a panacea. Still, mediation-friendly lawyers have increased career and life satisfaction. By sparing a family the ravages of court battle and ending strife more quickly, we can reduce that family's pain. Many mediations catalyze communication, awareness of parenting needs, and the transformation of the spouses from fiery foes to collaborative colleagues as described in The Good Divorce by Dr. Constance Ahrons.[17] Guiding a family into mediation and modeling effective problem solving can provide profound personal satisfaction. Clients frequently express their appreciation, and you can be a major contributor to positive systemic family transition. Increased awareness of how to solve problems without threats or tantrums and increased understanding of our own underlying interests improves our decision making and personal relationships outside the office.

Such total turnabout in professional and personal orientation is not mandatory, of course. However, we believe you will find value if you are open to enjoying this new approach, whether it generates new career and personal directions or simply makes your current family law practice more satisfying.

Notes

1. http://www.manchestertimes.com/?p=14886.

2. Some critiques *of* mediation include Richard E. Crouch, *The Dark Side of Mediation: Still Unexplored*, in ALTERNATIVE MEANS OF DISPUTE RESOLUTION 39 (Howard Davidson et al. eds., 1982); Penelope E. Bryan, *Killing Us Softly: Divorce Mediation and the Politics of Power*, 40 BUFF. L. REV. 441 (1992); Diana Richmond, *Torture by ADR*, FAM. L. MONTHLY 66 (April 1994).

3. David Dolovich "Mediation: A Process to Regain Control of Your Life," Mediate.com.

4. The following is adapted from Forrest S. Mosten, Lawyer as Peacemaker, *Lawyer as Peacemaker: Building a Successful Law Practice Without Ever Going to Court*, 43 FAMILY LAW QUARTERLY, Fall 2009.

5. https://nacmnet.org/sites/default/files/images/StaffCannotGiveLegalAdvice.pdf. *See*, e.g., California Court Form MC800, which details what court clerks can and cannot do for litigants. http://www.courts.ca.gov/documents/mc800.pdf.

6. CALIFORNIA STATE BAR COMMITTEE ON DELIVERY OF LEGAL SERVICES FOR MIDDLE INCOME PERSONS, LAWYER'S GUIDE TO BEING A CLIENT COACH (Steven Elias ed., *1994)*; Donald King, *Save the Courts—Save the Family,* CAL. LAW., Jan. 1992. Forrest S. Mosten, *Unbundling of Legal Services and the Family Lawyer*, 28 FAM. L.Q. 421 *(1994)*. Forrest S. Mosten, Unbundled Legal Services Today and Predictions for the Future, ABA FAMILY LAW ADVOCATE, Fall 2012, 14.

7. BRUCE D. SALES ET AL., SELF-REPRESENTATION IN DIVORCE CASES, ABA STANDING COMMITTEE ON DELIVERY OF LEGAL SERVICES (1993); Julie Macfarlane. *Identifying and Meeting the Needs of Self-Represented Litigants* (May 2013) REPSONDING TO THE NEEDS OF THE SELF REPRESENTED DIVORCE LITIGANT, ABA STANDING COMMITTEE ON THE DELIVERY OF LEGAL SERVICES (1994).

8. www.americanbar.org/content/dam/aba/administrative/delivery_legal_services/ls_del_self_help_center_census.authcheckdam.pdf.

9. ABA CONSORTIUM ON LEGAL NEEDS AND THE PUBLIC, COMPREHENSIVE LEGAL NEEDS STUDY (1994).

10. The trend among U.S. Supreme Court cases is to support entrepreneurial and consumer-oriented marketing *of* professional services. *See* Bates v. State Bar of Arizona, 433 U.S. 350 (1977) (holding blanket bans on lawyer advertising unconstitutional); Edenfield v. Fane, 113 S. Ct. 1792 (1993) (permitting a Florida certified public accountant to personally solicit clients).

11. *See* ABA STANDING COMMITTEE ON PROFESSIONAL LIABILITY, LAWYER'S DESK GUIDE TO MALPRACTICE (1992); Miller v. Metzinger, 154 Cal. Rptr. 22, 27 (Ct. App. 1979) ("When a party seeking legal advice consults an attorney at law and secures that advice, the relationship *of* attorney and client is established prima facie."); *see also* Forrest S. Mosten, *Unbundling Legal Services in 2014: Recommendations for the Courts*, 53 ABA JUDGE'S JOURNAL 10 (January 2014).

12. Nancy Neal Yeend, *How ADR Benefits Law Firm Management,* in CALIFORNIA ADR PRACTICE GUIDE § 31.04 (1992).

13. COMPREHENSIVE LEGAL NEEDS STUDY, *supra* note *5, at 32–35* (High satisfaction was generated with respect to the lawyer's honesty and explanation *of* the process and for keeping the client informed *of* the progress *of* the case and promptness in carrying out document work and returning phone calls. Much less satisfaction was experienced with courts than with lawyers). In Australia, a longitudinal study *of 723* divorcing people found high satisfaction with lawyer services until and unless the dispute was decided by a court. P. MCDONALD, SETTLING (1986).

14. Junda Woo, *Entrepreneurial Lawyers Coach Clients to Represent Themselves,* WALL ST. J., Oct. 13, 1993, at B1, B6.

15. Name withheld on request. Facts modified to protect identity.

16. Noted antitrust lawyer Maxwell Blecker in Katrina M. Dewey, *Meet Them in Court: What California Top Litigators Have in Common: Guts and Glory*, CAL. BUS. L. REV., July 10, 1995, at 10.

17. CONSTANCE AHRONS, THE GOOD DIVORCE, 57–58 (1994).

CHAPTER 2

Family Lawyer as Dispute Resolution Manager

Persuade your neighbors to compromise whenever you can. Point out to them how the nominal winner is often a real loser—in fees, expenses, and waste of time. As a peacemaker, the lawyer has a superior opportunity of being a good man. There will still be business enough.

—Abraham Lincoln[1]

Courts are often seen as the dispute resolution forum of first, rather than last, resort. Law schools focus on the study of appellate cases that, in every single instance, resulted from an appeal of an adversarial court proceeding. Continuing education and specialist training for judges and lawyers concentrate on substantive law and litigation strategy. Years ago, in courses on family law specialization, the subject of alternative dispute resolution (ADR) was barely even mentioned.

Clients are increasingly hiring lawyers who are committed and trained to effectuate early, low-cost settlements. Accepting the reality of settlement, client attention should be shifted to when the case will settle and what process will be utilized to effectuate settlement.

Recognizing this reality, the family court of Australia has established court rules that accept mediation as the norm and litigation as the exception in resolving family law matters. In this jurisdiction, mediation, collaborative law, and negotiation (bottom-up processes) are labeled primary dispute resolution (PDR) and litigation, evaluation, and arbitration (top-down processes) have been renamed alternative dispute resolution (ADR). Just as the change in custody language (e.g., "time-sharing" and "parental decision making" as opposed to "custody") in Florida and other states has changed the mind-set in handling parenting of divorced children, perhaps the Australian labeling change will be the start of a movement to rethink the language of the process of dispute resolution.

Dispute Resolution Manager as Lawyer of Record

When a client engages a lawyer for full-service representation, the lawyer can be a manager of dispute resolution in addition to being a courtroom barrister. Dispute management includes educating the client about dispute resolution options both inside the courthouse and in the private sector, helping the client select the appropriate option(s), and effectively representing the client within that process to obtain a settlement.

Ethical Duty to Advise About ADR

The role of the dispute resolution manager requires a different orientation and an evolved set of skills that go beyond courtroom advocacy. The modern lawyer continually stresses client education and client-centered decision making to ensure informed consent of the client in the process of dispute resolution as well as informed consent about substantive rights and court procedures. This duty to advise clients on appropriate dispute resolution options has been the subject of regulation of professional responsibility, federal and state legislation, bar association policy and activity, and extensive comment within the academic literature.

Rules of Professional Responsibility

The lawyer's obligation to discuss options to litigation is consistent with ABA Model Rule 1.1, which requires a lawyer to ensure that client's best interests are served. Model Rules 1.4 and 1.2a require competent lawyers to consult their clients about resolution options so that the client can make an informed decision about the terms and transactional costs of settlement.[2]

"A study of large-firm lawyers found that although lawyers often initially express the 'standard take' of a duty to seek every possible advantage, most acknowledge that some hyper-aggressive tactics are inappropriate even if they are legal."[3]

Colorado was the first state to include an explicit ADR provision in its Rules of Professional Conduct. Rule 2.1 of the Colorado Rules of Professional Conduct, enacted on January 1, 1993, provides that "in a matter involving or expected to involve litigation, the lawyer should advise the client of alternative forms of dispute resolution which might reasonably be pursued to attempt to resolve the legal dispute or to reach the legal objective sought."

While the rule says a great deal about the growing importance of ADR, the language is merely aspirational. The rule does not say that lawyers have a duty to use ADR in a case where it is appropriate; instead, lawyers should simply advise a client about the use of ADR—and leave the decision up to the client. To advise means "to offer judgment"—competently and in the best interests of the client. A duty to advise is not satisfied by merely casually mentioning ADR options. The new rules require lawyers to be adept and comfortable with ADR and to advise clients about it knowledgeably.

In the prefatory comments to the Uniform Collaborative Act (2010), the reporter (Professor Andrew Schepard) provides a comprehensive overview of this duty to advise:

> In many states lawyers are required to present clients with alternative dispute resolution options—mediation, expert evaluation, arbitration—in addition to litigation. Professionalism creeds in Texas ("I will advise my client regarding the availability of mediation, arbitration, and other alternative methods of resolving and settling disputes."[4]) and Ohio, for example, require such discussion between lawyers and clients. In other states, similar obligations are imposed on lawyers by statute or court rule. See, e.g., Ark. Code. Ann. § 16-7-204 (1999) ("All attorneys . . . are encouraged to advise their clients about the dispute resolution process options available to them and to assist them in the selection of the technique or procedure"); N.J. Ct. R. 1:40-1 (giving attorneys the responsibility to discuss alternative resolution procedures with their clients).[5]

Georgia has also addressed the issue of whether lawyers have a duty to advise clients about alternatives to litigation. According to Georgia Ethical Consideration 7-5, enacted in 1993: "A lawyer as adviser has a duty to advise the client as to various forms of dispute resolution. When a matter is likely to involve litigation, a lawyer has a duty to inform the client of forms of dispute resolution which might constitute reasonable alternatives to litigation." The Georgia rule has led to a requirement that lawyers, so that they have the requisite knowledge to inform clients about options to litigation, educate themselves about these options through a mandatory three hours of continuing legal education in ADR.[6]

A 1994 advisory opinion by the Kansas Bar Association states: "Lawyers are required to discuss alternative dispute resolution methods with clients when ADR is proposed by court or opposing counsel or when lawyer's professional judgment indicates ADR is a viable option." The Kansas opinion tells the lawyer that to serve a client competently, a lawyer must advise a client about ADR where applicable. While there is no rule or statute recommending or requiring ADR competence or advice, the advisory opinion is based on various rules on competent advising and lawyering in general.[7]

In their chapter on interviewing and counseling in California ADR Practice Guide (1992, Shepards/McGraw-Hill), Nancy Neal Yeend and Terrence N. Church contend that lawyers already have an ethical duty to advise: "Ethical considerations, as well as rules of professional responsibility, require competent representation and all but mandate an attorney to advise the client on resolution procedure options and their ramifications insofar as cost, confidentiality, efficiency, and the like are concerned."[8]

The most stringent requirement for informed consent of options is imposed on Collaborative Lawyers in Rule 14 of the Uniform Act due to the higher informed consent requirements of a limited scope engagement:

Before a prospective party signs a collaborative law participation agreement, a prospective collaborative lawyer shall:

1. assess with the prospective party factors the lawyer reasonably believes relate to whether a collaborative law process is appropriate for the prospective party's matter;
2. provide the prospective party with information that the lawyer reasonably believes is sufficient for the party to make an informed decision about the material benefits and risks of a collaborative law process as compared to the material benefits and risks of other reasonably available alternatives for resolving the proposed collaborative matter, such as litigation, mediation, arbitration, or expert evaluation; and
3. advise the prospective party that:
   A. after signing an agreement if a party initiates a proceeding or seeks tribunal intervention in a pending proceeding related to the collaborative matter, the collaborative law process terminates;
   B. participation in a collaborative law process is voluntary and any party has the right to terminate unilaterally a collaborative law process with or without cause; and
   C. the collaborative lawyer and any lawyer in a law firm with which the collaborative lawyer is associated may not appear before a tribunal to represent a party in a proceeding related to the collaborative matter, except as authorized by Rule 9(c), 10(b), or 11(b).

An interesting proposal that was never enacted was authored in California by Senator Newton Russell, a strong advocate of mediation, who introduced the following straightforward bill [Senate Bill 1427 (January 24, 1996), adding Section 6068.7 to the Business and Professions Code], which would impact the way lawyers advise clients about mediation:

6068.7. In any county that has established court-approved mediation services . . . it is the duty of every attorney to advise a client in a matter involving or expected to involve litigation of alternative forms of dispute resolution which may reasonably be pursued to attempt to resolve a legal dispute or to reach the desired legal objective.
  a. When a complaint is filed in a civil action, a plaintiff shall serve on each defendant and counsel for a plaintiff shall provide to each plaintiff that he or she represents, a notice concerning California's policy to promote the use of mediation. The notice, which shall be prepared by the Judicial Council, shall educate parties and attorneys about mediation and encourage them to evaluate

their cases earlier for possible use of mediation and to agree to a mediation process without court intervention.

b. In the mediation process, the attorneys may use reference materials already developed including, but not limited to, materials prepared by the legal profession, the Judicial Council, and the State Bar.[9]

Several family law presiding judges have taken the discussion directly to litigants in two main ways. The first is posting large-print recommendations to use mediation directly on court forms (see San Mateo, California forms in the Resources section).

Other presiding judges communicate directly to litigants about ADR in a letter sent to all family law parties. The Los Angeles Superior Court Letter printed in both English and Spanish is set out in the Resources section.

A litigation midpoint scheme often requires that parties attend an ADR Status Conference or otherwise elect an alternative process somewhere along the litigation timeline. California Civil Procedure (Section 1775-1775.16) requires an ADR Status Conference after both sides' initial pleadings have been filed and requires parties to engage in either court-mandated mediation or arbitration in all civil cases (no money was authorized to pay the neutrals to provide this statutory required process).

In addition to the varied focus of required court mediation and settlement conference, the public policy of settlement is reflected in allocating lawyers' fees. For example, California Family Code Section 271 permits the court to "base an award of attorneys' fees and costs on the extent to which the conduct of each party or attorney furthers or frustrates the policy of the law to promote settlement of litigation and, where possible, to reduce the cost of litigation by encouraging cooperation between the parties and attorneys."

In essence, the statute motivates lawyers and parties, through the distribution of fees and costs, to "out-nice" the other side. To do this and to engage in behavior that promotes settlement, the parties must be informed by their lawyers of various non-litigation alternatives that promote settlement.

At the Mediation Table

Tit for Tat
Despite the best motives, sometimes the other side plays dirty. What do you do? Robert Axelrod's brilliant book *The Evolution of Cooperation* may offer an approach based on his extensive game theory research.

Axelrod has two important tips. First, cooperation maximizes overall economic wealth for each party and for all parties collectively. Parties who cooperate get more than those that compete for individual gain.

Continued

> ### At the Mediation Table *Continued*
>
> Second, if the other party plays dirty, the best way to maximize ultimate cooperation is to retaliate, fast! The purpose of retaliation is not to punish, but to motivate the dirty player to return to cooperation. It turns out that if one waits to respond to uncalled-for defections, there is a risk of sending the wrong signal. The longer defections are allowed to go unchallenged, the more likely the other player will draw the conclusion that defection can pay. By responding right away, it gives the quickest possible feedback that a defection will not pay.
>
> Balancing quick retaliation with an unwavering commitment to cooperation is a major challenge.[10]

Voluntary ADR Pledges

Voluntary ADR pledges provide the inspiration for many family lawyers to inform clients about various alternatives to litigation. Although voluntary pledges lack the enforcement mechanisms of statutes or court rules, they do create a major incentive for lawyers to inform clients about alternatives to litigation. By prominently displaying an ADR pledge in your office, you have marketing tool that will attract clients who are searching for a lawyer who emphasizes ADR. Of course, you must live up to this pledge and develop an earned reputation for informing clients about and exploring various alternatives to litigation.

In 1993, the Beverly Hills Bar Association (3,000 members) adopted an association-wide ADR pledge designed to educate its members about the duty to inform clients about and to initiate ADR options and to have its members publicly declare their commitment to utilizing alternatives to litigation. A copy of the pledge is included in the Resources section. ADR pledges and ADR advice projects have been adopted by other lawyer groups, trade associations, individual businesses, and consumer groups. For example, in 1990, the Colorado Bar Association initiated a pledge program to encourage Colorado businesses to consider ADR. Hundreds of major businesses have agreed to the following: "In the event of a business dispute, our company is prepared to explore with the other party resolution of the dispute through ADR techniques before pursuing litigation." The California Association of Realtors has gone one step further by inserting a mediation clause in its standard home sale contract, requiring brokers to discuss this issue with both parties involved in the transaction.

Malpractice Exposure

Family lawyers are now in a catch-22. A plethora of cases holds lawyers liable for professional negligence if a settlement is entered into without reasonable discovery. Lawyers who settle difficult cases—trading off legal rights for a complete package—are far more likely to be sued for legal malpractice than are lawyers who litigate fully to judicial resolution. This causes defensive over-lawyering. However, many family lawyers would rather over-lawyer and risk nonpayment of their bill or escalation of conflict than be vulnerable to a malpractice claim from a remorseful client.

Paul Lurie and Sharon Press state:

> We could imagine clients bringing malpractice claims against their lawyers for
> 1. failing to properly consult with their clients about discovery and motion practice alternatives and their cost implications and
> 2. failing to properly use the mediation process to reduce the costs of settlements.[11]
>
> Now, with the emerging duty to inform clients of ADR alternatives, you could be liable for litigating competently but having a client complain that the lawyer did not diligently and prudently explore settlement—even when the client clearly declares: "I am not open to compromise. I will not settle."

Lurie and Press cite Federal District Judge Patrick Walsh who echoes this warning:

> The scorched-earth practice many lawyers employ, attempting to discover "everything" without regard to cost and aggressively litigating when production is not forthcoming, seems inconsistent with the goals of the civil rules—the just, speedy, and inexpensive resolution of the case—in what one assumes is the client's goal: obtaining the best possible result for the least amount of money.[12]

If you think we are kidding, ask the partners of the Severson law firm who were required to stand trial when a client who had instructed the lawyers not to settle later sued the same lawyers for failing to take reasonable steps to settle. In 1988, in a now de-published California attorney malpractice case, *Garris v. Severson*,[13] the Court of Appeal reversed a trial court's grant of summary judgment in favor of the attorneys. It held that attorneys may be liable for malpractice exposure for failing to reasonably inform clients of procedural and factual developments that occur during litigation, explain the legal consequences of those developments, take affirmative steps to explain the advantages of settlement, and reasonably attempt to effectuate settlement. The court viewed a lawyer's duty toward settlement as being proactive. Not only was a full disclosure of facts affecting settlement mandated, but the court held that lawyers should explore settlement even with clients who oppose it:

> The fact the client is initially opposed to settlement does not excuse the duty to advise and counsel the client about settlement if such advice and counsel is otherwise appropriate. After all, the lawyer's superior skill and knowledge is what the client is paying for. . . . It is not uncommon for the client to have unwarranted faith in the righteousness of his position. The lawyer's job is to bring rationality, objectivity and experience to bear on the matter. *Id.* at 207.

The outcome of Garris seems to undermine the historical distinction between overall client objectives, which require client consent, and technical/tactical concerns traditionally reserved for lawyer discretion.

A clear distinction between objectives and means sometimes cannot be drawn, and in many cases, the client-lawyer relationship partakes of a joint undertaking. In questions of means, the lawyer should assume responsibility for technical and legal tactical issues but should defer to the client regarding such questions as the expense to be incurred and the concern for third persons who might be affected adversely.

Although professional rules make a point of asserting that they do not apply in malpractice suits, courts have applied various mandatory requirements to measure an appropriate standard of reasonable care for lawyers.

Implicitly sanctioning the underlying purposes of statutes, court rules, and voluntary pledges incorporating the emerging duty to advise on ADR options, the comments of Rule 2.1 of the ABA Model Code of Professional Responsibility state:

> Advice couched in narrowly legal terms may be of little value to a client, especially where practical considerations, such as cost or effects on other people, are predominant. Purely technical legal advice, therefore, can sometimes be inadequate. . . .

A client may expressly or impliedly ask the lawyer for purely technical advice. When such request is made by a client experienced in legal matters, the lawyer may accept it at face value. When such a request is made by a client inexperienced in legal matters, however, the lawyer's responsibility as advisor may include indicating that more may be involved than strictly legal considerations.

The Garris court translated the duty of informed consent into a standard of reasonable care:

> It is a duty requiring attorneys to advise and counsel a client as to all facts, circumstances and consequences which are necessary to enable the client to make an informed decision on matters such as . . . desirability of attempting settlement. . . .[14]

Shouldered with the duty to attempt to effectuate a reasonable settlement, the family lawyer clearly has a duty to initiate conversations with the client about the desirability of settlement and to counsel the client as to the best means to effectuate the settlement if it is determined that settlement is appropriate. Although Garris dealt with attorney-to-attorney negotiations within the framework of non-family law litigation in the court system, the principles of Garris go beyond this setting. We must inform our clients about the relevant facts and circumstances concerning the process of settlement. In today's sophisticated family law practice, those facts should include non-judicial alternatives such as private mediation, private adjudication, mini-trial, and other appropriate alternatives to resolving disputes (ADR). These options may have a significant impact on cost, privacy, timing of adjudication, emotional turmoil, and family relationships.

Monitor Your Negative Assumptions

Lawyers are trained to focus on the problem. If you were a good student, you may have learned this lesson too well and may have developed a bit of cynicism and mistrust not only toward the other side, but also toward your client.

Just think about the following:
- Do most people tell the truth most of the time?
- Do most people honor most of the agreements that they make?
- Do most people want harmony in their divorced family rather than conflict?

If the answer to all three questions is no, is it possible that your lens of people has become unfairly jaded?

Because some people lie, do you focus on being vigilant against deception rather than working productively with the facts as related by your client and the other spouse?

Because some people breach or default on their agreements, should you focus on this problem rather than build agreements that will most likely be kept?

Because good people going through a divorce sometimes act their worst, can you focus on what they do well and use such positive behavior as a foundation?

We are neither naïve nor unrealistic when we suggest that you reflect on your assumptions about the families you serve. If you have learned the lesson of "Letting It Go" to prevent unnecessary posturing, perhaps you can take the next step to challenging negative assumptions that often prevent agreements from forming.

How to Advise Clients Properly About Alternatives to Litigation

In our mediation course at the UCLA School of Law and in conducting CLE programs for practicing lawyers, we have found that the teaching module that seems to gain the most traction is the step-by-step protocol of advising a client about options to litigation.

Veteran lawyers often resist such training with a dismissive "I have done this for years." However, even lawyers with many years of experience generally concede that performing the following protocol goes far beyond what they had been doing prior to this training.

1. Explain to Client the Purpose of This Portion of the Consultation (Learn Options to Litigation to Have Full Information Before Making a Decision and Certainly Before Filing a Lawsuit)

In their seminal book The Lawyer as Counselor, David Binder and Paul Bergman discuss the importance of a "prefatory introduction" to each phase of the client counseling process. In this protocol, the prefatory introduction explains to your client that to have full information before making a decision about an effective course of action, and certainly before taking a major step such as filing a lawsuit, the client must have full information about what the options are, what the positives and negatives of each option are, and how they compare to each other given the client's situation.

The Louis M. Brown and Forrest S. Mosten International Client Consultation Competition (affiliated with the International Bar Association, www.brownmosten.com) adopts the work of Binder and Price and accepted ABA Professional Rule 1.2 (c) in assessing the counseling skills of international law students using two central criteria that may be of guidance to you in your daily work with clients:

> Criterion 3: Learning the Client's Goals, Expectations, and Needs
>
> The lawyer should learn the client's goals and initial expectations and, after input from the client, modify or restate them as necessary, giving attention to the emotional aspects of the problems.
>
> Criterion 6: Developing Reasoned Courses of Action (Options)
>
> The lawyer, consistently with the analysis of the client's problem, should develop a set of potentially effective and feasible options, both legal and nonlegal. The lawyers may discuss appropriate use of creative peacemaking and alternative processes such as unbundled legal representation (in which the lawyer performs discrete tasks as part of representation that is limited in scope), collaborative law, mediation, arbitration, expert consultation and evaluation, and prevention of future disputes.

2. Explain Litigation—Benefits and Mythology

Although our clients may talk about going to court, very few truly understand what litigation entails and how their understanding of litigation from Perry Mason and *Boston Legal* may differ significantly from that of their local family court.

Your explanation about litigation should include the following topics:

1. The court that is involved and its location
2. The judges available and their backgrounds and suitability
3. The timeline for completion of a court-contested divorce
4. The client's personal involvement: witness in discovery and hearings, preparation of documents, attendance at meetings with lawyer, mandated and anticipated negotiation and mediation sessions, and time in the courthouse
5. The range of costs
6. The impact of litigation on key family relationships
7. The emotional toll on the client

As part of your explanation, you should test what myths the client has about courts and the litigation process and help debunk any myths that exist, including the following: the judge will be perfectly unbiased and impartial; the judge will be a former family law practitioner and therefore a family law expert; the process will be speedy because "Justice Delayed Is Justice Denied"; your client will be able to tell his or her story to the judge; the law is clear and will be fairly applied to the client's situation; your ability to cross-examine the other spouse will ensure that the truth will come out in court; and once there is a judge's decision, the other side will comply with the ruling.

3. Explain the Existence of Options (Within and Outside Courthouse)

The following chart lays out both court-based and private sector options:

Family Law Alternative Dispute Resolution Options

Inside the Courthouse	Private Sector
Court-staffed mediation for custody and visitation cases	Self-help
Custody evaluation	Informal third-party assistance
Mandatory mediation for financial issues	Divorce counseling
Meet and confer requirements	Community mediation centers
Special masters or referees	Mediators, licensed and unlicensed
Mandatory settlement conference	Binding arbitration
Negotiated settlement in the hall	Med-arb and arb-med

As demonstrated in this chart and discussed throughout this book, there are many options for dispute resolution. Just as mediators who may have been trial lawyers often lose their edge in witness examination and court argument, many litigators do not take the time or have the interest in staying current with evolving options and techniques for settlement. More important, many litigators feel very comfortable in their roles as advocates within the courtroom setting, using the leverage of litigation pressure to obtain negotiated results. They often do not view conflict in a mediated way—although clients often expect them to. This fear of change is understandable. Few professionals want to pioneer untested new products that may not be accepted easily by their clients. The answer is not that we should force our clients to use mediation in every situation. Rather we should be diagnostic problem solvers who widen the universe of client choices to improve client process decision making. By increasing the options, mediation will be utilized more frequently to the benefit of the individual client and to the family law system as a whole.

4. Explain Options—Benefits and Downsides

Clients have many options for dispute resolution, each of which has benefits and downsides. Some don't even involve attorneys or third parties. One option is client self-resolution—when based on reflective self-interest, the client simply takes one of his or her claims off the table. Sometimes this kind of resolution prevents the client from giving in or taking an appeasement route and can constitute one of the best decisions of the client's life. Another option is party-party resolution. You would be surprised how often clients seek legal services without having explored the option of sitting down for a cup of coffee with the other party to try to work out a problem. Sometimes they don't realize they have that choice. Sometimes they are afraid to try. Although such conversations can be challenging, with our support and coaching, clients often make more progress with the other party directly than they ever imagined.

As soon as attorneys are involved, there is an opportunity for lawyer-lawyer resolution. Even if your preference would be to have the parties more actively involved, you can still support your client's desire to avoid conflict and honor your client's informed decision to use you as a buffer. Another choice is a four-way settlement conference. With a peacemaking approach to this customary process option, attorneys can maximize the possibility of reconciliation and healing. For example, attorneys can encourage clients to speak directly to each other using their own words, choose not to use jargon or legalese, and make it okay for clients to choose to subordinate legal rights and financial gain in favor of a settlement with which they can live and that meets other kinds of needs.

Of course, there are formalized dispute resolution processes involving third-party neutrals and/or team members besides attorneys and clients. For a collaborative settlement conference—which may resemble a traditional four-way settlement conference but is functionally different—your mission would be to explain the benefits and costs of signing a disqualification clause, explain different models of collaborative practice, and explain how the other party might react in a collaborative settling compared with other process options. If you are not trained in collaborative practice or offer only one model of collaborative practice that might not be the best fit for a particular client, part of your peacemaker approach will be to refer clients to other lawyers in your community who offer other models. Finally, there is the option of mediation. Given the many models of mediation and choices of mediators with different orientations, backgrounds, and areas of substantive expertise, your peacemaker responsibility is to explain this menu of possibilities. If you invest in mediation training, you will enhance your ability to encourage clients to consider mediation early and seriously.

5. Compare and Contrast Options with Litigation and with Each Other Using the Following Factors

Speed: How quickly can each process get started, and how long will it take to conclusion?

Privacy: How will each process protect the privacy of the family members from unwanted publicity or oversight? Will problematic personal and financial behavior stay behind closed doors?

Control Over Process: How will each process give your client a say and control over what the ground rules are, who the decision maker is, and how comfortable the process will be?

Control Over Result: How does each process permit your client to influence the result and to walk away if the result is not satisfactory?

Relationships: How will each process impact your client's relationship with the children, the other spouse, business associates, members of a religious or geographic community, and others in your client's life?

Impact on Children: How will each process affect your client's children's functioning, happiness, and welfare?

Financial Cost: What amount of money will your client spend for each process option?

Family Heath: Divergence During Divorce

The following chart illustrates how the use of mediation can accelerate completion of the divorce process, which will facilitate healing of the parties. Leading researchers Mavis Hetherington and John Kelly have found that separation engenders crisis and psychological symptoms and that it takes approximately two years to return to normal baseline functioning.[15] Prolonged conflict leads to polarization, development of self-protective believe systems, and exacerbation of personality disorders.[16] This chart captures this research. You should make copies of it and use it with your clients to explain why the speedier resolution of mediation will benefit them and their children.

32 THE COMPLETE GUIDE TO MEDIATION, SECOND EDITION

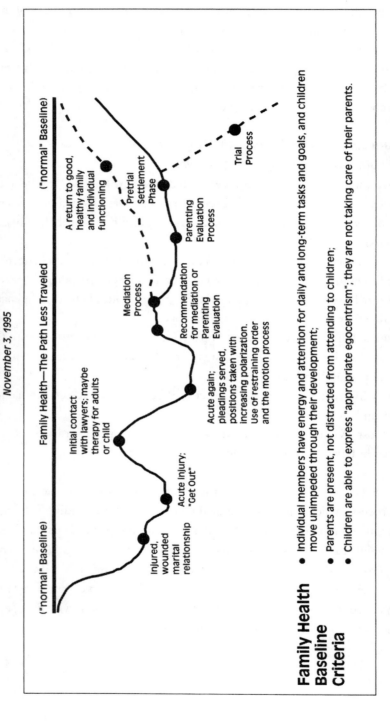

ADR Pledge of the Beverly Hills Bar Association

This document can be framed and displayed prominently in a law office. It may be accompanied by an ADR pledge certificate from the Bar recognizing the signatory as being committed to the use of mediation and related processes.

A signed copy of an ADR pledge can be sent to clients or referred to in promotional literature. It can also be sent to opposing counsel as an introduction or as part of an attempt to commence mediation or another alternative dispute resolution process. A copy of the ADR pledge is in the Resources section.

Practice Tips

1. Prepare a summary of the dispute resolution options for your website so that a potential client can start thinking about these issues before your first appointment.
2. Provide the client with a brochure or other materials explaining your philosophy to promote settlement and providing an explanation and comparison of mediation and other non-litigation options. The comparison of options authored by John Lande and Gregg Herman in the Resources section is a good start.
3. Offer the client an opportunity to view a video or read books in your office concerning the litigation process and alternatives.
4. Display an ADR pledge in your office and provide the client with a signed copy.
5. Include a provision in your attorney-client fee agreement in which the client acknowledges receipt and understanding of information about the benefits of mediation and other ADR options.
6. Before filing of the first contested court action or filing of a response, send your client a confirming letter concerning non-litigation options.
7. Advise your client on selection of mediators and other professionals who will support your views of client self-determination and informed consent.

Notes

1. Abraham Lincoln, *Notes for a Law Lecture,* in SELECTED SPEECHES, MESSAGES AND LETTERS 33 (T. Harry Williams ed., 1957), *quoted in* MARY ANN GLENDON, A NATION UNDER LAWYERS: HOW THE CRISIS IN THE LEGAL PROFESSION IS TRANSFORMING AMERICAN SOCIETY 55 (1994).

2. Paul Laurie and Sharon Press, *The Lawyer's Obligation to Advise Clients of Dispute Settlement Options*, ABA DISPUTE RESOLUTION MAGAZINE 34, Summer 2014.

3. Ibid citations omitted.

4. Supreme Court of Tex. Court of Criminal Appeals, The Texas Lawyer's Creed: A Mandate for Professionalism § II(11) (1989), *available at* www.texasbar.com/Template.cfm'section=pamphlets&CONTENTID=7227&TEMPLATE=/ContentManagement/ContentDisplay.cfm.

5. The Uniform Act Reporter also cites the following: *see also* Marshall J. Breger, *Should an Attorney Be Required to Advise a Client of ADR Options?*, 13 GEO. J. LEGAL ETHICS 427, apps. I and II (2000) (providing a comprehensive list of court rules, state statutes, and ethics provisions). *See generally* Bobbi McAdoo, *A Report to the Minnesota Supreme Court: The Impact of Rule 114 on Civil Litigation Practice in Minnesota*, 25 HAMLINE L. REV. 401 (2002) (discussing the Minnesota rule requiring ADR to be considered in civil cases); Bobbi McAdoo and Art Hinshaw, *The Challenge of Institutionalizing Alternative Dispute Resolution: Attorney Perspectives on the Effect of Rule 17 on Civil Litigation in Missouri*, 67 MO. L. REV. 473 (2002) (empirical studies analyzing the impact of rules requiring lawyers to discuss ADR with clients).

6. Comments of William Schroeder, LEXIS Counsel Connect, October 17, 1995.

7. KAN. BAR ASS'N, Op. Kan. Bar Ass'n 94-101 (Ethics Advisory Serv. Comm. 1994); Comments of Karin Bergener, LEXIS Counsel Connect, October 12, 1995; October 16, 1995; and October 18, 1995.

8. Nancy Neal Yeend and Terrence N. Church, *Interviewing and Counseling,* in CALIFORNIA ADR PRACTICE GUIDE § 35.07 (1992).

9. CA S.B. 1427, 1993-94 Reg. Sess. (1994).

10. Jeffrey Kichaven of Los Angeles, a member of the ABA Section of Dispute Resolution Council, has prepared an informative and entertaining presentation based on Axelrod's EVOLUTION OF COOPERATION—replete with cartoons and old movie photos. Lectures and workshops are an excellent introduction to mediation for the general lawyer population.

11. Lurie and Press, ibid.

12. *Id.*, citing Patrick J Walsh, From the Bench: Rethinking Civil Litigation in Federal District Court, 40 ABA J SEC OF LITIG 6 (2013).

13. *See* 207 Cal. Ct. App (1988) ordered not published by the California Supreme Court, February 2, 1989; Forrest S. Mosten, *The Duty to Explore Settlement: Beyond Garris v. Severson*, 14 FAM. L. NEWS, Sept. 1989, at 1. Both *Garris* and this article are cited by Nancy Rogers and Craig McEwen in their treatise MEDIATION: LAW, POLICY, AND PRACTICE 4:03 n.1-3 (2d ed., 1994). The authors also cite Muhamed v. Strassburger, 526 Pa. 541, 587 A 2d 1346 (1991), *cert denied* 112 S. Ct. 196 (1991), in which a federal district court held that a lawyer had a duty to explain settlement and to tell clients about settlement offers in a timely fashion.

14. Mosten, *supra* note 8, at 1.

15. E. MAVIS HETHERINGTON AND JOHN KELLY, FOR BETTER OR FOR WORSE (2002).

16. JANET JOHNSTON AND LINDA E. G. CAMPBELL, IMPASSES OF DIVORCE (1998).

CHAPTER 3

Mediation Confidentiality

A principal purpose [of mediation confidentiality] is to assure prospective participants that their interests will not be damaged, first, by attempting this alternative means of resolution, and then, once mediation is chosen, by making and communicating the candid disclosures and assessments that are most likely to produce a fair and reasonable mediation settlement.

—Cassel v. Superior Court (2011) 51 Cal.4th 113

A Core Principle

Confidentiality is a core principle of mediation. Confidentiality, in fact, is expressly identified as the prime concern of the Uniform Mediation Act (UMA). The underlying premise is that the effectiveness of mediation depends on the candor of the participants. As the drafters of the UMA put it, "Parties engaged in mediation, as well as non-party participants, must be able to speak with full candor for a mediation to be successful and for a settlement to be voluntary." This is in keeping with the common law principle that settlement discussions are precluded from discovery.

The UMA's prime concern is keeping mediation communications confidential. Parties engaged in mediation, as well as non-party participants, must be able to speak with full candor for a mediation to be successful and for a settlement to be voluntary. For this reason, the central rule of the UMA is that a mediation communication is confidential and, if privileged, is not subject to discovery or admission into evidence in a formal proceeding [see Sec. 5(a)]. In proceedings following a mediation, a party may refuse to disclose, and prevent any other person from disclosing, a mediation communication. Mediators and non-party participants may refuse to disclose their own statements made during mediation and may prevent others from disclosing them, as well. Thus, for a person's own mediation communication to be disclosed in a subsequent hearing, that person must agree and so must the parties to the mediation. To be effective, waiver of these privileges must be in a record or made orally during a proceeding. There is no waiver by conduct. Per Mediation Act Summary, by National Conference of Commissioners on Uniform State Laws.

There are many reasons why protection of confidentiality is so important. Brainstorming of options is an essential component of mediation, and the willingness to share new ideas requires a sense of safety. If participants feel as though admissions, positions, and proposals made in mediation could be used against them later, this will chill the kind of free, honest communication that is necessary to feed the mediation process.

Interest-based negotiations require that participants identify their underlying needs and concerns honestly. Posturing, to the extent it masks interests, is contrary to the goals of mediation. In *Lake Utopia Paper Ltd. v. Connelly Containers, Inc.*, 608 F.2d 928 (2d Cir., 1979), cert. denied, 444 U.S. 1076, 62 L.Ed.2d 758, 100 S.Ct. 1093 (1980), the court noted, "If participants cannot rely on the confidential treatment of everything that transpires during these sessions then counsel of necessity will feel constrained to conduct themselves in a cautious, tight-lipped, non-committal manner more suitable to poker players in a high-stakes game than to adversaries attempting to arrive at a just resolution of a civil dispute." *Id*. at 930.[1]

Confidentiality: A Key Benefit

Parties benefit from mediation confidentiality. It stands in stark contrast to the public nature of traditional litigation. In many states, some or all of family law cases are matters of public record and the ability to seal them or restrict access to them is limited by First Amendment concerns and strong public policy favoring the transparency of the judicial system. Clients are increasingly vigilant about informational, as well as personal, privacy. Personal information in divorce files (financial, medical, etc.) can damage business relationships, render parties vulnerable to fraud or identify theft, and may be accessed directly by the children later on, causing irreparable psychological damage to the children and to the remaining family system.[2] In this Internet age, privacy is a commodity whose value is on the rise.

Family court records may contain personally identifying information, including names and birthdates of minor children, address records, school information, financial records, and account information. The records may also contain especially sensitive information such as medical and mental health records and employment histories. It is easy to attach documents inadvertently to court filings that contain Social Security numbers, and it is expensive and cumbersome—if not impossible—to redact or retract confidential information from a public court file once it has gone in. One has only to peruse the examples of identity theft schemes set out on the IRS website to see the myriad ways in which personal information available via public court records could be criminally appropriated and misused.[3] Disclosure of personal information in public records is of particular concern in cases involving stalking, harassment, and domestic violence. Even if the appropriation of personal information is not criminal, but commercial (direct marketers, potential employers), you should advise clients to be aware of the implications of personal information being available for strangers to access and disseminate.

In addition to identity theft and fraud, there are other profound reasons you should advise clients to keep the details of their family law cases out of public reach to the greatest possible extent. High-profile or high-net-worth clients, for example, may be sensitive to release of their personal data, given the heightened risk of harassment and/or interest in information "going viral." Just think of how former Dodgers owners Frank and Jamie McCourt and billionaires Ronald W. Burke and Kirk Kerkorian were portrayed in the media during their divorces.

For other clients, financial allegations in the public record (e.g., unreported cash income, employees paid off the books, excessive perquisites) could raise red flags with taxing authorities, exposing your clients to possible civil and criminal consequences. In some states, trial judges, as officers of the court, are obligated to report to the proper authorities evidence of any illegal activity.[4] In other states, even if they are not required to report the activity, judges may elect to alert tax authorities to issues of which they become aware during the litigation process.

Privacy can be of particular concern to parents of children with special physical, emotional, or educational needs. Clients should consider how public disclosures concerning a child's physical and/or mental health might impact access to health insurance, affect the child's ability to obtain accommodations or services from school districts, or subject the child to embarrassment, social stigma, or discrimination.

Finally, there may be cultural reasons that clients value confidentiality. If you have clients who are members of tight-knit religious or neighborhood communities, you may want to discuss mediation confidentiality with them and explain how it can limit public access to their private disputes. In this way, you can demonstrate your sensitivity to cultural attitudes toward divorce and/or preferences for private ordering of familial disputes.

Mediation confidentiality is not absolute (see discussion below), and mediation may not be the panacea for all privacy concerns. For example, there may be an ethical duty to terminate a mediation that is furthering criminal activity or an IRS audit may trump mediation confidentiality. But for most parties, you need to inform them that mediation does offer significantly more privacy and confidentiality than does traditional litigation.

Sources of Confidentiality Rules

There are various sources of rules governing mediation confidentiality in the family law context. It is crucial for you to be familiar with the specific rules at play in your jurisdiction in order to properly advise clients as to the parameters of their participation in a given mediation and the impact of that participation on concerns of privacy confidentiality.

The ABA Model Standards for Mediators address confidentiality. Specifically, per ABA Model Standard VII, "A family mediator shall maintain the confidentiality of all information acquired in the mediation process, unless the mediator is permitted or required to reveal the information by law or agreement of the participants." Application of these standards, of course, may be affected by laws, rules, or contractual agreements.[5]

The UMA contains detailed provisions regarding mediation confidentiality. However, among the states that have adopted it,, many have added, deleted, or altered confidentiality provisions, creating exceptions and limiting the scope of the confidentiality protections in the UMA.[6] Often the state variations involve confidentiality of mediation statements in child abuse and neglect proceedings. In Nebraska and Ohio, for example, there is an absolute exception to confidentiality (i.e., "no privilege") for a mediation communication that is a threat or statement of a plan to inflict bodily injury or commit a crime of violence; intentionally used to plan a crime, attempt to commit a crime, or conceal an ongoing crime or ongoing criminal activity; sought or offered to prove or disprove a claim or complaint of professional misconduct or malpractice filed against a mediator; sought or offered to prove or disprove a claim or complaint of professional misconduct or malpractice filed against a mediation party, nonparty participant, or representative of a party based on conduct occurring during a mediation; or sought or offered to prove or disprove abuse, neglect, abandonment, or exploitation in a proceeding in which a child or adult protective services agency is a party.[7] California's statutory scheme, which is arguably the most protective of mediation confidentiality in the world, does not exempt any such statements from mediation confidentiality. Every state currently has some statute that addresses mediation confidentiality. State laws and court rules on the subject vary widely in scope, approach, and application.[8]

There are a wide range of possible consequences (formal, informal, serious, and nominal) for disclosing information protected by mediation confidentiality. Such conduct may be sanctionable by the court. It could form the basis for a mistrial. It could anger the judicial officer or compromise your client's credibility or your own. It will undoubtedly impact the willingness of the opposing party or counsel to participate in settlement discussions or mediation with you in the future. If egregious enough, it can result in dismissal of the case with prejudice.[9]

For state-by-state information about privacy policies vis-à-vis court records, see the National Center for State Courts website: http://www.ncsc.org/Topics/Access-and-Fairness/

Privacy-Public-Access-to-Court-Records/State-Links.aspx?cat=Privacy%20Policies%20for%20Court%20Records.

Conflicting Public Policies

Though confidentiality can be a key benefit and a selling point of mediation, there are instances in which it conflicts directly with other compelling public policies such as transparency of process, full financial disclosure, attorney professional responsibility, and even the promotion of fairness of result and treatment of parties. Where mediation confidentiality conflicts with other important public policies, there are potential pitfalls as well as opportunities for sophisticated, client-centered lawyering.

For example, in states with laws that are highly protective of mediation confidentiality, it may be virtually impossible for clients to set aside mediated agreements—even those that turn out, for example, to have been based on inaccurate or incomplete financial disclosures. This is because much of the evidence on which a set-aside claim would necessarily be based (e.g., what was disclosed and when) is protected by mediation confidentiality and therefore is inadmissible in court.[10] Buyer's remorse is frequent in family law settlements, and before entering mediation, you need to advise your clients in advance that it will not be easy for them to "undo" deals once they are done.

Similarly, even potentially incompetent advice rendered to a client by an attorney may be covered by mediation confidentiality and thus inadmissible to show attorney malpractice.[11] This means you should inform your client before starting a mediation that by participating they may essentially be relinquishing claims for malpractice against you. Most clients would not otherwise understand that their agreement to mediate their family law matter could operate as a legal malpractice waiver. As fiduciaries, with ethical obligations to bring to clients' attention areas in which your own interests conflict or may conflict with theirs, you should disclose this issue and obtain informed client consent before proceeding with mediation. A sample letter to your client setting out these risks before entering mediation is contained in the Resources section.

On the other hand, a 2014 federal bad faith insurance case in California not only admitted mediation communication when there was no objection during the trial, but also went further to say that any objection would have been overruled because the mediation statements were necessary to rule on whether the parties were acting in bad faith and for the court to understand why a settlement could not be reached.[12]

Exceptions to Mediation Confidentiality

You must advise your clients that mediation confidentiality is not absolute. Even in states with broad confidentiality protections, confidentiality does not attach in every context and various exceptions exist. In most jurisdictions, for example, confidentiality can be overruled by duties imposed on mediators to report child abuse[13] or criminal acts, by constitutional rights of defendants in criminal cases, or by other requirements, regardless of the parties' agreements.

Evidence otherwise admissible or subject to discovery outside mediation or mediation consultation does not always become inadmissible or protected from disclosure solely by reason of its introduction or use in a mediation or mediation consultation.[14] Legislators are understandably loathe to have mediation used as a pretext to shield materials from disclosure in other situations.

Many statutory schemes governing mediation confidentiality apply only to legal proceedings. This is an important limitation, for oftentimes no law prohibits your client or client's spouse from disclosing through mainstream or social media what took place during mediation. Your client must be informed that there is no legal bar stopping the client's spouse or another participant in the mediation from talking about such matters with business or professional colleagues, extended family members, or friends and others in the neighborhood or religious community. If parties want to bargain for confidentiality agreements to cover these nonlegal contexts, they are generally free to do so in a separate confidentiality or non-disclosure agreement that needs to be negotiated before the mediation begins or during the mediation itself.

Given the complexities of mediation confidentiality and its exceptions, counseling a client simply that "mediation is confidential" and leaving it at that will not result in informed consent by clients and arguably falls below the standard of care.

Settlement Agreements

If a settlement is reached during mediation, can a party introduce the settlement agreement in a court proceeding for enforcement? It depends. With 50 state jurisdictions in addition to federal jurisdiction, there is no uniform or cohesive body of law governing the enforcement of settlement agreements achieved through a mediation process in the United States.[15]

Although there is strong policy protecting mediation confidentiality, an equally strong policy promotes the enforcement of settlement agreements. After all, as cases are diverted to alternative dispute resolution (ADR), including mediation, court efficiency improves. Reduced caseloads, in turn, increase the public's satisfaction with the judicial branch as other matters move through the system more efficiently.[16] Section 6 of the Uniform Mediation Act provides that a written agreement signed by all parties is an exception to mediation confidentiality. This kind of confidentiality exception enables litigants to rely on a written settlement agreement produced in mediation and to bring it to the court for enforcement even when the agreement is the result of a confidential mediation.

> There is a general consensus that the UMA requirement of a written agreement, which makes evidence of oral agreements inadmissible, is correct and will eliminate many disputes and many situations in which mediation confidentiality would be breached.[17]

Whether you are acting as the mediator or representing a party in mediation, there are practical steps you can take to help maximize the likelihood that a mediated agreement will be admissible and enforceable in court. These include:

1. Make sure all of the material terms of the parties' agreement are included and clearly stated.
2. Include a statement that the parties intend the agreement to be binding and enforceable by the court and/or that the court shall retain jurisdiction over the parties to enforce the settlement until it is fully performed.
3. Include provisions expressly addressing the admissibility of the agreement in evidence in any enforcement proceeding.[18]
4. Include provisions expressly addressing whether mediation confidentiality will be waived and, if so, to what extent in any enforcement proceeding.
5. Include representations by the parties as to capacity, access to legal counsel, voluntariness, authority to act, and lack of duress.
6. Have the parties individually, as well as counsel, sign the settlement agreement.

Practice Tips

1. Advise clients about the strict confidentiality protections in mediation.
2. Understand the specific laws/rules governing mediation confidentiality in your jurisdiction, including what constitutes a "mediation" for confidentiality purposes? When does it begin and when does it end? Who is covered? What communications are covered? Does the protection attach only in the context of civil litigation, or is it broader?
3. Ask clients whether they have any concerns about confidentiality. If they do, ascertain the specific nature of those concerns.
4. Contract specifically in the mediation agreement regarding mediation confidentiality.

5. Obtain and document informed consent from clients on mediation confidentiality issues.
6. Draft mediated settlement agreements carefully to anticipate and forestall conflicts between confidentiality and enforcement.
7. In addition to any law promoting mediation confidentiality, make sure all parties, counsel, mediator (and co-mediators), and other participants (experts, family members, business associates) sign a separate mediation confidentiality agreement.
8. Advise clients that the mediator's role is to facilitate settlement and that the mediator cannot later be a witness in court.
9. Advise clients that they cannot rely on deals made or later use communication between spouses outside the presence of the mediator if those deals or communication are not written up or if counsel of record do not sign off.
10. Make sure the mediator follows the confidentiality rules in the mediation contract and conduct and takes steps to ensure that all mediation communication and writings are marked as confidential. For example, ask the mediator to put the following header on all summary letters and draft agreement: "Confidential and Inadmissible: Prepared During the Course of Mediation."
11. Attempt to negotiate a mediated case management protocol regarding negotiations of ultimate settlement terms and resolution of discovery, law and motion, and other contested pretrial issues.
12. Advise clients that evidence existing before a mediation will not be immune from disclosure if used in a mediation, for better or for worse.
13. Be prepared to guide your client and even participate in sessions as a non-adversarial resource and coach to improve the quality of the agreements reached so that difficult challenges to confidentiality and mediation settlements will not be necessary.
14. Never ask the mediator to offer testimony in any form (written or oral) about the mediation. Be prepared with legal authority to object to any testimony offered by the mediator and put the mediator and other party/lawyer on notice of your position. Remember, written affidavits and declarations by a mediator are still testimony.
15. Be cognizant that lawyers or parties may still be permitted testify about the conduct during a mediation as long as mediation communications are excluded.
16. Make sure parties understand that there is no binding deal unless both parties (and counsel of record) sign a written agreement. The written settlement agreement should unambiguously and directly express the parties' intent to be bound and to permit disclosure and enforcement of the signed mediated agreement in a court of law and to request the court to enforce the provisions of the settlement reached in mediation.
17. If there are essential issues to be worked out after a basic agreement in principle has been reached, take the time to resolve those issue on the day of the mediation or schedule a return session.

18. Never represent to court that a matter is resolved in mediation unless all essential drafting terms have been worked out.
19. Advise your client never to initial or sign any document unless it is first reviewed by you and make sure the client knows that such document may be admissible in court as a binding agreement.
20. Advise your client prior to starting mediation that attorney negligence during a mediation may be inadmissible in a subsequent malpractice or fee dispute with a client even if such conversations are not in the presence of a mediator.

Notes

1. CONFIDENTIALITY AND OTHER ETHICAL ISSUES IN MEDIATION, Copyright 1999, Jacquelin F. Drucker, Esq., http://www.ilr.cornell.edu/alliance/resources/Legal/confidentiality_ethical_issues_in_mediation.html.

2. There is a vigorous public policy debate in progress over whether public records, including family court files, should be freely available by anyone via the Internet. The issue of online access to public records, with which court administrators are now struggling, will likely be an increasingly significant privacy concern in the coming years.

3. www.irs.gov/uac/Examples-of-Identity-Theft-Schemes-Fiscal-Year-2014.

4. *See*, for example, Sheridan v. Sheridan, 247 N.J. Super. 552 (Ch. Div. 1990).

5. ABA Model Standards of Conduct for Mediators at i (1995): "Various aspects of a mediation, including some matters covered by these Standards, may also be affected by applicable law, court rules, regulations, other applicable professional rules, mediation rules to which the parties have agreed and other agreements of the parties. These sources may create conflicts with, and may take precedence over, these Standards. However, a mediator should make every effort to comply with the spirit and intent of these Standards in resolving such conflicts." *See also*, *Model Standards of Practice for Family and Divorce Mediation* (2000) promulgated by The Association of Family and Conciliation Courts, The Family Law Section of the American Bar Association, National Council of Dispute Resolution Organizations (NCDRO) as well as many other organizations. http://www.afccnet.org/Resource-Center/Practice-Guidelines-and-Standards.

6. *See* The Uniform Mediation Act: An Analysis of Current State Acts, http://moritzlaw.osu.edu/epub/mayhew-hite/vol5iss1/student.html.

7. Ohio Revised Statutes 2710.05; NE ST § 25-2935(a)(7).

8. The numerous state statutes address mediation confidentiality and mediator protections and "are remarkable both for their variations in approach and the narrow subject matters to which they apply." (CONFIDENTIALITY AND OTHER ETHICAL ISSUES IN MEDIATION, Copyright 1999, Jacquelin F. Drucker, Esq.

9. J. Michael Hand v. Walnut Valley Sailing Club, Case No. 11-3228(Tenth Circuit, April 4, 2012). (No sanction short of dismissal "would adequately admonish [Mr. Hand] for his complete disregard for and willful violation of the confidentiality rule, deter similar conduct by others in the future, restore respect for [the] Court's authority, repair the damage caused by [Mr. Hand] to the integrity of the Court's ADR program, and minimize prejudice"); Paranzino v. Barnett Bank (1997) 690 So.2d 725.

10. A recent California case, Lappe v. Superior Court (2014) 232 Cal.App.4th 774, however, held that statutorily mandated financial disclosures are not "prepared for the purpose of mediation" within the meaning of the confidentiality provisions in the California Evidence Code and therefore those provisions do not apply. The trial court had determined that the California Supreme Court's rejection of judicially crafted exceptions to mediation confidentiality, coupled with the parties' stipulated agreement precluding discovery or admission of their mandated financial disclosure statements, meant that those disclosure statements were protected by mediation confidentiality. Presumably, any statement other than one reflected on a mandated financial disclosure would be protected.

11. Cassell v. Superior Court (Wasserman, Comden, Casselman & Pearson, LLP (2010) 51 Cal.4th 113 (California Supreme Court holds that mediation confidentiality protections extend to communications made outside mediation between a disputant and his or her attorney.)

12. Milhouse v. Travelers Commercial Insurance Co., __F. Supp.2nd __(C.D. Cal, 2013). As of the date of publication, this case is pending in the Federal Ninth Circuit Court of Appeals, Case numbers 1356959 and 13-57029.

13. *See* Mediators as Mandatory Reporters at www.law.fsu.edu/journals/lawreview/downloads/342/hinshaw.pdf .

14. *See*, for example, Cal. Evid. Code § 1120.

15. http://www.arbitralwomen.org/files/publication/5809170924333.pdf .

16. Mosten, www.callawyer.com/Clstory.cfm?eid=918251.

17. www.arbitralwomen.org/files/publication/5809170924333.pdf at 37. See Peter Robinson, "Centuries of Contract Common Law Can't be All Wrong: Why the UMA's Exception to the Mediation Confidentiality in Enforcement Proceedings Should Be Embraced and Broadened" (2003) J Disp Resol 135; Peter Thompson, "Enforcing Rights Generated in Court Connected Mediation—Tension Between the Aspirations of a Private Facilitative Process and the Reality of the Public Adversarial Justice" (2004) 19 Ohio St J on Disp Resol 509; Ellen Deason, "Enforcing Mediated Settlement Agreements: Contract Law Collides With Confidentiality" (2001) 35 UC Davis L Rev 33.

18. *See In Re* Tft-Lcd (Flat Panel) Antitrust Litigation, United States District Court (N. D. Cal.), Multi-District Litigation, Case No. M 07-1827 SI, C 12-02214 SI, relating to Sony Electronics Inc. et al. v. HannStar Display Corp. (December 3, 2013). Sony had moved for summary judgment, alleging HannStar had reneged on a commitment to pay a confidential settlement sum proposed by a mediator and arguing that a series of e-mails between the parties and their mediator formed a binding contract which was admissible in evidence to prove breach. The Court "reluctantly" denied summary judgment, holding that because the e-mails did not affirmatively provide that the

agreement the parties reached was enforceable or binding, mediation confidentiality rendered the purported settlement agreement inadmissible. It stated, "although it may be inequitable to permit HannStar to avoid its agreement to settle, such inequity alone does not permit the Court to fashion a new exception to the mediation confidentiality statute. Rather, because the parties failed to include an affirmative statement to the effect that they intended their settlement to be enforceable or binding, the e-mails are inadmissible as evidence of settlement." The moral of this story is that failure to include the "magic words" can sometimes lead to catastrophic consequences.

CHAPTER 4

Representing Clients in Court-Ordered Mediation

". . . THE COURT on its own volition finds that reducing conflict through a process that promotes an amicable agreement on the issues is in the best interest of the parties, therefore both parties are required to attend mediation to resolve the contested issues. . . ."
—Order of Referral to Family Court Mediation, First Judicial Circuit of Florida

"In an effort to provide an expeditious, expense-saving, fair and beneficial alternative to traditional litigation in the resolution of domestic relations controversies, these rules establish a program of court-annexed mediation which shall operate in cases pending in the Domestic Relations Division of the Circuit Court of Cook County. Parties and their representatives are required to attend mediation sessions, but are not compelled to reach an agreement. The program includes mediators employed by Cook County and private mediators. In addition, the parties may agree to utilize other forms of alternative dispute resolution ('ADR')."
—Cook County (IL) Circuit Court Rule 13.4(e)

"Most civil disputes are resolved without filing a lawsuit, and most civil lawsuits are resolved without a trial. The courts and others offer a variety of Alternative Dispute Resolution (ADR) processes to help people resolve disputes without a trial. ADR is usually less formal, less expensive, and less time-consuming than a trial."
—California Courts Website (www.courts.ca.gov/programs-adr.htm)

Many jurisdictions have court-mandated mediation requiring litigants to participate. In court programs, the mediation takes place in either the courthouse or the office of a court-referred mediator. The mediation might be conducted by court staff mediators, private providers under contract with the court, or pro bono volunteer mediators. In the National

Standards of Court Connected Mediation Programs (called National Standards from now on)[1], the exclusive use of volunteer mediators is discouraged. While child custody and visitation are the issues most often mandated by court-annexed or court-referred mediation, some court systems provide for mediation of economic distributive issues as well (support, property, lawyer fees, and costs). With the deluge of court budget cuts in recent years, many of the programs are in trouble or are being eliminated, regardless of format.

Court-Annexed Mediation

Court-annexed mediation is authorized by either statute or local court rule. Sometimes individual judges impose the requirement in their own courtrooms. *Mandatory* generally means the parties are required to participate in mediation before a court hearing is permitted, except in rare emergencies or with a waiver by the court. *Mandatory* does not mean that the parties are required to reach agreement, only that they must participate meaningfully.

Are Mandatory Mediation Proceedings Confidential?

There is a major split between practice and authority. In some jurisdictions, all communication is protected by confidentiality. Any disclosure of mediation communication by the court may be subject to contempt, monetary sanctions, or other judicially discretionary remedies. Any issues that remain unsettled can be resolved by the court. However, even in confidential jurisdictions, statutorily mandated reporting such as allegations or mediator suspicion of child violence or sexual abuse, physical danger to a party or third person, or threats to commit crimes may be reported to law enforcement or the court. Lawyer/mediators assume reporting obligations like therapists, who often have a duty to report child abuse or domestic violence, whenever it is discovered (even when they are not acting as treating therapists). Lawyers have an opposite duty of confidentiality and generally may not report past criminal acts or abuse. However, lawyer/mediators serving in a court mediation program may be required to report. On the other hand, private lawyer/mediators generally do not have a right to report unless so authorized in advance by written agreement or there is reasonable suspicion of imminent harm to a mediation participant or to others. This area needs further study and standardization.

In nonconfidential jurisdictions, if agreement is not reached, the mediator may be asked by the judge to give a report, including observations, findings, and recommendations. The report may be given in writing, orally in open court subject to cross-examination, or on camera on or off the record. In California, neighboring counties may have very different rules regarding confidentiality. For example, Los Angeles County has confidential child-custody mediation, whereas Ventura (immediately north) is nonconfidential. Absent a statute authorizing such nonconfidentiality, such jurisdictions operate contrary to the confidentiality proscriptions of 8.1 (e) of the National Standards and contrary to 12.1-3, which limits communication by a mediator to the court, and contrary to 11.5, which warns against a court's adverse response to non-settlement by the parties.[2]

When Does Court-Annexed Mediation Take Place?

Jurisdictions vary widely. Mediation may take place as late as the date of the hearing. Progressive jurisdictions require mediation soon after an action is filed; a few courts require mediation before a hearing date is set. Rules may differ from courtroom to courtroom within the same jurisdiction or based on the type of issue involved.

Who Participates in Court-Annexed Mediation?

Litigants are generally required to be physically present at the mediation. Lawyers may or may not be permitted to participate in the sessions. In some jurisdictions, lawyers are present at the beginning to set out the issues and give their perspectives. Parties are always permitted to consult with their attorneys, who may wait in the hall or be available by telephone.

Try Not to Second-Guess the Mediator or Micromanage the Process

With the best of motives, many lawyers have a difficult time letting go—trusting their clients and the mediator to get the job done. It's a bit of a control struggle. Most lawyers like control and have difficulty being the coach; they want to peel off their warm-ups and join the huddle! Here is one example:

After successfully resolving approximately 100 issues and subissues, Mike and Karen were down to the last issue: would spousal support be subject to downward modification if Karen cohabited romantically with another person? Both parties knew that under the law, such cohabitation was a statutory basis for reduction because there was a presumption of reduced need on the part of the payee spouse. Karen had already agreed to shave two years off her support period and was not willing to sacrifice her financial independence, being adamant on this point.

Mike's lawyer, screaming from the sidelines, was coaching him to hold firm: "She can't have it both ways. Every judge in the courthouse would reduce spousal support—many would even terminate payments—if a payee spouse was living with a member of the opposite sex." The lawyer called the mediator, faxed her, even bent her ear when they ran into each other picking tomatoes at the local farmer's market.

The twist in the story is that Mike wanted to wrap up the mediation, and he could even understand Karen's concerns. However, he was nervous and afraid—afraid of his own financial future, afraid of letting down his lawyer, afraid of looking like an emasculated wimp (Karen was the moving party in the divorce). He needed to talk out his concern and think aloud about his future.

Continued

> **Try Not to Second-Guess the Mediator or Micromanage the Process** *Continued*
>
> Mike then met with the mediator three times in private caucus—90 minutes each time. At the end, he was willing to concede the issue. He just wanted recognition from his wife that she appreciated his movement, that he was a good guy. Mike's lawyer was upset to the very end, but both Mike and Karen moved on without his consent.

In some court mediation programs involving economic issues, the parties may not be permitted to be in the mediation room or to speak directly to the other party or to the mediator. The lawyers alone might mediate and involve the clients only if an impasse occurs on one or more issues. In such models, the lawyers shuffle in and out of the mediation room, meet with their clients, and then return to the mediation room.

New spouses or non-married partners of the parties may be allowed to participate in mediation sessions if the mediator deems them necessary and/or helpful. In such situations, there may be a conflict. Quite often a problem between a new romantic partner and a party is driving the litigation. In such cases, opening up participation can be instrumental in achieving resolution.

Do the Parties Meet Individually or Together?

The mediator determines the agenda of the session and whether the sessions are to be individual or conjoint. It is common for the mediator to use several configurations within a single mediation: meet together, alone with each party shuttling in and out several times, jointly again, with or without counsel—the combinations are endless.

In cases of alleged physical or sexual abuse, statutory authority or local practice may require that the parties not meet in joint sessions and can only attend mediation in separate sessions when requested by the alleged victim for physical protection or to prevent coercion or duress. In California, for example, a statutory scheme affirmatively permits the victim to have a support person or an advocate in the mediation session to increase security and emotional support and to request that the parties not meet together.[3]

How Are Mediated Agreements Finalized?

Many jurisdictions have the parties recite their agreement verbally to a judge, at which time it becomes an order. Some models include the mediator working with the parties to finalize the agreement in writing. In other situations, the lawyers will draft the court stipulation and the mediator will participate only in case of drafting trouble. Some jurisdictions have a cooling-off period that permits either party to revoke the agreement for any reason within a specified number of days; otherwise, it automatically becomes an order of the court. A revoked agreement is generally inadmissible in any proceeding (but it probably remains in the court file, where the judge might read it!).

What Happens If a Party Refuses to Participate?

This is also an area of great variation. The general minimum requirement is for the parties to appear physically before the mediator, although this basic compliance is sometimes waived due to hardship (cross-country residence or illness) or the emergency nature of issues requiring an immediate hearing or just because the judicial officer has an open courtroom in which to start a hearing or otherwise grants an exception. Failure to appear at mediation may be sanctionable.[4] Once the parties show up, jurisdictions vary in the extent to which they monitor what actually happens before the mediator. In nonconfidential jurisdictions where the mediator is permitted to make a recommendation, the mediator often informs the judge when a party refuses to participate (and may identify the culprit). In some confidential jurisdictions, as long as the parties physically appear, the mediation requirement is fulfilled even if they stay less than five minutes and sit like sphinxes. Other models leave it up to the mediator to release the parties after there has been "meaningful participation," an intentionally vague term. If a party merely articulates a position, no matter how unreasonable, does this constitute meaningful participation? What if a party literally shouts down the other so that neither side can be heard?

Commentary to Section 5.1 of the National Standards takes the view that participants must show up but need not negotiate an agreement to avoid inappropriate pressure to settle:

> . . . the intention of the Standard is to clarify that by referring parties to mediation on a mandatory basis a court should require only that they attend an initial mediation session, discuss the case, and be educated about the process in order to make an informed choice about their continued participation.[5]

It is difficult to define meaningful participation in the mediation context. The National Standards provide for courts to establish deadlines that may be extended if continuation is found to assist resolution. Such vague requirements, however, do not provide the parties with sufficient guidance on what constitutes compliance and suggest the difficulty of defining meaningful participation.

Possible sanctions for failure to participate in good faith in mediation, depending on the jurisdiction, include attorney fee awards, payment of other reasonable expenses incurred due to failure to appear, civil or criminal contempt, revocation of counsel's *pro hac vice* status, a stay of proceedings pending compliance with court orders for mediation, entry of default judgment, preclusion of claims, or even dismissal with prejudice.

Courts have not hesitated, sometimes *sua sponte*, to sanction a party that did not abide by certain fundamental courtesies that went beyond filing the required documents and showing up with the proper representatives, as in *O'Donnell v. Pennsylvania Department of Corrections*, 2011 U.S. Dist. LEXIS 11438, at *18 (M.D. Pa. Feb. 4, 2011) (ordering attorney fees as monetary sanctions) (quoting *Taberer v. Armstrong World Industries*, 954 F.2d 888, 892 n.3 (3d Cir. 1992) (case involved sanctions of criminal contempt, a $5,000 fine, and revocation of counsel's *pro hac vice* status in all cases pending in that district): "While [it has been] suggested that, as a matter of law, the court is powerless to sanction parties for actions relating to settlement and mediation conferences, plainly under Rule 16 this is not correct. Quite the contrary, it is well settled that Rule 16 'is the usual vehicle for imposing coercive or punitive sanctions in these circumstances.'"[6]

What Issues Are Covered by Court-Annexed Mediation?

In many states, mandatory mediation is limited to custody and visitation disputes. In some states, the court mediation service (often inaptly named *conciliation court*) can be utilized for marriage counseling, domestic violence, or other issues of personal conduct and communication. Many court systems have mandatory parental educational components ranging from the required viewing of a video to a required lecture, classes, or training in parenting or divorced-couple communication that could span several weeks. Due to budget constraints, classes have been replaced with online mini-courses in many jurisdictions.

The PEACE Program developed by Professor Andrew Schepard of Hofstra University, Hempstead, New York, is probably the nation's most comprehensive parent education program. Some courts require court mediation for the economic issues, such as child support, spousal support, allocation of assets and debts, and disputes over payment of costs and lawyer fees. In court programs limited to children's issues, parents may not bring up economic issues. In other courts, staff mediators will be limited to custody/visitation, but economic issues may be mediated by volunteer lawyers or others selected by a community bar association. In such programs, qualifications and training vary widely, as do the techniques.

Mediation by Court Referral

An approach used in many jurisdictions is the mandatory referral of the parties to a mediator outside the courthouse. In some schemes, court-referred mediation replaces hearing-day mediation; in others, it supplements the courthouse system. Some mediators are paid by the court system or by the parties themselves, and others volunteer their time. The mediations may be time-limited (one or two hours) or left to the mediator's discretion and largesse. Some systems let parties select their mediator from a list, with the judicial officer assigning only in case of impasse. In others, the assignment of the mediator is imposed and final, except for challenge due to legal cause. Just as in courthouse programs, the issues, mediator skill, experience, and dispute resolution processes vary greatly. The National Standards recognize mandatory referral outside the court and underscore the court responsibility of such mediators to report information to the court to permit monitoring. The standards urge courts to set up a complaint mechanism. The standards also encourage the parties to have the right to substitute a private mediator unless a court specifically prohibits it. How the mediator gets paid varies throughout the country.

A successful model for outside mediation has been developed by New Jersey through its Complementary Dispute Resolution Program (CDR). The New Jersey program provides for not only referral to a mediator at no charge for CDR qualified mediators but also provides for party selection of a non-court-administered program in which the mediators are compensated. New Jersey family law specialist Cary Cheifetz of Skoloff, Wolfe reports that the program is well accepted by the Family Law Bar and has evolved beyond the initial rules:

> If the referral is made to an early settlement panel, . . . there is no fee associated; however occasionally a complex matter is referred to what is known as a blue ribbon panel, . . . i.e., two highly respected and experienced lawyers. It is customary that the panelists be compensated if the proceeding takes more than one session. It is usually negotiated among the lawyers for the parties, the judge, and the panelists. I know it sounds very informal, but our judges generally feel that non compensation can be a burden and that there are limits to pro bono work, especially if the parties have privately retained counsel and have assets.[7]

Another growing approach is referral to an outside mediator in which the parties initially bear the costs equally at market rates. This type of referral calls for early mediation in all civil cases with the court having the discretion to determine on good cause not to order early mediation.[8]

If this model (facetiously called a mediation work bill) continues to gain acceptance, the current oversupply of trained mediators might be transformed to a demand for many more mediators in both the courts and the private sector.

Malpractice Protection for Court Mediators

Many family lawyers who want to participate in court mediation may fear being sued by hostile litigants. Lawyers who volunteer their time may be particularly reluctant to offer this public service if the price is being named in a lawsuit.

In their seminal article on court mediation, Margaret Shaw, Linda Singer, and Linda Povich summarize statutory schemes for mediation immunity and indemnification. However, the National Standards takes an anti-immunity position, finding that "granting mediators immunity from liability inappropriately denies recourse to litigants injured by incompetent service, especially when litigants are required to pay for the service."[9] This position is in conflict with the California case of *Howard v. Drapkin* (1990) 222 Cal App. 3rd 843, which provides quasi-judicial immunity to protect mediators and to encourage them to provide mediation for the court system.

The Role of Lawyers in Court Mediation

Although it is becoming much less frequent today, some lawyers (particularly those with little family law experience), do not trust the court-annexed mediation process or want to use it solely as an adversarial tool. These lawyers may script their clients fully or give detailed coaching on what to accept during the mediation negotiations. They may even instruct the clients to leave the mediation room prematurely to avoid the potential for compromise and to get to court (and still avoid sanctions for not participating meaningfully). In attempting to avoid interfering with lawyer control (often alternatively labeled a litigant's confidence in the lawyer), some mediators will abort the mediation if one or both parties seem to be in an anti-mediation trance from their lawyers. Having the lawyers participate in the sessions and become part of the process may be a remedy for this problem. Participation of the lawyers in the sessions may have a downside in the form of causing interference, increasing the adversarial tone, removing control and empowerment of the parties, and increasing the complexity of the negotiation. The court-annexed system in New Zealand and the legal aid mediation conferences in Queensland, Australia, addressed this problem 30 years ago by requiring the lawyers to sit behind their clients and limiting the lawyers' participation unless the clients ask to consult with them. In that instance, the clients had to take the initiative to turn 180 degrees to make eye contact with their lawyers and initiate the lawyer-client conference outside. When the mediation resumes, it is the party (not the lawyer) who carries the dialogue with the other spouse and the mediator. This practice is less prevalent today and has not caught on in this country.

The Role of Lawyers in Court Mediation

The National Standards for Court-Connected Mediation Programs set out the following role for lawyers in court mediation:
10.1 Courts should encourage attorneys to advise their clients on the advantages, disadvantages, and strategies for using mediation.

> COMMENTARY: Lawyers have several possible functions to perform in connection with their clients' participation in mediation:
> 1. Before their clients decide whether to mediate, lawyers may give initial advice concerning whether it is in the client's best interest to participate in mediation and what substantive rights will govern if the case goes to trial.
> 2. Lawyers may attend mediation sessions and participate directly in mediation. Alternatively, they may participate indirectly by advising clients before, during or after mediation sessions.
> 3. Lawyers may review draft agreements reached in mediation or, alternatively, they may draft the agreements themselves.
> 4. Following mediation, lawyers may complete the legal process, by filing a consent decree if agreement is reached, or by continuing the pretrial process if issues remain to be resolved by the court.
> 5. If necessary, lawyers may act to enforce any agreements reached in mediation.

Mandatory Settlement Conferences

Most court systems have a built-in procedure for the parties to come to court with their lawyers to try to settle the case prior to a trial. Generally, the process includes an opportunity for at least the lawyers, and often the parties, to have some time with a judicial officer. A mandatory settlement conference (MSC) is generally held within 30 to 60 days of trial. The parties are expected to have completed all discovery; exchanged witness lists and documents; and received court rulings on pretrial motions such as joiner of necessary parties, summary judgments, and necessary discovery compliance. In short, prior to an MSC, lawyers and parties are expected to have explored settlement, to have completed their preparations, and to be ready for trial. To ensure that the parties are truly ready, most courts require the parties to submit in advance some form of MSC brief setting forth the facts of the case, issues in contention, a proposal for settlement with supporting argument (including legal authorities), and limited support documentation. This can be a very expensive process.

In progressive jurisdictions, the MSC can be effective in stopping the litigation by adopting a number of rules to facilitate settlement, inducing rules and procedures affecting judicial attitude, which include:

- Setting MSCs early to allow sufficient time prior to the trial for meaningful negotiations that won't be aborted in favor of preparing for trial.
- Allocating judicial resources so that the judge assigned to preside at the MSC is skilled, energetic, patient, and devoted to quality settlements. It is crucial that MSC judges

be freed from competing trial or administrative duties so that they can have the time and focus to serve the parties and lawyers attending the MSC.
- Setting a low number of cases so that the MSC judge can devote sufficient time and attention to each matter. Many courts utilize experienced family lawyers to serve as MSC judge pro tem or to handle less complex matters, warm up the parties while waiting for the judge, act as a co-settlement officer with the judge, or take over the process.
- Making sure that all people necessary to accomplish settlement are present. Quite often a spouse's parent (holding a promissory note or being ready to fund a buyout), a business partner, a real estate broker or mortgage lender, accountant(s) (personal, business, and/or forensic), a personal injury lawyer handling a spouse's personal injury or disability claim, a child-care provider, a therapist, a vocational counselor, or another relevant person might hold the key to settlement and should be present.
- Devote sufficient court space, auxiliary resources, and amenities to the settlement process. Private, carpeted, air-conditioned rooms with round tables and sufficient comfortable chairs for all in attendance affirm settlement as a court priority.

Is the MSC Judge the Trial Judge?

There is a difference of opinion here. Many judges and lawyers contend that the all-purpose judge system as used in the federal district courts makes parties accountable in settlement discussions because an unreasonable negotiating position that propels the case to the court will be remembered and resented by the trial judge. Also, aware of the jurist's read of the case, parties will adopt more realistic settlement positions. The other school of thought is that by utilizing a different settlement judge, parties will be encouraged to take more expansive and creative and less positional settlement proposals without the trial judge's being aware of such positions—thereby easing the concerns of the more polarized and inflexible party.

It should come as no surprise that many courts do not have the resources or the will to meet these proposed standards. Unfortunately, many MSCs are held within days of trial (or simultaneously on the date of trial); many cases are set on the same day; the judge's other duties limit the time available; only the lawyers, not the parties, see the judge (then perhaps only in separate sessions); and the parties wait on wooden benches in public corridors. Lawyer discussions are conducted (if at all) in the hallways and on the courthouse steps, driven by fatigue, frustration, and fear of continually rising costs and the impending trial.

Mediation Versus Mandatory Settlement Conferences

Even in progressive jurisdictions, many lawyers view MSCs as synonymous with mediation. If a lawyer's client or the opposing lawyer suggests early mediation (either inside or outside the courthouse), a common response is, "Why should my client spend money to pay a mediator or pay additional lawyer fees when we'll have to mediate at the MSC anyway?"

MSCs differ from mediation in many ways, including:

- The black-robed jurist (even if the robe is temporarily on a hanger) represents the court authority, which often has an arm-twisting effect on parties. Such authority often produces settlements—based in part on reliance on that authority. Although a mediator may provide neutral legal information, including predictions of outcome in court, the mediation is premised on the parties controlling the outcome through negotiation facilitated (not controlled) by the mediator.
- The MSC judge often does consider emotions and values and how the family will function after the settlement. However, the main motivation of the court is to settle the case and remove it from the trial docket. Therefore, the MSC judge may focus the parties on the anticipated legal outcome and encourage, persuade, and sometimes threaten the parties to accept that outcome by settlement rather than have it imposed judicially after a costly trial. In mediation, the parties are encouraged to reach agreement only if it is in their best short- and long-term interest. The mediator will explore underlying fears and concerns of the parties and work with them to fashion an agreement that addresses those concerns.
- The MSC is generally held in the courthouse, and the parties are often treated with polite impersonal efficiency at best and callous disregard (or even rudeness) at worst by the courthouse staff or even by the judge. Unfortunately, some citizens who haven't settled their divorces prior to an MSC are viewed by the court personnel as failures or troublemakers—surly irritants or unwelcome problems foisted on the court. In private mediation, only one case is set and the mediator has been booked to devote exclusive time to this matter. The mediation starts at the appointed time and continues uninterrupted by other business for the time that was blocked off in advance.
- Many MSC judges are the best settlement judicial officers in the courthouse, and those assigned to family law matters often have extensive family law experience, both in practice and on the bench. Even these judicial stars have rarely received training in progressive negotiation theory or have been trained in advanced mediation techniques. In other venues, the MSC judge may have little experience in family law or the training, talent, or desire for taking a proactive settlement role. In misplaced deference to the autonomy of the lawyers, many MSC judges quit early when the settlement gap appears insurmountable rather than proactively jawbone attorneys and parties into

movement. Due to a myopic view of the nature and causes of conflict and an inadequate inventory of impasse-breaking skills and techniques, some judges take a quick hard look and choose to use their limited time to resolve cases that they believe have a chance of settling with a reasonable investment of time. Many times this short-shrift approach is the correct call because the case might never have settled or might have settled only after many hours of direct judicial intervention. In many other situations, a lack-of-settlement focus might ensure the drain of judicial time not only in the present trial, but also in possible subsequent litigation.

- In jurisdictions where the date on which the MSC is set is also the deadline to serve witness lists and exhibit lists for trial, the clients will have already paid for a substantial level of trial preparation and will not enjoy the full economic benefit of early settlement.

In contrast, professional mediators are specially trained in proactive settlement and are paid to ply their craft in such difficult cases. Helping the parties work through an impasse by acknowledging those areas of agreement that may be preserved even if some issues need a decision imposed by a judge is a common auxiliary mediator skill.

The MSC judge is generally free to the parties, whereas paying for a private mediator is an additional out-of-pocket cost. However, the initial cost differential needs further exploration. The preparation for an MSC in both generating quality advocacy and complying with court requirements can be very expensive. Yet, competent preparation for a mediation is probably not much less expensive, if at all. The major costs of an MSC are the hours and hours of waiting for available judicial input and the price of lost opportunity by lack of time and settlement expertise of the MSC judge, resulting in a trial. Also, once they have reached an equitable and enforceable agreement through mediation, the parties may be better prepared to settle follow-up matters on their own or can return to mediation to build on their prior success at resolution, resulting in major cost savings from reduced relitigation. A generic estimate of private mediation costs is included in the Resources section.

Practice Tips

1. At the beginning of client representation, learn about the court-annexed mediation requirements and options in your jurisdiction, including timing, staffing, settlement styles of staff mediators and MSC judges, courthouse facilities, and permitted roles of counsel.
2. At the earliest available opportunity, educate the client about the philosophy and procedures in court-annexed mediation. Compare and contrast court-annexed mediation with court hearings and with dispute resolution options in the private sector.

3. If there is any emergent need to reschedule a court-annexed mediation, promptly advise the opposing party and the mediator both orally and in writing and make efforts to reschedule as soon as possible.
4. Confirm in writing that the client is aware of the date, time and location of the court-annexed mediation. Send a written reminder.
5. Prepare written materials and a DVD or online visual presentation to teach clients about court-annexed mediation. Encourage clients to take a field trip to the courthouse to eyeball the mediation and MSC processes to gain comfort and information to make informed process decisions.
6. Prior to the date of court mediation or an MSC, schedule a client conference to explain every anticipated step of the day's activities, including the highlighting of unknown variables (how long the day will last, which decisions will be made, and where and with whom the various configurations of discussions will take place). Discuss the need to have emotional support at the courthouse and to bring reading material and/or work to pass the time. Also stress the importance of not booking any appointments for the afternoon and arranging child care so that time or child pressures will not add to the client's anxiety.
7. Find out whether the court-annexed mediation is confidential or nonconfidential. If it is nonconfidential, carefully educate your client about the use of mediation statements and the power of the mediator to make recommendations to the judge.
8. If your client is a victim of spousal violence, request separate sessions to reduce intimidation and fear. Also arrange for your client to have an emotional support person or victim advocate.
9. During the court mediation, if lawyers are not permitted to participate, be available for client consultation in the hallway or by telephone.
10. When an MSC is scheduled, suggest the possibility of private mediation first, giving the parties two chances (with different formats) to settle.

Notes

1. Margaret Shaw, Linda Singer, and Linda Povich, *National Standards for Court-Connected Mediation Programs*, FAM. & CONCILIATION CTS. REV., Apr. 1993, at 156-225. NAT'L STANDARDS OF COURT CONNECTED MEDIATION PROGRAMS § B.4 [hereinafter NAT'L STANDARDS].

2. NAT'L STANDARDS, §§ 8.1(e), 12.1-3, 11.5.

3. CAL. FAM. CODE § 6303 (West 1994).

4. *See*, for example, Roberts v. Rose, 37 S.W.3d 31, 33 (Tex. App. 2000) "The appellants argue that the trial court erred in granting sanctions against both Murr and Roberts in that there was

neither an allegation nor a finding of bad faith on their parts. Murr and Roberts were not sanctioned, however, for failure to mediate in good faith. They were sanctioned for failing to appear. . . . [W]hile parties cannot be forced to peaceably resolve their disputes through alternative dispute resolution procedures, a trial court can compel the parties to sit down with each other."

See also Black v. Sakelios, No. CA2013-10-094 (C.A. Ohio, June 16, 2014) (A death in the family was a sufficient reason for a party to miss a court-ordered mediation, but failure to let the mediator or other side know was nonetheless grounds for imposing sanctions); Rommel v. Torpey, No. 68804-9-I (C.A. Wash., April 28, 2014) (trial court did not err in dismissing ill plaintiff's case after she twice failed to participate in court-ordered mediation); U.S. Bank v. Sawyer, 2014 ME 81 (S.C. Me., June 24, 2014) (Supreme Court of Maine upheld the dismissal with prejudice of a complaint, following a warning, after multi-session mediation in which party exhibited lack of good faith.)

5. NAT'L STANDARDS, § 5.1 cmt.

6. https://casetext.com/case/odonnell-v-pennsylvania-department-of-corrections-7.

7. NEW JERSEY RULES OF GENERAL APPLICATION 1:40, COMPLEMENTARY DISPUTE RESOLUTION PROCESS [adopted September 1992 to adopt Report of Supreme Court Committee on Complementary Dispute Resolution, 130 N.J.L.S. 578, 1 N.J. LAW. 170 (1992); [Cary Cheifetz, Comments on LEXIS Counsel Connect, December 22, 1995. NEW JERSEY RULES OF GENERAL APPLICATION 1:40, COMPLEMENTARY DISPUTE RESOLUTION PROCESS [adopted September 1992 to adopt Report of Supreme Court Committee on Complementary Dispute Resolution, 130 N.J.L.S. 578, 1 N.J. LAW. 170 (1992)]; Cary Cheifetz, Comments on LEXIS Counsel Connect, December 22, 1995.

8. CA S.B. 1429, 1995-96 Reg. Sess. (1996).

9. Shaw et al., *supra* note 2.

CHAPTER 5

Using a Limited Scope Approach (Unbundling) to Represent Clients Outside and Inside the Mediation Room

The combined use of unbundled legal services can give otherwise unrepresented parties greater access to justice. . . . By using unbundling, attorneys can expand their practices, gain additional clients and increase their revenue all by helping represent the otherwise unrepresentatable.[1]

—Professor Kristen M. Blankley, University of Nebraska

A system based solely on the paradigm of full representation means either a litigant has the resources or luck to obtain beginning-to-end assistance from a lawyer, or is left alone to languish in the inexorable demands of the legal system. Unbundling offers flexibility that benefits the great majority of the public.[2]

—Hon. Michael B. Hyman, Chicago, Illinois

For decades, America's favorite hot drink was brewed coffee served in ceramic mugs. In recent years, coffee has been given a boost in its popularity and sales by changing its preparation and presentation. The coffee industry responded to consumers with new processes, innovative presentations, and creative marketing. This industry remodeling helped stimulate the coffee industry and give it life when many thought the health and fitness craze might devastate it.

Similarly, approximately 30 years ago, dentists feared that widespread introduction of fluoride would render dental services obsolete. Rather than defensively reacting to battle the fluoride movement, the dental profession embraced this discovery with the theme "The American Dental Association supports regular brushing with fluoride toothpaste as a necessary component of twice-a-year dental checkups for overall dental hygiene."

Changing its image from tooth drillers to managers of preventive dental health preserved and revitalized the dental profession.

Family lawyers have much to learn from these tales of flexible reinvention. We have an opportunity to buff up our inventory of service products to rise to the very challenges that appear to threaten our livelihood. Consumers are choosing to do without lawyers because of the high economic barriers of entry, loss of control, perceived pejorative attitudes and condescending treatment by lawyers, and fear of lawyers being deal breakers and family wreckers. Over half of these self-represented litigants could afford to hire a family lawyer but choose not to. Rather than blame the public, overcrowded and underfunded courts, the organized Bar, or the press, family lawyers can revitalize their own economic future by exploring new and more responsive ways of meeting consumer demand and increasing their profitability.

Unbundling: Rethinking How to Package and Deliver Legal Services

The Traditional Full-Service Package

Most family lawyers offer one legal service product: the full-service representational package of legal services. Upon being hired by a client and without otherwise limiting services, the lawyer explicitly or implicitly undertakes to provide the following services:

- Gathering facts
- Advising the client
- Discovering the facts of the opposing party
- Researching the law
- Drafting correspondence and documents
- Negotiating with the other lawyer (or unrepresented party)
- Representing the client in court

Although not all services are performed in every engagement, both clients and lawyers assume that the lawyer, as tactical captain, will decide what services are needed and who will perform them. It is also assumed that the lawyer, not the client, will perform these services on behalf of the client. While the client may be a resource for factual information, the lawyer is responsible for doing all of the work. In fact, many lawyers discourage involvement of the client in preparing correspondence or written court documents. (Some less responsive lawyers even fail to send the client copies of all correspondence.) And once at the courthouse, it is clear to everyone that this is a lawyer-directed production.

In full-service representation, the client has the right to approve decisions regarding the final settlement and to be informed about the progress of the case as it goes along. At its very essence, much like hiring a surgeon to handle an operation while the patient is under anesthetic, the client selects a lawyer based on a client's feeling of trust in the lawyer's competence and judgment. If either the competence or the judgment is questioned to the point of undermining client confidence, the client's remedy is to go it alone or hire another lawyer—probably also operating under the full-service representational package.

In return for the responsibility of controlling the case management and doing the work, lawyers and clients contract for the lawyer to be paid for the work performed, generally on an hourly basis. Applying pure economic motivation, the lawyer makes more money if more lawyer work is done. Clients, while suspicious of this motivation, generally trust lawyer integrity and judgment, and because they view full service as increasing the quality of legal services, clients sign on for this model—until they lose confidence, run out of money, or both.

Lawyers often "unbundle" by employing a cost-benefit analysis to determine what services are to be rendered. For example, you might decide which depositions to take and who will take them. Because lawyers fear malpractice claims should the client later be unhappy, defensive over-lawyering to do all possible work becomes more common—with clients paying the bills. Over-lawyering doesn't run up costs for just one spouse. The other spouse must defend and will often choose to escalate the response. Such over-lawyering can pollute the value system of an entire legal community, becoming the "safe and prudent" standard of customary law practice under the guise of protecting clients' rights.

Unbundling Defined

Unbundling (also called *limited scope* or *discrete task representation*) offers clients a middle ground between dispensing with lawyers altogether and signing on for the full-service package. With the help of a lawyer, the client determines which services are to be performed by the client, which services are to be performed by the lawyer, and the extent or depth to which the lawyer shall perform the designated services. The division of these tasks should be clearly and specifically spelled out in the initial attorney-client engagement letter. Here are 17 choices:

1. Legal advice: office visits, telephone calls, fax, mail, e-mail
2. Advice about availability of alternative means to resolve the dispute, including mediation and arbitration
3. Evaluation of the client's self-diagnosis of the case and advice to the client about legal rights
4. Guidance and procedural information for filing or serving documents
5. Reviews of correspondence and court documents
6. Preparation and/or suggestion of documents to be prepared

7. Factual investigation: contact of witnesses, public record searches, in-depth interview of the client
8. Legal research and analysis
9. Discovery: interrogatories, depositions, requests for document production
10. Plans for negotiations, including simulated role playing with the client
11. Plans for court appearances made by the client, including simulated role playing with the client
12. Backup and troubleshooting during the trial
13. Referral of the client to other counsel, an expert, or a professional
14. Client counseling about an appeal
15. Procedural assistance with an appeal and assistance with substantive legal argumentation in an appeal
16. Preventive planning and/or legal checkups
17. Other agreed-upon services

The lawyer only has responsibility to perform those services that are specifically checked off and authorized by the client. The lawyer is not entitled to payment for services that have not been checked off unless the limited scope arrangement is modified in writing by both lawyer and client. In the same vein, if the client makes ineffective or self-destructive decisions or actions in handling (or not handling) a task for which the lawyer is not responsible, the client cannot blame or take legal action against the lawyer. Rather than being treated paternalistically, clients are afforded the control to choose the scope of engagement and must therefore live with the result.

Family lawyers are currently offering a number of new service products to serve both self-represented litigants and represented clients. After reviewing some of these common unbundled services, the balance of this chapter will focus on your limited scope role representing clients as a consulting lawyer outside the mediation room as well as a limited role of being at mediation sessions without necessarily being counsel of record for the rest of the case.

Attorney Coach: Educator and Adviser

The 1993 ABA study on self-represented litigants in Maricopa County, Arizona, found that what most hurt litigants without lawyers was the lack of legal advice. While court forms and procedures have been simplified so that working people can process a divorce themselves, processing a divorce without some legal advice can adversely affect the life of the pro se litigant. The ABA study found that, compared with litigants who had a lawyer's help, self-represented litigants received lower child and spousal support and less temporary relief through *pendente lite* orders, lived with outdated orders due to getting fewer modifications, and did not take advantage of tax breaks due to receiving less advice on tax consequences. Equally important, self-represented litigants knew less about alternative dispute resolution (ADR) and used it less frequently than people who were represented by lawyers. This means that although self-represented families got their divorces more easily and cheaply, conflict and parenting deficiencies were not addressed as adequately as if the agreements had been mediated or the parties had been taught how to resolve disputes in the future by lawyers serving an educational role in regard to diffusing conflict.[3] By serving as a client legal coach (attorney coach), you can offer self-represented litigants a nonthreatening and less expensive alternative. Clients decide when, for which issues, and at what depth they want to consult with their lawyers. Accustomed to handling the whole case or not helping a person going through divorce, you must be willing to alter your expectations about decision making, fees, and handling of the nuts and bolts of the case.

How can you as an attorney coach provide value to your clients by delivering such limited service for limited fees? Here are a few suggestions:

- You can help a client calculate income and statute-allowed deductions, exemptions, and hardships and then print out statutory guidelines for support. This will provide the client with a reality check and help the client prepare for direct negotiations with the other spouse or a court hearing without your being present.
- You can help your unbundled client fill out court forms. Even with simplified forms, experience and training are needed to complete them out. As an attorney coach, you can assist lay litigants who otherwise would be flummoxed or who often make self-destructive choices by checking the wrong box.
- You can help your unbundled client fill out court forms. Even with simplified forms, experience and training are needed to fill them out.
- Going to the courthouse can be frightening and overwhelming. As an attorney coach, you can orient clients, including where to park, which courtroom to go to, and how much time to allocate, and double-check that all forms needed for a court hearing are prepared, the filing fee is ready, and other requirements have been met.
- Figuring out budgets for post-divorce expenses is a daunting process. As an attorney coach, you can help a client budget for and talk through the inevitable choices that living in two households entails.
- Clients may need the help of other professionals, such as accountants, therapists, vocational counselors, or financial planners. As an attorney coach, you can help the client assess the need for these professionals and offer alternatives for referral.

> ### Red Flag Warning
>
> In a 2013 unbundling presentation, Toby Rothchild, Executive Director of the Legal Aid Foundation of Los Angeles, and Wendy Wen Yun Chang, a lawyer who represents lawyers in legal malpractice actions, described the types of clients that pose challenges for unbundling:
> - The Principled Client: claims to be acting on "principle"
> - The Great Expectations Client: expects to triumph on every issue
> - The Emergency Client: every task becomes a last-minute crisis
> - The Coy Communicator: withholds pertinent information
> - The Control Freak: unable to let go of tasks or delegate
> - The Client with Cognition Issues: may lack understanding of relationship
> - The Client Who Cannot Handle It: needs broader attorney support
> - The "Paralawyer" Client: micromanages attorney work
> - The Favor Client: Scope creep as result of requests for extra help

- Clients often need emotional support. As an attorney coach, you can help clients get through their reactions, which can paralyze them or escalate the conflict. By referring clients to the literature on the stages of the emotional divorce (denial, resistance, anger, acceptance) and the various types of divorce (Maccoby and Mnookin's four types of divorce—spousal divorce, parental divorce, economic divorce, and legal divorce),[4] as legal coach, you can help normalize their experience.
- As an attorney coach, you can discuss legal issues and give advice on legal position that the client should take. You can provide the client with a duplicated statute (such as the factors considered in permanent spousal support) or give the client an article, such as one describing the choice between accepting a buyout or reserving court jurisdiction on defined benefit plans. Like a physician prescribing a particular medication, you can improve client decision making just by providing resources of which you are aware.
- If you have a client library, you can recommend books, websites, or DVDs to help your client. For example, the State Bar of Wisconsin's DVD *Your Divorce Deposition* may be a tremendous resource in helping the client prepare for taking or defending a deposition. Similarly, the new DVD *Split* and the websites www.uptoparents.org and www.ourfamilywizard.com can be invaluable in educating clients who are trying to represent themselves.
- You can be available to answer the client's questions and concerns. Just having you available throughout the divorce process often makes it easier for a self-represented litigant to get through the divorce.

General Conflict Management Client Coaching

This chapter discusses legal coaching within limited scope representation within the family law context. It is important that you be aware of (if not actively explore) conflict coaching in a more general context.

In this regard, and of special interest to attorneys, the coaching specialty of conflict management coaching—also known as conflict coaching—has steadily emerged with the field of ADR. Toronto-based Cinnie Noble, one of the world leaders in conflict management coaching, describes this process as follows:

> Coaching is partnering with clients in a thought-provoking and creative process that inspires them to maximize their personal and professional potential. Coaching is an ongoing relationship which focuses on clients taking action toward the realization of their visions, goals, or desires. Coaching uses a process of inquiry and personal discovery to build the client's level of awareness and responsibility and provides the client with structure, support, and feedback.[5]

Unlike sports coaching, conflict coaching, like many other types of coaching, does not entail advising people on what to do to improve their actions and reach their goals. Rather, one of the cornerstones of the field of coaching is self-determination and one of the main skills of trained coaches is the use of powerful questions that increase insight and awareness that help people help themselves.

Conflict management coaching may be used instead of or in tandem with mediation in a number of ways:

1. As a pre-mediation process, to help clients anticipate and prepare for any challenges that may impact their ability to effectively participate in the process or otherwise engage with the other party
2. As a post-mediation process, to help clients in the aftermath of sessions to address any unresolved matters and identify ways to manage ongoing interactions
3. To help clients improve their negotiation skills and their comfort and confidence to actively participate in mediation and/or
4. To provide a self-reflective method that helps your clients interact in sessions with increased proficiency and confidence

You can also use professional coaching to strengthen your own mediation and negotiation skills, to adapt to the new lawyering roles, and to integrate those roles to expand your law practice.

Although the balance of this chapter will focus on your craft of offering limited scope legal services to your clients, training in conflict management coaching or engaging a conflict management coach will accelerate your own development in this field.

Coach or First Class?

In addition to giving advice and being a teacher, you can help the client wrestle with the central issue in unbundling: if problems arise, should the client continue to self-represent with you as a coach or should you convert the lawyer-client relationship into a full-service engagement? Just as a patient diagnosed with cancer is inexperienced in determining the best medical treatment, a self-represented litigant needs the attorney coach's advice about what role to use. Therefore, you must provide advice to help the client understand how limited scope coaching and full service differ and the costs and benefits of various options.

To begin, you must help the client assess his or her legal needs by answering three questions: (1) Is a lawyer needed at all? (2) If so, for which tasks? (3) How will the lawyer-client relationship be structured? Determining the scope of the coaching relationship requires a blend of education, negotiation, and shared control.

Education is a two-way street. You must educate the client about the benefits of using (and paying for) your experience, knowledge, and skill on a limited basis while the client remains in charge of case strategy and implementation. This education flows naturally from a discussion of the client's needs.

- Is the assessment conference the only client-lawyer meeting, or will another meeting be planned now or be left to client discretion?
- Will the client handle every aspect of self-representation (fact gathering, discovery, correspondence and pleadings, negotiations, court appearances), or will some of these tasks be delegated to you?
- You also can educate the client about the extent of any service you might provide as a limited service attorney coach. For example, your client may want to handle (with limited lawyer coaching by you) all court filings, discovery, negotiations, and court appearances short of trial but have the lawyer convert roles from coach to lawyer of record at the trial itself. Your client can educate you as well. In other words, the client must clarify his or her goals, values, experience, and ability to handle various tasks, given the time and money available. Based on what they learn from each other, *the lawyer and client decide together whether to establish a coaching relationship and to what extent.*

> ### Coaching the Rich and Vulnerable
>
> When you think of coaching, you probably think about helping a middle-income self-represented litigant process a divorce without complex life-threatening issues. However, coaching is also being requested more and more by professionals and those who earn well over $100,000—people who can afford the full package but want to both save money and keep lawyers out of their divorces!
>
> Mary earned $500,000 a year as a corporate executive, and due to an emotionally deprived childhood, she picked men very poorly. She had totally supported her husband for three years and now was being harassed by him at work and home.
>
> Mary did not want a lawyer speaking to Todd. As with Mongo in *Blazing Saddles*, a lawyer's presence and power would only enrage Todd and send him more out of control. So Mary customized and limited her lawyer's work. The limited scope lawyer drafted the restraining orders, and her legal assistant accompanied Mary to the court, where Mary processed it herself. The lawyer guided Mary through the criminal complaint process and consoled her when the prosecutor rejected the case. The lawyer was on call during the Christmas holiday when Mary called from the Caribbean to report that Todd was in her house removing items: "What should I do?" The lawyer advised Mary concerning a lump-sum buyout of her spousal support liability and drafted the final agreement, which Mary and Todd negotiated in a bar. Was this frustrating professional work? Yes. Could the lawyer have helped Mary more if he had been the full-service counsel of record? Yes. Could he have made more money, and could Mary have afforded it? Yes and yes. Were limited unbundled services what Mary wanted and was willing to pay for? Yes.

This mutual process lessens the conflict of interest that naturally arises when a lawyer advises a potential client about retaining his or her services. Some clients' rights advocates say that a client should have a lawyer's advice in negotiating a contract for legal services due to the financial and role complexities in that relationship. Are you as a family lawyer the best person to advise your client as to whether your services are reasonable and necessary and if so what financial terms are appropriate? Should you advise your potential clients on this business transaction? In the unbundled situation, the attorney coach still has a financial conflict in advising whether the client needs further coaching. However, because coaching implies that someone other than the coach (the client, a different lawyer, or another professional) may handle the legal services recommended by the coach and because the coach's fees are much lower, the conflict of interest is greatly reduced.

Negotiation Coach

In this coaching role, the negotiation on a variety of issues can take place with the client and the other spouse directly, between the client and the other spouse's lawyer, between the client and child or other member of the client's family (including in-laws), with a court clerk, with an IRS agent, with a former lawyer, or with a present significant other. The client can be negotiating with anyone involved in the family maelstrom and may need help in the process.

By working with your client in understanding their underlying needs and goals and anticipating those of the other spouse, you can help your clients develop priorities and clear objectives for their negotiations. The rest is downhill. As coach, you can educate the client about the psychological profiles of the parties and teach the client basic negotiation principles such as determining each party's underlying needs and negotiation techniques such as how to formulate an offer.

The major coaching functions for negotiation include the following.

Teaching Divorce Dynamics: Using this coaching function, you educate your client about general divorce dynamics that may give your client additional insight into the current situation. If you can teach your client about the four distinct divorce relationships mentioned earlier (emotional, physical, financial, and legal), the client may find it easier to understand the negotiation process.[6] For example, if the spousal (emotional) divorce is almost complete, the couple will probably be less raw and can focus on other issues. If all four divorces are at early stages, there will be more work to do on all fronts. Similarly, teaching the client about the long-term effect of anger may provide a perspective that makes it easier for the client to get through the divorce.[7]

Assessing the Legal Strengths and Weaknesses of Each Party's Position: This is a traditional lawyer function. Instead of merely sharing this information with the client to obtain settlement authority, helping the client learn this assessment makes it available for the client's use in discussions with his or her spouse.

Analyzing the Personalities of the Parties, Communication Dynamics, Emotional and Financial Leverage: These insights are utilized by experienced negotiators, and you need to transfer this experience to your client for use at the family dining table or restaurant, when the spouses are hammering out a deal themselves. In short, skilled lawyers have the ability to insightfully read their clients, opposing parties, counsel, and others involved in and affected by a negotiation. In addition to your own experience, you probably have direct knowledge of and access to negotiation resources that can help.

You can be invaluable in helping the client understand negotiation dynamics. By sharing your impressions and teaching the client how to appreciate and empathize with the underlying needs and goals of their spouse, you can help your clients to maximize their effectiveness in formulating and presenting their proposals. Overall conflict can be reduced by helping your client recognize the behaviors of his or her spouse that pushed the client's buttons and understand what destructive behaviors the spouse may unleash in reaction to the client. As one client admitted after a coaching session, "I want to thank you for 'beating me over the head' this morning. I needed it. I began to see the whole picture more clearly again . . . what was happening to me and the level I was permitting myself to sink to. I didn't like the picture at all. I am going to start writing the letter [to my wife's lawyer], which I think you'll be pleased with."

Teaching Negotiation Theory and Techniques: The only negotiation training to which many family lawyers have been exposed has been OJT (on-the-job training). That is all that many family lawyers who are naturals in negotiation may need. The recent boom in negotiation training and literature has made less talented lawyers more knowledgeable and competent in negotiation skills and generally has made the naturals even better. Regardless of formal training, you can give the client a customized crash course in the relevant negotiation skills needed to aid the client in reaching his or her goals. This project is greatly facilitated by having a collection of client-friendly negotiation books and tapes available for study. See the Appendices for a fuller discussion on developing and maintaining a client library.

Developing a Negotiation Plan: Regardless of the techniques and interventions that the client actually displays during the negotiation, experts in this field generally concur that the quality of the negotiation plan and the degree of pre-meeting preparation are the keys to a successful outcome.[8] Coming up with an initial settlement position is often the most difficult task facing a lawyer representing a client in a negotiation. It is no less difficult (probably more so) for you to help a client develop a plan with several backup positions and prepared responses for anticipated concerns raised by the other spouse.

Preparing Through Role Playing: Progressive law schools emphasize role playing for teaching law students essential skills such as client counseling, negotiation, and trial practice. In effect, you can become the client's clinical instructor by rehearsing a negotiation and then giving constructive feedback to the client's performance (often recorded) to prepare for the real thing. You can do this type of rehearsal in front of the client's friends or even office staff to get comments that might help the client.

One method of preparing the client for negotiation is to role-play the scene in advance. Clients can play themselves, and you can play the opposing spouse or other negotiation participant. Both client and coach stay in role and try to work out the issue(s) at hand. This exercise helps the client practice by saying the words that will affect the outcome during the real negotiations as well as anticipate at least some reactions of the other spouse.

Another negotiation preparation technique is to have the coach and client reverse roles: the client plays the other spouse, and the coach plays the client. This role reversal can be very illuminating, increasing understanding of the other's needs and concerns. The client can also see what to do or not to do because the client gets to react to proposed actions as if he or she were on the receiving end. This exercise is a cousin to the mediation technique of reframing, which is often used to break an impasse.

Consulting in Mid-Negotiation: Although remaining on the sidelines, the coach often remains available by telephone during (or shortly after) a spousal meeting to serve as a resource and emotional support for the client.

Court Coach

Historically, courts have been seen as the private preserve of the legal profession. The unwanted children of the court system, self-represented litigants often do not speak the correct language, dress in appropriate uniform, or know where to stand or when to speak—or not to speak. They are perceived as being unprepared and taking too much court time. So it is not surprising that many feel they have already been burned due to their status as a self-represented litigant.

Nevertheless, people represent themselves in record numbers, and they certainly want help from lawyers who are willing to provide it. You can accommodate self-represented litigants by helping them with many concrete tasks:

- Ghostwriting court pleadings and briefs or reviewing and editing the client's product
- Organizing, arranging, and marking documents for court exhibits
- Advising clients as to appropriate pretrial motions
- Drafting or reviewing the client's work
- Educating the client about court procedures and giving advice, such as explaining the right to disqualify a judge, which judges the litigant should consider disqualifying (if any), when to act, and what to say
- Helping the client prepare opening and closing statements and direct and cross-examination; ghostwriting, reviewing, or simulating court conditions through role playing; and staying available for telephone consultation during last-minute preparations and while the client is in court

Fear of Malpractice as a Barrier to Unbundling

Under current ethical rules and case authority, malpractice exposure and vulnerability to professional discipline frighten many lawyers away from experimenting with unbundling. Malpractice exposure exists for lawyers who render incomplete advice or who fail to give needed advice in areas ancillary to the client's presenting problem. For example, a lawyer's failure to sufficiently advise a client who comes in for a worker's compensation claim about a potential third-party claim may give rise to a malpractice action.[9] This malpractice exposure increases when the client comes in for a limited time and explicitly restricts the lawyer's time and activity in unbundled situations. If legal research is required and the lawyer is authorized to spend only 30 minutes, a rushed or an inadequate job might lead to wrong advice. The exposure is increased by the fact that clients receiving unbundled service are extremely vigilant about lawyer overbilling. Those choosing discrete task representation are often schooled in competitive shopping for lawyer services and often have a do-it-yourself mentality. Such clients may be inherently mistrustful of lawyers, extremely stingy with their legal fees, or both. Lawyers need to make sure they are not compromising their ethical duties as attorneys when performing unbundled services.

To give you comfort, Lawyers Mutual, a leading lawyer malpractice insurance company, not only does not discourage its policy holders from offering unbundled legal services, but encourages them to do so in a competent and responsible manner. Toward that end, in 2014, Lawyer's Mutual produced a one-hour video highlighting best practices of unbundling, Debunking the Myths of Unbundling.[10] The State Bar of Oregon's malpractice plan has taken a similar position of support for responsible unbundling since 1997.

Another ethical problem surfaces when a lawyer coaches the self-represented client on negotiation strategy and scripts the client in how to talk with the other party. With regard to representation of the opposing party, the California State Bar has issued a formal ethics opinion holding that this "scripting" violates the rule of professional responsibility prohibiting indirect communication with a represented party.[11] Such a rule conflicts with the organized Bar's stated policy of encouraging client coaching and widening legal access. Lawyers who ghostwrite clients' correspondence and court documents to help improve the quality of the work at a fraction of the cost may also face liability and judicial condemnation. Although Colorado is an unbundling-friendly jurisdiction, a federal district judge in that state excoriated a lawyer who ghostwrote court pleadings for a self-represented litigant and indicated that such conduct may be punished by sanctions or contempt for committing a fraud on the court.[12] Such statements by judicial officers cannot help having a chilling effect on lawyers who are considering unbundling and who desire to service clients within the clients' ability to pay.

Notice of Limited Scope Role

Some of the challenges facing your attempts to unbundle and serve as a coach to unrepresented litigants are that other lawyers or judges may not be aware that you are representing a party in a limited scope role or they are unaware of the tasks, issues, or court processes to which your role is limited. This can mean that a judge may not permit you to appear in court just for one hearing or to prepare court pleadings without become a full counsel of record.[13] Also, other lawyers may become confused or reluctant to deal with your client on the same issues or with you on other issues. Such reluctance is understandable if you do not communicate clearly the existence and details of the scope of your engagement.

The California Judicial Council has addressed this problem head-on by developing a set of unbundling-friendly rules and family law forms to permit lawyers and their clients to give clear notice to other lawyers and judicial officers. The form, Notice of Limited Scope Appearance (FL-950), is provided in the Resources section. This form has several benefits:

1. It is filed with the court and served on other lawyers so that actual notice is perfected.
2. The form permits "vertical unbundling," which means that the client and lawyer can allocate tasks and such allocation is binding on the court and other lawyers. For example, the lawyer might limit his or her scope to negotiation only. In such case, the client would be responsible for all other tasks.
3. The form also permits "horizontal unbundling," which means that issues or different court appearances can also be allocated between lawyer and client. For example, the lawyer might handle all tasks and court appearances in respect to retirement plans and the client is responsible for all other issues. Or the lawyer might attend an initial hearing involving several substantive issues. Once that hearing is concluded, the lawyer has no further responsibility.
4. The form also provides that the client agrees to sign a substitution of attorney, relieving the lawyer when the scope of work is completed. When a client fails or refuses to do so (which happens rarely), the California Judicial Council has developed forms for a limited scope attorney to withdraw without a hearing if there is no written objection and a form for clients to make such objections—leaving the decision of relief of counsel up to the court.

Even if your state does not have such forms, you can develop your own based on the California template as well as work toward obtaining such forms in your jurisdiction in the future. However, without a court rule or ethical opinion permitting limited scope, there may be uncertainty in your jurisdiction. To check unbundling rules state by state, see www.americanbar.org/groups/delivery_legal_services.html.

Using an Unbundled Approach Outside the Mediation Room
The first step is for you to make it clear to your clients (and potential clients) that you are available and interested in helping them through a mediation without becoming full counsel of record. For several reasons, clients will appreciate your willingness to be a consulting lawyer in mediation. First, while many people may want to mediate, fear of being overpowered by the other party or a lack of confidence in their ability to hold their own may weigh against entering mediation. Second, although your assistance may be appreciated, clients often want to keep your time to a minimum to save costs. Working outside sessions can accomplish that. So instead of billing four hours for a three-hour session (assuming a half hour for travel time), you can limit your time to under an hour for session preparation and de-brief with the client. If you are in your office during the

session, you can remain on call for a possible telephone conversation if your client faces a question or a problem.

Some of your key tasks in helping clients when you do not attend the session include:

1. Help your client set an agenda that will meet his or her concerns. You can help frame the issues so that when the mediator calls for the agenda, your client is ready.
2. Make sure your client can handle the proposed format of the mediation. Some mediation participants can stay focused for a four-hour session; others wear out after 90 minutes.
3. Help your client prepare an opening statement that is effective and within the client's ability to deliver. For example, some mediation parties need to write out every word and maybe even read their statement, others can refer to their draft, reading occasionally, some may only need an outline, and still others will speak from the heart. Help your client use this opportunity to speak in aspirational terms and objectives rather than use the statement to make a negotiation demand. For example, instead of saying, "I want $3,500 per month in child support," your client can learn to say, "I hope you and I can ensure that the children continue to have sufficient resources to meet their needs." You can even play the role of mediator or other party and offer your client an opportunity to practice the statement and then offer some gentle hints for improvement.
4. Make sure your client has backup documents prepared and available at the mediation with sufficient copies for the other party and the mediator.
5. Alert your client to the possibility of bringing important people to the mediation. For example, if your client's father has been bankrolling the family or is owed outstanding loans, having the father attend a session might pay dividends. If the father's presence could inflame the situation, this dynamic needs to be discussed before your client suggests that he attend.
6. Make sure your client has copies of statutes, cases, or other information to share at the session. For example, if an issue will be the interest rate applied to a deferred payment, you can provide various options for presentation at the session Department of Labor rate of inflation, bank or mortgage rates, current investment rates of family bonds, for instance.
7. Make sure budgets, income information, and schedules of assets and debts are collected with backup documentation and ready for discussion.
8. Discuss primary and second negotiation options on each issue so that your client is ready.
9. Help your client link issues together or be willing to concede a point if the other party agrees to a reciprocal concession.

10. Read the summary letters prepared by the mediator so that you both know how progress is being made and what trade-offs are being considered.
11. Be ready to draft or review interim, partial, or temporary agreements.
12. Alert your client to be vigilant about when it might be best for you to attend a session.
13. Work with the other party's lawyer to defuse conflict and find compromise positions in support of the mediator's efforts. Be willing to write letters to the mediator or participate in conference calls to move the mediation along.
14. Be ready to suggest the addition of other professionals to help the process. The addition of a neutral forensic CPA or financial planner might cut through unproductive and expensive discussions.
15. Be ready to suggest an ancillary process to take place within the mediation to break an impasse or accelerate progress. For example, if the parties cannot seem to work out a school schedule after several sessions, you might wish to bring in an evaluator to conduct a confidential mini-evaluation to provide a nonbinding recommendation after interviewing the parties, children, significant others, teachers, coaches, and other persons (collaterals).

Using an Unbundled Approach in the Mediation Room

Even though you may not be representing your client in court proceedings before or after the mediation, your limited role can be expanded to being at mediation sessions with your client. Such increased service may be cost-effective for your situation in any of the following situations:

1. Your client refuses to make any decisions or agreements in the mediation until speaking with you. You should advise your client to be careful about making impulsive agreements or saying yes when he or she does not understand the ramifications of a decision, However, some parties hide behind the absence of their lawyer to do nothing—frustrating the other party and putting the mediation at risk.
2. When your client is stumbling through sessions and making bad deals or blowing up good deals, your presence might make a big difference.
3. When your client explicitly asks you to come or where the other party has announced his or her intention to bring a lawyer.
4. The mediation seems to be stalling or taking too long or the expense is getting out of hand. In such situations, lawyers can expedite the process, resulting in savings of money and time.
5. A deadline has been imposed by the court or another reason has come up (e.g., a deadline is looming to sign up for application to a school, escrow is closing on the sale of a house, or health insurance coverage is running out).

If a decision is made to have you attend sessions with your clients, several ground rules should be followed to maximize your effectiveness:

1. Always give notice to the other lawyer and to the mediator that you are coming. Your client might be the one to give notice to the other party and the mediator. Showing up unannounced is not only discourteous, but also could cause the other party to retaliate in some way or at least reduce your high ground and ability to convey trust to the mediator and to the parties.
2. Ask the mediator how you can help when you are in the room. The mediator might indicate that your client's active role in speaking might kick-start the agreement-making process. On the other hand, the mediator might believe that a quiet, steady presence on your part would anchor progress already being made.
3. Ask the other lawyer how you can best work together. Find out if the other party has needs and concerns that you might be able to address.
4. Ask your client before your arrival and continually check your client's temperature to make sure that the client is comfortable with your input. Remember that the parties and mediator had been a system before your arrival, so your presence (and that of the other lawyer) may significantly change the dynamics—and not always for the better.
5. Support the mediator overtly in session and privately with your client. To help your client, you do not have to show how smart you are or how the mediator is not up to the job. You are not getting paid by the word or the number of times you are proven to be correct. What counts is the ultimate result. Try coming up with brilliant solutions and paving the way for your client or the mediator to present the solution. You will receive your acknowledgment and credit through the gratitude of your client in graduating from mediation with an agreement.
6. If you have a limited scope role, the best way to get fired is for the mediation to terminate prior to a settlement being reached. Therefore, it would be foolhardy for you to threaten litigation unless certain conditions are met. Termination of mediation has major costs for your client and the entire family, so your job is to do everything possible to keep the process going forward and prevent premature or preemptive threat or termination of the process.

Practice Tips

1. Any unbundled legal service products you choose to offer can supplement (not replace) your central existing product—representing clients in litigation.
2. By offering limited scope services to clients who would otherwise self-represent, you will be receiving revenue from clients who otherwise would not have hired a lawyer.
3. By serving as an unbundled client coach, you can provide guidance, information, and support to self-represented litigants without having the responsibility of being counsel of record.
4. You should develop your assessment skills to help clients decide whether to use discrete task lawyering or to hire you as counsel of record in a full-service package.
5. You should customize your coaching so that the level of lawyering fits the needs, ability, and value system of each client.
6. Education is a two-way street. As coach, you educate the client; the client educates you on what working relationship is desired and will work best.
7. In drafting correspondence, the client can initiate drafts for you, the lawyer coach, to review; conversely, you can prepare drafts to be sent by the client. In some situations, the client will ask you to send a letter on law office letterhead.
8. Before a negotiation, offer the client an opportunity to consult with you to develop a strategic plan and to role-play making and responding to offers.
9. Consider being a court coach to help prepare your client to go to trial on his or her own.
10. Lawyers who offer mediation-related service products often receive calls from prospective clients and colleagues. These callers may be interested in the concept of unbundling generally or in specific service products offered by your office. By organizing materials in advance to include in packets, you can send out these educational and marketing materials quickly as well as minimize staff cost.
11. Malpractice carriers in many states (e.g., Minnesota) have developed forms and publications offering guidance about unbundled legal services. Check with your carrier for these useful resources.

Notes

1. Blankley, Kristen M., *Adding by Subtracting: How Limited Scope Agreements for Dispute Resolution Representation Can Increase Access to Attorney Services* (2013). COLLEGE OF LAW, FACULTY PUBLICATIONS. Paper 175. http://digitalcommons.unl.edu/lawfacpub/175.

2. Hon. Michael B. Hyman, *Why judges should embrace limited scope representation*, Illinois State Bar Association Bench & Bar (April 2014).

3. For a comprehensive overview of unbundling rules, see An Analysis of Rules That Enable Lawyers to Serve Self-Represented Litigants: A White Paper by the ABA Standing Committee on the Delivery of Legal Services (2014). www.americanbar.org/content/dam/aba/administrative/delivery_legal_services/ls_del_unbundling_white_paper_2014.authcheckdam.pdf. Among topics discussed are rules authorizing limited scope services, communications between counsel and parties, document preparation, and appearance and withdrawal in court.

4. Eleanor E. Maccoby & Robert H. Mnookin, Dividing the Child: Social and Legal Dilemmas of Custody, 103, 300. (1992).

5. Cinnie Noble, Conflict Coaching, A New ADR Technique, Ontario Bar Associations' Alternative Dispute Resolution Newsletter, Volume 17, No.1, December, 2008.

6. *Id.*

7. Judith S. Wallerstein and Sandra Blakeslee, Second Chances: Men, Women, and Children a Decade After Divorce 7–8 (1989). ("Divorce is the only major family crisis in which social support falls away. . . . [W]hen a man and a woman divorce, many people tend to act as if they believe it might be contagious. The divorced person is seen as a loose cannon. We have names for them: rogue elephant, black widow. Despite the widespread acceptance of divorce in modern society, there remains something frightening at its core.")

8. Carrie Menkel-Meadow, *Toward Another View of Legal Negotiation: The Structure of Problem Solving*, 31 UCLA L. Rev. 754, 818-21 (1984).

9. *See* Nichols v. Keller, 19 Cal. Rptr. 2d 601 (Ct. App. 1993); *see also* Peter Spero, *The Attorney's Duty to Advise Beyond Scope of Representation*, L.A. Daily J., Dec. 19, 1994, at 7.

10. *See* www.lmic.com and contact Kim Spirito (spiritok@lawyersmutual.com), Vice President of Loss Prevention and Claims to discuss access to the video and supporting materials.

11. California State Bar Comm. on Professional Responsibility, Formal Op. 1993-131 (1993). This opinion is based on Model Rules of Professional Conduct Rule 4.2 (prohibiting a lawyer from directly or indirectly communicating with a represented party).

12. Johnson v. County of Fremont, Civil Action 93-K-2465 (1994) at 13, 14–15 (Hon. John L. Kane): "Having a litigant appear to be *self represented* where in truth an attorney is authoring pleadings and necessarily guiding the course of the litigation with an unseen hand is ingenuous to say the least; it is far below the level of candor which must be met by members of the bar. . . . I have given this matter somewhat lengthy attention because I believe incidents of ghost-writing by lawyers for putative *self represented* litigants are increasing. Moreover, because the submission of misleading pleadings or briefs to courts is inextricably infused into the administration of justice, such conduct may be contemptuous irrespective of the degree to which it is considered unprofessional by the governing bodies of the bar. As a matter of fundamental fairness, advance notice that ghost-writing can subject an attorney to contempt of court is required. This memorandum opinion and order being published thus serves that purpose.") *See* U.S. District Judge John L. Kane's

comments, *in* Leigh Perkins, *Unbundling Your Services Makes Some Clients Happy,* LAW. WKLY. USA, Dec. 18, 1995, which include "The courts of justice are not soda fountains where clients can choose the toppings they want."

13. The law varies from state to state in terms of whether limited court appearances are permitted. For a state-by-state directory of rules governing unbundled services, see www.americanbar.org/groups/delivery_legal_services/resources/pro_se_unbundling_resource_center/court_rules.html.

CHAPTER 6

Representing Clients in Mediation with a Collaborative Lawyering Approach

Lawyers involved [in Collaborative Practice] are as committed to the resolution of the issues as are the parties. . . . The Collaborative Process centers on a discovery of personal needs and interests and how those are prioritized by each spouse.
    —Nancy J. Cameron, *Collaborative Practice: Deepening the Dialogue* (2004)

The previous chapter discussed how you can use your lawyering skills to help mediation participants effectively without taking on the full role as counsel of record. This chapter will stretch you a bit further by asking you to consider incorporating the values, protocols, and roles of collaborative lawyering while serving as consulting lawyer or unbundled coach in support of your client's efforts in mediation.

Collaborative Lawyering

Collaborative law is an unbundled service in which lawyers limit the scope of their services by contracting to bilaterally withdraw if the matter is litigated. It shares a core mediation principle, namely, that the process should empower the parties and make their interests central. Not only are lawyers less adversarial toward each other, but they also join together to ensure that the negotiation belongs to the parties. The lawyers expressly sign on to treat their own clients and the other party in a respectful and peaceful manner for the collective benefit of all members of the family.

While a collaborative law process generally does not include a mediator, it dovetails nicely with mediation to the extent that collaborative lawyers sign on to the following peacemaking principles:

- Respect and dignity for the other party and other professionals
- Direct and open communication with the other party and professionals
- Voluntary and full disclosure of relevant information and documents necessary to make agreements
- Commitment to the healing of the family
- Use of interest-based negotiation to try to meet the needs of both parties

Be a Beacon of Hope

One of a mediator's greatest attributes is to be the one person in the room who has an optimistic demeanor and belief that regardless of the conflict, progress toward an agreement, if not a written settlement, is possible.

The mediator does not need to be so lonely. As lawyer for one of the spouses, you can be a second beacon of hope.

When the other spouse or lawyer makes an outrageous offer, try to find the nugget of movement upon which to build. When your offer is rejected or gutted through an aggressive modification, shrug it off and come up with another proposal with more chance of acceptance.

If you are the target of verbal abuse, literally "turn the other cheek" and don't respond in kind.

Your rose-colored vision and grounded behavior will not only model positive negotiation behavior for your client, but also get you the respect of the other side and appreciation (and help) from the mediator.

Collaborative law encourages the respectful use and cooperation of lawyers, mental health professionals, and financial professionals on behalf of divorcing families. The world's largest collaborative organization, the International Academy of Collaborative Professionals (www.collaborativepractice.com) is based on an interdisciplinary approach, and its mission is defined as collaborative practice that encompasses many models.[1]

Collaborative law puts a buffer between the parties and the courthouse by taking away the customary lawyer tools of threats and court action. The absence of such power and leverage tactics permits parties to focus on their own needs and those of people in their lives (children, business associates, members of their religious community, for instance) to build agreements. While in mediation, we make participants aware of the risks and disadvantages of litigation alternatives to incentivize settlement, in collaborative law, we incentivize settlement by also contractually eliminating the litigation alternative.

In the collaborative process, a contract, the participation agreement, provides for the inadmissibility of collaborative communication and documents. Privacy and confidentiality incentivize many clients to turn to mediation as well. The participation agreement can be a private agreement among parties and professionals or a court order. The disqualification clause is a safe "container"[2] for the parties and professionals to use in working out issues without the imminent, looming specter of litigation.[3] As we discuss later in this chapter, such disqualification of mediation consulting lawyers can benefit mediation participants as well.

Why You Will Get More Work by Offering a Collaborative Approach

When Woody first started his mediation practice in 1979, he lived off the crumbs referred by other family lawyers. Over time, the flow of family law referrals has reversed. In recent years, mediators have become major referral sources for family lawyers for several reasons:

1. Many divorcing spouses make their first call to a mediator. Competent and trained mediators routinely encourage mediation participants to consult an attorney at some point in the process.
2. When making a referral for their clients, mediators want to select attorneys who will support the mediation, not blow it up. When referred lawyers have collaborative training, the mediator can facilitate an agreement with expected help of lawyers who understand and value mediation principles and do not have one foot in the courthouse and the other in the mediation room.
3. If you have a practice that favors consensual dispute resolution rather than litigation, mediators know that you are a prime referral source for them. If you also offer a collaborative approach, this increases the expectation of mediators in your community that a referral to you might be reciprocated in the future.

How to Use a Disqualification Agreement in Your Mediation Representation Work

At the beginning of a mediation, in determining what role lawyers will play, many mediators offer a protocol for how parties can maximize their use of lawyers during the mediation process. Mediators differ in whether they will offer any protocol or whether they will provide lawyer recommendations.

The following is a template protocol that we proactively provide to mediation parties early in the process. We offer it for your consideration, not as what you should expect, but as a summary of possible issues your clients (actual and potential) should consider in their relationship with you. After each point of the template protocol, we discuss some issues and alternative approaches for you to consider.

1. If either of you wants to consult an attorney, you will let the other party and the mediator know promptly. Under the law in most states, anyone (even a party in mediation!) has the absolute right to consult an attorney at any time. The fact that a party in mediation sees an attorney can be a private and confidential event between the party and the lawyer. The content of the communication between lawyer and client is statutorily privileged in virtually all jurisdictions. This means that without the proposed notice provision offered by this template protocol, the traditional and legally supported view is that if a mediation party wants to consult a lawyer, that is a private decision and act and the other party or the mediator need never know.

In fact, in determining the standard for confidentiality of limited scope representation, California has parted company with many other states by providing complete confidentiality for anyone using an unbundled lawyer. Neither self-represented litigants nor their limited scope attorneys need to inform the court or the other party or lawyer if documents were prepared by or with the help of a lawyer. A few other states permit drafting assistance without disclosure; for example, Illinois Supreme Court Rule 137 makes it clear that an attorney may assist a person who is representing himself or herself in drafting or reviewing a pleading or other paper without making a general or limited scope appearance and without the attorney signing the pleading or other paper. Missouri Rule 55.03(a) and Montana Rules of Civil Procedure 11 also permit a lawyer to draft pleadings or motions for self-represented litigants without signing the documents or disclosing lawyer involvement.

However, most states (Florida and Colorado being the leaders) have opted to require self-represented litigants to inform the court and the other party when a lawyer is providing ghostwriting help on court documents.

So why does this template protocol swim upstream against the legal current? The reason for this protocol is support transparency of communication. Providing the other party and the mediator with notice if a lawyer's advice may come into play serves several positive mediation goals.

First, many mediation parties who start without lawyers are afraid that the other party is getting coached from the sidelines to the disadvantage of the party going it alone. Such fear can escalate into paranoia or even to a premature termination of mediation. By agreeing to this notice provision, the fearful party has his or her own consultation, if he or she so chooses. A less positive consequence is that such a provision could deter one or both parties from consulting an attorney out of fear that by doing so, two lawyers might wrest control away from the parties in the mediation.

Second, by alerting the mediator that lawyers are about to be consulted, the mediator can strategically plan and work with the parties to better address their concerns and provide more neutral information as requested by either party. If lawyers are to become involved, the mediator can help improve selection and integration of the lawyers into the process as allies for settlement.

What is your approach to a prospective client who consults you and asks whether he should agree to this protocol offered by the mediator? We suggest that you inquire of your prospective client:

1. What is your understanding of the protocol for use of lawyers in mediation proposed by the mediator? Do you have a copy in writing?
2. What are your concerns or questions about this protocol?
3. Would you like to know what options there are to this protocol?
4. Would you like to discuss the benefits and downsides of the protocol proposed by the mediator and options we have discussed so that you can compare?

You also need to share any professional reservations or support that you have in working with prospective client under the template protocol. If the mediation party is in favor of sharing attorney-client meetings and communications but you are not comfortable working with this approach, the most professional thing to do is turn down the assignment. However, it is important that you do so in a way that still empowers the client to make his own decision.

2. You will only consult collaborative or mediation-friendly lawyers whom the mediator approves, unless a different agreement is made. The mediator has your authority to provide these referrals to you or your client privately without compromising the mediator's neutrality. The purpose of this aspect of the protocol is to give mediation parties the advantage of selecting a lawyer who will maximize the opportunity for settlement. You should consider two factors: the amount of mediation-supportive training you might have (or are planning to obtain) and the proven success record you have with a particular mediator.

A mediation participant has the right to select any attorney of her choice. Actually, some parties may want to select an aggressive litigator to create leverage and power in an effort to get the best deal possible. A downside of selecting an adversarial attorney is that such pressure could result in an impasse or mediation termination rather than agreement. Yet, it is still the client's choice.

The underlying basis for an agreement requiring the parties to work with attorneys who have mediation or collaborative law training may be more obvious to clients than it is to lawyers. While many litigators do represent clients in mediation, those lawyers with mediation or collaborative training offer clients two advantages. First, these lawyers often understand the mediation process at a more sophisticated level. They know from training (and perhaps through experience as a mediator) what strategies and perspectives the mediator may be using. Such a lawyer will have training on how to prepare clients to give their opening statements; build an agenda; and even better, negotiate with the mediator. A second advantage of lawyers trained in mediation and collaborative law is that such lawyers generally support client-centered decision making and may provide excellent support for their clients going through the challenges of mediation.

If you do not meet these training qualifications presently, you might find available mediation training through the Association of Conflict Resolution (www.acresolution.org) or collaborative training through the International Academy of Collaborative Professionals (www.collaborativepractice.com) or your local Collaborative Law Group.

Mediators generally want to minimize risk of lawyer domination or adversarial posturing that often occurs when lawyers enter the mediation process. Past success with the mediator is one indication of lowered risk. Also, as experts in their field, mediators know which lawyers work well with them and have the skills and perspectives that result in satisfied clients. Some of the lawyering qualities that mediators appreciate through experience are to be knowledgeable and supportive of the mediation process, responsive to client needs, open and respectful to the other party, and nimble and creative in supporting a client-based solution that may fall outside the legal parameters. If you work to develop these qualities, you may find that you receive more mediator referrals.

3. You and your client need to discuss and agree as to whether all communications with your attorney will remain confidential or whether you will share the advice if it provides information or different perspectives than have been discussed in mediation. As discussed earlier, the attorney-client privilege permits clients to keep all attorney-client communications confidential. This essentially protects secrets. In mediation, the fear of secrets or the actual secret strategies can cause some lack of trust between parties that may destroy the possibility for successful mediation. Therefore, in evaluating whether you would participate in such a protocol of disclosure, you must decide whether your long-standing devotion to the lawyer-client privilege can give way to having your client share what you have told him or her with the other party and the mediator.

But why should you give way? What are the advantages of your client sharing these otherwise privileged and sacrosanct communications?

The key is transparent information and informed decision making. For example, what if during a mediation session for which you were not present the parties are considering $1,500 a month in child support? You are representing Mom, who happens to be the primary custodial parent, and your calculations show $2,200 a month in child support. You have also told your client that you cannot see any legal reason why she should accept less than $2,200.

What would be the advantage of your client not sharing this otherwise privileged advice? Perhaps, your client does not want to anger Dad or has other issues that she wants to negotiate that dwarf the importance of the $700 difference in child support.

However, if your client has received this legal advice, what would be the advantage of sharing this with the other party and the mediator? First, your client would not have to keep a secret. Secrets beget more secrets, and secrets beget fear, which in turn begets preemptive aggressive moves, termination of mediation, or both. Second, your client could share your advice in a mediation session and Dad might agree with your assessment, resulting in an agreement (perhaps on modified terms). And third, if Dad does not agree, at least he is informed of what Mom knows and they can discuss the issue of child support with the benefit of fuller information.

4. Once you engage an attorney, you need to discuss and agree whether the mediator should send summary agreements to the attorney, whether the mediator may communicate with the attorneys, and whether such communications shall be confidential or disclosed to the other party. It is becoming commonplace for mediators to send out summary letters following mediation sessions. These letters are also known as minutes or progress notes. These summary letters contain agreements reached in session, discussions that resulted short of agreement, assignments for either party, and the mediator's observations and recommendations for substantive agreements and for an improved process. For example, in a summary letter, the mediator might state:

You agreed to arrange transitions of parenting care in a way that would reduce conflict during the transition itself. Toward that end, you agreed to always greet each other in a friendly way, not conduct business (negotiate children's events or finances) during the transition, and, for the parent dropping off, to say good-bye and kiss the children in the car before the transition and to leave as quickly as possible to reduce the loyalty conflict of the children during these important moments. You also agreed to try and arrange dropoffs and pickups at school or activities so that only the parent starting parenting time would be present. I called these "blind transitions."

These summary letters are not binding. They are used to help parties remember what happened during sessions and serve as a structured anchor for out-of-session work.

It is important for lawyers to be aware of these letters with their clients for two reasons. First, it gives us a heads-up as to what is going on the mediation so that lawyers can discuss midcourse corrections with their clients. Second, and equally important, if lawyers are fully engaged during the agreement-making process, they can appreciate and understand the trade-offs leading to a final agreement so that their agreement review is more accurate and supportive than if they were coming in from the cold.

5. If either of you want your attorney to attend a mediation session, this may occur without the agreement of the other party. However, the party intending to have his or her lawyer attend must give at least three days' notice to the other party and to you so that the other party may bring her or his lawyer. If a set time for a mediation is not convenient for either

lawyer, it is agreed that the date of the mediation will be changed to accommodate both you and your client and both lawyers. You may be accustomed to attending mediation with your client to offer protection and advice and to be in charge of the negotiation. This occurs most often in cities and regions in which mediation is viewed as a late-stage process in litigation consisting of a single session presided by a third-party neutral (generally, a retired judge or a veteran litigation lawyer) who evaluates the strengths and weaknesses of each party's position and gives directive recommendations for compromise settlement terms. This view of mediation is often accompanied by the mantra "A good settlement is one that makes both parties equally unhappy."

The above view of mediation is heavily steeped in an "old paradigm" view of negotiation and settlement. This "old paradigm" is rights-based and lawyer-centered, and settlements are seen as compromises reached primarily to avoid the uncertainty of litigation.[4]

The mediation process underlying this protocol is very different. First, rather than assuming that a mediation will be a one-time conference or hearing, it is based on sequential sessions. Each of these sessions is two to four hours in duration. Rather than assuming that a global agreement will be reached at the end of a session, the sequential session model prepares parties and lawyers to work toward an agreement over time rather than pressuring everyone to come up with an agreement by the end of the session.

Although lawyers often attend sequential sessions with their clients, this protocol is designed for the many situations in which parties attend sessions with the lawyers absent or on the sidelines. The protocol is designed to accommodate a smooth and nonthreatening procedure if one party wants a lawyer to attend a session. Notice is given to prevent fear and pressure. Also, once one party has decided to have a lawyer, two changes in the mediation process result. First, the other party is afforded the same opportunity to attend. Second, scheduling must accommodate both lawyers in addition to the parties and mediators—no session will be scheduled without the entire mediation "team" present.

Mediation Disqualification Agreement

As discussed above, the key element defining collaborative practice is the attorney disqualification clause. This definition is ratified by the Uniform Collaborative Law Act, state statutes, court cases, and virtually all definitions of state and local Collaborative Law Groups.

The same benefits of an attorney disqualification clause apply to lawyers involved in the mediation process. By agreeing to terminate services upon the termination of mediation or initiation of court action, you create a barrier to the courthouse steps. Your client may always avail himself of court action, but if your client does, he or she will need to hire another lawyer.

We firmly believe in the mantra "Every day out of court is another day out of court!" We have seen many seemingly intractable situations somehow work themselves out through further discussion and modification of the mediation process. However, once the Maginot Line of a contested court hearing is crossed, the unintended consequences and harm are usually far worse than anticipated.

Many clients will not be comfortable with this disqualification process. They either want the negotiation leverage that threats sometimes provide or do not want to start looking for another attorney should mediation terminate. It is not uncommon for clients to have such pessimistic attitudes. After all, they are often mediating the biggest deal of their lives with someone with whom they have little trust and a poor negotiation history.

Your mission, should you choose to accept it, is to be open to the possibility of working with such a disqualification clause should the client want it. A sample clause is provided in the Resources section. Because over 60 percent of court-ordered mediations end in full settlements (much higher in self-selected mediations), the odds are that no litigation will be necessary anyway. And if it should come to that, there are many litigators from whom your client can choose. Your true focus should be in making mediation the last stop on the dispute resolution highway. If your involvement with a disqualification agreement can smooth the path for mediated agreement (or help the client feel better about that possibility), we suggest that you familiarize yourself with the disqualification option and consider accepting engagements involving this option.

Use of Other Collaborative Professionals in Mediation

If you have some experience in representing clients in mediation, you should be well versed in the involvement of therapists working as mediators or co-mediators. They also enter the mediation process as evaluators, consultants, and treating therapists for the parties and their children.

Financial professionals also are involved as neutral or party consultants, providing opinions about business valuation, marital lifestyle, or cash flow analyses for support as well as advice on tax issues. Financial planners can help with the preparation of budgets and explanation of the long-term financial ramifications of particular settlement proposals, and insurance or real estate professionals offer help in obtaining appraisals and necessary policies.

One of your key goals should be to find those professionals who have substantive expertise as well as knowledge of and commitment to the mediation process. We have found many child custody evaluators who truly are directive toward the parties and resistant to mediative roles. The same is true of many financial professionals who are ingénues to the mediation process.

A resource in your community for professional recommendations in mediation are the mental health and financial professionals listed on your local collaborative practice website (for the collaborative practice groups in your area, consult www.collaborativepractice.com.) Most of the professionals listed have had mediation training and experience. The following are some of the roles these professionals play in collaborative practice that can be adapted for mediations.

Divorce Coach/Process Facilitator/Communications Coach

Most collaborative practice groups require divorce coaches to be licensed therapists from a variety of backgrounds: clinical psychologists, social workers, and marriage and family therapists/counselors. These collaborative divorce coaches may be in addition to parenting coaches consulted by the parties. While their roles may differ, the following are some descriptions of how you might involve a collaborative divorce coach in a mediation.

To manage and contain emotions, coaches can work directly with the parties to help them and their children get through the divorce process with a minimum of pain and long-term negative impact. Rather than providing therapy to treat disorders or produce long-term behavior change, coaches educate and support the parties through the divorce crisis period. The coach avoids using diagnostic labels or getting caught up in symptoms and complaints. The coach is looking for positive "can-do" solutions to help the client overcome emotional barriers to reaching agreement.

Experienced mediator and coach David Kuroda LCSW in Los Angeles sets out the following clear, limited goals for coaches:

- **Identify and prioritize client concerns.** Help the client identify his or her concerns and emotions and assist in helping the client to share these emotional issues with his or her spouse. At the same time, help each client understand and appreciate how his or her own power and behavior impacts the spouse. The coach can give tips to the client to modulate the impactful behavior to reduce reactions from the other party. In the tradition of the prolific Dr. Murray Bowen, coaches can help parties reduce the emotional reactivity toward each other by helping them to "differentiate"—get some distance from the emotional enmeshment of the parties so that they can think things through rather than react with tantrums or cold withdrawal.
- **Prepare the client to succeed in the collaborative process.** The coach can teach the client what to expect in joint sessions and how to maximize progress by giving ideas about how best to work with lawyers and other professionals as well as with his or her spouse. Discuss and rehearse for the emotional fallout of seemingly "safe" legal and financial issues. The coach can help the client normalize common emotional reactions and make problems seem solvable by showing how most people going through divorce deal with them. For example, coaches can discuss how most people are caught up in roles and communication patterns that did not work in the marriage and will not work in the divorce negotiations. By identifying such patterns, the coach can help the client avoid such negative repeated interactions altogether, take a detour if they come up, or minimize the reaction if the pattern comes up during a session.

- **Catch the client doing well.** It is somewhat of a miracle that anyone going through divorce is able to be mature, reflective, and nonreactive with the person that they are divorcing during the most important negotiation in their lives! If there is ever a time to regress or act immature, this is it. Yet, we expect parties to mediation or the collaborative process to be at their best—or even better than their best. Rather than try to remake the client going through one of life's toughest challenges, coaches often try to identify the positive and constructive behaviors exhibited by the client, point them out, and encourage the client to do it again. Coaches can help parties recognize their best personal attributes and call on them during this family crisis.
- **Educate the client about tested parenting and communication guidelines and help them practice.** Coaches can teach parties what to say and not say to each other and to their children as well as how to say it. Coaches can effectively use Web resources such as www.uptoparents.org or DVDs such as *Split* as learning tools to improve behaviors.
- **Educate parties about the impact of different parenting plans; help the client select the most appropriate plan and discuss the plan with the other spouse.** There are wonderful books (e.g., *Mom's House, Dad's House*) and court-sponsored websites about parenting plans.[5] Coaches can review this material with clients and help them make sense out of them.
- **Assess and screen for signs of domestic violence or child abuse.** In addition to their process skills, many coaches have undergone specialized training related to domestic violence and can play an invaluable role in screening and providing protections within the collaborative process. Coaches also are attuned to child-related issues that can be addressed within the privacy of the collaborative process.
- **Contribute to the communication and teamwork of the collaborative team.** Coaches can play an invaluable role in coordinating the efforts of different professionals and facilitating teamwork.
- **Provide emotional support for the client during and between mediation sessions.** Mediation sessions can be overwhelming even for the strongest of divorcing parties. Some legislation allows parties who are ordered by the court to attend mediation (especially alleged victims of abuse) to have nonlawyer resource persons available to to lend support. Coaches are trained to handle outbursts and breakdowns and prevent premature termination of the process. Some parties can contain their behavior during sessions, yet need a shoulder to cry on or helpful hints between sessions. Coaches can be invaluable in that role.

Child Specialist/Co-Parenting Coach

While a mental health professional with child specialist credentials may also serve in the broader role as coach described above for one party or as a neutral, the parties may choose to engage a child specialist in addition to parties' coaches. In such engagements, the child specialist is generally a neutral resource for the parties. Information about the child's point of view or suggestions about co-parenting strategies are likely to be heard and respected more fully when they emanate from a qualified neutral person as opposed to the other party.

In the limited role as neutral child specialist, the mental health professional is the "voice" for the child(ren). The child specialist's main focus is to keep the children's concerns and needs at the top of the agenda and to maximize the children's sense that they are being heard by the adults who are handling the reorganization of their family. In joint meetings with the parents, the child specialist can take a family history and assess the parental concerns and the parenting needs of the parties. The specialist may use a number of data collection instruments, including parent and child questionnaires, psychological written testing, and review information such as parental and children e-mails, report cards, medical records, videos and photos, and reports from other professionals.

In serving a facilitative, non-evaluative role, the child specialist can help the parents set boundaries and lessen derogatory or pejorative behavior toward the other parent, handle concerns about parental incapacity due to substance abuse, improve and increase consistency on discipline, diet, bedtime, homework, and coordination of activities, handle the appropriate integration of new romantic partners, and help the parties reduce their conflict in front of the children.

The child specialist can serve as a consultant for the children and can educate the parents and answer their questions about children's needs in general based on the specialist's training and experience as well as research. In meetings with children, the child specialist can explain to the children how their parents are handling the divorce in a child-centered way, describe the divorce process to the children, create a sense of comfort and safety for the children, and provide honesty and transparency toward what is happening in their lives. Child specialists can also assess and work with the children in reducing their risks from divorce and increasing their resilience and ability to adapt during this stressful and often disruptive period in their lives.

In addition, the specialist translates the children's needs for the family in one of several ways:

- Meeting directly with the children and reporting their needs to the parents alone or in a five-way feedback session involving attorneys and coaches
- Discussing the children's needs with other therapists, teachers, and "collateral providers" of the children (e.g., nanny, sports coaches, tutors, clergy) and reporting back through a written report and or feedback session
- Facilitating the children's direct involvement with the parents

Sometimes, even with the involvement of a child specialist, parents will have unresolved disputes over key parenting issues. The use of a confidential or nonconfidential evaluation, focused on one issue or comprehensive, can be conducted within the mediation process.[6]

Financial Professionals

The use of neutral financial professionals (e.g., CPAs, financial planners, tax lawyers, pension specialists) rather than separate experts retained by each party is common in mediation. Every collaborative financial professional has undergone at least the basic course in collaborative practice and often has taken advanced courses in collaborative practice, mediation, and conflict resolution. Collaborative financial specialists also attend dispute resolution conferences and typically participate in ongoing collaborative and mediation study groups. This means that in addition to their financial expertise, these specially trained financial professionals are skilled at active listening, discussion facilitation, and interdisciplinary teamwork.

Some of the typical duties of financial professionals include:

- Gathering and organizing financial documents.
- Developing a statement of assets and liabilities-marital balance sheet.
- Preparing a marital standard of living analysis.
- Running hypothetical computer searches for statutory guidelines for child and spousal support.
- Analyzing cash flow (income and living expenses for each party and expenses for the children in each home).
- Determining imputed income for non-income producing investment property and for support purposes.
- Performing present value calculations for deferred streams of income such as spousal support, defined benefit plans, and annuities.
- Analyzing ability of each party to purchase a new residence or the need to sell the family residence.
- Preparing written financial disclosures for each party.
- Valuing and distributing retirement assets.
- Valuing business interests.
- Providing advice on income tax filings, capital gains, support deductibility, and other tax issues.
- Determining college expenses and recommending financial plans.

Neutral financial professionals can provide financial advice and analysis for the parties in an impartial way. Financial professionals contribute their views of the common financial interests and goals of both parties and creatively develop options for review by the parties, lawyers, and mediator. Financial professionals can be active participants in the negotiation process, offering financial perspectives and input on various proposals. They can provide analysis and practical advice for long-term outcome of proposed financial agreements. For example, they can factor in inflation, increased needs of parties and children, and return on investments and can help parties identify and evaluate various settlement options.

The key role of financial professionals is to educate the parties. As there are many technical and nuanced concepts and terms, a competent financial professional will patiently explain (in understandable language, not "accountant-ese") what the concepts mean, what work is needed, who will do the work, and how the work fits into the overall resolution of the divorce.

One of the key roles you can play as a consulting attorney is to be a resource of ideas and personnel. By incorporating the people and concepts of collaborative practice and involving professionals who have a demonstrated commitment to non-adversarial divorce, you increase your value not only to your client, but also to the mediation process.

Practice Tips

1. Build relationships with collaborative and mediation-friendly professionals in your area. Get to know their strengths, weaknesses, specialties, and demeanor. The more professionals you know, the better able you will be to suggest people who are a good fit for a given case.
2. Don't be afraid to import concepts, roles, and interventions from collaborative law into your mediations when appropriate.
3. Obtain informed consent when involving a collaborative professional in your mediation. Define the collaborative professional's role carefully and explicitly.
4. Enlist the input of the collaborative professionals in determining how they might best be used to solve a particular problem or impasse.
5. Be prepared to discuss your preferred qualifications for a consulting attorney and draw from the ready pool of collaboratively trained attorneys in your community.
6. Study the aspects of attorney disqualification in collaborative cases and consider importing them into your representation of mediation parties.
7. Attend trainings, seminars, and conferences in collaborative law.
8. Prepare your client to raise the issue of an agreed-upon protocol for using collaborative attorneys at the start of mediation so that the other party is less likely to engage a litigator to serve in that role.

9. Utilize collaborative websites as resources for mental health and financial professionals to get involved in mediation.
10. Even if the other party or mediator resists, remain flexible, tolerant, and collaborative in your approach toward non-collaborative behavior.

Notes

1. The principles of Collaborative Practice on the website of the International Academy of Collaborative Professionals (www.collaborativepractice.com) state, "While Collaborative lawyers are always a part of collaboration, some models provide child specialists, financial specialists and divorce coaches as part of the clients' divorce team. In these models the clients have the option of starting their divorce with the professional with whom they feel most comfortable and with whom they have initial contact. The clients then choose the other professionals they need. The clients benefit throughout collaboration from the assistance and support of all of their chosen professionals." IACP, *Principles of Collaborative Law*, Jan. 24, 2005, www.collaborativepractice.com/lib/Ethics/Principles%20of%20Collaborative%20 Practice.pdf.

2. *See* Pauline H. Tesler and Peggy Thompson, Collaborative Divorce (2007).

3. To train as collaborative lawyer, we recommend taking a basic course in Collaborative Training and several advanced Collaborative Training courses, studying the growing literature, and joining a local Interdisciplinary Collaborative Practice Group.

4. In a law review article *Is That All There Is? "The Problem" in Court-Oriented Mediation*, George Mason Law Review, 2008, 15(4), 863–932, Len Riskin and Nancy Welsh describe mediation as lawyer and legal culture-dominated in much the same way as described here.

5. The Arizona State Court website is a useful model that can be used outside Arizona as well, http://www.azcourts.gov/portals/31/parentingtime/ppwguidelines.pdf.

6. Forrest S. Mosten, *Confidential Mini Evaluations: Another ADR Option*. 45 Family Law Quarterly (ABA) No. 1, Spring 2011.

CHAPTER 7

Setting Up the Mediation

Short of dueling, mediation is the form of dispute resolution that puts clients most directly in control. Clients make their own cases instead of playing roles in dramas created by lawyers.
—Jeffrey G. Kichaven and Vicki Stone, *Litigation* (Journal of the ABA Section of Litigation), 1991

Selecting the Mediator

Once a decision has been made to mediate, the next step is determining who the mediator will be. Mediators have different professional orientations and take a variety of approaches. You must advise the client about the importance of selecting the appropriate mediator and take steps to ensure a fair process that will meet your client's needs.

You need certain expertise to ensure that your client's consent to the mediation is appropriately informed. You need to be conversant in mediation orientations and philosophies (e.g., evaluative vs. facilitative). You should also know the field of locally available mediators well enough to speak to the skills and orientation of possible mediators, their reputations in the community, their level of experience, and any particular skill set they offer that might be relevant to the dispute at hand. If you don't have this information, poll your trusted colleagues, review mediator websites, and gather information about potential mediators just as you would if you needed a referral to an attorney in a different practice area.

If your dispute is cross-cultural, you should look for cultural competency. Successful cross-cultural interactions require mutual awareness of cultural differences and respect for these differences. Culture is not merely a function of a person's region of origin; cultural identity can shaped by a multitude of factors, including without limitation faith, ethnicity, race, physical abilities, educational background, class, gender, sexual orientation, geographical location, and profession. Culture influences perspective, and differences in perspective can lead to conflict. A mediator's ability to navigate the cultural differences among disputing parties is paramount for success of dispute resolution. Cultural competence" (i.e., the capacity to navigate cultural differences effectively) is an essential aspect of the mediation toolkit. "Cultural competence is about acknowledging implications of cultural differences for a dispute and its outcomes, and then transcending them in a respectful and productive manner to arrive at an optimal resolution for all disputing parties."[1]

> ### An Uneven Playing Field Doesn't Mean Ending the Game
>
> Jim and Marta wanted to get married. Marta had been the housekeeper for Jim and his first wife before their separation. (Remember *Down and Out In Beverly Hills*?) Jim wanted a premarital agreement, and Marta wanted anything that Jim wanted. Jim wanted to mediate the agreement to cut out the lawyers.
>
> Sounds imbalanced? It was. Language difficulty, financial naïveté, immigration problems, and deep infatuation spelled out duress if not coercion. If you ran away from this one as either a lawyer or a mediator, no one would blame you. But Marta and Jim wanted to get married. Jim wanted the agreement to provide for his children and to protect himself from a possible divorce. All they both wanted was help.
>
> The first challenge as mediator was to work with Jim to allow him to understand why it was in his best interest for Marta to have a lawyer and an interpreter at the sessions. At his request, Woody took on the assignment of finding Marta a lawyer and accompanying her to the lawyer interviews. Four interviews later, Marta had a lawyer who was both independent from and supportive of the mediation. The lawyer was the key to the mediation. Three sessions later, Jim had his agreement, and he and Marta have their new life together.

Many family law mediators are retired judicial officers or family law litigation veterans. Although their substantive knowledge may be impressive and their instincts about likely litigation outcomes finely honed, these family law experts may be new to mediation and/or may not have received mediation training to qualify them to handle your case. Training over a 40-hour period provides a mediator with at least a basic understanding of the nuances of mediation, imparts key skills, and helps ensure that mediators live up to the promise of mediation and meet the clients' needs. Also, if an evaluative approach is not likely to further settlement in a particular case, the substantive expertise and litigation or judicial experience of the mediator—while valuable in a courtroom—may not be so valuable to the client sitting at the mediation table.

Keep in mind not only the needs, preferences, and temperament of your own client, but attempt to meet those of the other party as well. Find out from your client what kind of approach he or she feels is most likely to resonate with the other party. For example, your client may be far along into the process of grieving the loss of the relationship, ready to settle and committed to mediation. The other side, however, may be more emotionally raw and less comfortable with the idea of getting a divorce, let alone starting mediation. In such a situation, you may wish to maximize chances of the other side coming to the table and staying there by selecting a mediator with a facilitative, gentle approach or personality type likely to appeal to the *other* client.

Once you have researched which mediators are available and formed some preliminary opinions about who might be a good fit and why, talk this through with your client. Set aside sufficient time for this crucial conversation. Send the client links to Internet information about potential mediators you have found. Compare and contrast each potential mediator's strengths and weaknesses to help your client make an informed choice. Explain what you know about the potential mediators and how what you know might affect the client's mediation experience. If you have an existing professional relationship with the mediator, discuss that fact with the client.

Some clients will take the initiative and come up with a mediator or mediators themselves. You should encourage clients to do this. One of the goals of mediation is to locate power in the participants, and if clients believe they have participated actively in the selection of the mediator, they will be empowered, invested, and generally more optimistic about the mediation process.

Letting the Other Spouse/Counsel Nominate a Mediator
Schooled in the trench-warfare mentality of litigation, you may be accustomed to jockeying for tactical advantage over even the most technical and minute issues: jurisdiction, venue, judge, evaluator, and even location of the settlement talks (your office or theirs). As in most process decisions involved in setting up a mediation, we generally favor using the mediator proposed by the other side. Because resolution of settlement terms in mediation is ultimately consensual, a client rarely will be harmed by the choice of the mediator. Remember, unlike judges and arbitrators, mediators do not make binding decisions. Moreover, your primary goal is to set up the mediation so that the parties can work out their problems and come to a fair settlement. It is possible that you get so bogged down in trying to game the logistics of the mediation that the opportunity to mediate gets lost. All of the strategic micromanagement in the world won't make a difference if the parties never get to the table! Also, as an attorney, you can model for clients how they should approach the dispute, and you can have a profound impact on the parties' attitudes merely by setting a tone conducive to the mediation. Flexible, accommodating behavior by counsel models an agreement-making mode that increases settlement momentum for the parties.

There are, of course, circumstances in which specific factors render deferring to the other side's choice of mediator impractical or unwise. You should exercise a veto if you suspect a proposed mediator has a demonstrable bias toward the other party or lawyer.

What if the other lawyer has worked with this mediator ten times and you only once? What if the other lawyer and the mediator are golfing buddies? What if the other lawyer and the mediator have spoken together on a recent continuing education panel? What if the mediator's office is in the same building or suite as the other lawyer? These factors could cause concern that the mediator favors the other party, and in some cases, such suspicions might be valid. However, several safeguards built into mediation favor letting it go.

First, mediators build their practices based on their reputations for neutrality and fairness. Most mediators are zealously committed to preserving this reputation.

Second, mediators have a growing obligation to disclose prior contact with lawyers and parties. In our local area, many mediators specifically list all the matters in which they have previously participated with each counsel and often circulate that list in the same packet as the mediation agreement. Retired judicial officers tend to be especially aware of this issue and comfortable disclosing prior matters involving counsel. Detailed, unsolicited disclosure itself should give your client a feeling of comfort concerning the mediator's integrity. (Of course, a failure to disclose or a "fudge" disclosure could raise major concerns.)

Third, if the mediator ever does display bias in favor of the other side, you can end the mediation immediately. Although such delayed termination could result in wasted fees for mediation and possibly hurt settlement momentum, it is generally more important to get the mediation started in the first place.

Fourth, if a party expresses a concern about bias, the mediator may be consciously on guard and may even increase his or her vigilance for fairness. Because the other lawyer proposed the mediator, you and your client can gain comfort that if the mediator presses the other spouse during the mediation, the mediator is to be respected and given increased credence.

Barring specific information tending to indicate that the other side's choice would do your client palpable harm, we presumptively favor the use of the other side's recommendation. Instead of constantly maneuvering to improve your client's position, your test should be "If it doesn't hurt my client, let it go." This may be a novel and frightening approach to many lawyers who worry that their zealousness may be called into question if they miss a single opportunity to control a decision. But if you have worked with the nominated mediator before and feel good about the mediator's integrity, fairness, process experience, reputation, and competence in the area of dispute, it is probably best to let the issue go.

The Mediator Nominating Process

Generally, the mediation setup process is facilitated when the party or lawyer most resistant to commencing mediation has the option of nominating the mediator. However, the resisting lawyer may be inexperienced in mediation and may not have the knowledge to make a nomination. In addition, the other lawyer may be busy (or lazy) and willing to let you make the nomination. In such situations, you should be careful not to abuse the trust reposed in you by the other side. You should discuss your intended process with the other lawyer and attain consent along the way rather than be accused of introducing any surprises. Allying with the other lawyer starts with the selection process and can continue until the settlement agreement is signed, and beyond.

The first step in mediator nomination is to identify the type of mediator background and style that most suits the parties and the nature of the dispute. It is then important for the family lawyer to assemble background on each of several possible mediators (three is a good number) with a gender mix if possible. In addition to a curriculum vitae and the mediator's standard mediation agreement, you should request a sample of articles written by or about the mediator and any promotional material the mediator can provide. Many family lawyers keep files on a diverse group of mediators so that nominations can be sent out as needed. The nominations should be sent with a cover letter making it clear that the other party has the unilateral right to choose among the mediators proposed. You may also clarify the other party's option to reject all three, in which case other names will be provided. The letter should contain a full disclosure of your past professional and personal involvement with each of the nominated mediators. If there are any pending court hearings, you should indicate a willingness to continue the dates of the hearings, preserving the status quo of any current orders, retroactivity, or other issue that may be necessary for the protection of the clients. If agreement cannot be reached on an issue, indicate a willingness to address that issue first in mediation. Finally, it is helpful if the other party is offered an opportunity to interview any or all of the nominated mediators (with your client paying half the cost). Of course, your client should also have the right to interview the mediator finally selected by the other party.

Designing the Process

Setting up a mediation can be as simple and straightforward as the parties and lawyers want it to be. Certain steps can enhance the success of a mediation, and pitfalls can abort it from the start.

Approving the Mediation Agreement

Most (if not all) competent mediators require the parties to sign a written mediation contract before any negotiation takes place. Such an agreement contractually protects confidentiality (many states preserve mediation confidentiality by statute even without agreement), spells out the mediator's basic rules, and provides for payment of the mediator's fee. (See the sample mediation agreement and the model standards in the Resources section).

While every clause is subject to negotiation, the "let it go" standard also applies here. Mediation agreements vary from mediator to mediator. You and your client should review the agreement closely so that both of you understand the text and consequences. However, unless the agreement contains language that is prejudicial to your client or omits some protection that cannot be dispensed with or obtained down the road, usually it is far better to sign the agreement and move to the next stage of the mediation.

Orientation with the Mediator

In elementary school, many of us learned the lesson of the five Ps—Prior Preparation Precludes Poor Performance. The same is true in mediation. Many lawyers' only experience with mediation occurs in the courthouse, where the parties (and often counsel) sit down cold with a mediator and within an hour reach complete agreement or give up and proceed to court. Because court-annexed mediation has an approximate success rate of 60 percent, many lawyers believe that mediation works quickly or not at all and that the odds are four in ten that a particular case will end up in a contested hearing. Private mediation works very differently. Our own experience and informal survey of competent family law mediators and mediation-friendly lawyers indicate that 85–90 percent of matters starting in private mediation end in a complete agreement. The remaining cases often settle soon thereafter, having used the mediation as a foundation for negotiated agreement or as a forum for streamlining the litigation. The lawyers and parties benefit by receiving a tour of the mediation landscape so that they know what to expect in the process. In turn, the mediator needs to understand the needs and concerns of both the parties and their lawyers to better design, convene, and facilitate the mediation.

Telephone Conference Call

At a minimum, counsel should arrange to have a joint conference call to set up the date(s) of the mediation and the briefing schedule and to determine who should be at the table, how food is to be arranged, the time of day, and other administrative details. You should consult with your client as to whether having the parties join that conference call is important. Of course, the other party or lawyer may feel differently about such client involvement and you may need to work this out or just "let it go" and handle it the way with which the other side is most comfortable.

Setting the Date for the Mediation

The success of a mediation may depend on when it is scheduled and how much time is reserved for the mediation itself. The goal should be to set the mediation for the earliest possible date while allowing sufficient time for the parties and counsel to prepare adequately. The lawyers' attitudes toward mediation are just as important as openings on everyone's calendar. Lawyers who are experienced in representing clients in mediation understand that the probability of success at the mediation is very high if it is scheduled before further acts or posturing or conflict (involving parties or counsel) extinguish the interest in settlement.

Actually, the long wait for an appointment with a courthouse mediation or an impending hearing date may be the primary motivation to initiate private mediation. If lawyers are going to be meeting with the mediator along with their clients and/or be present at the mediation sessions themselves, no more than two to six weeks should elapse between the date of agreement to mediate and the commencement of mediation. If the parties will be mediating without lawyers, it is often possible to commence mediation within a few days.

As more mediators are being trained, the supply of qualified mediators increases. This increased supply offers more choice and makes waiting weeks or months for an opening less acceptable. In any community, the top echelon of mediators will be in high demand and the waiting time for them will be the longest. The involvement of such highly regarded mediators does in fact increase the odds that a case will be resolved in a satisfactory manner. However, lag time between agreement to mediate and start date may decrease the chances of settlement, cause the mediation to be more protracted or conflictual, or increase the risk that the mediation never actually begins. Balancing the best choice of mediator with an accelerated start date is a key area of mediation strategy for lawyers.

Invite All Parties to the Table

Here is one of Woody's mediation stories:

My client was the son of a powerful industrialist. Father and son were co-owners of the company but wouldn't talk with each other. They sent faxes even though their offices shared an adjoining wall. The presenting reason for the spat was that Howard, the dad, had been rude to his son's wife. My client, Steven, and his father started fighting—but so did Steven and his wife—which led him and his business litigator into my office.

Steven loved and hated his father. He didn't want to stay in business with his father, but was equally agitated that his estranged wife was keeping the children from seeing their grandparents. Steven did not have much love for Howard's new wife (who was the same age as Steven).

Before starting work on the divorce, I spent considerable time with Steven and his business lawyer to get their approval to initiate an invitation to Dad, his new wife, and Steven's sister to mediate their future as a family and as business owners. With the changing and widening context that included all of the players, Steven had an opportunity to improve his overall legal health (not to mention stomach lining) as well as simplify the divorce negotiation. In my role as dispute resolution manager and negotiation coach, creating two negotiations instead of one may have been unorthodox—but it created opportunities for long-term solutions.

Format

There are two general formats in family law mediation: single-session and multisession. When clients are selecting a mediator or participating in designing the format of the mediation, they need to understand the information set forth visually on the following chart.

MEDIATION FORMATS

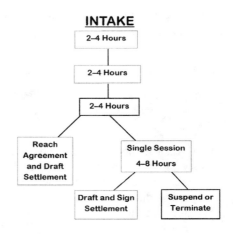

Reprinted from Forrest S. Mosten, *Mediation Career Guide*, Jossey Bass, 2001, All rights reserved.

Traditionally, most civil mediations are set up to take place in a single session. Sometimes these sessions can last days and nights—exhaustion often contributes to settlement as much as skill. Another choice is to have a series of shorter sessions (two to four hours each). Mediators may send out summary letters following each shorter session; these serve as minutes and outline the agreements made and the remaining open issues. The parties continue to meet in shorter episodic sessions pending full agreement or termination. In planning your mediation, you can offer either model or a combination of the two. In the hybrid model, parties usually begin with sequential sessions. If an impasse develops, the parties can try to resolve it in a single-session marathon.

Single-Session Format. In the single-session model, parties and counsel generally meet at the appointed date and time and mediate until an agreed-upon end time (unless agreement is reached sooner) or until an agreement is reached or an impasse on one or more issues blocks further progress. Sometimes exhaustion, the need for further information or reflection, or other factors cause the mediation to adjourn for the day, with a set date agreed on to finish up the agreement. Mediators differ as to whether the mediation session concludes when a document is drawn up and signed by the parties or an agreement in principle is reached on all issues with the drafting of a formal settlement agreement or court order to follow.

Multisession Format. In the multisession model, after the mediation orientation and any private sessions with the mediator to prepare for the first joint working session, the parties and mediator (and lawyers if they shall attend sessions) work out a schedule of sessions ranging from one and a half hours to four hours in length. The goal for each session is to accomplish as much as possible, with the understanding that the parties will continue their work and continue meeting until all of the issues have been resolved. Between sessions, the parties will gather documents, meet together to resolve defined issues (such as personal property or holiday schedules), wait for expert reports such as home appraisals or accountings, meet with their consulting lawyers, think about the issues, plan negotiation strategy, and reevaluate underlying priorities and positions. To increase productivity of the recess periods between sessions, many mediators send the parties (and the lawyers, if agreed) summary letters or minutes of the prior session, setting forth tentative agreements reached, areas of continuing differences, concerns of the parties, homework, and observations of the mediator on both the substantive issues and the mediation process. A sample summary letter appears in the Resources section.

We have found the optimum timing to be three hours for mediation sessions without lawyers present and four hours when lawyers participate. If the sessions are much shorter than three hours, by the time everyone is seated (tardiness is unfortunately quite common) and discussions have occurred about additions and corrections to the last summary letter, new or emergency concerns have been raised, or a topic has been started to develop underlying concerns and options and to explore the consequences of an issue, little time is left to allow for resolution. If three hours is too long for your client or for some reason the session runs out of steam, you can instruct your client to be vigilant and ask whether a session can end early (hopefully without charge) This mediation interruptus can occur regardless of the length of session but seems particularly frustrating to the parties if they have just started when it is time to leave. Since many professional mediators, like therapists and unlike most lawyers, book back-to-back sessions, parties generally do not have the option of continuing past the stop time. Actually, you should caution your client against staying beyond the time set for the appointment. Early in our careers, we both experienced the impact of no ending time. In one situation, after reaching the end time, the parties agreed to buy another 30 minutes of the mediator's time, then another and another—finally extending the mediation five additional hours for a total seven-hour session. Agreement was reached, but everyone's previous plans and nervous system were shot! We both have vowed "Never again" and we have (for the most part) kept that vow.

If lawyers are present at the mediation, time for sessions should be increased between 50 and 100 percent for several reasons. One is the simple reality that there are more people in the room to talk— and most lawyers are good talkers. Second, a major purpose of having you present is to give your client the opportunity to consult with you on the spot, and such consultations can often run to 30–45 minutes when a difficult issue is involved or when emotions are running high. When one side is conferring, the mediator may meet with the other side or it may just be dead time. Finally, in addition to bringing up additional issues and fully (sometimes too fully) advocating their clients' positions, lawyers might increase the conflict in the mediation room, requiring extra time to reach resolution.

Hybrid Format. As in most models, the two major formats are subject to innovative alteration or may be combined into a hybrid format. For example, the parties alone may commence mediation in a multisession format. When the parties get close to final agreement and need a little boost over the last hurdle, a single closing session with counsel may be scheduled. On the other hand, if the parties meet with you and the other lawyer in a single session, the parties may work together better than anticipated. In such a situation (or just to save money), the parties may agree to meet in multisession format with the mediator and without counsel, each side reserving the right to include counsel in sessions down the road.

Preliminary Private Planning (PPP) Sessions

Some training programs advocate starting with private meetings, and there is extensive couples' therapy literature in supports of the concept that starting with individual sessions establishes comfort and rapport with each participant and allows the parties to raise and explore issues privately before dealing with them in open session. Mediators who begin with private sessions try to induce movement in each party's attitude and negotiating position by getting them to "earn" the opportunity to meet directly with the other party. They implement the Edelman (*The Tao of Negotiation*) theory of facilitating agreement by having both individuals reevaluate and reflect to weed out or modify their own unreasonable positions before negotiating directly with the other side.

Family mediation clients seem to want and expect more direct contact with the other party—largely because direct contact is one major difference between mediation and litigation. The most common and traditional mediation format is to start with the parties meeting jointly with the mediator. This process is taught in most mediation training programs and is utilized in community and private mediations. This approach makes both parties feel a part of the process, creates or reinforces trust that there will be no secrets or hidden agendas, and allows the parties to negotiate directly with each other rather than through a shuttle messenger.

We recommend a cross between the two models, incorporating the approach of Dwight Golann, who in his 2014 book, *Sharing a Mediator's Power: Effective Advocacy in Settlement*, argues strongly for lawyers to take a preventive planning role, including encouraging the mediator to counsel a client on how to approach bargaining. After having a joint orientation meeting with both parties (or a conference call with the lawyers), we suggest that mediator meet with each party individually for a private session (one to two hours; if the consulting lawyer attends, two to two and a half hours are reserved for the private session). During the private sessions, clients are encouraged to raise any concerns they may have about the mediation process, the behavior and attitude of the other spouse, and their views about the emotional, financial, parenting, or financial issues in the mediation. This time is used for the mediator to learn the facts of the case and to help the clients prepare for the negotiations by gathering documents and getting information from professionals and institutions (e.g., bank records, insurance rates, retirement benefits, listing reimbursement claims). A major benefit of these sessions is for the client to be educated by the mediator to refine and perhaps eliminate a position as the client is affected by the mediator who assumes the role of reality agent, testing each side's position with legal information, research findings, and practicality. You should prepare your clients to be open to the mediator's help to better achieve their goals, see how some goals may conflict, and explore options and reassess positions. You should stress that the mediator may start pointing out the areas of commonality and the values the parties share. These private sessions can be used to reinforce basic negotiation skills that you can teach, helping both sides think about what they want to present during the joint session and how to make such a presentation. Finally, you should point out that your client can benefit from such private time to assess whether the mediator will truly listen to and understand your client's underlying concerns. Your client should know that the mediator can be available for additional private time during or between sessions.

One of your tasks is to help your client decide whether the mediation should commence with joint or private preliminary planning sessions. If private sessions are agreed upon, you can orient your client about what can be accomplished and help your client be prepared to articulate concerns and develop goals and positions subject to the mediator's input. If you attend the private session, you can be a resource for and a supporter of your client by raising issues he or she may have forgotten, asking questions that your client previously asked you, articulating the client's position from your perspective, and raising your own concerns as consulting lawyer about the process or the negotiation. For example, you may want to reaffirm that all tentative and preliminary agreements are to be subject to the overall agreement that you, as consulting lawyer, want to review carefully. You may want to emphasize your desire to receive all summary letters or other correspondence directly, your availability to the mediator, and your commitment to be an ally to the mediator throughout the process.

Even if you haven't used this approach before, be open to reflecting on your process. For example, New York mediator Daniel Burns had never used preliminary private planning sessions during his 25-year career, but after attending Mosten mediation training in 2014, he endorsed this strategic approach as a new feature of his mediations.[2]

Mediation Briefs

Generally, briefs are utilized in the single-session format, but nothing prevents counsel from agreeing to submit briefs in the multisession format as well. Lawyers who have not participated in mediations may treat the use of briefs as perfunctory or be wary of revealing their legal theories and supporting facts. Some lawyers may propose that briefs be sent confidentially only to the mediator and not be shared with the other side. This wariness may be caused by a trial lawyer's desire to preserve the surprise factor or by skepticism about the potential success of mediation combined with desire to keep legal bills low.

There are no hard-and-fast rules about what a mediation brief should contain. Often, like a trial brief, it contains an outline of the disputed legal and factual issues and a summary of the submitting party's position on each disputed issue. Because mediation is not litigation, a helpful and effective mediation brief might also cover other topics of relevance in the mediation context. For example, it can contain specific proposals for resolution of each disputed issue and an explanation of why the proposed resolution is fair, workable, and responsive to the interests of both parties. It can explain the nonfinancial interests or concerns of the submitting party. It can address what obstacles have prevented settlement of the dispute. It can address the nature of the past and contemplated future relationship between the parties.

Once mediation has been agreed upon (or ordered by the court), you should view it as the last dispute resolution process in the case—the end game during which the case *will* be settled. Success rates of mediation back up this more hopeful view. Therefore, if briefs are utilized, you should not hold back; you should utilize research and careful drafting to use the mediation brief as a tool to persuade the other party. You should not write your brief directed solely at the mediator or even the opposing lawyer. In mediation (as in all negotiations), the real judge, the last decision maker, the relevant audience is the other party. The mediation brief should be drafted with the other spouse in mind: what will persuade that party? The brief should also be submitted far enough in advance for the other spouse to discuss it with his or her lawyer, accountant, family, and other respected people. Try to work out a protocol with the other lawyer so that the mediation briefs can be sent directly to the other spouse to expedite the reflection and reassessment process and to absolutely confirm that the briefs will be seen and studied by the parties.

Costs of the Mediation

Just as knowledge of a lawyer's hourly rates and the amount of required retainer is insufficient to plan for the total cost of a lawyer's fee in divorce litigation, that information is insufficient to determine a mediator's total fee. The variables that determine the total fee are the complexity of the legal and financial issues and the emotional and negotiation chemistry of the parties. Sizable assets may not necessarily mean a prolonged mediation, particularly when no community business exists and most of the assets are in cash or other liquid assets that are not difficult to value and allocate. A negative asset case may be far more difficult because every dollar may affect basic living needs. As to emotional and negotiation variables, naked conflict is never pleasant and will extend the mediation time. However, other less overt styles of the parties may even be more difficult.

If parties are midscale in both complexity and style, experienced mediators generally estimate one full day for a single session or three to six shorter scheduled sessions. Although complex and emotional cases may take more than ten sessions, it is more common that parties without children, complex assets, or difficult dynamics can resolve their dispute in one to three sessions. In the multisession format, it generally takes one hour of outside mediator time for every session, allowing for telephone with parties and counsel, contact experts, draft summary letters, and review correspondence and other documents sent by the parties.

A handout detailing mediation expenses is useful in educating clients before they start mediation. Such knowledge helps avoid sticker shock, and understanding the variables that run up mediation fees might help your client reflect about and change his or her behavior to a more helpful mode.

Who Pays the Mediator?
Who will pay the mediator's fees is often a subject of major negotiation and sometimes is a hurdle to starting a mediation. The two most common options are for each party to pay half the total fees and for the parties to pay proportional to their respective gross incomes. Many lawyers believe that the contribution of the parties should be equal to give each spouse an equal stake in the outcome of the mediation and also to level out an imbalance of power so that the less affluent spouse need not be apprehensive that the mediator might kiss the hand that feeds the kitty. Some variations in fee arrangements include reserving the final allocation of the mediator's fee for negotiation within the mediation or decision by the court if necessary. The spouse unable to pay could receive a preliminary advance

distribution from the marital estate or even a personal loan from the other spouse to pay the fees. Of course, parties could borrow or otherwise obtain fees from extended families or by other means. Many mediators accept credit cards, and the parties can then negotiate that obligation along with other marital debts.

Even if the parties agree to pay equally, it may be necessary for you to negotiate that the obligation be joint and several (causing one spouse to pay the bills of the other defaulting spouse) or if the mediator must look to each spouse separately for that spouse's share of the bill. Of course, just as in lawyers arranging other services and experts, it is good practice for your client, rather than you personally, to be directly and exclusively financially liable for the mediator's fees.

Under the second option, the parties make unequal contributions to the mediator, yet each spouse has some stake. If one spouse is totally without funds, the other spouse may pay or merely advance all of the mediator's fees. In such a situation, there may be resentment on the part of the paying party and fear about fairness on the part of the spouse paying less than half or nothing at all. It is important for you to address these concerns with your client, the other side, and with the mediator before the start of the session. Professional mediators are quite accustomed to these unequal payment arrangements. Once retained, experienced mediators rarely, if ever, think about how much each side is paying and do not favor the party paying the bill while it is current. Few mediators can avoid negative countertransference against parties who do not pay as promised, which can affect a mediator's impartiality and effectiveness.

Another nuance of payment of mediation fees deals with the common situation in which one party meets much more with the mediator than does the other party. We generally recommend that parties pay equally for both parties' time regardless of any time imbalance. The mediator is using that time to help both parties reach an agreement. In fact, if the other party is eating up the clock, you can advise your client to be grateful: it is far better for the mediator to deal with these concerns than have the situation blow up. Of course, if parties cannot see the benefit of equal payment, you can negotiate with the mediator to have all joint sessions paid equally (or another way) and have each party billed separately for their individual time with the mediator in person, on the phone, or by e-mail.

Methods of Payment

Mediators differ in the payment arrangements they offer. Hourly charges are most common. Some mediators bill by the day, and others negotiate a flat fee with certain parameters, such as $2,000 per day up to 7 p.m. and then hourly. The noted alternative dispute resolution (ADR) firm of Gregorio Haldeman Piazza in San Francisco charges a flat fee and is available for a 24-hour day (rarely used because everyone else is exhausted, but a very compelling marketing tool). Some mediators (generally lawyer/mediators) charge for out-of-session time; others do not. Some mediators ask for an advance deposit to be applied against hourly charges; others require clients to pay the current charges and the remaining deposit is applied to the final bill.

Many mediators do not even send bills, but are paid in full at the beginning or end of each session. (There are vibrant conversations at mediator conferences as to whether payment at the beginning or end of session is better practice.) Therapist/mediators are accustomed to billing for a 45- to 50-minute hour and so may charge for three and a half sessions for a 3-hour mediation session.

Most mediators are open and not defensive about discussing their fee arrangements. There is a general spirit of disclosure and informed client consent about which mediators receive training and which mediators are generally committed.

The Site of the Mediation

The mediator's office is the obvious first choice—it is neutral. Some mediators do not have offices, but rent only their working space without access to sufficient breakout rooms or other amenities; some reside in other cities and are traveling to a locale to mediate a dispute. In such situations, parties with sufficient means may elect to rent space at a hotel, another consensual dispute resolution firm, a court reporter's office, or some other space to ensure neutrality. Perhaps one has access to a colleague's office that can be used. However, it might come down practically and economically to using your office or your colleague's. [We often call the other lawyer our "collaborative colleague," particularly when we both sign a disqualification clause (see Chapter 6).]

Again, you should invoke the "let it go" mantra. If the other lawyer has sufficient space and wants to host, you should agree to travel there, as long as you work out a number of logistics. You must be assured that the mediator has exclusive use and control of a room of sufficient size to accommodate all parties, counsel, and others present for the mediation. The room should contain a whiteboard, a flip chart, or other settlement-inducing features that the mediator might request. You as the visiting lawyer and your client should have exclusive use of another room with a door that closes, ensuring privacy. The mediator, you, and your client should all be given access to telephones, fax, and wireless Internet facilities. You should be assured that your messages and documents will be delivered promptly, with confidentiality protected. The hosting lawyer should commit to not taking telephone calls that interrupt mediation work, going through e-mail or snail mail, directing staff, or otherwise conducting customary office business that would interfere with the mediation. In short, as with other process issues, it is important for you to discuss any concern that might make someone uncomfortable and to attempt to approximate a neutral setting to the best possible extent.

Food and Drink: Agents of Collaboration

Unlike the courtroom, in which litigants are restrained from bringing in food or beverages at the threat of bailiff intervention, mediations should provide a nurturing atmosphere. It is harder to dislike those with whom one has broken bread. The arrangements for providing caloric and tasty sustenance should be discussed explicitly and not left for the day of the mediation.

Mediation authority Laurence Boulle addresses the ritual importance of food and drink in his book *Mediation: Principles, Process, and Practice*: "Mediators may also provide food, drink and other refreshments which can be 'ritually' served in a way which shows respect for and the equality of all parties present. Consumption becomes a common activity, participated in equally by all participants, which temporarily distracts attention from the negative features of the dispute during the settling-in phase."

The following discussion assumes a single-session format (even if such session is designed to last several days). In the multisession model, the meetings are generally at the mediator's office, which is accustomed to providing drinks, cookies, candies, and other tideovers. During day-long sessions, there are usually four feedings: breakfast, lunch, midafternoon snacks, and evening food.

Space permitting, the ideal setup is to have a neutral food room that all parties and lawyers can enter at any time to replenish their plates. The host is responsible for having the food set up, ice freshened, and cleanup completed. Some of the most important settlement discussions are initiated casually while participants engage in the common goal of enjoying the repast. The positives of a generous spread go beyond creating a warm atmosphere and putting people together. If personal needs are provided for, the participants will not need to go off-site and have hunger as an excuse to leave early or to blame for an inability to focus on the issues.

Who is to arrange and pay for this catering? The options are the lawyers, the parties, or the mediator. Although we usually suggest that the lawyers be given the responsibility for arranging the meals, the food negotiations themselves are fun (especially when the clients are paying) and help you and your colleague test out your working collaborative relationship. The office host may provide local purveyors and caterers. We have had many lawyers report that the task of arranging and feeding both parties and lawyers felt good and contributed to the day's settlement success. Other mediators opt to arrange for and provide the food, under the theory that the subtle, reciprocal social obligations created between guest and host and between joint guests can grease the wheels of the negotiation and help things proceed more smoothly.

Setting up the mediation properly and preparing for it diligently not only will increase the odds of success, but also will expedite a settlement process that reduces conflict and lowers the parties' costs. If you play a proactive role in getting the mediation set up, you will help settle a case and help start the family healing process.

Practice Tips

1. Advise your client to take care in selecting the mediator and support the client by gathering and presenting information about possible mediators.
2. Consider any information you have about the needs of the other party and counsel.
3. Unless the mediator is clearly incompetent, unqualified, or biased, agree to the one proposed by the other party.
4. "Let go" of unimportant issues in setting up the process. Reassure the client that flexibility is not weakness.
5. Establish a collaborative team approach with the opposing lawyer in setting up the mediation; you are both allies in the quest for amicable resolution—even if you differ on the issues or in your views of the parties.
6. Make it easy for the other side to try mediation; provide full background information of proposed mediators and disclosure of your past contact, give the other side wide control, and be willing to continue court actions to schedule the mediation.
7. Educate your client and the opposing party and lawyer about the 85–90 percent success rate in private mediation—far higher than the 60 percent in court-annexed mediation.
8. Do not cut corners or hold back important facts or law in preparing for the mediation.
9. Schedule the mediation as quickly as possible with sufficient time for preparation—one to six weeks should be the range.
10. Select the best mediator the parties can afford; be willing to compromise that choice to begin the mediation more quickly.
11. Explain the difference between the single-session and multisession mediation formats and propose the format or hybrid that best serves your client.
12. Use the time between sessions to the client's advantage: review the negotiation process, gather documents, revise positions, and prepare for the next session.
13. Schedule sufficient time for each mediation session; double the time allotted if lawyers are present.
14. Make sure your client understands how much the mediator is being paid, when payment is due, what the client is paying for, and what additional fees are expected and when. Urge mediators to offer a written estimate of their costs.
15. Define allocation of payment between the parties.
16. Try to use a neutral site, but invoke the "let it go" principle if the other lawyer wants to host.

17. Think about strategic options to arrange for food and drink.
18. Discuss the advantages of having a private session with each side before commencing the mediation.
19. Discuss the advantages of having you attend the sessions.
20. Direct your mediation brief and verbal presentation at the other party—not at the opposing lawyer or mediator.

Notes

1. The Mediator's Toolkit: Cultural Competence—Transcending Culture Differences in Mediation, Dave Aschaiek, November 2011 (Mediate.com). *See also Cultural Competence in Family Mediation*, Allan Barsky, David Este, and Don Collins, MEDIATION QUARTERLY, Vol. 13, No. 3, Spring 1996.

2. Daniel R. Burns, Preliminary Private Planning Sessions—Do They Work? http://burns-mediator.com/preliminary-private-planning-sessions-do-they-work.

CHAPTER 8

Building an Agreement Your Client Can Live With

"A mediator I was working with recently told me that he saw a well known divorce attorney talking to a client in one of the corridors of the court house where I practice. This attorney was telling his client that mediation will not work. He told his client to only do what he told him. He also said that the client should not make any decisions unless it is agreed to by the attorney. This is a recipe for disaster and failure. If the client is encouraged to go into mediation with that closed mind attitude, then it is doomed to fail."
—Henry Gornbein, "How Lawyers Can Sabotage Mediation," Huffington Post, 2012

Once the mediation is set up, lawyers can work proactively with their clients, the mediator, and opposing counsel to further the goals of the mediation. Mediation's popularity is largely due to the availability of lawyers who are willing and prepared to be team members. The overall purpose of attorney involvement is self-evident: to offer information, advice, and assistance to ensure that the client is protected and that the underlying needs and goals are maximized. The consulting lawyer's assignment, however, is far different from the role of zealous courtroom advocate. The lawyer's ultimate job in mediation is to help the client successfully complete the mediation, resulting in an agreement that feels fair and workable to the client based on the reasonably available information. The job is not to negotiate for the last dollar, vindicate every single one of the client's legal rights, or look under every last stone. Leaving some money on the table or passing up possible legal protections may be worthwhile to the client if the overall agreement satisfies other needs, such as finality, preservation of an amicable parenting relationship and healthy children, or privacy. Informed consent means that the client is the one who makes these value judgments.

Clients can choose to have the lawyers heavily involved in the mediation, attending and participating actively in the mediation sessions. Clients can also choose to "go it alone" during the sessions themselves and keep attorneys in reserve, even if the lawyer could have elevated the client's comfort level during the mediation and/or affected the settlement terms. In mediation, the client is in charge—not only of the ultimate settlement, but also of whether, when, and how to use the attorney's services. (An unbundled approach, its nature, and its ethical ramifications are discussed in Chapter 5.)

In a 2014 article, John R. Phillips, a former chair of the ABA Dispute Resolution Section, summed up conflicting roles of the lawyer in mediation: "Advocates often err on the side of extremes, either trying to control the mediation process or sitting idly by, expecting the mediator to be knowledgeable and effective in soliciting information from the parties to bring about compromise."[1]

Adviser and Coach

When mediation participants hire legal counsel, most are seeking both advice and emotional support. Even though a mediator might provide comprehensive information and a full menu of possible options and consequences, clients often want to know what their lawyers recommend because such a recommendation is neither neutral nor impartial, but wholly partisan and based on the client's interests. While a mediator may point out, for example, that a healthy family system collectively benefits everyone in it, the attorney's concern is the client's individual interests.

Many clients are unwilling to try mediation without the backup advice of their own lawyer, but their feelings about retaining counsel are ambivalent. They want comfort and protection, but worry that the lawyers will take over the mediation and that the lawyers' maximizing control over their future will be compromised. Many have chosen mediation specifically for the self-empowerment and control it affords, and they don't want to have to convince a lawyer to support the resulting agreement or be told how shortsighted or stupid their actions have been. And they certainly don't want to spend their children's college funds fighting each other.

On the other hand, going through a divorce is frightening, stressful, and profoundly unsettling. It is the single largest and longest-lasting financial transaction most people have ever entered into. They are deciding critical issues involving every aspect of their lives when their judgment is clouded by emotion. Both spouses fear the unknown—how will their lives turn out—as well as the known—few families live as well after a divorce, children are put at emotional risk, and it takes a long time to recover. It is normal and appropriate for people to be afraid, and fear creates reluctance to mediate.

Consulting family law attorneys offer clients the opportunity to enjoy the self-determination and other benefits of the mediation process without sacrificing the security and comfort of having received independent legal advice. They make it possible for clients to have the best of both worlds.

Educating and Advising on the Client's Legal Position

Just as in full-service representation, a major job for the family law attorney is to identify legal issues, educate the client about the law, and help the client formulate legal positions. Clients with the benefit of this preparation tend to be far more effective in negotiation sessions. They are not surprised by legal information, and they have a chance to process it and adjust their own expectations in advance. They have a greater sense of mastery over the subject matter on the table. They are able to articulate vital issues with greater confidence and focus, and they are equipped to recognize and respond to issues raised by the mediator and the spouse. If the client hears assessments of the law and/or the merits of a given position that diverge from their attorney's assessment, the client can explore and resolve those differences during the session with counsel, or both. Informed consent requires information—the more the better. Input from counsel facilitates critical thinking and improves the quality of client decisions.

Franklin Garfield and Frederick Glassman offer the following insights about early lawyer involvement: "The vast majority of parties who choose to mediate their cases have an incomplete and incorrect knowledge of the law. If they are involved early in the process, consulting attorneys can largely remedy this problem."[2]

Compiling the Client's Financial Information and Assessing Needs

Given that the exchange of detailed financial disclosure statements is a prerequisite for a divorce judgment, a customary mediation assignment calls for each party to prepare a written statement of assets, debts, income, and expenses and bring it to the session to facilitate discussion of financial issues such as support, division of property, and allocation of debt.

Seldom does the mediator have time to help a party prepare financial disclosures, and even if time did permit, it is questionable whether such help would be consistent with the mediator's role. Clients have fiduciary obligations to make full and fair financial disclosures, and mediators have no way of verifying or investigating the disclosures made. Most clients would benefit from having their lawyer make sure all expenses are included, all potential claims are identified, and all backup information is attached.

You may also suggest that the client receive help from a CPA, financial planner, or budget-savvy family member or friend. Various designations have developed in recent years for financial professionals who work with divorcing parties (e.g., Certified Divorce Financial Analyst (CDFA), Certified Financial Divorce Practitioner (CFDP), Certified Financial Divorce Specialist.) Another resource is www.collaborativepractice.com or your local collaborative practice group to find financial professionals trained in client-centered interdisciplinary services (including mediation and collaborative law).

Often all the lawyer does is review the financial need data and communicate approval to the client. The lawyer does this by briefly quizzing the client to verify that the client truly understands the situation and that the information is complete and well put together. This act of confirming legal health is reassuring to clients participating in mediation, and its importance should not be understated. Just as people are willing to pay for health checkups and feel better when the doctors tells them that everything is fine, mediation participants are willing to pay a consulting attorney to review basic financials and receive a clean bill. Lawyers can anticipate the questions the spouse or mediator will ask and help the client prepare an explanation. This not only helps clients feel prepared, but also can streamline the mediation sessions. Although lawyers routinely work with financial forms and are not daunted by them, many clients become bogged down, procrastinate, and hit major emotional roadblocks when faced with the financial disclosure forms and worksheets. For clients emerging from a marriage in which the informal division of labor located financial information and decision-making power in the spouse, this may be their first foray into budgeting, a skill which will be crucial for the in the future. Your support can give clients much-needed confidence not only in their ability to participate effectively in mediation, but also in your services and judgment.

Obtaining the Documents Needed to Make an Informed Decision

A major criticism of mediation in family law matters is that spouses might make lifelong decisions based on inadequate information. A spouse who does not get to play with the full deck of property (both assets and liabilities) or income can be deprived drastically of essential rights designed to provide a fair standard of living and distribution of the marital estate. Whether discovered before or after an agreement is reached, playing with half a deck or having the cards dealt from the bottom of the deck creates mistrust in the other spouse and the mediation process. This may in turn lead to a challenge to the finality or enforceability of the agreement, further conflict or litigation between the spouses on other issues, or possible claims against the professionals involved.

Consequently, many family lawyers routinely advise their clients to postpone even considering mediation on financial issues until formal discovery, governed by the traditional statutory process, is completed. Such discovery can range from a demand to fill out required court forms for income and property with documentary backup to full-scale interrogatories, requests to produce documents of the other party, subpoenas on third parties (banks, employers, family members), and depositions of witnesses that can go on from a few hours to many weeks.

Lawyers know well that a failure to conduct adequate discovery can lead to malpractice exposure. This exposure often leads to defensive over-lawyering and a negative attitude toward mediation early in the process. However, the best use of mediation is early in the process, before positions become entrenched and brutal battles (including those over discovery) can dissipate resources and inflame conflict.

To reconcile the need for adequate disclosure with the benefits of early use of mediation, you can advise your client that such financial disclosure is required whether mediation is used or not. Informed consent is also the foundation of a successful mediation. It is important to advise less knowledgeable spouses about their rights to full discovery of their financial lives. Receiving documents and other backup is not just a legal right, but a necessary element in good mediation participation. The more knowledgeable spouse is often the party pushing for mediation, partly to maintain the more powerful position by muting the role of lawyers and the litigation process, including formal discovery. Yet, it is ironic that the more powerful spouse actually benefits by making early full financial disclosure with documentary backup. The powerful spouse can then demonstrate a good faith commitment to fairness that will expedite the mediation. The other party and the mediator need sufficient information to have meaningful discussions—the prelude to reaching a fair agreement. Such disclosure will also increase the comfort level of the less powerful spouse's attorney and accelerate the review and approval process. Finally, once agreement is reached, such financial disclosure is like an insurance policy for the more powerful spouse's reliance on the finality of the agreement reached in mediation. Such disclosure, in addition to the involvement of counsel by the less powerful spouse, will increase (if not guarantee) court approval of the agreement and virtually obliterate any attempt to set the agreement aside at a later date. Many states have mandatory financial disclosure forms or other requirements of mutual financial disclosure that are non-waivable preconditions for obtaining a judgment of dissolution of marriage or legal separation.

In our mediations, parties use the mandatory forms for income, expenses, and property developed by the California Judicial Council. The parties prepare their own forms and exchange them during the fact-gathering process. The same forms (generally updated) are finalized and exchanged as a condition for obtaining a judgment of marital dissolution.

Therefore, it is important to pave the way for full disclosure even before mediation commences. If the parties are communicating directly with each other, the less powerful spouse should be advised to express the expectation that the other party will provide disclosure early in the mediation process. The more powerful spouse should be advised to start gathering documents and to put them in an indexed mediation notebook (resembling a trial notebook) so that both spouses, the mediator, and counsel can work with that information. Such a notebook should include tax returns, bank and stock statements, real estate deeds, purchase and improvement information, credit card and other debt details, reimbursement claims, and the like.

> **Sample Mediation Notebook Contents**
>
> 1. Tax returns—personal (last three years)
> 2. Tax returns—corporate (last three years)
> 3. Cash disbursements analysis reports
> 4. Summary of household expenses
> 5. Summary of child-related expenses
> 6. Schedule of assets and debts
> 7. Narrative from Richard Moore regarding management of the community estate
> 8. Real estate deeds
> 9. Deal memorandum and MCA contract
> 10. "Celebrity Goodwill: Enjoy It While It Lasts: It's Not an Asset" by F. Expert, Esq.
> 11. Documentation of loan to brother
> 12. Greenpeace donation
> 13. Pension plan
> 14. Corporate records
> 15. Real property and furniture
> 16. Contingent tax liability

Even with expectations for disclosure in place, some parties delay or resist providing documents. Every effort should be made to work out these problems during the mediation. Most experienced mediators are capable of assuming the role of mediated case manager as well as working on the settlement. Even if the court process would be invoked to compel production of documents or obtain other discovery, many states require in-person or telephonic meetings between counsel before any motion is filed. These meet-and-confer conferences can be conducted with the mediator. Sometimes the mediator can be helpful in facilitating negotiation between the lawyers.

Therefore, in situations of discovery impasse, concern should be raised with the mediator either by the spouses or by a letter from consulting counsel. Even if the parties may have started without counsel, if a looming discovery battle appears on the horizon, rather than throwing in the towel on the mediation and having the entire case head to court, it is preferable for the lawyers to attend a mediation session devoted to this issue. Even if resolution is not achieved, with the help of the mediator, counsel can work out an agreement to bifurcate the proceeding. The discovery problem can be decided by a judge or an arbitrator, and the mediation can continue with other issues not affected by this problem, such as parenting, personal property, and disposition of the house. As an alternative, the parties involved can reach an agreement to stay committed to the mediation process but take a recess in the negotiations until the discovery dispute is resolved.

Review of Documents

In helping the client evaluate and formulate a negotiation position, you can review legal documents such as deeds, promissory notes, employment contracts, partnership agreements, and prior court orders, among others. The principal task is to educate the client about what the documents mean, identify which documents are important, and advise the client as to how to use the documents during the mediations. It is important for you and your client to have a clear agreement on what documents the lawyer will review and in what depth. As in other aspects of discrete task representation, the client is ultimately in charge of the lawyer's scope of representation. However, you have the right (and perhaps the duty) to advise the client about the dangers of unduly restricting your work and to refuse to undertake an assignment unless it can be done so competently so that the client is reasonably protected.

Monitoring the Progress of the Mediation

There are two views on when a participant in a mediation should engage counsel. The first school of thought argues that the lawyer should be brought in after the parties have reached an agreement. The lawyer's function is to review the terms and drafting of the agreement and to play a technical role in processing the agreement already reached. The underlying support for the "review only" role is that the parties are capable of reaching their own agreement with the mediator and that earlier participation by lawyers will only muck it up and be a deal breaker. Further, by waiting until the end, the parties can make substantial progress and simply fine-tune the agreement once lawyers are involved.

The second view on timing the lawyer's involvement is that by waiting until after an agreement to involve a lawyer, mediation participants make deals without full information. When the lawyer has a concern about a deal point and recommends renegotiation of that portion of the deal, the client is faced with a major dilemma. If the client follows the lawyer's advice and reopens negotiations, the other spouse might react by feeling betrayed and accusing the other party of bad faith. As a result, the cost of the mediation will increase.

We see merit in both views. We have seen mediations sabotaged by adversarial attorneys who overnegotiate and push people around. We have also seen mediations virtually start from scratch after lawyers began reviewing an agreement in which they had no prior input. Everything else being equal, we favor having the parties start the mediation without lawyers present but having the mediator send summary letters to counsel if the parties so authorize. Parties should be encouraged to consult counsel early and often. In this way, even if they are not in the actual mediation room, attorneys become part of the process. If after review of a summary letter or consultation the lawyer does not like a particular agreement or direction of discussions, that view can be raised by the client or directly by the lawyer through a letter to the mediator or to opposing counsel. The parties and mediator can then deal with the concern head-on and resolve it in the agreement.

Once the review process starts, it generally goes more smoothly because the lawyers are familiar with and have participated in the agreement.

To Caucus or Not to Caucus?

Once the mediation starts, you should know the mediator's policy about holding private caucuses. Some mediators, concerned that it makes the subjectivity of the mediator too powerful a factor in the process and creates mistrust, oppose any use of caucus and have all communications in open session. Others routinely use caucuses to establish rapport and help make sure parties feel that they are fully heard. While some lawyers feel very strongly about whether or not to caucus, usually it works out best if such process decisions are left to the mediator. It is important that your client know whether caucusing will take place, whether such communications will remain confidential or can be shared with the other party, and how to use caucuses to the best negotiating advantage.

Caucus Tips for Clients

1. When the mediator asks to speak to the other party, leave quickly without attitude and do not try to get the last word in.
2. While alone outside the mediation room, do not obsess about what the others are discussing. Try to relax and shake any anger or tension. The mediator may be working with the other party on issues you cannot control.
3. If the caucus lasts longer than anticipated, be patient. You could be benefitting from the discussion taking place.
4. If the mediator requests a caucus with you, acquiesce politely and let the mediator direct the conversation.
5. Be candid with the mediator. If the caucus is confidential, trust the mediator to keep your secret. If it is not, trust the mediator to use appropriate discretion in handling your confidences. If you are bursting at the seams, it will not hurt you to express sadness, anger, or other emotions to the mediator.
6. If you are uncomfortable with something the mediator says or does, bring it up with the mediator.
7. If you feel you are losing control during a joint session, ask for a break and a private caucus with the mediator.
8. If you have a settlement proposal but are unsure about certain aspects or how best to present it, ask for a caucus and run it by the mediator.

Lawyers at the Mediation Table

More frequently, family lawyers are present at the mediation session. Although mediation still offers parties the opportunity to communicate directly and generate their own agreement, having the lawyers present at the table may be the added help that brings a settlement home.

When Lawyers Should Be Present

Assuming that the mediator (or court/organization) permits the lawyers to participate in the session, in the following situations, it is advisable for clients to be accompanied by their lawyers:

- One or both parties will not start or continue mediation without having counsel present.
- One or both lawyers will not permit their clients to start or continue mediation without counsel present.
- Due to a gross imbalance of power, sophistication, knowledge, or emotional readiness, the mediator recommends that counsel be present.
- After considerable effort, an impasse develops on one or more issues and the lawyers could be catalysts for settlement.
- The issues or timing of the mediation impacts on ongoing litigation or court management of the cases, and the lawyers' input would be helpful.
- Direct communication between the parties is so disruptive or harmful that the support and buffering of lawyers would be helpful.

A general guide is that absent harm, the parties should be encouraged to work without lawyers first. However, if any of the preceding criteria kick in or there is doubt about whether lawyers should be involved, the prudent (but more expensive) path is to have the lawyers present. It is critical to understand that these concerns should not threaten the life of the mediation. When things get tough or technical, many lawyers or clients pull the plug prematurely. Instead of terminating or considering lawyer involvement to be the demise of a mediation, consider it another approach or format of a mediation in progress.

The Role of Lawyers at the Session

There are three basic ways in which lawyers participate in mediation discussion. First, the lawyer speaks for the client, much as in traditional negotiations. This occurs when the client feels overwhelmed by the other party or when the lawyer cannot surrender control. The second approach is for the parties to conduct the discussions with the lawyers remaining rather mute. Here the lawyer serves as an adviser, a coach, and a legal expert resource, but does not change the dynamics of the direct party negotiation. Third, the lawyer and client are members of a negotiation team, and either speaks at any time. The team power may not necessarily be equal.

In his 2014 book *Sharing a Mediator's Powers: Effective Advocacy in Settlement*, Dwight Golann suggests that you combine roles by asking the mediator for advice in formulating a settlement proposal. In his review of this book, John R. Phillips cites Golann's proscription that if a mediator is reluctant to take authorship of a proposal, the mediator may be willing to endorse the proposal as a good-faith step that the other party should consider reciprocating.[3]

All three models are in play at mediation tables around the country. In fact, we have mediated and served as mediation counsel in all three formats—sometimes all three during the same mediation or even during the same session. It is important for you to educate the client about the choices available and for the client to be involved in deciding what role you should play.

During a session, when in doubt, keep quiet or say less. Many mediations are thrown offtrack by lawyers who believe that their clients want or need them to be highly assertive, articulate, and controlling. In fact, clients might even say that's what they want, but what they really want is to end up with a mediated agreement that meets their needs. No matter how silver tongued you are in the session, if your eloquent words derail the process, you have not done your job. This does not mean you should give away the store. Your clients deserve agreements that are fair to them and that meet their needs. If the mediation is not going well, rather than walking out or giving in, find a way to reshape its direction with fresh ideas for settlement or structure of negotiations (e.g., designating time to brainstorm creative solutions, exploring an apology, suggesting other dispute resolution processes).

Many family lawyers find it difficult to share control with a mediator. Because mediators have no ultimate decision-making authority, some lawyers either dismiss their input or struggle with them over procedural and substantive issues, large and small. Successful mediative lawyers use the mediator as an ally and a coach. Quite often the mediator can provide important insights, information about the other side, and recommendations for what to say and how to say it effectively. By having a neutral perspective and being trusted by both sides, a mediator can be a helpful third member of your team.

Finally, many family lawyers, comfortable with other lawyers and familiar with pitching an argument to a judge, will direct comments primarily to the mediator and secondarily to the other lawyer. Big mistake! The real decision makers are the parties. Effective lawyers in mediation address the other party as often as possible. If the other party buys your pitch, you've almost made the sale. However, the other co-judge in the room is your client. Don't forget to take care of the emotional and informational needs of your own client. Use the mediator to help you inform, educate, and persuade your client. Often clients finally hear what you have been trying to say when they hear the same thing from the mediator.

A helpful part of the lawyer's role is reviewing summary letters of each session that the mediator may send to parties and counsel. A sample letter from a consulting attorney to a mediator, commenting on a mediation summary letter, is included in the Resources section.

Use of Experts

In selecting a mediator, it is important to ascertain the prospective mediator's views and customary practice in regard to experts. Many family lawyers are accustomed to using neutral experts, and this option works particularly well within the mediation context. When each side retains its own expert, the expense to the family is doubled and the two results (all too often advocating the client's best-case scenario) are often compromised at some point. In many high-asset and complex marital estates, the professional fees of the dueling forensic accounts dwarf even the lawyers' fees.

By utilizing a neutral third-party expert, both spouses can benefit. The fees are reduced for the following reasons: The parties are paying one expert, not two. By agreeing consensually on the expert, cooperation by the parties in complying with the expert's requests may be increased, reducing conflict and expense. Rather than pandering to the client who hired the expert, the professional is retained through the mediation and will make judgment calls neutrally, starting with a more middle-ground report that facilitates follow-up negotiation. Finally, because both parties are involved in selecting the expert, rather than hearing from the other side's hired gun or having the expert imposed by the court, the expert's findings may be better accepted by the parties.

You can play a major role in the use of experts in mediation. First, by supporting the initial use of a neutral expert, you might elicit the client's consent to a process that could be instrumental in resolving the major issues in the case. The only risk to the client is the possible future cost of retaining his or her own experts if the matter is not resolved. While possible, this additional cost rarely occurs. The client can take comfort knowing that unless otherwise agreed upon, the neutral expert's report and comments are confidential and inadmissible by statute or such confidentially can be agreed to at the outset. Also, even if the neutral report is detrimental to the client, the results are not binding and can be the starting point for negotiations at the mediation table. The client retains control to negotiate, negotiate, and continue to negotiate until a satisfactory resolution is reached—no result will be imposed.

You can be of great help in identifying potential experts for the client to propose at the mediation table, and the selection can be negotiated by counsel in or out of session. Choosing an expert consensually rather than having one appointed by the judge affords clients the opportunity to meet the expert in advance separately in the expert's office, jointly with both spouses in the expert's office, or with the mediator in session. If either party feels uncomfortable, the parties can agree to continue interviewing until they both agree.

You can also advise the client as to the recommended scope of the expert's services and even assist in the negotiation and/or drafting of the joint engagement letter. We have found that experts generally prefer to have lawyers and clients absolutely clear about what work is expected and what the cost might be. Rather than engaging the expert for a soup-to-nuts job, the parties may agree to unbundle the expert's work and use services on a tiered step-by-step basis. For example, if the parties agree to jointly retain a vocational counselor to evaluate the wife's earning capacity neutrally, perhaps the counselor could meet with the wife for two hours, do two hours of job research, and report back with a brief letter. If this amount of work does not settle the issue, the parties may then want the counselor to administer standardized vocational assessment tests and prepare a detailed written report (still confidential unless otherwise agreed upon) or even come to a mediation session to discuss the findings. As an alternative, one vocational counselor could perform a confidential mini-evaluation, reserving the right for either party to compel a formal evaluation with another vocational counselor, whose report would be sent to the court if not resolved in mediation.

The same unbundled approach could be used with any type of expert. The parties retain control and calibrate their use of expensive professional services, opting first for the least invasive, least protracted, least binding, and least expensive approach. Regardless of the approach taken, you can help the client understand and interpret the significance of the expert's report and advise the client as to a workable negotiating position, using the report as one measure of objective reality.

The Lawyer as Negotiation Coach

Most family lawyers are skilled negotiators. The lawyer coach can teach the client some of the essentials of negotiation theory and give supervised individual training to the client in preparation for the mediation session. As a start, superb books on negotiation are available that the client can be encouraged to read and discuss with friends or with you. A list of these books is included in the Resources section. Viewing videos on negotiation and actual mediation sessions might give clients an appreciation for the process and some ideas on how to approach the discussions.

Helping the client develop creative options and a plan for the negotiation may be one your most important roles. In her groundbreaking article "Toward Another View of Legal Negotiation," Professor Carrie Menkel-Meadow makes a persuasive case that thorough and creative negotiation planning, not style of presentation, is most effective in achieving negotiation success. You can help the client assess the strengths and weaknesses of various proposals and help the client develop not only an initial proposal, but also backup proposals based on anticipated responses. Mediators often report that the most difficult job is not convincing the other side of the merit of a particular proposal, but having one party (either party) actually put a proposal on the table. By providing the client with a negotiation plan in advance, the consulting lawyer can help the momentum of the mediation and help the client in the process.

Understanding itself may not be enough to do the job. Another function of the consulting lawyer is to walk the client step-by-step through the negotiation process that will occur in the mediation. A role play where your take on the role of the other spouse might help the client articulate underlying concerns and proposals for each anticipated issue. Clients benefit greatly from this dress rehearsal and report greater comfort and familiarity with the issues once the curtain goes up at the mediation.

Practice Tips

1. Educate your client about the difference between legal information provided by the mediator and your advice recommending a particular course of action.
2. Collaboratively determine with your client what scope of service you will provide during the mediation, what tasks the client will perform, and what discrete tasks you will perform.
3. Make sure your client completes a financial budget, income information, and property and debt schedules and is conversant about the information set forth on the forms; determine who will complete the forms (your client, a CPA, a financial planner, or you).
4. Make sure your client fully discloses all relevant income and property information and that you receive adequate disclosures from the other side.
5. If you represent the more powerful, more knowledgeable spouse, urge early and full financial disclosure—it may be the key to a mediation's success.
6. You are not a potted plant. As consulting lawyer, you can offer input to your client's opposing counsel and directly to the mediator.
7. Acknowledge and praise clients when they are successful in representing themselves in mediation. Clients need your support as well as your guidance.
8. Instead of immediately filing for court relief, if an impasse develops on document production, failure to attend a deposition, or any other discovery issue, use the mediator as a case manager to mediate an expedited process.
9. Review important legal documents and advise your client about their meaning and importance in the mediation. Make sure your client keeps you in the loop so that you receive the documents *before* agreements are made in mediation.

10. Make a deal with your client about how often lawyer and client will communicate, who will initiate contact, and how proactive you should be.
11. If outside experts are needed, consider using a neutral expert rather than having both parties retain their own. You can be helpful in determining the level of the expert's service and fee and in interpreting findings for your client.
12. To stimulate negotiation, consider mini-confidential reports from experts so that the parties get a feel for an expert's opinion.
13. Help your clients understand the negotiation process, develop a strategic plan, and simulate the negotiation process ahead of time. Be a negotiation coach.
14. Remember, your job as a consulting lawyer in mediation is to help your client *complete* a fair agreement that the client believes is fair—not to win legal points or get the last dollar in the negotiations.
15. Protect your client in a manner that supports and honors the process they have chosen.

Notes

1. John R. Phillips, *Making the Best Use of Mediators and Their Role*, ABA Dispute Resolution Magazine, 26 (Summer 2014).

2. *In the Beginning: Independent Counsel's Place in Dissolution Mediation*, February 14, 1994, Los Angeles Daily Journal.

3. *Id.* at 27.

CHAPTER 9

Reaching Agreement

If an agreement is reached, mediators can try to create an atmosphere in which the parties savor their successes together. This can include congratulatory and complimentary statements by the mediator, stressing the hard work and sacrifices made by all involved and the ways in which agreements the parties have reached are preferable to their court or other alternatives.
—Douglas N. Frenkel and James H. Stark, *The Practice of Mediation: A Video-Integrated Text*, 2nd Edition (2012).

The goal of mediation is to help parties discuss their concerns with the concrete purpose of reaching agreements that can be carried out by the parties voluntarily or enforced by a court if necessary. In this chapter, we will explore the approaches, skills, and tools to help you help your clients achieve this goal.

Typical Divorce Agenda

After dealing with immediate emergency issues, most mediators work with the parties to establish an agenda, and you can help your client make sure that important concerns and needs are raised. In a comprehensive (parenting, support, and property) mediation, a customary agenda may include the following:

- Personal conduct and separation issues such as agreements regarding sexual contact (between the parties or third persons), physical separation of the households (who will move and when), couples living together in the same home, physical safety, diminishing emotional enmeshment such as repeated and lengthy telephone calls, derogatory

remarks, handling of relationships with extended family and friends, and other issues and concerns raised by the parties
- How the parties will handle negotiation of issues outside sessions and regarding which issues and in what format such out-of-session discussion will take place
- Immediate issues concerning time-share of the children
- Immediate issues concerning support, payment of current debts, and management of assets
- Decision making over issues involving the children and labeling
- legal custody (e.g., sole, primary, joint, or no label at all)
- Time-sharing of the children, including a school schedule, holidays, vacations, and special days
- Identification, valuation, and allocation of assets and debts
- Permanent child and spousal support
- Miscellaneous issues such as filing taxes; handling insurance; and filing court documents and ancillary documents such as deeds, partnership resignations, QDROs for retirement, and vehicle registrations

A client handout for a divorce agenda is included in the Resources section.

Your client should be prepared to start working issue by issue and building the overall agreement step-by-step. Success is incremental. If you are in the mediation room, try to recognize even the smallest indications of agreement and overlook many of the setbacks. Your belief in and support for your client that there will eventually be full agreement plays an important role in building an agreement.

Agreement Readiness

Most parties and lawyers believe that the key to getting a deal in mediation is "bargaining": trading positional positions back and forth until the parties compromise.

Although we provide tools for effective bargaining around the mediation table, we also stress agreement readiness as a necessary condition to negotiate. Are the parties ready to settle, or are they still infatuated with their own positions?

Here is the key to assessing agreement readiness. If either or both parties are constantly saying "yes . . . but . . ." to you, to the mediator, and to each other, each party needs more work to achieve readiness. For example:

Husband: I am willing to agree to return the children at 7 p.m., but she never has them ready on time for pickup.
Wife: I would get them ready on time, but he is usually so late in arriving that I no longer worry about the agreed-upon time for pickup because he never is there on time."

The key to overcoming the "yes . . . buts . . ." is to ask your client to be responsible and accountable for his or her behavior and request reciprocity from the other party.

Identify and Acknowledge Initial Positions of the Parties
An essential tool that you can use to help your clients and their spouses get past their positions is to acknowledge the *positions* as stated by your client and the other party. This identification and acknowledgment of the position demonstrates that you understand and empathize with what a party says that he or she wants. This builds trust and rapport that are essential in your effectiveness.

> Husband: "I want the house sold now so that I can get my share of the equity."
> You: "It is my understanding that for you to have use of your share of the house, you would like it sold as soon as possible."

Ask the parties to acknowledge that they need a new approach to solving their problem.
Until parties understand and indicate an awareness that they are open to exploring a new option, they can "yes . . . but" and they might remain stuck.

> Husband: "I want the house sold now."
> Wife: "I want us to own it together for the next 12 years until all of the children graduate high school."
> You: "It sounds as though you both agree that neither of you is willing to accept the other party's position. Am I right?"
> Wife: "Yes."
> Husband: "Yes."
> You: "Do I also understand that you both want to work out the issue of the house in mediation rather than have a judge do it?"
> Wife: "Yes."
> Husband: "Yes."
> You: "Because you agree that you want an agreement and neither of you is willing to accept the other's position, the only way I know is for both of you to agree to a new third way—not yours, Wife, or yours, Husband. Are you each willing to try to find that third way?"
> Wife: "Yes."
> Husband: "Yes."
> You (to the mediator or other lawyer): "Do either of you have a sense as to how to get us back on track?

When you are attending a session, ask the parties, the other lawyer, and the mediator for permission to suggest an alternative or make a suggestion.

If you want to avoid or reduce resistance to any ideas or advice that you would like to offer to help, try this preliminary step of asking for permission before giving advice:

> You: "You seem very set on your views about the house. I have an idea that I'd like to explore. Would you like to hear it?"
> Wife: "Yes."
> Husband: "Yes."
> You: "All right. I can't promise that this will solve the problem or that either of you will like it. But regardless of the outcome, are you willing to hear the entire idea and at least consider it?"
> Wife: "Yes."
> Husband: "Yes."
> You: "What would you think of the possibility of Wife finding a way to buy out Husband's share of the equity at today's value (we would need an appraisal), have Husband's share bear interest at an agreed-upon amount, have principal and interest accrue with no monthly payments, and permit Wife an agreed-upon amount of time to pay off this amount or sell the house? There are several details to work out, but what does each of you think of this overall concept?"

Try using this tool with your client, with the other party, with the mediator, or with another collaborative professional.

Encourage Ground Rules

Structure is a safety net for parties who are drowning in conflict. Mediators are trained to have the parties agree to clear boundaries in their behavior toward each other and reflect those boundaries in agreements. For example, mediation ground rules may include no cell phones or name calling and you can encourage your client to not only abide by ground rules, but also ask for the mediator to establish additional ground rules if needed.

A key issue in virtually every divorce mediation is to identify the ground rules for parties to use in communicating with each other in session and outside. While it is common for many mediators to convey Party A's offer to Party B, whenever possible, you should be supportive of having the parties present their own offers directly to each other. By stating each term and provision of their own proposals, the parties "own" every position they take during negotiations. When the parties say the words themselves, the proposals better reflect their needs. Equally important, as one party listens to an offer being presented by the other party, a working trust may begin to build.

Although many lawyers feel more comfortable when they mediate in private caucuses, if the mediator communicates the offer, the party is at least one step removed. In addition, direct party communication also prevents possible distortions or errors (by the mediator) in relaying the positions of the parties.

Some mediation participants are reluctant to present their own offers. Many feel inadequate or unprepared to articulate their own negotiating positions. Others may be excellent negotiators at work or at a car dealership, but fall apart when negotiating with their ex-spouses.

To maximize the parties' success in presenting their offers to each other, you should coach your clients to help them determine what they want and how to ask for it. Framing an offer is a difficult challenge—so is finding the right way to communicate the offer so that it will be heard and considered by the other party. You should be willing to spend time with your client prior to a proposal being communicated.

In addition, you should coach your client who is receiving an offer. You can "preview" an offer by helping your client to listen closely to the offer and not to interrupt or lose control. Provide an opportunity to meet after your client hears the details of an offer to discuss the pros and cons and to prepare a response.

We have found that with this type of help, parties appreciate having their own voice in the mediation and having the opportunity to assess the behavior and position of the other party.

Red Flag Rule

This is a ground rule that you can suggest to prevent things from getting out of hand. You could offer it like this:

> You: "So I understand that you are planning to divide up the family photos next Saturday between 2 and 3 p.m. while the children are with their friends and that you have asked for some guidelines. Can we focus on one rule?"
> Parties: "Yes."
> You: "If either of you feels uncomfortable during the selection process, either party may raise your hand and say, "The red flag is up." This means that discussion is over for the day. Neither of you may call the other that day to try and reengage. No reason needs to be given, so you can't argue over the reason. You can also raise the red flag verbally if either of you is uncomfortable during a phone conversation. If there is a problem, you can discuss it with either of us (lawyers) or with the mediator. Are you both comfortable with this ground rule?"
> Parties: "Yes."
> You: "Do you have any questions or concerns about it?"

Interest-Based Negotiations

A key approach for negotiation is a focus on the interests of the parties. Interest-based negotiation derives from Fisher, Ury, and Patton's seminal book *Getting to Yes: Negotiating Agreements Without Giving In*. Interest-based thinking is quite different from the type of negotiation traditionally used by litigators, which reflects the adversary system and is focused on the vindication of legal rights. Inherent within this "old paradigm" is a view held by both lawyers and their clients that lawyers are in charge and that if the other side won't compromise sufficiently, courts will produce justice. Power, leverage, and fear are used to create self-doubt in the parties to push for compromise. The conflict is considered a zero-sum game in which every dollar paid to the other side is seen as coming out of our client's pocket.

Because the focus of this adversarial approach is to maximize the financial gain on each issue, there is little or no consideration of or value ascribed to the ongoing future relationship between the parties in determining a successful outcome of the negotiation. The assumption is that both parties will be equally unhappy about the result and that somehow they will go on with their lives, heal or not heal, but the impact of the negotiation is rarely linked with the long-term viability of family relationships.

Under the new paradigm of interest-based negotiation, the focus is to dig below the stated positions of the parties to identify and meet underlying interests and concerns as opposed to legal positions. The goal is client-centered, not lawyer-centered, decision making. Although financial considerations are important, factors such as impact on the emotional functioning of the parties and children, speed of resolution, control over result, and costs of the negotiation are factored in. The input and advice of nonlawyer experts such as therapists and financial professionals are considered just as important as or more important than lawyer expertise. As in the old paradigm, negotiators try to create dissonance in the parties to reflect upon their positions. The difference is that instead of using threats and fear of litigation as the sole means of creating dissonance, interest-based negotiators create dissonance by exploring each party's BATNA (Best Alternative to Negotiated Agreement). Win-win scenarios are not only possible, but also quite common. Candor and transparency in communication are viewed as essential to building the trust necessary to reach effective agreements, and the process defines the long-term relationship between the parties as valuable and worth preserving to the greatest possible extent.

> ### De-Position with Positive Self-Interest
>
> Interest-based negotiation may seem like a great thing, but do you have just a bit of doubt as to whether you can pull it off or whether the other side will play with you?
>
> Here is a strategy that we bet will work (most of the time).
>
> Be smart, not nice. To negotiate, start with the self-motivation of your client or the other side. And rather than challenging, accept what they say. People generally trust others who value, acknowledge, and don't challenge them at the start.
>
> Let's see how this works. Your client is the wife who wants to stay in the house. Husband wants it sold. You know that if it goes to court, no one can predict the outcome.
>
> How do you help your client be open to another possibility other than staying in the house? Here it goes.
>
> 1. Restate her position: "I understand that you want to stay in the house."
> 2. Give her what she wants: "For our discussion today, let's pretend that Husband agrees that you can stay in the house."
> 3. Transition to the positive self-interest of your client getting what she wants: "So if you aren't fighting about whether you get to stay in the house, how do you benefit from such an outcome?"
> 4. As your client gives her underlying concerns and needs, go through each one and keep asking for more—never challenge them regardless of how unrealistic or unworkable: I will benefit:
>   "Stay in the housing market because I could not otherwise qualify"
>   "Make money as the house appreciates"
>   "Have stability by staying in the neighborhood"
>   "Make my husband keep his word"
> 5. For each of the underlying concerns and needs, reframe them mutually so that they lead to other options and will be accepted by the other side as well.
>   "Find a way to continue owning your own home"
>   "Increase your current assets with sound investments"
>   "Make sure you and your children maximize your stability and minimize chaos through the separation process"
>   "Build trust with your husband by being accountable to promises and commitments"
> 6. After restating all of these reframed concerns and needs, ask your client for the following commitment: "If I could assure you that we will focus on each of your needs and concerns as you stated [in #5], would you be open to exploring a solution other than staying in the house. Just be willing to explore; you do not have to accept."
>
> Your client (or the other side in a negotiation) may not say "yes" every time, but you may be surprised with how many yeses you do get.
>
> Try this baby step. It just might work.

The fact that the new paradigm is a departure from the traditional lawyer-centric, adversarial approach does not mean that the law is invisible in an interest-based negotiation. Educating clients is part of client-centered decision making. Knowing about the law matters, but it should not dictate a particular result or define the best result for each family. Moreover, because issues such as determination of a parenting plan and spousal support involve a great deal of discretion by judicial officers, the "legal" result (especially over the long term) is difficult to predict.

> ### You're Not the Judge—The Clients Are
>
> When families operate within the court system, the rule of law prevails. Most lawyers are comfortable with, if not totally supportive of, resolution within the legal system. In mediation, the parties may arrive at a solution that is personally idiosyncratic or governed by values and authority far different from the law. If it makes sense to your client and seems fair, practical, and enforceable, when do you stop being a naysayer and start being supportive?
>
> We know of a mediation for a couple who had a clear agreement providing for a sexually open marriage; each partner was free to engage in unlimited sexual opportunities outside the relationship. Problem: Sharon fell in love with a new partner and wanted to move out. Keith had promised to give Sharon $200,000 from his separate estate in case of a breakup but felt his promise was null and void due to her desire to move out and stop sex with him.
>
> The parties spent several sessions discussing the intricate details of their contract and the consequences of breach. Was it within the contract that Sharon could be away from Keith for more than a week at a time? Was she required to leave a phone number? When she was at home, was it OK to e-mail her lover from the marital bedroom? Was it bad faith for her lover to coach her in the negotiations?
>
> No judge would have listened to this private, *irrelevant* stuff. Few lawyers would engage in negotiations over these points! However, this was Sharon and Keith's life. Through mediation, they were able to work out a deal that was fair to them and made sense to them.
>
> In a joint holiday card, they wished their mediator well and indicated that they were still the best of friends.

In preparing your clients for negotiations in mediation or in participating in agreement building yourself, you should be respectful and interested to listen to the positions of your client and the other spouse on any given issue. Mediators are trained to then reframe the positions in an effort to tease out the interests underlying the stated position. However, you can participate in this reframing as well. One of your greatest assets in a mediation is to bond with the other party and lawyer so that your ideas and proposals get a fair hearing as well. If you can reframe the positions of your client and the other party in a fair way that points out mutual interests, this bonding and trust building will accelerate.

As explained in *Getting to Yes*: "Interests motivate people. They are the silent movers behind the hubbub of positions. Your position is something you have decided on. Your interests are what caused you to so decide." Interests can be substantive (e.g., housing, financial security); emotional (e.g., anger, fear, anxiety, revenge); relationship-related (e.g., with children, with the former spouse); or process-related (e.g., momentum, a feeling of being heard). Once you have worked with the mediator and the other attorney to help uncover both clients' interests, it is crucial to link the mutual interests of both parties so that they can build from commonality (e.g., both clients want to keep the children in the same neighborhood, both want to live close together to facilitate parenting, both want certainty and finality).

After identifying the mutual interests, you can help your client brainstorm options for resolution. Brainstorming is having each party think of all possibilities. After all options are put on a flip chart, you can help the mediator and parties prioritize and evaluate the identified options based on criteria such as cost, impact on children, privacy, speed of resolution, and impact on the future relationship of the parties. The parties talk through the positives and negatives of each option. This discussion is what leads the parties to agreement.

> ### At the Mediation Table
>
> **You Cut—I'll Choose**
> During the dark hours of a mediation, when an impasse looms, the parties can collaborate to build a hypothetical dummy model of resolution—putting off for a while who will get what. The mediator uses a "what if?" approach. Both parties want the same thing, such as the house, so they work out all of the terms—without initially deciding who will get each portion. More often than expected, the positive energy from the model building can break the impasse, making it easier to resolve who will get what.
>
> There are quirks, however. In a mediation, deferring the decision as to who would get the house, a couple built a dummy model on a house buyout. In the dummy model, the couple agreed that the light fixtures (including an expensive chandelier) would stay with the house at no cost to the party who would eventually be awarded the residence. Well, when Sara found that she could not afford the house, she chose the tax-free buyout—and surrendered the right to stay in the house to Joe. But here's the rub: Her parents had given the couple the chandelier as a housewarming gift. Sara was willing to give up the house but not the chandelier. An angry session later, Joe agreed to buy her a new chandelier if and when Sara ever bought another house and if she was not involved in a romantic relationship at the time of purchase!

Normalcy and Solvability

In a divorce, spouses will often concentrate on their own misery and pain, ignoring the condition of the other spouse. Or a spouse will actually blame the other spouse for his or her pain. One twin set of tools to stop the blame game is to help parties see that the problem is normal for other divorcing couples and that the problem is solvable.

> Husband: "If I agree to let Wife live in the house, the kids will never want to spend time with me. I think it would be better if we just sold the house and each purchased new residences."
> You: "Many Dads have this same concern, and they find ways to establish a new home for the children, who then enjoy their time just as much with Dad as with Mom in the family residence.

Use Professional Articles and Research to Offer Commonality

Objective criteria or expertise can often settle an argument. If Mom says that a 4-year-old should not have overnights and Dad says he wants overnights, rather than pushing anyone to compromise, you might say this: "Would either of you be interested in what child development research says about this issue? If so, I have an article by _____. Let's look at her findings and recommendations." You can do the same thing by referring to mediation research on process issues. A summary of highlights of mediation research is included in the Resources section.

Experiment and Test Solutions

Mediation allows parties to experiment and test out agreements without fear of establishing a binding legal precedent. Agreements can be time-limited and reviewed for viability within days or weeks. Agreements can also be modified to take into account the impact of new agreements. You can reassure your client that there is no final binding agreement until all of the parts are cross-stitched into a whole written agreement subject to review and final signatures. However, if both parties choose to make incremental final agreements on bifurcated issues, let your client know that you will support such incremental agreements and will help draft it in a timely way.

Involvement of Children

Participation of children is controversial and subject to mediator discretion. Dr. Florence Bienenfeld, a noted mental health professional, strongly urges the involvement of children: "Including children in the mediation process gives them an opportunity to hear, to be heard, and to gain perspective about the difficult situation in which they find themselves.

Most children leave the mediation session less burdened and better fortified for whatever will happen to them."

She is not alone. There has been a worldwide shift in attitude toward children's involvement in parental conflicts. When we began practicing, the general consensus was that any direct involvement in the parental dispute was inappropriate and harmful to children. The United Nations as well as state agencies and private child education and advocacy groups are increasingly recognizing a child's right to be heard in matters that affect him or her. Research and expert opinion support this increased respect for the child's voice.

Professor Cassandra Adams argues that mediation is an appropriate and beneficial method of addressing and listening to the voices of children. She argues that a holistic mediation process that includes the voices of parents and children will promote the integration of interests and recommends specific child-oriented education and training for mediators who handle family law issues.

Children generally do not participate in the negotiating and bargaining stages of mediation. Before children are invited to a session, discuss this issue carefully with your client. You must work out whether siblings should come in together or separately and/or whether the parents should also be present. Your client should get assurance from the mediator that the children want to be present and that they are not to be given the impression that they are responsible for the decisions being made or that they have the power to veto or alter their parents' agreements. Your client should know that mediators are trained to reassure the children that their parents are choosing the peaceful and less destructive option of mediation in large part because their parents love them. Often by meeting the mediator and sitting in the mediation room, children fill in their concrete reality of what is happening at the mediation, which can help ameliorate their fears and concerns.

In the case of many older adolescents and adult children, parents more readily choose to have them sit at the mediation table and participate as important (if not equal) parties or as resources for their needs and desires (which are important to their parents) or about factual matters such as the operation of the family business or investments. Although children should never be given the impression that they get to decide issues affecting them, a teenager's buy-in after the opportunity to be heard may make the difference between a parenting plan that is workable and one that isn't.

Starter Toolbox for Reaching Agreements

Here are some sample tools (by no means exhaustive) for you to start using the next time you attend a mediation session.

Emotional Reframing

Use this tool to capture the feelings your client or the other party has expressed. He or she will feel heard and appreciate your sensitivity, which instills confidence and reduces fear.

> Wife: "He never brings Josh home on time."
> Reframe: "You must be frustrated/angry/worried when this happens."

Bifurcate Divorce Issues: Salvage Agreements, Plan for Contained Litigation

Some mediations just will not settle all issues. Rather than throw out the progress and good work, one strategy is to use the progress and goodwill developed in the mediation to isolate the issues to be litigated and join the mediator to write up the agreed issues for a final settlement. This tool will not only remove the "all or nothing" scenario, but also permit parties to get resolution in a rational manner. The lawyers and mediator can work with the parties to work out which issues will be litigated and how they will be litigated. For example, within the mediation process, parties can work out expedited and limited discovery as well as how the spouses will interact with each other and the children through the end of litigation. Parties can also agree to return to mediation after the judge makes a decision to discuss how to live with the decision, heal, and plan for the future.

Negotiating with the Mediator

Unlike a judicial officer, a mediator's role and interventions can be greatly influenced by the requests and needs of the parties. As your client's representative, you can take a proactive role in negotiating with the mediator in a number of ways:

1. If your client expresses that he or she is not being given the opportunity to present his or her concerns or facts, you can request the mediator to make additional time during the sessions or in stand-alone private sessions.
2. If you or your client believes that the discussion in mediation is not considering necessary legal, financial, or parenting criteria or factors, you can supply the mediator with cases, statutes, articles, reports, or other material to enhance the quality of the discussion.
3. If the format being used is not meeting the needs of your client, you can request a modification. For example, the time between sessions may need to be compressed or delayed, the length of the sessions may need to be increased or reduced, your client may need more breaks, the other party may be taking too many breaks, or your client may need more or fewer ground rules.

4. If your client is making impulsive decisions or cannot make any decisions at all, contact the mediator to discuss a possible change in approach.
5. If the mediator is a flabby drafter, you may request that the lawyers jointly draft agreements and other documents.
6. If the parties have reached agreements on key issues, you may ask the mediator to suggest writing up binding partial agreements and have those agreements turned into enforceable court orders.

There are many other issues in which you can weigh in tactfully and collaboratively. Remember, you are not a potted plant. Most competent mediators welcome the input and suggestions of lawyers who are knowledgeable and supportive of the process. Your client is spending considerable money and is relying on the mediation process, and a key part of your job is to make sure the process is working to its full capacity.

Working with Mediator Proposals

Although the goal of mediation is to facilitate agreements by direct negotiation between the parties, sometimes snags develop. We have discussed how working in separate caucuses or having lawyers play a more active role in negotiation can accelerate agreement.

Another strategy to break impasse is the use of a mediator proposal. If the parties are stuck on one issue or are having difficulty linking an overall settlement, many mediators are willing to provide their own proposal for settlement.

A mediator proposal can work in several ways:

1. A proposal is suggested by the mediator or requested by the parties.
2. The proposal can mirror a court resolution or reflect an integration of proposals by the parties.
3. The proposal can be offered as take it or leave it or as a catalyst to more negotiation.

During bargaining, you should be vigilant about the timing and use of mediator proposals. If a mediator proposal is offered too early, it can cut off creativity and exchange of ideas that might morph into a settlement with such direct intervention by the mediator. If impasse hardens and parties start saber rattling or packing their briefcases, a mediator proposal may come too late.

In selecting a mediator, one aspect of your due diligence is to learn whether and how a proposed mediator uses this strategy. If the mediator is flexible about how mediator proposals are used, you might discuss their possible use with your client, the other lawyer, and the mediator.

If you and/or your client begin to feel that the discussions are stalled on any particular issue or an overall agreement, you should raise the possibility with the other lawyer and the mediator of using a mediator proposal. However, it is important to be clear about how the process will work and how the mediator's neutrality and trust can be preserved during and after the mediator proposal is presented.

You might consider using the following protocol in setting up and implementing a mediator proposal:

1. You should request that the mediator neutrally describe the state of negotiation. This can be done privately with the mediator or with the other lawyer.
2. You should request that the mediator set out areas of agreement in joint session.
3. The mediator should set out issues (and subissues) that need further work in joint session.
4. The hope is that the mediator will then check with the parties regarding their reaction to the mediator's sense of agreed-upon issues and those issues that need work and suggest other areas that need work to achieve overall agreement.
5. You should discuss with the mediator what facts or objective criteria are needed to bridge the gap.
6. You should discuss whether there are additional decision makers who should be involved in receiving, reviewing, and responding to a mediator proposal.
7. You should discuss whether the parties are ready hear the mediator proposal at the session or whether the mediator should send a proposal by e-mail in days following the session.
8. You should know whether the mediator proposal is "take it or leave it" or is a compilation of the mediator's ideas as to what might meet the interests and concerns of the parties.
9. You should request the mediator to prepare a written term sheet listing all agreed issues, all issues to be subject to a mediator proposal, and a detailed proposal by the mediator as to each issue.
10. Discuss whether the mediator proposal will be presented in a joint session or with the parties separately.
11. Make sure there is ample time to discuss questions and concerns with the mediator either jointly or privately.
12. Be nimble to using a mediator proposal to completely resolve issues or to kick-start further bargaining.

"Notes for My Mediation"

During a particularly tense mediation, the wife was reading this poem to herself sotto voce. She had written the words in a mood of hopeful prayer to give her comfort through several stressful and important weeks for every member of her family. This poem can be sent to clients in the mediation packet or handed out during a difficult mediation.

Notes for My Mediation
- Stay centered/relaxed/focused.
- Concentrate on positive aspects of this process. We will get through it, and it will end.
- Change is difficult, requires patience and perspective. The bigger the change, the greater the requirements. The outcome will be a good one.
- Our mediator understands the dynamic and can help—let him be in control. He has been through harder mediations. He has the experience to help.

This process requires tolerance, forgiveness, and going the extra mile
- I will continue to be responsible for myself and try to do well for our child. She is my major focus.
- I can only control myself.
- I will respond to my spouse's anger and judging with perspective and forgiveness.
- I will not allow my spouse to hurt or anger me by anything he says or does.
- I will not react personally or negatively to my spouse.
- I will continue to act affirmatively whenever possible.
- My spouse cannot help it and is not acting out of malevolence or intentional hurtfulness.
- I will continue to act with integrity, sensitivity, and with my eye on the goal of completing the process with the best possible outcome.
- I will keep my eye on the prize of peace.
- I deserve it and have worked hard for it.
- I believe I will come out of this a stronger, better person.
- I believe God will help me and take care of me.

My Vision

There will be a time within the next year when I will catch myself smiling or laughing without even thinking about it.

I will wake up with a mind and heart clear of fear of the unknown and the unanticipated financial and emotional threats that now burden my life and relationships.

I will return to being an innately happy person who values recreation, relaxation, and relationships.

I will be able to regenerate.

I have carried the burden for many years; I can continue to carry it quietly for another few weeks. It has been a long road. I can keep going a little bit longer. I have done a good job. I will get to the end and start a new beginning.

Continued

"Notes for My Mediation" *Continued*

Editor's Note: Poem submitted by attorney Forrest Mosten. Identity of the author is withheld by request. Salient facts are fictitious. Published in the Family & Conciliation Courts Review, January 1996.

CHAPTER 10

Reviewing and Drafting Mediated Agreements

(V)irtually all divorce mediators, lawyers or not, now urge both husband and wife to consult their own lawyers before, during or after the mediation. The role of such "outside" lawyers also is unclear. Just how deeply must they delve into the bases of the mediated agreement? One danger, of course, is that some reviewing attorneys undermine a mediation by inappropriately imposing an adversarial perspective. But sometimes a strong adversarial impetus is just what the client needs.
—Leonard L. Riskin and James E. Westbrook, *Dispute Resolution and Lawyers*, 1987

It is generally accepted that the family lawyer's major role in mediation is to review and give approval to the settlement agreement and court documents. You must inform your client that nothing is binding until the final agreement is signed by both parties. This encourages flexibility and creativity in negotiations. Once signed and submitted to the court, the agreements entered in mediation can become enforceable court orders with the same validity as any order negotiated directly between lawyers or rendered by a judge. This impending legal finality often makes spouses anxious and can cause clients to reconsider elements of the agreements, both major and minor. The finality can also be a catalyst for emotional turmoil. Fear and uncertainty about the future can overcome the euphoria of having reached agreement and the anticipation of moving past conflict and on to the next chapter of their lives. It is definitely a nervous time!

Clients are not the only nervous ones. With the increasing trend to grant mediators and other alternative dispute resolution (ADR) neutrals immunity from malpractice liability, as the reviewing family lawyer, you may be the only pocket (deep or shallow) to which a dissatisfied or remorseful client can later look. Because clients rely on lawyers more in the review process than at any other time in mediation, clients are dependent on the sometimes conflicting lawyer roles of supporting the client's deal and vigilantly protecting the client's legal and financial position now and for the future. It is no wonder that lawyers are also nervous as signing time approaches. Lawyer anxiety may be intensified as clients put time and emotional pressure on the reviewing lawyer to churn out settlement documents quickly, to be extremely careful in viewing both deal points and draft language, and to keep the fees low. After all, one of the chief client motivators in choosing mediation is to save money—and high bills from you in your role as the consulting lawyer can defeat that purpose.

Juggling conflicting goals and demands is not a new skill for most family lawyers. It is indeed possible to render competent and needed services, to provide legal information and advice, and to be supportive of the client's productive work at the mediation table. We are no strangers to dealing with client's remorse. We are skilled at holding deals together when they begin fraying at the seams. We perform these feats week in and week out—on the agreements we ourselves have negotiated. The big challenge in mediations is for you to rise to the challenge of keeping your client's deal together—especially when you may be critical of the terms reached or believe that your client "gave away the store." It is very tempting for the reviewing lawyer to indulge in comparisons between the agreement brought in after mediation and the hypothetical deal that "might have been" had the lawyer been the client's negotiating arm from the beginning or had the agreement been left to the judge to decide.

The "let it go" mantra that works so well in working with opposing counsel in setting up the mediation can also be applied to reviewing an agreement. It is your duty as well as the client's expectation for you to point out problems that you find. We would never suggest that a reviewing lawyer ignore present or future difficulties that the agreement might cause the client. However, how you inform the client about these difficulties is as critical as the substance of your critique.

First, you should assess the weight and magnitude of a deficiency and communicate it accurately to your client. Some problems are nits, others are ticking time bombs, and still others are fires presently raging out of control. Not all of your valid concerns are raging fires! Many lawyers review an agreement by sending a client a letter exhaustively detailing every problem in the proposed draft settlement agreement. Many lawyers write such a letter defensively to protect themselves against their client's complaints or claims rather than to help the client better understand the agreement and to consider carefully whether to propose changes to the other party to obtain an improved agreement. The information delivered to the client may be the same in both approaches. The first approach is lawyer-centered, and the second approach is client-centered. Client-centered approaches usually work better, especially for mediation participants who have grown accustomed to an empathic client-centered approach in dealing with their mediator and expect and appreciate a similar client-centered manner from their reviewing lawyer.

Your concerns about the presented agreement should be balanced, as much as possible, by your appreciation for the client benefits that have been achieved in the agreement.

Consistent with using the approach that finds every problem encouraged by most legal education, many lawyers are obsessive about finding and talking about what does not work. Pointing out the good things that help your client not only makes the client feel more confident about their mediation performance (we are not suggesting unrealistic hubris), but a balanced approach is also a more realistic overall assessment of the agreement. In mediation classes that we teach, we have many times encountered mediation trainees who have raised their hands and said: "I wish the world was as rosy as you paint it. In the real world [i.e., the trainee's perceived world], people don't want to pay for gratuitous solicitous comments from me. My clients think that I am pandering them. My clients want my straight opinion about the agreement's defects. They know the good aspects; after all, they negotiated it."

Many lawyers (and other people too!) unequivocally attribute their world view to others and are shocked to learn that their view is not universally held. Most people keep agreements. Most clients do not expect their lawyers always to be right. They expect you to try to understand their concerns and to try to be right given the circumstances. And we have found that clients like and are willing to pay for your affirmations about benefits of the mediated deal.

Be open and ask about your client's motivations and actions that led up to the agreement. Use the word *why*. For example: "Why did you agree that your spouse could be awarded her car worth $20,000 without requesting an equal amount ($20,000) of marital property or an equalizing payment of $10,000 from her share of the house proceeds?" Your client may not have been crazy to give up dollars that were possible to obtain by negotiating or by taking the case to trial. The client may have received equalizing dollars in other issues of the agreement or may have chosen to give up dollars for expeditious closure, for a better parenting relationship, for payment of a moral debt, or for some other non-monetary reason. It is important to delve into the trade-offs leading up to the final agreement and to appreciate them from your client's point of view before even thinking about trashing the deal.

Review Summary Letters and Have Your Client Prepare a Memorandum

You should carefully review any summary letters from the mediator as a first step in reconstructing the history of the negotiations. You should ask your client to prepare a memo for you that (1) gives the client's view of the trade-offs and (2) articulates your client's view of the benefits of the agreement as well as any concerns your client might have.

The summary letters and client memo are excellent supplements to the draft agreement or deal memo prepared by the mediator in your review of the agreement. Many agreements are clear enough that your comments can be contained in a balanced letter to the client. Even in the simplest agreement, it is important for you to ask your client to come into the office for a face-to-face consultation to go over the agreement clause by clause.

Child support agreements can last ten years or more, and spousal support awards can last decades—for example, $2,000 a month for ten years is $240,000 in support payments alone! With this type of present and future impact on their lives, most clients benefit from a personal meeting with you, their trusted professional, to discuss the terms and ramifications of the agreement. Clients need to understand the consequences, legal and practical, of their agreement and need your help to have a reality test to make sure the agreement is workable. Be sure to initiate a preventive discussion to both help your client handle with family-relationship issues. Also, you can diagnose other legal soft spots facing the client in the future so you can recommend preventive solutions. (See Chapter 11.)

In addition to the issues you have spotted, most clients have some questions or concerns of their own in regard to the agreement. If you take on the assignment of reviewing settlement agreements, you owe it to your client to set aside sufficient time (one or two hours) during which there can be a wide-ranging discussion about the agreement and how it will impact your client's life after the settlement is signed.

Even the clients who are the biggest penny-pinchers generally find this review conference to be well worth the fees that you charge. If there is resistance to paying for your time, your response can be something like: "Very few homeowners like paying 6 percent to a real estate broker to sell a house. However, the stakes are high enough, so most people consider the broker's commission to be a necessary cost of selling a house. You are now entering into the most important agreement of your life, and I have found that my clients benefit greatly from sitting down with me before signing on the dotted line. We both have done a great job in keeping your fees down to this point, and now we are almost at the finish line. Just consider this review to be a necessary cost of getting a divorce."

Will There Be a Writing? What Is the Product of Successful Mediation?

Mediation grew out of a desire for a more holistic, less adversarial process for divorcing families. In her 2014 article, Rebecca Aviel stated: "There is ample room in family law for expertise without advocacy, for the exercise of legal judgment and skill without full fledged partisan loyalty to an individual client."[1]

Typically, family law mediations result in Stipulated Judgments or Marital Settlement Agreements which resolve pending issues contractually and/or via court order, and a final binding writing is something that the participants value and expect.

Many other mediation participants, however, may just be seeking information or clarifying discussions and neither need nor expect a writing of any kind. To some, the demand that an agreement be reduced to writing can in and of itself evoke resistance or imply lack of trust.[2]

Spouses may have diametrically opposed hopes and expectations about the results of their mediation. One spouse may enter mediation hoping for reconciliation (the "leaning in" spouse) and the other spouse may enter mediation expecting and hoping for a final, enforceable divorce decree(the "leaning out" spouse). Dr. William J. Doherty of the University of Minnesota has found that 30 percent of couples coming into marital therapy are "mixed-agenda" couples: one spouse is leaning out and the other spouse is leaning into the relationship.[3] While the number of mixed agenda couples entering mediation or coming into our offices is probably lower than 30 percent, most experienced family lawyers are familiar with this challenge.

It is by no means a foregone conclusion that a final, enforceable, written document will be the result of mediation, Consider the following range of possible outcomes:

1. A discussion with the mediator that leads to the parties returning to the marriage.
2. A referral by the mediator to discernment counseling to explore whether both parties wish to commit to couples counseling.
3. A Reconciliation Agreement that may include a referral to a couples counselor and may also include parenting and financial issues requiring review and drafting by an attorney.
4. A Post-Marital Agreement that will be a binding private , with the assumption that the parties will remain married. Physical separation may be contemplated or provided for in such an agreement. In most states, attorney representation is encouraged or required for such agreements, especially where spousal support rights are affected.
5. A Temporary Physical Separation, with or without a written agreement.
6. A Long-Term Separation: with Memorandum of Understanding (Non-Enforceable Private Separation Agreement). Given that the parties do not want this agreement to be involved in court enforcement, the lawyer level of review may vary from very light to very involved.
7. A Long-Term Separation: with Enforceable Private Separation Agreement. In some states, mediators, even if they are lawyers, are not permitted to draft final documents.[4]
8. A Marital Settlement Agreement with No Filed Court Documents. The difference between a MOU and a Marital Settlement Agreement is that the MSA is considered an enforceable binding document which many mediators are not permitted to draft and which needs greater review by the parties' lawyers.
9. A Public Marital Settlement Agreement with Filed Court Documents and No Final Decree. Many states permit bifurcation of the divorce proceedings so that parties can finally resolve all parenting and financial issues and obtain a partial court decree/judgment while reserving the dissolution of marital status for a later second/further decree/judgment.

10. A Court Decree/Judgment of Marital Dissolution (Divorce) with Public Terms of Settlement. In some states, the terms of the marital settlement are merged into the decree/judgement so that there is no necessity of a Marital Settlement Agreement. In other states, the Marital Settlement Agreement is submitted to the court and either adopted as a Court Judgment/Decree or as an Exhibit to the Judgment/Decree.

11. A Court Decree/Judgment of Marital Dissolution (Divorce) with Private Terms of Settlement. In order to protect privacy of financial and other settlement terms, some states permit the parties to obtain a Judgment/Decree of Marital Dissolution resolving some or all of the financial and parenting terms and reserving the balance of the terms for a completed and signed private judgment/decree to be held by the parties and not filed in court at the time the first Decree/Judgment is approved. In turn, the terms contained in the private judgment are not subject to court enforcement unless and until the private judgment is submitted and approved by the court. In our experience, the vast majority of such private judgments/decrees are never filed with the court since parties tend to comply with such terms without court assistance.

It is important for you to discuss what outcome your client wants from the mediation and the level of review/drafting that may be required.

Is the Mediator a Lawyer?

If you do a survey of all people who mediate family issues in your community, you may find that most family mediators are not lawyers, and many of these mediators do not have a professional license. Most of these mediators do not draft enforceable final documents. This is due to both training, custom, and state laws that define drafting of final documents as the practice of law and requiring licensed lawyers to perform that function.

Therefore, when nonlawyers are selected to mediate your client's matter, your role in review and drafting will be increased and you need to estimate your work and fees accordingly from the outset.

Even if the mediator is a licensed lawyer, that mediator's role in drafting depends on your jurisdiction. Some states prohibit any mediator, including those with law licenses, from preparing documents beyond a MOU. The rationale behind such a prohibition is that lawyers who mediate assume a neutral, nonlawyer role in deal making, but drafting necessarily converts that neutral role into a dual representation role in which the parties have conflicting interests.

In states that permit lawyer mediators to draft binding agreements, there are two basic schools of thought. The first is that while drafting does constitute the practice of law, but the mediator can appropriately do so if parties provide an informed conflicts waiver and are encouraged to consult and retain independent lawyers to review and supplement such drafting.[5] The second does not define a mediator's work as the practice of law and permits lawyer mediators to draft as neutral mediators.[6]

Having competent lawyer mediators draft as either a neutral or intermediary can benefit clients, since the person who was present during the negotiation can often most accurately capture the spirit and substance of the parties' agreements. In addition using the mediator's draft as a point of departure can reduce the number of disputes between counsel over agreement terms and permits the mediator to facilitate resolution of any such disagreements. Mediator drafting is also consistent with the desire of many mediation participants to have a "one stop shop" with attendant lower transaction costs.

The Level of Review

Just as lawyers who unbundle their services to coach self-represented litigants need to determine the depth of their service, so do lawyers who take on the assignment of reviewing mediation agreements. The scope of representation must be defined explicitly between you and your client to avert misunderstandings and increase client satisfaction. It is not unusual for a client to call a lawyer, wanting a full review within a low budget and requesting a cap of not more than $500. While it may be possible to do a review within the requested budget, it is crucial for both the client and lawyer to understand what a *full review* means. As with all areas of ensuring competence, if you are presented with a nonnegotiable review budget that would not permit you to provide competent service, you should consider turning down such an engagement rather than taking on malpractice exposure or a dissatisfied client (or both!).

Client-centered control and decision making has its limitations. Although the client has a right to negotiate the level of service and fees, you also have the right to decline to perform the requested services if you cannot to them in a competent manner. If you indicate a need for legal research before giving an opinion, your client has a right to limit the research time to, for example, two hours. If you agree to work under those conditions, you have made a deal which defines the parameters of your work for this professional task. You do not need to promise to have a full answer, or in fact any answer, within that limited time period. Your client pays for your best efforts and may be rewarded with a full answer (with the hope that it supports the client's desired outcome) that you reached in less than two hours. The client might not get the right answer that more exhaustive research could have yielded. But as long as the client understands the basis of the bargain, he or she has a right to make an informed choice, even if it is a destructive one, the client may be well served.

However, what if the client wants to limit research to 15 minutes, wants the agreement reviewed with a supporting letter in one workday, or walks in at 4 p.m. on a Friday without an appointment and wants custom drafting of a step-down spousal support order in 30 minutes—while you keep another client waiting for a scheduled appointment? In each situation, to ensure competence, you have the right to pass on the assignment or to demand conditions. The client has a choice to accept your conditions (or an agreeable compromise) or to look elsewhere for professional assistance. It is a two-way relationship, and both you and your client must agree to the scope and expectations of the assignment.

Between the extremes of dealing with unreasonable working conditions or telling the client to look elsewhere, there is a wide area for a compromise in regard to the scope of your review. For example, you can do a full legal audit and look at every check and bank statement of the other spouse for the last three years or merely look at an income and expense court form or do something in between. You can provide four optional clauses for each deal point or merely read the proposed draft for glaring unfairness or technical mistakes—or do something in between. You can insist that the client have an independent CPA to calculate tax liability and future capital gains or indicate that there may be tax liability and the client should consult appropriate professionals or do something in between. These are clearly judgment calls about the scope of review that the lawyer should raise for joint decision making between client and lawyer.

In contrast to the pure unbundled form of providing discrete task service in which you are not full counsel of record, here there are two differences. First, you may or may not be the lawyer of record who is responsible to the client for court litigation as well as the mediation. Second, the task of lawyer service is clear: review the agreement and advise your client accordingly. Even if you are counsel of record, it is rare that you perform every task or take on each task in 100 percent depth. Every day you most likely dispense with taking depositions at all or limit the number of depositions taken or you rarely ask every possible questions within any one deposition. When you litigate, you probably don't subpoena every possible witness for each court hearing and you may dispense with live witnesses altogether. You probably rarely document by letter every conversation you had with or request by your client. Simply, few, if any, clients can afford to pay for perfect and complete lawyering, and it is rarely cost-effective, requiring weighing the dollars expended for the marginal benefit gained.

You and your client can agree that the only task you will perform is reviewing the mediation agreement. Filing documents, making court appearances, conducting discovery, or handling the range of other lawyering functions can be excluded by contract. However, you still may be liable for any negligence in performing the tasks agreed to be within the scope of representation: review of the mediated agreement.

Geoffrey Hazard, a recognized authority on legal ethics, believes that a lawyer can limit the scope of representation ethically, but also cautions about maintaining professional competence:

If a lawyer says, "What I will do for you is review the papers and tell you if you have a claim, but I'm not going to take the case on," I can't see why that's troublesome. Many lawyers do it, and many clients would like to know that you can engage a lawyer to do this alone. But if I agree to make an opening statement, but only to spend five minutes giving it; or if I agree to do a real estate mortgage but not to do any personal property security matters in a commercial transaction, that would be improper. If the limitation is inconsistent with what a reasonable lawyer could plausibly suggest he's going to do for the client, it's a limitation of liability in disguise, and is unethical. And lawyers are always responsible for advice that they give.

Therefore, if you advise a client on an issue that comes up during your review, you may be subject to malpractice liability.[7]

Drafting the Agreement

Because many mediators will not or cannot draft the actual settlement agreement or draft any court documents,[8] one of the consulting lawyers may have to take on that job. In such situations, the mediator generally will provide a memorandum (aka Memorandum of Understanding, or MOU) with the essential deal points. The quality and depth of that memo varies depending on the professional background and skill of the mediator. Nonlawyer mediators often keep the memo brief and to the point, explicitly deferring the legal drafting to lawyers. Depending on their training orientation, family law experience, drafting skills, and the law in various states, many lawyer/mediators also do not draft agreements, and the depth and clarity of their deal memos vary widely. Generally, the binding effect of the mediation is also deferred until the parties and counsel approve and sign the final legal agreement.

In drafting an agreement from a deal memo, the "let it go" mantra should kick in. It may be tempting for you to try to improve your client's position by resolving any and all uncertainties in drafting choice in favor of your client, putting the burden on the other lawyer to catch the problem and start a negotiation over drafting. Unfortunately, we have been involved in mediations that resulted in "successful agreements," only to have the drafting process take months and dwarf the original mediation costs in dollars and acrimony.

Therefore, in drafting, proactive restraint should be the standard. If new terms are necessary to carry out the intent of the agreed-upon principle, try to limit the new terms to what is minimally necessary to do the job. Even more seriously, make every effort not to change or water down deal points the parties agreed to in mediation with which you are less than enthusiastic. Again, the purpose of drafting is to complete the mediation, and often this means pulling punches and not seeking advantages that you might have won had you negotiated the deal yourself.

As in drafting agreements arising from direct lawyer negotiation, best practice and professional civility dictate that you clearly point out any changes from the deal memo in a cover letter and/or a redlined version of the proposed draft. This means that you should use a computer program that invites the other lawyer and party to insert proposed modifications directly on your draft. Call up the other lawyer and run new terms by him or her to obtain agreement or to work out compromises before sending the redlined draft. In mediation, it is also helpful to consult with the mediator before sending out drafts to get a preview of the mediator's reaction.

If snags in drafting occur, schedule a meeting with the other lawyers (and sometimes the parties as well) to meet with the mediator (or have a telephone conference call) to discuss drafting issues before a full draft is sent out. Copy the mediator on all correspondence between counsel so that the mediator is up to speed in dealing with the lawyers or parties if questions or problems should arise.

Due to the problems inherent in having one side's lawyer do the drafting, you should be open to having the mediator neutrally draft the settlement documents (particularly if the mediator is also a family lawyer). In fact, if you are not attending the mediation sessions, you can advise your client to request that the mediator prepare the initial draft of the agreement. The advantages of this approach are that having worked with the parties, the mediator is intimately familiar with the parties' agreement. Second, being trusted as impartial, the mediator's attempts at neutral drafting will most likely be very middle ground. A fair and balanced initial draft of the agreement may obviate adversarial posturing between you and the other side that could cause delay and cost—often putting the mediation into jeopardy. The option of having the mediator do the initial drafting is often very attractive to mediation participants who have developed a trusting bond with the mediator. Even when you were present at the sessions and are fully aware of the agreement terms, having the mediator do the drafting increases the chances that a writing will actually be completed and signed. Of course, it is always an option to have the agreement drafted and signed on-site to prevent later remorse or backtracking. However, you must also factor in the importance of giving the client time to reflect on the terms and have a chance to read and reread proposed language. While obsessing over drafting and backing out of deals are clear risks, so is putting excess pressure on a client to sign. Your support for the client to "think about it" rather than sign a deal exhausted after many hours of negotiating is particularly important considering the reluctance of courts to set aside mediated agreements.[9]

Sharing Boilerplate Early

"Boilerplate" is legal slang for the customary clauses that appear in most agreements. However, lawyers have their pet boilerplate and may have different perspectives on what boilerplate is and what constitutes "new negotiation." You can work out agreements that both lawyers will share their pet boilerplate early. In this way, settlements may not be held up once the final substantive points are resolved.

Single Text—Track Changes: One of mediation's great benefits is limiting or eliminating turf issues between parties and professionals. Some traditional lawyers refuse to share "electronic drafts" via e-mail due to a desire to control the drafting process or due to fear that the other lawyer might tamper with the draft. To move above this game playing and increase collaboration, consider a consensual process that has everyone working off one document and using color (not just "red" changes). This will feel more mediative, and the drafting will probably go faster and obviate the need for elaborate letter writing.

Don't Forget Aspirations

It is customary for lawyers to limit drafting to provisions that can be enforced by a court. This means that "nonenforceable terms" are often viewed as irrelevant, surplusage, or worse, contrary to or undercutting the effect of enforceable provisions.

As indicated earlier in this chapter, there are many reasons for parties to be in mediation other than walking out with an agreement that can be enforced in court. One key motivation is to identify and memorialize the aspirations and intent of parties even when agreements are not reached. Such language can remind parties of the context of their discussions.

You can provide an important service if you support the work of your clients around the mediation table by accurately incorporating even nonenforceable terms.

Some common examples include:

1. Imprecise, intangible, but meaningful aspirations of the parties. Such aspirations may include a desire to act "cooperatively," "supportive," child-centered," or otherwise positively toward the other party;
2. Set out the fact that an issue has been discussed but that no agreement has been reached and memorialize the positions of the parties. Example: *Husband is willing to pay 30 percent of any bonus as additional spousal support. Wife is not willing to accept 30 percent of any bonus of the husband as additional spousal support. No agreement has been reached and the issue shall be reserved for future discussion in mediation or shall be determined by the court. The positions of the parties in respect to this issue may/may not be considered by a court in resolving this issue.*
3. Describe an agreement and indicate that the parties do not want such agreement to be the subject of any court enforcement. Example: *Each party intends to contribute*

to the college expenses of the children in the amounts that each party is capable and desirous of paying, and neither party nor the children may enforce this clause in a court of law."

4. The parties can decide which issues will be discussed or reevaluated in the future. *Example: The parties currently agree that the children shall live in the Springfield School District. This issue shall be evaluated by the parties returning to mediation on or before January _____ . The criteria for such evaluation shall be _____ . If no additional agreement is reached, during such reevaluation, the children shall continue to attend school within the Springfield School District unless there is a court order to the contrary.*

This expanded view of "proper" drafting may feel foreign at first. However, as you gain more experience in the jurisdiction of mediation in which the interests and needs of the parties supersede state law and court procedure, you may find both a comfort and satisfaction that you had not anticipated.

To Sign or Not to Sign?

If the parties choose to use a mediator to help them negotiate their own agreement, should you be willing to sign the final judgment? If you refuse to sign, does the client have a nonbinding or a nonenforceable document negating time and money invested in mediation?

Although there is no hard-and-fast answer, it is essential that you raise the question of signing at the outset of the lawyer-client relationship. Whether your signature (or lack thereof) affects the validity of the agreement or your malpractice exposure is a gray area. Some lawyers won't sign or will condition their signatures with the words "Approved as to Form Only" or other such defensive maneuvers. The essence of professional responsibility and liability is whether you provided advice and assistance that was negligent. If you believe an agreement is not in the client's interest, *you and your client* cannot negotiate a compromise that will satisfy you, and your client chooses to go forward, you must clearly communicate your reservations in writing to your client and should not sign the agreement in *any* form. If the other party requires a lawyer's signature, the client is then in a position of trying to find another lawyer or signing the agreement without a lawyer's signature. The other side then must decide whether to go ahead with the deal. In any event, you will have one unhappy client, and you should not be surprised if you also have an unpaid fee.

The best way to avoid this problem is to have early involvement in the mediation so that you are a co-architect of the ultimate agreement. As Garfield and Glassman write:

> If they are involved early in the process, consulting attorneys can serve the interests of the mediator and their respective clients by discussing tentative agreements with

their clients, addressing collateral issues that ultimately need to be resolved, but that may not be particularly controversial, and documenting the agreement the parties have reached in order to keep the process moving forward.

Eventually, all agreements must be documented; eventually the parties will end up with a comprehensive Judgment of Dissolution of Marriage and perhaps a marital settlement agreement as well. But there is no reason to postpone preparation of those documents until the end of the process. Indeed, there is good reason to prepare successive drafts of those documents as agreements are reached during the process. Preparing successive drafts of documents that will eventually embody the parties' final settlement accomplishes a number of important goals. First, it gives the parties an opportunity to see their tentative agreement expressed in the formal provisions of the settlement agreement or judgment. Second, it enables the consulting attorneys to collaborate with respect to a whole host of issues that are subsidiary to the parties' main agreement, but important nonetheless. The provisions added by the consulting attorneys to the draft document may range from "boilerplate" provisions to provisions that may be considered "standard" or "customary" to provisions that serve mainly to supplement the parties' general agreement with important detail. If consulting attorneys are involved in the process from the outset, it is very likely that the final agreement will turn out to be better than if consulting attorneys are retained only at the end to "review" an agreement that is a fait accompli. By the end of the process, the parties are heavily invested in the agreement they have negotiated. Even if there are problems that will predictably lead to friction later on, the parties come to their attorneys for *approval* of what they have already done. While it may not be fair to say that the parties want their attorneys to do no more than rubber-stamp the deal, the parties are resistant to the idea of making changes. They want the consulting attorneys' review of the agreement to be quick and inexpensive; they want to be reassured that they have succeeded in negotiating a favorable agreement. Rarely, unless assailed by doubts, are they genuinely interested in being told that their agreement may be ill-advised in any significant respect.[10]

The public's confidence in mediation depends, to a large extent, on the competent yet nonintrusive involvement of lawyers in the review process. Many divorcing spouses will not enter mediation without such review. Once invested in the process, people need their lawyer's expertise to feel informed and confident that the agreement worked out in mediation is indeed in their best interest.

Practice Tips

1. Advise your client that nothing is final until the agreement is signed and that review and possible renegotiation and clarification of terms are part of the mediation process.
2. Be clear about what constitutes a "review," what specific tasks you will do, and what is expected of the client to make your review successful.
3. Work out your level of review: is this a full audit of every aspect of the divorce, or does the client just want you to refine drafting language?
4. Balance your support of the client's efforts and the need for improvement of agreement terms.
5. Never suggest starting from scratch or chastise the client for making poor decisions in the mediation process or trying to negotiate agreement without you. Take what was mediated and build an improved agreement.
6. Do not bomb the agreement. Be judicious in what you criticize and what you leave alone.
7. Fully understand the history of the negotiation and your client's reasons for agreeing to trade-offs. Review all mediator summary letters and compare them to the proposed written agreement.
8. Set aside plenty of time for the client to ask questions and share concerns. Your client's feeling about being supported is just as important as your competent legal and practical suggestions.
9. Be clear about what documents you will be drafting from scratch compared with reviewing the work of the mediator or other attorney.
10. Be gracious, whenever possible, in deferring to the neutral drafting of the mediator and assuming that the mediator is competent to draft.
11. Let it go: Do not tussle with the other lawyer about who will draft the documents and whose language is "better."
12. Do not "overdraft" or consistently write in favor of your client. Attempt to write the deal points in acceptable language for both parties. Lengthy drafting negotiations and/or delay often undercut the goals of your client.
13. Use one text drafting with Word or another program that invites and permits redlining (modifications on the text). Surrender the control that PDF affords you for the collaboration of a single text. (If you work from a single document such that all revisions are public, make sure that you do not use that document for private communications with your client.)
14. Be clear at the beginning of your engagement whether you are willing to sign the agreement and in what form.

15. Offer your suggestions as determined by the parties in mediation. Some parties and/or mediators prefer that the parties convey the ideas of consulting lawyers, and others prefer direct communication with you.
16. Be prepared to solve any drafting problems with the parties and professionals in a collaborative and nonthreatening way. Remember: a good job is defined as an agreement based on informed consent resulting from a positive process.

Notes

1. Rebecca Aviel, *1099 Counsel for the Divorce*, 55 BOSTON COLLEGE LAW REVIEW (September 2014).

2. See DOUGLAS, FRENKEL, AND STARK, THE PRACTICE OF MEDIATION, 2nd Edition (2013), at pp 287–288.

3. WILLIAM DOUGHERTY, DISCERNMENT COUNSELING TRAINING MATERIALS, 2015.

4. Tim Pierce, Ethics Counsel for the State Bar of Wisconsin, wrote the following in 2010 about lawyers drafting final documents:

> Utah Ethics Opinion 05-03 (2005) opined:
>
> *When a lawyer-mediator, after a successful mediation, drafts the settlement agreement, complaint, and other pleadings to implement the settlement and obtain a divorce for the parties, the lawyer-mediator is engaged in the practice of law and attempting to represent opposing parties in litigation.*
>
> Likewise, Ohio Ethics Opinion 2009-4 (2009) stated:
>
> *At issue is whether upon completion of a domestic relations mediation and preparation of a mediation report, a lawyer-mediator may prepare necessary legal documents, such as petitions, decrees, and ancillary documents, for filing by or on behalf of one or more of the parties to a domestic relations proceeding. Examples of these documents might be a Separation Agreement, Shared Parenting Plan, Petition for Dissolution of Marriage and Decree for Dissolution of Marriage, Ohio Child Support Guidelines Worksheets.*
>
> *A domestic relations lawyer-mediator who goes beyond preparing the mediation report, which is required of the mediator by law and rule, into the preparation of necessary legal documents for filing by or on behalf of the parties to a domestic relations proceeding is engaging in a legal representation subsequent to the mediation.*
>
> These opinions reflect the generally agreed-upon consensus that the preparation of pleadings or other documents for filing in court constitutes the practice of law.

5. Leading states permitting lawyers to draft final documents as intermediaries are Massachusetts (Massachusetts Bar Association—Ethics Opinion No. 85-3), New York (New York State Bar Opinion 736, 2001), and Utah (Utah Rule of Professional Responsibility 2.4).

6. Maine and Oregon are leading states permitting mediators to draft as neutrals with certain conditions.

>Rule 2.4 Lawyer Serving as Mediator
>
>(a) A lawyer serving as a mediator:
>
>(1) shall not act as a lawyer for any party against another party in the matter in mediation or in any related proceeding; and
>
>(2) must clearly inform the parties of and obtain the parties' consent to the lawyer's role as mediator.
>
>(b) A lawyer serving as a mediator:
>
>(1) may prepare documents that memorialize and implement the agreement reached in mediation;
>
>(2) shall recommend that each party seek independent legal advice before executing the documents; and
>
>(3) with the consent of all parties, may record or may file the documents in court.
>
>(c) Notwithstanding Rule 1.10, when a lawyer is serving or has served as a mediator in a matter, a member of the lawyer's firm may accept or continue the representation of a party in the matter in mediation or in a related matter if all parties to the mediation give informed consent, confirmed in writing.
>
>(d) The requirements of Rule 2.4(a) (2) and (b) (2) shall not apply to mediation programs established by operation of law or court order.

Maine accomplished the task in 1993 by adding the following provisions to its version of 2.4 which is identical to ours:

>(c) The role of third party neutral does not create a lawyer-client relationship with any of the parties and does not constitute representation of any of them. The lawyer shall not attempt to advance the interest of any of the parties at the expense of any other party.
>
>(d) The lawyer shall not use any conduct, discussions or statements made by any party in the course of any alternative dispute resolution process to the disadvantage of any party to the process, or, without the informed consent of the parties, to the advantage of the lawyer or a third person.
>
>(e) When acting as a mediator, the lawyer shall undertake such role subject to the following additional conditions:
>
>(1) The lawyer must clearly inform the parties of the nature and limits of the lawyer's role as mediator and should disclose any interest or relationship likely to affect the lawyer's impartiality or that might create an appearance of partiality or bias. The parties must consent to the arrangement unless they are in mediation

pursuant to a legal mandate.

(2) **The lawyer may draft a settlement agreement or instrument reflecting the parties' resolution of the matter but must advise and encourage any party represented by independent counsel to consult with that counsel, and any unrepresented party to seek independent legal advice, before executing it.**

(3) The lawyer shall withdraw as mediator if any of the parties so requests, or if any of the conditions stated in this subdivision (e) is no longer satisfied. Upon withdrawal, or upon conclusion of the mediation, the lawyer shall not represent any of the parties in the matter that was the subject of the mediation, or in any related matter.

7. You should be aware of the new liability relief offered by the 2012 California Supreme Case *Cassel*. In *Cassel*, the court held that mediation confidentiality extends to all lawyer-client communications conducted during mediation, even outside the presence of the mediator. This means that a client is precluded from testifying about wrongful advice provided by the lawyer—which virtually eliminates most malpractice claims. This holding has been vastly criticized by consumer groups and the plaintiff malpractice bar, and legislation attempting to gut the *Cassel* holding is pending in the California legislature. Also, the *Cassel* court may have been viewing mediation as a single session rather than sequential sessions over weeks or months. Many questions remain about whether a court would uphold the *Cassel* result if you were to provide negligent advice in your office several weeks after a joint mediation session rather than in a conference room with the mediator working in the same office suite.

8. Many drafting issues involve professional responsibility for mediators with law licenses and other issues involving mediators without a law license in respect to the unauthorized practice of law.

9. *See* James R. Coben and Peter N. Thompson, *Disputing Irony: A Systematic Look at Litigation About Mediation* (Sp. 2006). 11 HARV. NEG. L.REV. 43. California is also developing significant law around mediation.

10. Franklin Garfield and Frederick Glassman, *In the Beginning: Independent Counsel's Place in Dissolution Mediations*, LA DAILY J, February 14, 1996, at 7.

CHAPTER 11

Preventing Future Conflict

Legal problems can be prevented altogether by lawyers who operate in a fast forward rather than rewind mode, designing environments and facilitating relationships that are less conflictual or problem-producing.
—Thomas D. Barton and James M. Cooper, *Preventive Law and Creative Problem Solving: Multi-Dimensional Lawyering* (2009)

Getting the divorce does not mean the family is free and clear of family court. Especially when there are minor children, long-term support payments, or continuing financial entanglements—deferred sale of the family residence, ongoing joint business or investments, deferred compensation, and the like—the parties are likely to need ongoing legal and dispute resolution assistance in the future.

This chapter will explore three methods of preventing conflict in the family: incorporating dispute resolution clauses into the judgment, using preventive mediation to form new family relationships, and maintaining and expanding the legal health of all family members through legal wellness checkups.

Drafting Future Dispute Resolution Clauses

After spending thousands of dollars on legal and mediator fees to handle a divorce, most clients are open to learning about how to prevent future disputes. The goal of preventive planning is to raise concerns and solve problems before they reach the level of conflict. A second working concept is that absent emergency, consensual methods of dispute resolution are preferable. Therefore, parties should try to start with the least invasive method of dispute resolution. If the conflict remains unresolved, parties should consider agreeing to having more control imposed on them until, finally, they agree to have someone else makes the decision for them. Finally, even as more invasive methods are utilized, the parties should build in a return to mediation with the benefit of new information from the more invasive process as a catalyst for a mediated result returning control (or part of it) to the parties themselves.

The following are some options you can incorporate into settlements to prevent conflict and to keep the parties away from the courthouse in the future.

Although the enforceability of mediation clauses is not guaranteed in every jurisdiction, courts routinely enforce contractual or statutory obligations to mediate as a condition precedent to litigation.[1] Concerns about enforceability are relatively insignificant in practice: "Given the relatively minor time, risk or expense of compliance and the likelihood that noncompliance would be used to block any later clauses, most parties to mediated clauses probably will comply."[2] A sample mediation clause is included in the Resources section.

Written Notice of Dispute

Completing a legal divorce rarely means ending a relationship with a former spouse. Even with a well-drafted agreement and a detailed parenting schedule, opportunities for contact and conflict seem inevitable and unending. Being a parental and business partner with a former spouse may be one of the most challenging relationships in modern life. When the challenges become excessive, explosions can occur in areas such as choosing the children's school, dividing up Thanksgiving, paying for lessons or camp, or figuring out new support if income fluctuates or either party becomes involved with a new spouse or live-in partner.

Hopefully, parties will be able to communicate by telephone or in person and make whatever accommodations or changes are requested. Even if both parties try with good faith, impasse sometimes develops. When one party feels aggrieved and believes that a dispute remains unresolved, step one in the dispute prevention chain should be for that party to write a note or letter to the other party, detailing the concern and suggesting a proposal for resolution.

Once receiving proper notice, the other party can accept the proposal in full, in which case the matter is resolved. With most divorced couples, even if tensions have escalated to the point of requiring the notice, the dispute ends right here. There are no more meetings, lawyers, mediators, or judges. The family just carries on.

If the proposal is not accepted, the party receiving the notice should have a duty to respond in writing within a specified time period, setting forth that party's concerns about the proposal. From this point on, either party has the option of continuing the correspondence exercise or calling for the next step: an in-person meet-and-confer session.

Parties Meet and Confer

Following the entry of the decree, divorcing spouses might build in contact by correspondence, telephone, or in-person meetings to take care of ongoing matters between them. Such joint business can include regular parental meetings as well as intermittent accountings to reconcile finances; to tote up contributions and reimbursements for post-divorce joint expenses; or to divide up receipts, dividends, or sales proceeds of jointly owned property. These post-divorce meetings are premised on legal wellness—the parties are doing necessary business to meet the ongoing needs of the divorced family. The preventive dispute resolution provision to meet and confer is somewhat different. It is designed to kick in when there is a dispute between the parties that cannot be resolved and that might otherwise be headed for court. When the written notice and subsequent correspondence are unable to resolve the problem, a personal meeting constitutes the last clear chance to avoid bringing in a mediator or going to court. The judgment should spell out when the parties should meet and confer. The party requesting the meeting should offer a choice of neutral sites (unless a mutually agreeable site has previously been worked out) and several possible meeting times within the time period prescribed by the notice requirement. The other party should be required to acknowledge the meeting request in writing, but also should have the right to choose among the provided options of venue and time. If none of the meeting times are acceptable to the party receiving the notice of personal meeting, that party should have the duty to respond within a specified time frame and to offer several reasonable alternatives.

Because the vitality and effectiveness of this dispute resolution matrix—in fact the entire post-divorce relationship—depends on compromise, integrity, and commitment to manage conflict, the outlined procedures are intended as default fallbacks. The real hope is that parties will circumvent them and set up the meeting in a 30-second phone call—if not quickly resolving the underlying controversy during the call itself.

Required Mediation

If the in-person meeting does not resolve the issue, either party should have the right to compel mediation. A drafting issue is whether to require the use of the mediator who successfully handled the divorce or leave the choice of the mediator up to mutual agreement of the parties. For a host of reasons, one or both parties may have concerns about using the same mediator again. On the other hand, using a mediator with flaws might be better than having the parties start over again. In contrast, the underlying purpose of this mediation clause is to get the parties into mediation and get them there fast! Arguing about the choice of mediator defeats that goal.

The clause should deal with the minimum amount of mediation required. At the very least, one or two 3-hour sessions will get the parties to sit down with a neutral and make an attempt at resolution. If there is progress, additional sessions can be mutually agreed upon. The other view is that there should be three or four required sessions (possibly adding initial private meetings) or a full day in the single-session format.

Finally, allocation of cost for the mediator should be considered. The options for payment discussed earlier apply to future disputes as well, with one change in perspective. Although the higher earner may be willing to advance or totally pay for mediation costs during a divorce, he or she may be more reluctant to sign on to an open commitment to pay for mediation regarding an undetermined number of issues for the next several years. Due to this concern, parties may be better off agreeing to a fixed split—if not 50-50, then 60-40 or 75-25). It also may be less prudent to have a split based on future comparison of adjusted gross income because this would require a disclosure of income information (maybe involving joint returns with a new spouse) that could cause additional conflict in and of itself.

In about 2005, Woody finished mediating a high-profile, complex matter and he suggested that because the parties had experienced such success, they should discuss having a mandatory mediation clause. The wife, the wife's lawyer, and the husband wanted such a clause. The husband's attorney, a well-regarded litigator, stated that although he was very satisfied with how mediation had worked to settle the divorce, he never (and repeated the word *never*) would permit his client to give up his right to go to court without trying mediation. While the wife and wife's lawyer pointed out that the clause was neutral and applied to both parties and that emergency situations were excluded, the person with the veto won! You know the coda of the story. Two years later, the husband wanted the wife to participate in mediation and the wife refused—14 months of virulent and expensive litigation followed.

Confidential Mini-Evaluation (CME)

This process is available when mediation does not resolve a parenting dispute and the parties might benefit from having a nonbinding confidential expert's opinion to defuse the conflict. Initially developed as an alternative to the costly and adversarial formal court custody evaluation,[3] the CME is a balancing act that gives the parties the input of an experienced custody evaluator without the cost, delay, adversarial posturing, and virtually binding decision of imposing a court-appointed evaluator on the family and making the decision part of the permanent court record. The CME evaluator is selected by the parties and will customize the process based on the mutual instruction of the parties. For example, the evaluator may do the entire evaluation in one day without any home visits, psychological testing, or interviews with collateral witnesses such as teachers, child-care providers, or physicians. To save both time and expense, no written report is prepared. In addition, such written reports often become indelible parts of the family history. They usually expose the least attractive aspects of both parents. Furthermore, such written reports often create smoldering resentment in the parent described or are used as weapons. The CME evaluator gives oral feedback containing recommendations, and the parties then can use that report to stimulate negotiations. If resolution is not reached, either party can compel a formal evaluation, but the judgment should provide that in any subsequent evaluation or court hearing, the parties are restrained from making reference to the communications or recommendations adduced during a CME.

Although the CME can be started by the parties themselves or by their lawyers, it works best when initiated and conducted in the mediation setting. The parties can have prospective evaluators come to the mediation for joint interviews under the mediator's guidance. The mediator can facilitate negotiations over the final selection and scope of the evaluator's assignment. Being present during the evaluator's oral feedback session (hopefully along with the parties' lawyers), the mediator can be an objective neutral witness to what the evaluator actually did say and then use that information to help negotiate a resolution.

The CME process can be adapted for experts in financial issues as well. Instead of the parties hiring two forensic CPAs to do a cash available report for support or a business evaluation, each of whom might take adversarial positions in submitting their lengthy reports replete with bells and whistles, one neutral CPA can be hired on a customized assignment to give an oral report to the parties. The same can be true if the parties need real estate appraisers or vocational counselors to determine suitability for employment, for example.

At the Mediation Table

Mediation Fills the Family Album
Mediation is a malleable, custom-designed process that can adapt to the changes in a divorced family. The first time Kate and Samuel came in, they had one daughter, Rebecca, age 2, and a baby on the way. Samuel was involved with Cheryl. A divorce settlement was reached.

Three years later, Kate and Samuel returned, urged strongly by Cheryl, who had a son in her arms. Samuel's company had gone out of business, and he wanted a reduction of the overgenerous support agreement made at the time of divorce.

Four years later, seven years after the divorce, Kate and her new husband, Peter, initiated a mediation when they wanted to move to an adjoining county, radically changing a long-standing joint physical custody arrangement. The move was worked out, with Samuel having additional control on weekend activities, putting driving responsibilities on Peter and Kate.

After another two years, the family was back, this time with lawyers in the room. Tensions had simmered over driving and lifestyle differences. After two all-day sessions, the parties agreed that Cheryl and Samuel would move close to the other home with a return to an equal time-share arrangement.

While less than a perfect situation, the family has a history of resolution, and only they know when the mediation will recommence. A mediation file rarely closes—yet the timing and format of the next stage to resolve family conflict are subject to later determination.

These CME evaluators permit parties to get the expert information needed to facilitate negotiated agreement without being stuck with an adverse written report that could be submitted to the court. A sample court stipulation for a CME appears in the Resources section.

Formal Evaluation Report

If a parenting or financial dispute does not settle after the results of a CME are reported by the CME evaluator at a mediation session, one of the parties may require the use of a neutral full evaluation as provided in the judgment. The full evaluation capitalizes on the benefits of having one impartial expert instead of two, and because it entails a written report that can be sent to the judge and admitted into evidence, it may provide extra motivation for the parties to settle. On the other hand, because it is an unabridged full-service job, the expert will probably take longer and it will cost quite a bit more compared with a CME.

As with the CME, the parties should provide for mandatory mediation at the request of one party after the report is complete and before it is submitted to the court. This mediation will give the parties an opportunity to resolve the matter based on the new information of the expert's findings (for which they probably paid dearly) and before the party feeling wounded goes out and pays another evaluator to prepare still yet another report (unless the dispute resolution clause makes the full evaluator's findings binding on the parties). The opportunity to mediate before sending the report to court allows the family to keep the matter private rather than airing the linen (clean or dirty) in public.

Binding Adjudication

Despite all the hoops, some disputes just won't settle. The parties need someone to make a decision for them. However, before automatically assuming that the binding adjudicator will be a judge in the public court system, consider several other options in drafting the future dispute resolution clauses.

Arbitration

Although arbitration is binding and enforceable like a court order, the parties can streamline the process to make it faster and cheaper than the court system. The trend is to give the arbitrator virtually absolute power to decide the matter with little right of court review or appeal unless specifically reserved.

The dispute resolution clause can call for all issues to be resolved by arbitration or merely delineate single issues that can be arbitrated with court having jurisdiction to decide everything else. It is customary to designate which rules of arbitration service providers will govern. If you are unfamiliar with the specifics of the designated rule scheme, look it up to make sure it is appropriate for your type of dispute.

Liz recently reviewed a draft cohabitation agreement that provided for future arbitration of disputes under the rules of a major provider. When she looked up the rules, she discovered that although various subsets applied to specific types of disputes, no subset existed for family law, and it was not apparent which set of rules would apply to a family law dispute. Because the goal of these kinds of clauses is to limit areas of future dispute, be mindful that you are not inadvertently opening new lines of miscommunication.

Also, different arbitrators can be designated to handle different disputes. For example, if a deferred house sale is provided for in the judgment, the parties may agree to a modified step process, such as meet and confer, mediation, full appraisal report, then straight to arbitration, eliminating the CME. In so doing, for this issue only, perhaps they could name a real estate broker at the time of judgment or at the time of the dispute. The same approach can be taken by naming a CPA to arbitrate tax filing, audit, or refund conflicts.

In high-conflict custody cases, there is a trend to designate a therapist or another mental health professional to serve as arbitrator or special master to have binding authority over some but not all parenting disputes. For example, the binding decision maker decides issues such as holiday and vacation periods, selection of medical providers, and struggles over extracurricular activities. The major decisions, such as time-share, location of residence, and choice of school, remain in the public court system.

Private Judges

An alternative to arbitration is a private judge. Very popular in California,[4] this option is providing steady employment for retired judges (and some lawyers) and is an available option for those who choose to pay for more accessible justice. There has been considerable criticism that the popularity of private judging has created two types of justice: one for those who can pay and the public court system for everyone else. The draining of talent from the judiciary and the conflicts of interest created by repeat buyers of the same providers are other issues of current public debate.

The benefit for the family of providing for a private judge is that the major costs to litigants result in complex prehearing court procedures and waiting time to both get and finish a hearing. Some courts are so overburdened that it takes months to start a hearing. Once it has started, the judge may have to bifurcate and trifurcate the proceedings to squeeze in three hours one day and four hours several weeks later. It can be very frustrating for parties and lawyers—and very expensive. Private judging offers the speed and possible customized, streamlined procedures of arbitration with the safeguards of the rules of evidence and rights of appellate review guaranteed in the court system. Many private judges wear their robes, most private trials have a court reporter to preserve the record, and many private courtrooms have been built to accommodate demand. The prestigious Los Angeles family law firm Trope and Trope has even built such a courtroom in its well-appointed office suite, which is available for rental to other lawyers in the community. These amenities can be the subject of discussion and drafting in the judgment.

Once a private judge is selected, the scheduled hearing time is virtually guaranteed to go on that date. The judge works six to eight hours a day without the interruption of other cases—which is more than enough for any trial lawyer! In December, a dad wanted an immediate change of custody because his son had received Fs in four of six subjects in seventh grade. After considerable negotiation and preliminary procedural wrangling in court, in early January, the parties stipulated to use a respected retired judge. By February 1, the parties had completed an eight-day hearing and the child had changed his residence.

Mediation to Follow a Binding Decision

Of course, if the parties cannot agree on the terms of arbitration or private judging, the parties can still use the public court system as their binding-decision option. Regardless of which binding option is included in the scheme, it is generally worthwhile to have it followed by mandatory mediation if requested by one party after the binding decision is rendered. After beating each other up in a contested hearing and receiving a result that may satisfy neither party, the parties may welcome the return to the mediation process, which helps them restore some control to their lives as well as facilitate healing from the wounds of litigation. Many clients do not realize that even after the judge rules, the parties can generally negotiate a modification of the court order that may better meet their needs.

Many lawyers are unaccustomed to drafting dispute resolution clauses. Traditional litigation mind-set has been "We have enough to do in working out agreements on the current disputes. If there are problems in the future, parties can always seek a modification in court (except in final determinations such as property divisions and nonmodifiable spousal maintenance orders) or enforcement actions. Let's just wrap it up fairly and let the future take care of itself." This school of family law may be suspicious of a step-by-step, calibrated approach to future dispute resolutions. The cure may be seen as worse than the disease. Fears of unnecessary hoops and expense when the case might end up in litigation anyway are quite reasonable.

Robert Theobald, a well-regarded futurist and adviser to the Oregon Legislative Task Force designing the court of the future, has said that the essence of professional competence is trying to use one's best judgment in making the very best decisions at the moment given the people involved.[5] It is true that at times, negotiating and drafting future dispute resolution clauses may take more time and money than actually litigating a dispute later. Also, by detailing a step-by-step approach, the parties may incur unnecessary fees and conflict in addition to the costs of litigation. This concern may also be valid. In fact, when presented with that concern, many clients opt to leave everything open or just have a mediation option without all of the rest. Yet others, even when advised about the dangers of uncertainty, may choose to invoke the calibrated process set out here, a hybrid, or a wholly original concept. In rendering the most competent service, modern family lawyers are keeping their eyes on the road ahead as well as in the rearview mirror—sharing those observations with their clients and working collaboratively to enhance informed client decision making.

Preventive Mediation

If mediation helps preserve relationships during and after a divorce when parties have differing interests and life paths, the process should also work when the parties form new relationship commitments. Preventive mediation may be discussed by divorcing spouses as a way to spare family members (especially the children) future conflict and pain if either spouse breaks up with a new romantic partner. However, the main use of preventive mediation during divorce mediation is to educate both parties and their lawyers in how to stay out of trouble (but not just with each other) after the judgment is entered. Any conflict affecting any member of the new family system can have a ripple effect.

Preventive mediation is used most frequently in forming committed life partner relationships such as domestic partnerships and marriage or sharing a residence. As exciting and promising as these relationships can be, they are also frightening, especially for divorce survivors. People fear not only an acrimonious breakup (perhaps another one), but also the new problems that might be presented by this new commitment. These concerns go beyond the legal ramifications of sharing income, buying real estate, and having joint bank accounts or obligations to a broad range of issues: "How will I communicate and resolve problems with my new partner (better than I did the last time around)?" "How will we work out budgeting and managing our money?" Will it hurt our new relationship to have separate incomes?" "Should we have a baby? If so, what would that do to our lives?" "How will we deal with controlling in-laws or the need for a sibling to live with us or be supported by us?"

Binding legal agreements may be helpful in protecting against the disaster of a breakup, but what people really want is information and guidance about leading a happy and satisfying life together. Maximizing their opportunities for harmony and mutual gain may be far more important to an engaged couple than protecting against the ultimate demise of the relationship.

All that having been said, you might be concerned that premarital agreements are walking malpractice time bombs. Some lawyers won't do them, and many who will do them charge extremely high fees because of the explosive risk of professional liability. Regardless of the fees charged, think about the appropriateness and real value of having two lawyers, pledged to get the best financial and legal deal for their respective clients, haggling over terms while their clients are more interested in just living their new lives together. Yes, marriage and cohabitation can entail great risks in case of failure. These issues must be discussed—but how?

Some divorced couples are now consulting mediators when they form new relationships. They want a supportive, relaxed educational setting in which to speak with a professional who wants to help them. They have heard that many family lawyers do not want to handle relationship formations. Even though mediators generally work with divorces, the orientation of healing and looking beyond rights toward underlying needs and concerns is a very attractive alternative to having two lawyers writing letters and running up big bills. Most important, while understanding that they should face problems, most parties are afraid of lawyers planting mistrust or doubt about the other party—either to them or the other.

In preventive mediation, client education may be even more important than writing up the agreements of the parties. However, written agreements can actually help relationships! Worrying about the loss of property or financial insecurity in case of a breakup can cause relationship anxiety. The same is true of worrying about the other partner worrying. If people can talk about sex, intimate emotions, and family secrets, why can't they talk openly about money, property, and legal rights? If an agreement can ameliorate fears and then be put in the drawer, it can actually strengthen the relationship—as long as the process of making the agreement doesn't do too much damage. To be married by clergy, some religions require a couple to participate in education and counseling about the responsibilities and pitfalls of marriage. The overriding goal is that such education may make a marriage stronger.

Preventive mediation is based on the same principles. It is interesting that the same lawyers who use mediation for divorce never think of mediation when they have a client who is trying to save a marriage[6], getting married [7]or blending a family in a nonmarried relationship. Part of the problem is that the client calls and says:,"I'm getting married; I need help with a premarital agreement." The client's presenting request often determines the lawyer's actions, which might differ greatly from those flowing from the mediative approach of attempting to uncover the client's underlying goals and concerns—many of which have nothing to do with legal rights.

Ethically and practically, the lawyer's role in a preventive mediation is the same as in a dispute mediation: help the client achieve a result maximizing the goals and concerns that improve the client's life—which may or may not coincide with maximizing legal protection. A mediator can set the proper tone for doing this important business without intruding on the romance. The mediation can also cover wills, durable powers of attorney, deed drafting, and other estate planning needs, which often go hand in hand with marriage planning.

The recognition for marriage education, including informed consent for agreements, has spawned at least two successful Bar-sponsored preventive programs in addition to the activity in practitioners' offices. Under the leadership of former Chair Lynne Gold Bikin, the ABA Section of Family Law launched a partnering program designed to educate citizens before making committed relationships.[8]

If your client is reluctant about using and paying for a mediator for a premarital agreement, consider using a collaborative approach in building an agreement. In addition to choosing an interdisciplinary option and utilizing the values and guidelines of collaborative practice discussed in Chapter 6, this approach prevents much resentment that often is the fallout of one party wanting these agreements and the other being either neutral or opposed. Rather than having you draft a one-sided agreement to maximize the interests of your client and then sending it over with the message (either overt or covert) "Please sign this, sweetheart," both parties are involved in a facilitated meeting in understanding the concepts of the agreement and deciding it together. You and the other collaborative lawyer can then jointly draft the agreement so that much of the heat of these transactions is avoided.

Other Uses of Preventive Mediation

In addition to helping form a romantic relationship, preventive mediation is very conducive to forming a new parent-child relationship. Adoptions often cause tension and fraying among the participants. For example, as an alternative to working only through lawyers, mediation is a suitable process for having the birth mother, adoptive parents, and other concerned family members iron out concerns with the guidance of their lawyers. In surrogate situations, a sister is sometimes the birth mother, which results in the adoptive mother's family of origin being intimately involved in the future of that child—and not without conflicting interests. Finally, family businesses are rife with potential strife. Preventively working out parent-child issues while at the same time formulating business goals and agreements is a perfect application of mediation.

These opportunities for preventive mediation often arise from presenting problems around conflict—to wit, the present divorce. You may have run across conflicts involving parents and adult children, siblings, or quarrelling business partners. These sad cases are often symptomatic of underlying relationship dynamics that cry out for resolution—or at least workable agreements. Such matters also can benefit from the use of an intergender lawyer-therapist co-mediation team. A family experiencing the resolution of conflict may also be more open to learning about methods for preventing conflict and maintaining legal health in the future.

Preventive Legal Wellness Checkups

Mediation offers many benefits for resolving and managing conflict, but even its most ardent proponents concede that a successful mediation is focused on settling a dispute, not on helping people have happier, more satisfying lives. Research has shown that mediation does not bring about long-term behavioral change in the participants. Compared with the process of psychotherapy, client contact with a professional is rather superficial in psychodynamic terms.[9] Some mediation authorities, such as Robert A. Baruch Bush, Joseph P. Folger, and Gary J. Friedman, talk about mediation as a transformative experience.[10] Such transformation, when and if it occurs, may or may not be the motivation that propels people into future mediation and is not likely to occur unless the presenting dispute is settled in a fair and satisfying manner. Two esteemed mental health colleagues with whom Woody has co-mediated, Dr. Constance Ahrons and Dr. Mary Lund, have stated: "Mediation is not necessarily a growth experience. Fasten your seat belts and get ready for a rough ride. The best you can hope for is for it to stop hurting when it's over. Then you can start healing."

Having muted expectations for long-term behavior change through mediation is important in helping clients be satisfied with the progress they do achieve. Once resolution is achieved, having used mediation can significantly and positively impact a participant's future life. The benefits of saved money, expeditious finality, preserved privacy, salvaged relationships, and feelings of satisfaction rather than victimization can facilitate improved personal lives for the participants and/or limit any damage caused by the dispute that would be compounded by the transaction costs of resolution.

The legal wellness checkup is an unbundled service that you can use to improve the legal health of clients at every stage of representation. Just as a doctor will examine a lump on your nose even though the presenting problem is a stye in your eye, a preventive lawyer will inquire about a client's overall legal health when trying to solve the specific problems—for example, divorce, support or custody modification, or adoption—that brought the client into the office. The legal checkup can be brief, such as one question: "Do you have a will?" The client's answer can initiate a client-lawyer dialogue that focuses on the importance of having an up-to-date will, a durable power of attorney, beneficiary designations, and other related documents. It is the client's choice to take any action or have any legal work done. If work is desired, the client must decide whether to prepare documents without assistance, use the family lawyer who diagnosed the problem, or hire another lawyer or financial planning professional.

If you actively ask other questions concerning the client's life, the discussion can be more wide-ranging. Such questions could include the following:

- "I notice that your expenses seem to be exceeding your available cash of about $1,000 a month. How do you plan to solve this problem?"
- "You mentioned that you sometimes are feeling depressed these days—and that intensifies when the children are at their mother's home. What thoughts do you have about feeling better?"
- "I am delighted to hear that you and Jim are moving in together. You looked great together the last time he was in the office with you. He has custody of his three children, right? Do you have any concern as to how this might affect your relationship with your former spouse or your own children?"
- "You really do work long hours! I am sorry to hear that this work stress comes home with you. What are you going to do about it?"

Probing these hot spots through concerned lawyer-client conversation can encourage the client to think about possible solutions. The client need take no action at all. As a preventive lawyer, you have fulfilled an important function just by raising the questions. The client can ignore advice, cut corners, or make stupid or self-destructive choices once these questions are on the table. The client is ultimately in charge of the information and options provided by the lawyer in regard to legal health.

In addition to spontaneous conversation that sparks preventive counseling, many lawyers use preventive checklists to guide the conversation. Invented by Louis M. Brown, the internationally recognized father of preventive law, such checklists are available commercially. Sample checklists are provided in the Appendices.

People are more than willing to pay for a medical wellness checkup on a regular basis. They will go to their doctor's office for these checkups even if they have no symptoms or pain. They do not expect the doctor to find a problem. In fact, they are delighted and will pay their bill when given a clean bill of health. Why do lawyers generally believe that problems must be present before clients need to see us? Some preventive family lawyers schedule the next office visit before the client leaves the office. Others have implemented non-litigation calendars that alert the lawyer to contact the client on a regular calendar basis or on the occurrence of significant client events through life cycle dates or events that resulted from the executory provisions of the settlement agreement.

With respect to life cycle events, the non-litigation calendar can be set to trigger client contact one year before, six months before, three months before, and one month before important dates in the client's life, including the age of retirement eligibility, matriculation of children to a new school or college, and the date each child attains majority.

When negotiating or mediating custody and support agreements, you can educate the parties about the possibility of having wellness checkups with the mediator on a regular basis. Generally, these checkups are scheduled on a six-month or one-year basis. The contract specifies that the parties come to see the mediator even if there are no presenting problems. The appointment is generally one hour long, but if there is a pressing issue, more time can be booked. On occasion, spouses complete a wellness checkup without any repressed or latent issue arising. In that case, the parties deservingly get a clean bill of health and support from the mediator that they are doing well. However, usually something comes up—often parties save their concerns for the checkups, knowing that their discussion will be monitored and managed by the mediator and not get out of hand. These regular discussions can preempt and solve problems before they ripen into expensive and destructive conflict.

Sample Notice-Triggering Events for Nonlitigation Calendar

October 1, Year 1	Settlement completed that provides that the client reside in the family house until the oldest child, Mary, is 18 (on September 15, Y3). The youngest child (Johnny) is at local elementary school and will matriculate to middle school in February Y4.
October 2, Year 1	The preventive lawyer makes all of the following entries in the office's non-litigation calendar.
January 15, Year 2	Write client concerning upkeep and expense of house.
October 1, Year 2	Write client about house and general status. Remind client about buyout date and monitor efforts to save money for possible buyout. The mortgage interest is 9% on date of the Judgment (October 1, Y1). Check current interest rates for refi possibilities. Remind client of wellness checkup.
January 15, Year 3	Monitor buyout or sale progress. Discuss initiating negotiations with other spouse (either directly between the clients or through counsel).
May 1, Year 3	Monitor buyout or sale progress. Remind client to bring in listing agreement or any sales documents before execution and financing. Discuss seeking extension of September 15 deadline.
August 1, Year 3	Monitor house sale listing or buyout. Final check to ascertain if court action to extend deadline is required.
September 1, Year 3	Final monitoring of house sale listing or buyout.
October 1, Year 3	Write client to schedule wellness review re residence, insurance, estate planning, and status of possible career change.

Practice Tips

1. Work toward future dispute resolution processes that will not only resolve disputes, but also prevent conflict from developing.
2. Erect barriers to the courthouse so that, absent an emergency, filing in court is a last rather than first resort.
3. Encourage parties to work out problems themselves and to surrender control to an outside decision maker only when other options have been attempted unsuccessfully.
4. Include both a written notice and a personal meet-and-confer requirement for parties to use in resolving future disputes themselves.
5. Build in required mediation as the first and primary dispute resolution process.

6. Have parties return to mediation after more invasive processes such as expert evaluations, arbitration, and court. Parties can regain control by mutually modifying imposed decisions and begin to heal after conflict.
7. Use a confidential mini-evaluation (CME) to retain privacy and control and to cut costs in parenting and financial disputes.
8. Provide a safeguard for the parties not to file an expert's report with the court until the findings can be a basis for a mediated agreement.
9. Arbitration can be used on single issues or for an entire case, with the possible exception of child custody.
10. Consider using a private judge to select the best decision maker, expedite a hearing, and possibly save overall costs.
11. New family relationships can benefit from using preventive mediation. Marriage, adoption, and family business are prime candidates for using mediation to form and monitor the new relationships.
12. Provide legal wellness checkups to keep clients healthy legally and to provide a new source of revenue.
13. Establish a non-litigation calendar to monitor ongoing client events and to remind clients to come into the office for a regular legal checkup.

Notes

1. MEDIATION LITIGATION TRENDS: 1999–2007 by James R. Coben and Peter N. Thompson., World Arbitration and Mediation Review, Volume 1, No. 3.

2. NANCY ROGERS AND CRAIG MCEWEN, MEDIATION: LAW, POLICY, AND PRACTICE § 8:01 (2d ed., 1994). For an example *of* a dispute resolution clause, *see* Richard Chernick, *Dispute Resolution Assessment and Process Design in Professional Responsibility Disputes,* AMER. ARB. ASS'N (Prof. Resp. Panel/Panel Seminar No.2, Los Angeles, CA), May 15, 1996.

3. Forrest S. Mosten, *Confidential Mini-Evaluation,* FAM & CONCILIATION CTS. REV.., Jul. 1992, at 373–84; and Forrest S. Mosten, *Confidential Mini Evaluations: Another ADR Option*, 45 FAMILY LAW QUARTERLY (ABA) No. 1, Spring 2011.

4. *See* THE PRIVATE JUDGE: CALIFORNIA ANOMALY OR WAVE OF THE FUTURE? By Jill S. Robbins, www.iaml.org (2012).

5. Robert Theobald, Opening Address, 1995 Northwest Conference of Association of Family and Conciliation Courts, Nov 1995.

6. *See* Laurie Israel who writes and practices in the area of marital mediation http://www.ivkdlaw.com/practice-areas/marital-mediation/

7. Sandra M. Rosenbloom and Judith C. Nesburn, IsN'T IT UNROMANTIC? Collaboratively Negotiating Pre- and Post-Nuptial Agreements, http://www.judithcnesburn.com/CM/Custom/artice-collaboratively-negotiating.asp.

8. AMERICAN BAR ASSOCIATION, SECTION OF FAMILY LAW, PARTNERS CURRICULUM MANUAL FOR TEACHERS at Overview (1996). ("PARTNERS teaches students about the legal system as it impacts on marriages, families, and children. It also teaches basic relationships that can withstand the normal stresses of the daily interaction of family life.")

9. Joan Kelly et al., *Mediator and Adversarial Divorce: Initial Findings from a Longitudinal Study,* in JAY FOLDBERG AND ANNE MILNE, DIVORCE MEDIATION: THEORY AND PRACTICE(1988) at 465–66. "The mediator intervention was not powerful enough to selectively reduce major psychological distress beyond the passage of time."

10. ROBERT A. BARUCH BUSH AND JOSEPH P. FOLDER, THE PROMISE OF MEDIATION: RESPONDING TO CONFLICT THROUGH EMPOWERMENT AND RECOGNITION, 20–21 (Jeffrey Z. Rubin ed., 1994); GARY J. FRIEDMAN, A GUIDE TO DIVORCE MEDIATION: HOW TO REACH A FAIR, LEGAL SETTLEMENT AT A FRACTION OF THE COST, 365–66 (1993).

CHAPTER 12

Be a Peacemaker

There is a great and growing desire for change in the world; change that ushers in a renewed commitment to ethical and spiritual values, that resolves conflicts peaceably, employing dialogue and non-violence, that upholds human rights and human dignity as well as human responsibility.

—Tenzin Gyatso, H. H. the XIVth Dalai Lama, 2008

You now have the perspectives, concepts, and skills to work with clients and other professionals to produce informed, fair, and lasting agreements. You also have an opportunity to establish a lucrative and sustainable professional practice. As you cultivate your practice in the years to come, your skills will continue to develop and evolve and you will inspire the next generation of collaborative practitioners.

This is good. This is very good. But it is not the end of your journey. Frankly, if over the next 20 years you merely facilitate divorce settlements more effectively and build a profitable practice, you will still be treading the same path that traditional divorce professionals have been doing for decades. What would you need to do to take your professional identity to the next level? Not just to glide, but to soar?

You have an opportunity to help families and to improve your own life that goes far beyond settling divorces and making your living more sanely. Just as the absence of war does not constitute peace, helping divorcing people stay out of court does not make you a peacemaker. If you reach just a bit further—reach to become a peacemaker—you have a profound chance to transform the lives of the families you serve as well as your own. On Monday morning, start thoughtfully and deliberately down a peacemaking path.

What Is a Peacemaker?

A "peacemaker" is defined as "one who makes especially by reconciling parties in conflict."[1] *Reconciliation* is defined as "restoring or creating harmony in the family."[2] Peacemaking, therefore, as we envision it, is an active process. Peace does not just happen. It is the product of concrete and deliberate words, acts, and choices. Harmony is, at its essence, allowing individual voices to ring out together to create a collective whole. It requires listening. The individual voices are essential. If any individual voice is weak or silenced, the resulting music will be that much more anemic, and it is in the collective interest to repair and restore it. Harmony in the family means that the system as a whole functions and that each person in that system functions within it. When we choose to be peacemakers, we commit ourselves to working deliberately toward a world in which we function together as the sum of individual voices, each of which is integral to the beauty and success of the whole.

Many lawyers are peacemakers; many are not. Peacemakers can be litigators, teachers, negotiators, or client counselors. Lawyer peacemakers come from all backgrounds, and there is no litmus test to earn your peacemaker card. Being a peacemaker is not defined by what role you play, but by how you actively restore and create harmony in your interactions with clients, colleagues, opposing parties, children and other members of the family, judges, court staff, witnesses, experts, and others in your community. Peacemaking is not a process, but a set of values, personal attributes, goals, and behaviors that guide your work. In other words, your core values as expressed through your work as a family lawyer will define whether you are a peacemaker. Peacemaking means devoting lawyering efforts to the improvement and repair of the parties' individual lives, repair of their relationships, and prevention of future conflict.

So where should you begin? The following are some points of departure.

Foster Mindfulness

Peacemakers cultivate personal peace and mindfulness and harness their core values and strongest personal attributes. Over 25 years ago, Leonard Riskin wrote his groundbreaking book on ADR and lawyers. Although he has made many other important contributions to our field, perhaps his most enduring hallmark is his work on mindfulness. Riskin defines mindfulness as "Mindfulness . . . means being aware, moment to moment, without judgment, of one's bodily sensations, thoughts, emotions, and consciousness. It is a systematic strategy for paying attention and for investigating one's own mind that one cultivates through meditation and then deploys in daily life." Mindfulness concentrates on helping us to do our jobs better by acquiring compassion, help us provide professional distance so that we do not get caught up in the emotions and reactivity of our clients, and free us from habitual mind-sets that hinder our creativity in negotiation or in the courtroom. Clark Freshman adds to this insight for our work during negotiation: "Mindful negotiation training could include training people to label positional impulses as they arise rather than acting on them. Existing meta-analyses suggest negotiators fail to identify opportunities for trade-offs in nearly half of their negotiations. Training negotiators to note a 'competing impulse' before rejecting a potential trade-off may cut this tendency substantially."

Identify Your Core Values

Another of our field's most inspirational thinkers, Nan Waller Burnett, hails from the mental health field. Her groundbreaking book *Calm in the Face of the Storm*, devotes each of its 365 chapters to a peacemaking value and how to better understand it and apply it in our work Exploring these core values to identify which ones resonate most with you will help you formulate a peacemaking signature.

Examples of Use of Key Core Values

Empowerment—People should have control over their own destiny and reduce their dependence on professionals, courts, and other experts.

Cooperation—People work more effectively and are more satisfied when they are working together.

Fairness—People should get a fair shake out of life, and human action and institutions should be designed with fairness as an outcome.

Satisfaction—Although the customer may not always be right, what clients say and believe about their satisfaction is important in evaluating professional service.

Options—People do better with choice. Do you take the time to make sure that you and those around you have choices for what to have for breakfast to how to obtain and finance healthcare?

Creativity—The process of carving out time and devoting energy to create new ideas and opportunities is a value in and of itself.

Hope—Having a belief in the possible and believing it should be shared with others who are paralyzed with fear and pessimism.

Reconciliation—Actively seek out to apologize to others or to accept a heartfelt apology from someone who has hurt you or someone you care for.

Transformation—Believe that you and others can change for the better. In the divorcing context, such transformation can be facilitated and accelerated by the way the divorce is resolved.

Rational Problem Solving—People can find solutions by thinking through and talking about difficult issues.

Peacemaking—Peace and the act of being peaceful way toward those in pain and conflict are values to which you should devote time and energy.

Although Burnett's book is intended for spiritual growth and comfort, you can adapt peacemaking values in developing a signature for your work with clients and professional colleagues. Burnett uses her daily themes as a loom on which she weaves a living definition of peacemaking. We have selected some of Burnett's daily themes and linked them with our vision of peacemaking values to offer strategies for integrating peacemaking in your work at the negotiation table and in collaboration with other family law professionals. As you review each value, read each of the steps aloud and then write out your answers as you develop them. Take proactive steps to discuss these values with colleagues at conferences and lunches and with friends and family. This is not a one-time conversation—it will develop and evolve throughout the rest of your legal career.

1. Explain each value and its importance in your work.
2. Think about how you share and communicate each value with clients and colleagues and how you implement each value in your work.
3. Ask yourself how each value can impact the process that you utilize to create settlements.
4. Reflect on how you can implement each value into expanding the services that you offer to clients to increase your profitability.
    a. **Peacemaking:** Do you believe that peace and the act of being peaceful toward those in pain and conflict are values in and of themselves? What impact can your direct application of peacemaking have on negotiations between divorcing spouses and on meeting their children's needs? Do you talk about peace with your clients, colleagues, clients, and staff and share with them a vision of peace in the world that goes beyond your professional practice? Do you design your office to invoke and foster peace for everyone who comes through the doors?
    b. **Empowerment:** Do you believe that your clients should have control over their own destiny and should reduce their dependence on professionals, courts, and other experts? How do you develop protocols to help your clients gain such empowerment over their own parenting and financial decisions? What can you say and do to assist clients to gain empowerment given your expertise, experience and power as a professional? How do you assure that the other lawyer can be empowered to fully participate at the negotiation table? How do you use your commitment to client empowerment on your website, at initial meetings, and during other opportunities to grow your practice?
    c. **Cooperation:** Do you believe that people work more effectively and are more satisfied when they are working together? What can you do to encourage your clients to cooperate with their spouses, especially when your clients are not feeling cooperative? How can you better cooperate with your colleagues in sharing practice materials that you have developed and referring cases that you do not want or cannot take on?
    d. **Fairness:** How do you believe that fairness for everyone in the divorcing family fits in with your work? How do you approach your clients with the importance of "fairness" (as opposed to just getting the issue behind them)? What standards do you utilize to measure fairness in a divorce on any one issue and in a global

settlement package? How do you react when you perceive that you have been treated unfairly by a colleague or a client (especially in a billing matter)?

e. **Satisfaction:** How important is the client's expressed (and unexpressed) satisfaction with the final settlement and with your competence, efforts, and fees in evaluating your professional services? How do you assess the satisfaction of clients? How do you reach out to your colleagues to determine whether they are satisfied with you in handling their referrals and working with you on cases?

f. **Options:** How do you ensure that clients have a full array of options, opportunities, and help to make good choices? How do you employ options to determine different professional roles or fee structures that you make available to potential clients? Are you open to options that your staff can use to approach their working day and prevent burnout?

g. **Creativity:** As you start each day, what efforts do you make to approach people and problems in a different way? What innovative methods do you use to support clients to design their own solutions creatively? When you host a meeting at your office, what creative ideas do you employ to make everyone comfortable and to set the stage for a successful settlement?

h. **Hope:** Do you have a positive view of the future, especially when the past has been negative? How do you share that forward-looking belief with others who are paralyzed with fear and pessimism? What strategies have you put in your toolbox to motivate clients with hope during setbacks in negotiations? After investing time and money to develop your practice, if you hit setbacks or a flat growth period, how do you remain hopeful for a successful future?

i. **Reconciliation:** What approach do you use with your clients to help them stay in or return to a relationships in their families? How do you actively encourage your clients to explore the possibility of apology and forgiveness? How do you reach out to apologize to clients, colleagues, and others when you believe you have caused hurt or acted badly? How do you accept a heartfelt apology or express forgiveness from a colleague who has hurt you in your professional life?

j. **Transformation:** How do you encourage your clients to change for the better during or after a divorce? How do you accelerate your own professional and personal change regarding interaction with your family law colleagues and ideas and developments generated in your field? How do you continually breathe new life into your law practice so that it remains cutting edge and stimulating for you?

k. **Rational Problem Solving:** How do you bring about solutions to seemingly intractable problems by thinking through and talking about difficult issues? How do you motivate discussions when tough issues and a gap between positions verge on impasse? How do you increase your profitability when you want

l. **Trust:** What are your feelings about the importance of building trust between your client who is hostile to his or her spouse and the spouse to create lasting agreements and healthy relationships? How do you reestablish or initiate trust with the other lawyer? How do you react when you believe that your trust has been betrayed by a member of your staff or by a colleague?

m. **Compassion:** How do sympathy and concern for the misfortune of others impact your daily work? How do you demonstrate compassion for your client, the other party, and the other lawyer? If colleagues are struggling with their clients or with you in your case or in their personal lives, how do you express compassion for them?

You may have other core values that are not on this list, such as love and belief in family/children; devotion to a divine being or religion; commitment to economic justice and fair distribution of wealth; preservation of natural resources and our planet; or the eradication of tyranny, mass disease, or other social ills. Whatever your core values may be, think about how you can incorporate them into your work as a family lawyer.

Actively Prevent Future Conflict

Perhaps the greatest difference you can make as a peacemaker is to add conflict prevention to your lawyering work. By the time people enter into mediation, there has already been a failure because a dispute has escalated to the point that requires a mediator's intervention. Just as doctors try to prevent relapse or recurrence and promote future health when treating the symptoms of illness or disease, it is our duty and opportunity to help our clients minimize future recurrence of conflict and maximize future harmony. We can do that using tools such as dispute resolution clauses in contracts between parties, agreement implementation calendars to remind parties about what they have agreed to (and find out if additional facilitation is necessary), and conflict-wellness checkups (for examples, see www.mostenmediation.com/legal/wellness.html) as discussed in Chapter 11.

Apply Peacemaking to Your Daily Lawyering Work

You are in charge of whether there is a next step in moving toward peacemaking rather than just settling cases. If your choice is affirmative, the following are some avenues in which you might walk your peacemaking walk.

Get Training in Mediation and Collaborative Law

If you have spent most of your professional career learning substantive family law and how to write court motions and to better conduct cross-examination, you may need to go back to school to learn new skills and perspectives. If you invest the time and money to take such training, you will be learning more than the curriculum in your bulky training manual. The relationships you form during training seminars can give you support in your new career path. You will have a shared experiences and a common set of skills. During the training, pay attention to the other participants as much as to the material and process. Arrive early and stay late (as much as possible given your other responsibilities). Be open to invitations to go off-site for lunch or an evening meal. Treat training like a trip out of town so that you are not distracted by calls or other obligations of your practice. Follow up after the course with other training participants. They can be your core for a study group or structured reading program for representing clients in a peacemaking way.

Collaborate with Peacemaking Lawyers, Mediators, and Other Professionals

Generally, peacemaking lawyers are generous to colleagues. Be ready to accept an invitation to observe as a fly on the wall, attend a meeting or conference of a local interdisciplinary organization, or adapt the practice materials of others to your evolving family law practice. And be sure to return the favor. The input by another family lawyer or mediator about your performance in a recent case can be invaluable to you. Your reciprocal feedback can bring new ideas and approaches to your colleagues' work. Follow up on the help from your colleagues with acknowledgments for their generosity. Send them clippings or forward e-mail links that you believe will be helpful to them. Building your practice and reputation can have payoffs for decades to come.

Honor Your Colleagues

In this book, we have suggested the following mantra when reviewing mediated settlements: "Let it go!" This means that "winning" is not pushing every technical point or making sure that no money is left on the table. "Winning" means making sure that your client understands trade-offs and is comfortable with the overall deal.

The same mantra, "Let It Go," applies to working with other lawyers in your community. You might observe that a lawyer has intimidated your client. Let it go. If you hear the other lawyer misstating the rules for calculating capital gain on a family residence, let it go. Letting it go does *not* mean that you will be negligent or dilatory in making sure that your client gets proper information or is treated respectfully. Letting it go *does* mean that the goodwill and relationship of colleagues may mean more in the long run (including this case) than "calling out" someone and causing a loss of face or respect. Private debriefing sessions are the place to discuss what worked and what can be done better next time. Gentle humor can be an invaluable and disarming method of making a point about civility without attacking or putting someone on the defensive.

After one challenging settlement conference at Liz's office, knowing that the opposing attorneys had traveled far and were likely to get stuck in rush hour traffic if they drove straight home, she invited them to the restaurant downstairs for a drink. Everyone was able to move beyond the intractability and frustrations of the day and enjoy one another's company and insights in a spirit of mutual respect and collegiality. One of the opposing attorneys, who had been practicing law for over 30 years, commented at the end of the evening that this was the first time he had ever received this kind of invitation from another attorney after a settlement conference. Try to make deposits of positive acknowledgment and good acts and minimize withdrawals due to unnecessary conflicts or control struggles. It is a difficult balance, but one from which you and your family law colleagues will benefit.

Contribute to Family Law Organizations

In working with colleagues on issues of importance to our field, perhaps you have experienced or observed turf struggles and adversarial wrangling over issues that affect us and the public.

Our colleagues have strong views about issues that can be viewed from different perspectives. Regardless of the importance of any one issue, it is important that we dialogue rather than confrontationally debate these issues (see Linda Ellinor and Glenna Gerard, *Dialogue* 1998). How we speak with each other is not less important than the points we want to make. We need to watch the tone of our public discourse on listservs and during organizational outreach. We should stress our commonality and form alliances with other organizations and professionals regardless of differences over any one issue. Just like at the table with our clients, our model is more than what we say. Collaboration with colleagues has its own rewards, many of which are unforeseen at the time.

One doesn't have to hunt for concrete opportunities to work positively with family law colleagues toward common goals. There are nonprofit family law organizations in most communities that need committed, ethical support, and help. Promoting access to family law services for the indigent and working poor is one way in which collaborative efforts by family law professionals can effect positive change.

Your Next Steps in Using Peacemaking to Improve and Expand Your Practice

As lawyers, we often suggest to the parties we serve that they consider the "next steps" to take in implementing their agreement. A pledge to take "next steps," especially when they are specific and concrete, is an essential key to making key changes. Here are some "next steps" that can be taken to transform your lawyering work into peacemaking:

1. Make peacemaking your life's work. Talk about it; study it; create a personal mission statement. Create a career plan and have a vision of your role in the field—5, 10, 20, and 30 years from now.

2. Perform a peacemaker impact study in the work you do. Test every projected plan to gain skills, help your clients, or build your practice by whether and how such a plan reflects peacemaking.
3. Add new roles or services within your current job or practice to enhance peacemaking. For example, think about how to educate members of your local bar association Family Law Section about peacemaking or consider developing a mentoring program to help local lawyers who are going through disputes with each other or in their personal lives.
4. Become a preventive conflict-wellness thinker and provider. Use the preventive legal wellness checkup when clients first come in and after you have helped them achieve a settlement. Test settlement terms by how they will help restore future peace in the family.
5. Constantly reflect on your own professional behavior and monitor your humility and openness to new approaches. Make sure you treat your staff, court clerks, and clients' meddlesome extended family members with the same respect you offer to esteemed colleagues and others you value highly.
6. Embrace others through the implementation of peacemaking values. This can be a challenging and often lonely profession. We need mutual help and support—and to be reminded daily of the core values that shape our work, improve our lives, and contribute to our society.

Notes

1. Merriam-Webster Online.
2. *Id.*

Glossary

Active listening: The process of picking up another's message and sending it back in a reflective statement that mirrors what you have heard. Active listening responses can mirror both content and feelings. Active listening is important not only to show that you hear and understand another, but also to motivate that other person's full expression. [David Binder, Paul Bergman, and Susan Price, *Lawyers as Counselors 52–58 (1991)*]

Agenda setting: The process of working with clients to determine what issues must be addressed as well as the order in which these issues will be discussed. The order and manner in which issues are discussed is an important tool used by the mediator to minimize dispute and bring about settlement.

Alternative Dispute Resolution (ADR): Traditionally viewed as dispute resolution processes used as alternatives to litigation. ADR, which includes negotiation, mediation, arbitration, and various hybrid forms, focuses on new and creative methods used to resolve disputes. Today, ADR is institutionalized and incorporated into a variety of court processes.

Arbitration: A dispute resolution procedure, designed by the parties to suit their particular needs, that involves the submission of proof and arguments to a third-party neutral (selected by the parties) who has the power to issue a decision, which can be binding or nonbinding. Generally, arbitration hearings are more informal than court hearings, and the rules of evidence are not strictly applied. [Stephen Goldberg, Frank E.A. Sander, and Nancy Rogers, *Dispute Resolution: Negotiation, Mediation and Other Processes 199–200 (1992)*]

Bargaining range: A field of options, any one of which disputants would prefer to the resulting consequences of terminating negotiations. In the best possible scenario, the parties will have overlapping bargaining ranges so that there are mutually satisfactory solutions or divisions of resources. [Christopher Moore, *The Mediation Process: Practical Strategies for Resolving Conflict 219–21 (1986)*]

Best Alternative to Negotiated Agreement (BATNA): The notion that parties should know the likely results that will occur if they do not negotiate with another person. One who is unaware of the results that may be obtained if negotiations are unsuccessful runs the risk of entering into an unsatisfactory agreement or rejecting a satisfactory agreement. In addition, parties should know as much as possible about the other party's BATNA. [Roger Fisher and William Ury, *Getting to Yes (1981)*]

Brainstorming: The process by which ideas are rapidly generated by a group. Brainstorming is often useful because it separates the generation process from evaluation procedures so that the group has multiple options to consider. [Christopher Moore, *The Mediation Process: Practical Strategies for Resolving Conflict 193 (1986)*]

Breakout rooms: Rooms that are used during mediation for caucuses between parties and the mediator and discussions between clients and their lawyers. Breakout rooms can also provide a place for parties to wait when other discussions and caucuses are taking place. This function is particularly important in the family law context because estranged spouses are often uncomfortable waiting in the same room. These rooms should be equipped with a telephone that the parties and their lawyers are free to use.

Caucus: Part of the mediation session in which the mediator meets privately with each party or a combination of the parties. To allow parties to be more candid and explore various ideas that they are not comfortable sharing with the other party, caucuses are a very important tool for mediators. In addition, caucuses provide a good opportunity for the mediator to do reality testing with the parties.

Client coach: As part of a client's preparation for negotiations, a lawyer can teach the client some of the essentials of negotiation theory and give supervised individual training to the client in preparation for the mediation session. In addition, the lawyer can help the client assess the strengths and weaknesses of various proposals and help the client develop not only initial proposals, but also backup proposals based on anticipated responses.

Co-mediation: Mediation is frequently conducted by interdisciplinary teams, often consisting of therapists along with lawyers. Co-mediation can be effective as a result of the diversity of mediation teams (such as gender, expertise, style). The teams can work together at all times or meet with couples (or individual spouses in caucus) separately.

Comprehensive mediation: Mediation model in which a therapist/mediator works with couples on all issues involved in a family dispute. Issues related to child custody, economic distribution, child support, and alimony are addressed alongside the couple's emotional and conduct issues.

Conciliation: Traditionally used interchangeably with *mediation*, the term usually denotes a process that strives to minimize unnecessary conflict and build a positive psychological relationship between parties. Conciliation is the psychological component of mediation in which the third party attempts to create an atmosphere of trust and cooperation that is conducive to negotiation. [Christopher Moore, *The Mediation Process: Practical Strategies for Resolving Conflict* 124 (1986)]

Confidential Mini-Evaluation (CME): A nonbinding expert's opinion used to defuse custody conflicts when mediation does not resolve the dispute. The CME gives the parties the input of an experienced custody evaluator without the cost, delay, adversarial posturing, and virtually binding decisions of a court-appointed evaluator being imposed on the family and being part of the permanent court record.

Confidentiality: In most jurisdictions, negotiations concerning a disputed legal claim are not admissible in evidence to prove the claim or its amount (see Fed. R. Evid. 408 or comparable state rules). The rule results in exclusion of evidence in most, but not all, circumstances. Courts have found several types of evidence outside the purview of the rule (e.g., information that is also requested through the discovery process and negotiations not involving legal claims). [Steven Goldberg, Frank E.A. Sander, and Nancy Rogers, *Dispute Resolution: Negotiation, Mediation, and other Processes* 179–80 (1992)]

Conjoint sessions *(see also co-mediation)*: Mediation sessions involving mediation teams that work together throughout the entire session, including intake, joint sessions, and caucuses. During conjoint sessions, mediation teams, often consisting of lawyers and therapists, do not necessarily retain their separate professional roles.

Consensus building: A mediative process, often used with large groups, involving multiple conflicts. Consensus building often takes place over an extended period of time and is conducive to large public policy disputes, such as disputes involving environmental issues. [Kimberlee K. Kovach, *Mediation: Principles and Practice* 244–45 (1994)]

Countertransference *(see also transference)*: Countertransference involves not only the professional's distorted perceptions of the client, but also distorted expectations of his or her services and the outcome of those services. (Rhonda Feinberg and James Tom Greene, "Transference and Countertransference Issues in Professional Relationships," *Family Law Quarterly*, Vol. 28, Spring 1995, at 111)

Dispute resolution manager: Role played by attorneys that includes educating the client about dispute resolution options both inside the courthouse and in the private sector, helping the client select the appropriate options, and effectively representing the client within that process to obtain settlement.

Early Neutral Evaluation (ENE): A process, designed by federal district courts in northern California, that encourages parties to identify the real areas of agreement and dispute and helps them develop an approach to discovery that focuses promptly on central issues and discloses key evidence. The goal of ENE is to provide parties with an early opportunity to try to negotiate a settlement. [Joshua D. Rosenberg and H. Jay Folberg, *Symposium on Civil Justice Reform: Alternative Dispute Resolution: An Empirical Analysis,* 46 Stan. L. Rev. 1487 *(1994)]*

Flip chart: A large, prominently displayed pad of paper used by the mediator and parties. Flip charts are often used by parties in presenting proposals. Unlike information written on a white board, information on a flip chart can be preserved. In addition, various pages of the flip chart can be posted around a mediation room to serve as a review of previous discussions and/or settlement progress that has been made.

Framing *(see also reframing)*: The manner in which a conflict situation, issue, or interest is conceptualized or defined. Individuals generally frame situations according to history and direct experience (subjective reality). (CDR Associates)

Impartiality: The obligation of a mediator to maintain a posture toward parties free from bias or favoritism in either word or action. Impartiality implies a commitment to aid *all parties* in reaching a mutually satisfactory agreement. [Christopher Moore, *Center for Dispute Resolution Code of Professional Conduct (1982)]*

Impasse: In mediation, parties often reach a point where they are stuck on particular issues. Often a declaration of a bottom line by the parties does not mean they are unwilling to move; instead, it is a bargaining strategy. An important skill for mediators involves effectively dealing with situations where an impasse is evident. [Kimberlee K. Kovach, *Mediation: Principles and Practice 128–29 (1994)]*

Interest-based bargaining: Negotiation style focusing on the interests of the parties. Focusing on interests may uncover the existence of mutual or complementary interests that will make agreement possible. Negotiators can seek integrative solutions that meet as many of the needs of both parties as possible. [Roger Fisher and William Ury, *Getting to Yes*; Christopher Moore, *The Mediation Process: Practical Strategies for Resolving Conflict 35 (1986)]*

Intervention: Words or actions of the mediator that enter into the family system for the purpose of altering the power and dynamics by influencing beliefs or behaviors of individual parties, by providing knowledge or information, or by using a more effective negotiation process and thereby helping participants settle contested issues. [Christopher Moore, *The Mediation Process: Practical Strategies for Resolving Conflict 14 (1986)]*

Judicial case management: Process in which parties voluntarily give a judge all discretion to determine interim orders and amount and order of discovery and to hold settlement conferences. The judge is available to the parties by phone so that emergency court hearings are rarely needed. Parties waive not only their rights to appeal and other judicial review, but also their rights to sue their family lawyers who have consented to the use of the process.

Mandatory mediation: Most jurisdictions have court-annexed mediation programs that generally require participation by litigants. Mediations often take place in the courthouse and may be conducted by court staff mediators, private mediators, or pro bono volunteer lawyers. Although child custody and visitation are the issues most often mandated by court-annexed mediation, some court systems provide for mediation of economic issues as well.

Mandatory Settlement Conference (MSC): Procedure by courts that encourages the parties to attempt to settle their case before trial. Generally held within 30 to 60 days of trial dates, MSCs occur at a point when parties are expected to have completed trial preparation.

Med-arb: Process in which a neutral functions first as a mediator, helping the parties to arrive at a mutually acceptable outcome. If mediation fails, the same neutral then serves as an arbitrator, issuing a final and binding decision. [Stephen Goldberg, Frank E.A. Sander, and Nancy Rogers, *Dispute Resolution: Negotiation, Mediation, and Other Processes 226 (1992)*]

Mediation: A process by which a third-party neutral facilitates parties in resolving a dispute. The role of the mediator is to facilitate communications between the parties, assist them in focusing on the real issues of the dispute, and generate options for settlement. The goal of mediation is that the parties themselves arrive at a mutually acceptable resolution of the dispute. [Kimberlee K. Kovach, *Mediation: Principles and Practice 17 (1994)*]

Mediation brief: Generally used for single-session mediations, briefs are written for the purpose of educating and persuading the other spouse about a party's interests and goals. Briefs must be researched and drafted carefully to be used as a tool of persuasion.

Multisession mediation: Mediation model in which participants work out a schedule of mediation sessions ranging from one-half hour to four hours in length. The goal for each session is to accomplish as much as possible with the understanding that the parties will continue meeting until all of the issues have been resolved.

One issue mediation: Issues often arise in mediation that require experts from another field. These experts are brought in to mediate a single issue. For example, a real estate broker can be brought in to help the parties determine the fair market value of a house.

Positional bargaining *(see also zero-sum game)*: Negotiation style based on a perception that contested resources are limited and a distributive solution, one that allocates shares of gains and losses to each party, is the only solution. [Christopher Moore, *The Mediation Process: Practical Strategies for Resolving Conflict 35 (1988)*]

Power imbalance: In many instances, an imbalance of power between the parties might bring about an unfair result. Because mediation lacks many of the formalities and safeguards of adjudication, there is a concern that, as a result of gender, cultural, language, education, or class differences of participants, certain parties may have unfair advantages in the mediation process. In light of the mediator's role as a neutral, the extent to which mediators should address these power imbalances is unclear. [Trina Grillo, *The Mediation Alternative*, 100 Yale L. J. 1545 (1991)]

Preliminary joint session: The most common format of mediation involves the parties initially meeting jointly with the mediator. The rationale behind preliminary joint sessions is to make both parties feel part of the process, to create or reinforce trust in the mediator that there will be no secret or hidden agendas, and to show the parties that they can negotiate directly with one another.

Preventive mediation: The use of mediation in preventing future conflict. It can be used in the divorce context to educate both parties (and their lawyers) as to how to avoid future problems, not just with each other, after the judgment is entered. Preventive mediation can be especially useful in sparing family members (especially children) future conflict and pain if either spouse breaks up with a new romantic partner.

Reality testing: The role of the mediator in working with the parties to assess the realistic possibility of attaining what they are hoping for. Because reality testing often involves issues that are sensitive or personal to the parties, the mediator should do reality testing in private caucuses. [Kimberlee K. Kovach, *Mediation: Principles and Practice 166–68 (1994)*]

Reframing *(see also framing)*: The process of changing how a person or a party to a conflict conceptualizes his or her own or another's attitudes, behaviors, issues, or interests or how the structure of a situation is defined. Reframing can be used to identify underlying interests; make a transition from positional to interest-based bargaining; soften or harden demands, modify timing or deadlines, decrease or enhance the explicitness of threats, remove emotions from communications, and remove value-laden language from communications. (CDR Associates)

Settlement weeks: A court system's attempt to maximize judicial and volunteer lawyer resources to resolve outstanding cases through mediation and other settlement procedures.

Simulated coaching: As part of preparing a client for mediation, a lawyer can help clients by practicing several scenarios of issues likely to be raised in mediation. As a result of these simulations, the client receives an orientation about possibilities and an early reality check. In addition, simulations increase the client's comfort level in the actual mediation.

Single-session mediation: Mediation model in which parties, counsel, and mediator attempt to reach agreement in a single session. As a result of impasse or other issues that block progress, single-session mediations often must adjourn with an agreed-upon set date to continue the mediation.

Summary letter of mediation sessions: Correspondence initiated by the mediator to parties, counsel, and other authorized persons (e.g., accountants, therapists) to set forth agreements made, areas of disagreement, agendas, assignments of parties, and observations of the mediator to facilitate the process.

Transference *(see also countertransference):* A client's distortions in professional relationships where the client has expectations not grounded in current reality but on past personal history, self-image, adopted role in life, naïve hopes and expectations of a fairy-tale outcome of self-validation, or perhaps a self-fulfilling prophecy of defeat. (Rhonda Feinberg and James Tom Greene, "Transference and Countertransference Issues of Professional Relationships," *Family Law Quarterly*, Vol 29, Spring 1995, at 111)

Transformative mediation: A view of mediation that emphasizes its capacity to transform the character of both individual disputants and society as a whole. Because of its informality and consensuality, mediation can allow parties to define problems and goals in their own terms; consequently, the important role of these problems and goals in the parties' lives is validated. Rather than placing an emphasis only on reaching agreement, transformative mediation focuses on (1) empowerment by instilling the parties with a greater sense of self-respect, self-reliance, and self-confidence and (2) recognition by engendering acknowledgment and concern for others as human beings. [Robert Baruch Bush and Joseph Folger, *The Promise of Mediation 20, 21 (1994)]*

Trust building: Mediators strive to build trust between parties to reinforce beliefs that commitments and agreements will be carried out. Mediators can make specific interventions that will build trust between the parties and change their perceptions. These techniques include creating situations in which parties must perform joint tasks, vocally identifying commonalities, and facilitating a discussion of their perceptions of one another. [Roger Fisher, *International Mediation: A Working Guide (1978)]*

Unbundling *(also known as discrete task representation)*: Unbundling offers clients a middle ground between dispensing with lawyers altogether and signing on for full-service representation. In unbundling, the client determines which services will be performed by the client and the extent and depth to which the lawyer will perform the services engaged.

White board *(also known as dry erase board):* Large, erasable boards that are used by parties and the mediator to write down various ideas. Because white boards are erasable, they are particularly useful in brainstorming and formulating settlement proposals. To preserve information written on a white board, it is often necessary for participants to pause and copy information onto pads or flip chart paper.

Zero-sum game: The assumption that negotiations will end up with a winner and loser as a result of both parties trying to get equally valued limited resources. The adversarial paradigm often incorporates a zero-sum approach to negotiation.

Assumption of total competition of interests and zero-sum outcomes hinders the potential for creative solutions inherent in situations where parties attribute differing values to the issues. Because trade-offs between issues are possible, when more than one issue is discussed, negotiations often lose their zero-sum game qualities. [Carrie Menkel-Meadow, *Toward Another View of Legal Negotiation: The Structure of Problem Solving,* 31 UCLA L. Rev. *754, 783–89* (1991)]

Appendix A

Model Standards of Practice for Family and Divorce Mediation (2000)

Convening Organizations

The Association of Family and Conciliation Courts
The Family Law Section of the American Bar Association
National Council of Dispute Resolution Organizations (NCDRO)

Overview and Definitions

Family and divorce mediation ("family mediation" or "mediation") is a process in which a mediator, an impartial third party, facilitates the resolution of family disputes by promoting the participants' voluntary agreement. The family mediator assists communication, encourages understanding and focuses the participants on their individual and common interests. The family mediator works with the participants to explore options, make decisions and reach their own agreements.

Family mediation is not a substitute for the need for family members to obtain independent legal advice or counseling or therapy. Nor is it appropriate for all families. However, experience has established that family mediation is a valuable option for many families because it can:

1. increase the self-determination of participants and their ability to communicate;
2. promote the best interests of children; and
3. reduce the economic and emotional costs associated with the resolution of family disputes.

Effective mediation requires that the family mediator be qualified by training, experience and temperament; that the mediator be impartial; that the participants reach their decisions voluntarily; that their decisions be based on sufficient factual data; that the mediator be aware of the impact of culture and diversity; and that the best interests of children be taken into account. Further, the mediator should also be prepared to identify families whose history includes domestic abuse or child abuse.

These *Model Standards of Practice for Family and Divorce Mediation* ("*Model Standards*") aim to perform three major functions:

1. to serve as a guide for the conduct of family mediators;
2. to inform the mediating participants of what they can expect; and
3. to promote public confidence in mediation as a process for resolving family disputes.

The *Model Standards* are aspirational in character. They describe good practices for family mediators. They are not intended to create legal rules or standards of liability.

The *Model Standards* include different levels of guidance:

1. Use of the term "may" in a *Standard* is the lowest strength of guidance and indicates a practice that the family mediator should consider adopting but which can be deviated from in the exercise of good professional judgment.
2. Most of the *Standards* employ the term "should" which indicates that the practice described in the *Standard* is highly desirable and should be departed from only with very strong reason.
3. The rarer use of the term "shall" in a *Standard* is a higher level of guidance to the family mediator, indicating that the mediator should not have discretion to depart from the practice described.

Standard I

A family mediator shall recognize that mediation is based on the principle of self-determination by the participants.

A. Self-determination is the fundamental principle of family mediation. The mediation process relies upon the ability of participants to make their own voluntary and informed decisions.
B. The primary role of a family mediator is to assist the participants to gain a better understanding of their own needs and interests and the needs and interests of others and to facilitate agreement among the participants.
C. A family mediator should inform the participants that they may seek information and advice from a variety of sources during the mediation process.

D. A family mediator shall inform the participants that they may withdraw from family mediation at any time and are not required to reach an agreement in mediation.
E. The family mediator's commitment shall be to the participants and the process. Pressure from outside of the mediation process shall never influence the mediator to coerce participants to settle.

Standard II

A family mediator shall be qualified by education and training to undertake the mediation.

A. To perform the family mediator's role, a mediator should:
   1. have knowledge of family law;
   2. have knowledge of and training in the impact of family conflict on parents, children, and other participants, including knowledge of child development, domestic abuse and child abuse and neglect;
   3. have education and training specific to the process of mediation;
   4. be able to recognize the impact of culture and diversity.
B. Family mediators should provide information to the participants about the mediator's relevant training, education and expertise.

Standard III

A family mediator shall facilitate the participants' understanding of what mediation is and assess their capacity to mediate before the participants reach an agreement to mediate.

A. Before family mediation begins a mediator should provide the participants with an overview of the process and its purposes, including:
   1. informing the participants that reaching an agreement in family mediation is consensual in nature, that a mediator is an impartial facilitator, and that a mediator may not impose or force any settlement on the parties;
   2. distinguishing family mediation from other processes designed to address family issues and disputes;
   3. informing the participants that any agreements reached will be reviewed by the court when court approval is required;
   4. informing the participants that they may obtain independent advice from attorneys, counsel, advocates, accountants, therapists, or other professionals during the mediation process;

5. advising the participants, in appropriate cases, that they can seek the advice of religious figures, elders, or other significant persons in their community whose opinions they value;
6. discussing, if applicable, the issue of separate sessions with the participants, a description of the circumstances in which the mediator may meet alone with any of the participants, or with any third party and the conditions of confidentiality concerning these separate sessions;
7. informing the participants that the presence or absence of other persons at a mediation, including attorneys, counselors or advocates, depends on the agreement of the participants and the mediator, unless a statute or regulation otherwise requires or the mediator believes that the presence of another person is required or may be beneficial because of a history or threat of violence or other serious coercive activity by a participant.
8. describing the obligations of the mediator to maintain the confidentiality of the mediation process and its results as well as any exceptions to confidentiality;
9. advising the participants of the circumstances under which the mediator may suspend or terminate the mediation process and that a participant has a right to suspend or terminate mediation at any time.

B. The participants should sign a written agreement to mediate their dispute and the terms and conditions thereof within a reasonable time after first consulting the family mediator.
C. The family mediator should be alert to the capacity and willingness of the participants to mediate before proceeding with the mediation and throughout the process. A mediator should not agree to conduct the mediation if the mediator reasonably believes one or more of the participants is unable or unwilling to participate.
D. Family mediators should not accept a dispute for mediation if they cannot satisfy the expectations of the participants concerning the timing of the process.

Standard IV

A family mediator shall conduct the mediation process in an impartial manner. A family mediator shall disclose all actual and potential grounds of bias and conflicts of interest reasonably known to the mediator. The participants shall be free to retain the mediator by an informed, written waiver of the conflict of interest. However, if a bias or conflict of interest clearly impairs a mediator's impartiality, the mediator shall withdraw regardless of the express agreement of the participants.

A. Impartiality means freedom from favoritism or bias in word, action, or appearance, and includes a commitment to assist all participants as opposed to any one individual.
B. Conflict of interest means any relationship between the mediator, any participant, or the subject matter of the dispute, that compromises or appears to compromise the mediator's impartiality.
C. A family mediator should not accept a dispute for mediation if the family mediator cannot be impartial.
D. A family mediator should identify and disclose potential grounds of bias or conflict of interest upon which a mediator's impartiality might reasonably be questioned. Such disclosure should be made prior to the start of a mediation and in time to allow the participants to select an alternate mediator.
E. A family mediator should resolve all doubts in favor of disclosure. All disclosures should be made as soon as practical after the mediator becomes aware of the bias or potential conflict of interest. The duty to disclose is a continuing duty.
F. A family mediator should guard against bias or partiality based on the participants' personal characteristics, background, or performance at the mediation.
G. A family mediator should avoid conflicts of interest in recommending the services of other professionals.
H. A family mediator shall not use information about participants obtained in a mediation for personal gain or advantage
I. A family mediator should withdraw pursuant to *Standard IX* if the mediator believes the mediator's impartiality has been compromised or a conflict of interest has been identified and has not been waived by the participants.

Standard V

A family mediator shall fully disclose and explain the basis of any compensation, fees, and charges to the participants.

A. The participants should be provided with sufficient information about fees at the outset of mediation to determine if they wish to retain the services of the mediator.
B. The participants' written agreement to mediate their dispute should include a description of their fee arrangement with the mediator.
C. A mediator should not enter into a fee agreement which is contingent upon the results of the mediation or the amount of the settlement.
D. A mediator should not accept a fee for referral of a matter to another mediator or to any other person.

E. Upon termination of mediation, a mediator should return any unearned fee to the participants.

Standard VI

A family mediator shall structure the mediation process so that the participants make decisions based on sufficient information and knowledge.

A. The mediator should facilitate full and accurate disclosure and the acquisition and development of information during mediation so that the participants can make informed decisions. This may be accomplished by encouraging participants to consult appropriate experts.
B. Consistent with standards of impartiality and preserving participant self-determination, a mediator may provide the participants with information that the mediator is qualified by training or experience to provide. The mediator shall not provide therapy or legal advice.
C. The mediator should recommend that the participants obtain independent legal representation before concluding an agreement.
D. If the participants so desire, the mediator should allow attorneys, counsel, or advocates for the participants to be present at the mediation sessions.
E. With the agreement of the participants, the mediator may document the participants' resolution of their dispute. The mediator should inform the participants that any agreement should be reviewed by an independent attorney before it is signed.

Standard VII

A family mediator shall maintain the confidentiality of all information acquired in the mediation process, unless the mediator is permitted or required to reveal the information by law or agreement of the participants.

A. The mediator should discuss the participants' expectations of confidentiality with them prior to undertaking the mediation. The written agreement to mediate should include provisions concerning confidentiality.
B. Prior to undertaking the mediation the mediator should inform the participants of the limitations of confidentiality such as statutory, judicially, or ethically mandated reporting.

C. The mediator shall disclose a participant's threat of suicide or violence against any person to the threatened person and the appropriate authorities if the mediator believes such threat is likely to be acted upon as permitted by law.
D. If the mediator holds private sessions with a participant, the obligations of confidentiality concerning those sessions should be discussed and agreed upon prior to the sessions.
E. If subpoenaed or otherwise noticed to testify or to produce documents the mediator should inform the participants immediately. The mediator should not testify or provide documents in response to a subpoena without an order of the court if the mediator reasonably believes doing so would violate an obligation of confidentiality to the participants.

Standard VIII

A family mediator shall assist participants in determining how to promote the best interests of children.

A. The mediator should encourage the participants to explore the range of options available for separation or post-divorce parenting arrangements and their respective costs and benefits. Referral to a specialist in child development may be appropriate for these purposes. The topics for discussion may include, among others:
 1. information about community resources and programs that can help the participants and their children cope with the consequences of family reorganization and family violence;
 2. problems that continuing conflict creates for children's development and what steps might be taken to ameliorate the effects of conflict on the children;
 3. development of a parenting plan that covers the children's physical residence and decision-making responsibilities for the children, with appropriate levels of detail as agreed to by the participants;
 4. the possible need to revise parenting plans as the developmental needs of the children evolve over time; and
 5. encouragement to the participants to develop appropriate dispute resolution mechanisms to facilitate future revisions of the parenting plan
B. The mediator should be sensitive to the impact of culture and religion on parenting philosophy and other decisions.
C. The mediator shall inform any court-appointed representative for the children of the mediation. If a representative for the children participates, the mediator should, at the outset, discuss the effect of that participation on the mediation process and the

confidentiality of the mediation with the participants. Whether the representative of the children participates or not, the mediator shall provide the representative with the resulting agreements insofar as they relate to the children.
D. Except in extraordinary circumstances, the children should not participate in the mediation process without the consent of both parents and the children's court-appointed representative.
E. Prior to including the children in the mediation process, the mediator should consult with the parents and the children's court-appointed representative about whether the children should participate in the mediation process and the form of that participation.
F. The mediator should inform all concerned about the available options for the children's participation (which may include personal participation, an interview with a mental health professional, or the mediator reporting to the parents, or a videotape statement) and discuss the costs and benefits of each with the participants.

Standard IX

A family mediator shall recognize a family situation involving child abuse or neglect and take appropriate steps to shape the mediation process accordingly.

A. As used in these Standards, child abuse or neglect is defined by applicable state law.
B. A mediator shall not undertake a mediation in which the family situation has been assessed to involve child abuse or neglect without appropriate and adequate training.
C. If the mediator has reasonable grounds to believe that a child of the participants is abused or neglected within the meaning of the jurisdiction's child abuse and neglect laws, the mediator shall comply with applicable child protection laws.
   1. The mediator should encourage the participants to explore appropriate services for the family.
   2. The mediator should consider the appropriateness of suspending or terminating the mediation process in light of the allegations.

Standard X

A family mediator shall recognize a family situation involving domestic abuse and take appropriate steps to shape the mediation process accordingly.

A. As used in these Standards, domestic abuse includes domestic violence as defined by applicable state law and issues of control and intimidation.
B. A mediator shall not undertake a mediation in which the family situation has been assessed to involve domestic abuse without appropriate and adequate training.
C. Some cases are not suitable for mediation because of safety, control, or intimidation issues. A mediator should make a reasonable effort to screen for the existence of domestic abuse prior to entering into an agreement to mediate. The mediator should continue to assess for domestic abuse throughout the mediation process.
D. If domestic abuse appears to be present, the mediator shall consider taking measures to insure the safety of participants and the mediator including, among others:
   1. establishing appropriate security arrangements;
   2. holding separate sessions with the participants even without the agreement of all participants;
   3. allowing a friend, representative, advocate, counsel, or attorney to attend the mediation sessions;
   4. encouraging the participants to be represented by an attorney, counsel, or an advocate throughout the mediation process;
   5. referring the participants to appropriate community resources;
   6. suspending or terminating the mediation sessions, with appropriate steps to protect the safety of the participants.
E. The mediator should facilitate the participants' formulation of parenting plans that protect the physical safety and psychological well-being of themselves and their children.

Standard XI

A family mediator shall suspend or terminate the mediation process when the mediator reasonably believes that a participant is unable to effectively participate or for other compelling reasons.

A. Circumstances under which a mediator should consider suspending or terminating the mediation, may include, among others:
   1. the safety of a participant or well-being of a child is threatened;
   2. a participant has or is threatening to abduct a child;
   3. a participant is unable to participate due to the influence of drugs, alcohol, or physical or mental condition;
   4. the participants are about to enter into an agreement that the mediator reasonably believes to be unconscionable;

5. a participant is using the mediation to further illegal conduct;
6. a participant is using the mediation process to gain an unfair advantage;
7. if the mediator believes the mediator's impartiality has been compromised in accordance with *Standard IV*.

B. If the mediator does suspend or terminate the mediation, the mediator should take all reasonable steps to minimize prejudice or inconvenience to the participants which may result.

Standard XII

A family mediator shall be truthful in the advertisement and solicitation for mediation.

A. Mediators should refrain from promises and guarantees of results. A mediator should not advertise statistical settlement data or settlement rates.
B. Mediators should accurately represent their qualifications. In an advertisement or other communication, a mediator may make reference to meeting state, national, or private organizational qualifications only if the entity referred to has a procedure for qualifying mediators and the mediator has been duly granted the requisite status.

Standard XIII

A family mediator shall acquire and maintain professional competence in mediation.

A. Mediators should continuously improve their professional skills and abilities by, among other activities, participating in relevant continuing education programs and should regularly engage in self-assessment.
B. Mediators should participate in programs of peer consultation and should help train and mentor the work of less experienced mediators.
C. Mediators should continuously strive to understand the impact of culture and diversity on the mediator's practice.

Appendix: Special Policy Considerations for State Regulation of Family Mediators and Court Affiliated Programs

The *Model Standards* recognize the *National Standards for Court Connected Dispute Resolution Programs* (1992). There are also state and local regulations governing such programs and family mediators. The following principles of organization and practice, however, are especially important for regulation of mediators and court-connected family mediation programs. They are worthy of separate mention.

A. Individual states or local courts should set standards and qualifications for family mediators including procedures for evaluations and handling grievances against mediators. In developing these standards and qualifications, regulators should consult with appropriate professional groups, including professional associations of family mediators.

B. When family mediators are appointed by a court or other institution, the appointing agency should make reasonable efforts to insure that each mediator is qualified for the appointment. If a list of family mediators qualified for court appointment exists, the requirements for being included on the list should be made public and available to all interested persons.

C. Confidentiality should not be construed to limit or prohibit the effective monitoring, research, evaluation, or monitoring of mediation programs by responsible individuals or academic institutions provided that no identifying information about any person involved in the mediation is disclosed without their prior written consent. Under appropriate circumstances, researchers may be permitted to obtain access to statistical data and, with the permission of the participants, to individual case files, observations of live mediations, and interviews with participants.

Appendix B

Highlights in Divorce Mediation Research

The following brief summaries of research are both helpful to understand how mediation works and has been studied by empirical research.

The following compendia of research showcase research summaries that go well beyond this brief section:

- Constance Beck and Bruce Sales, Family mediation: Facts, myths and future prospects.(2001)
- Kenneth Kressel and Dean Pruit, Mediation Research (1989).
- Joseph Folger and Tricia S. Jones, New Directions in Mediation (1994).
- Morton Deutch and Peter Coleman, The Handbook of Conflict Resolution: Theory and Practice, 3rd Edition, Jossey-Bass, San Francisco, CA (2006).
- Christopher Moore, C.W. (2003), The Mediation Process: Practical Strategies for Resolving Conflict, Jossey-Bass, San Francisco, CA.
- Wall, J.A. and Dunne, T.C. (2012), "Mediation research: a current review", Negotiation Journal, Vol. 28, No. 2, pp. 217-244.
- Peter Coleman. Putting the peaces together: A situated model of mediation. (2014) [publication pending].

Who Chooses to Mediate?

- Those who voluntarily agree to mediate generally have higher socioeconomic status (education level, occupation status, income) than those who do not mediate. (Pearson [1989]: 13)
- Those who agree to mediate report better spousal communication patterns than those who do not agree to mediate. (Pearson [1989]: 13)

- Data do not support the view that those who choose to mediate are the couples with "easier" divorce cases or the couples who are more communicative with their spouses. (Kelly [1989]: 267)
- Marital conflict and poor communication, nonmutuality in the divorce decision, and strained cooperation do not appear to act as barriers to selecting mediation. (Kelly [1989]: 269)
- Lawyer support of the mediation processes influences parties to agree to mediation. (Pearson [1989]: 14)
- Men are significantly more positive about beginning the mediation process than women. (Kelly [1989]: 272)
- Whereas men's willingness to mediate is related to their recognition of a poor marriage, women's willingness to mediate is shaped by divorce-related anger they hold toward their spouse, their view of spousal integrity, and their perceived level of cooperation. (Kelly [1989]: 273)

The Mediation Process

- The factors during the mediation that were best able to predict settlement and willingness to recommend mediation are (1) the parties' perception of the mediator's ability to provide insights into their own feelings and (2) the mediator's ability to aid the parties in understanding the feelings of children and ex-spouses. (Pearson [1989]: 24)
- When parties produce complaint responses, mediators adopt a less (or non) confrontational intervention style. (Greatbach [1994]: 94)
- Back-and-forth blaming and fault-finding often become the central conversational activities of disputants in divorce mediation. (Tracy [1994]: 119)
- Children can escape the negative consequences of parental conflict when they are not caught in it by their parents, when their parents avoid direct aggressive expressions of their conflict in front of the child, or when they use compromise styles of conflict resolution. It is important to explore the extent to which the child is compromised by parental behavior that enlists the child in the parent's conflict agenda. (Kelly [1991]: 2)
- Mediators establish their impartiality to each party by defusing negative comments of one party toward another. (Tracy [1994]: 119)

Outcome and Satisfaction

- Research on mediator qualifications has failed to show a correlation between the mediator's education and rough indicators of performance, such as settlement rates or satisfaction by the parties. (Pearson [1988]: 435-441)
- Mediation outcomes are affected by three elements: (1) the skill and behavior of the mediator, (2) the characteristics of the disputants, and (3) the nature of the dispute. (Pearson [1989]: 23-24)
- Disputants consider mediation less damaging to relationships with former spouses than traditional courtroom proceedings (Pearson [1989]: 22-23)
- Mediation appears to have a very limited ability to alter basic relationship patterns or promote cooperation between divorcing parties. (Pearson [1989]: 23)
- The preexisting characteristics of disputes that are best defined when disputants would settle and recommend mediation are (1) the duration of the dispute, (2) the intensity of the dispute, and (3) the quality of the relationship with the ex-spouse. More recent and less severe disputes were most likely to be resolved, as were disputes between parties with at least a modest level of communication and cooperation. (Pearson [1989]: 24)
- Voluntary participation in mediation does not appear to produce higher settlement rates than mandated participation in mediation. (Pearson [1989]: 14-15)
- No evidence exists that voluntary versus mandatory mediation affects user satisfaction. (Pearson [1989]: 15)
- Mediation is effective in generating agreements on custody and visitation issues. (Pearson [1989]: 18)
- Mediation agreements relating to custody and visitation issues are no less stable than agreements generated in lawyer negotiations and court hearings. (Pearson [1989]: 18)
- No conclusive evidence about compliance and relitigation patterns associated with mediation and adjudicated agreements exists. (Pearson [1989]: 21)
- Users find that mediation identifies the real issues in a dispute. (Pearson [1989]: 19)
- Users find that mediation is less rushed and less "superficial" than courtroom proceedings. (Pearson [1989]: 19)
- Parties who terminate the mediation process before reaching agreement on all divorce-related issues are not easily distinguished from those who complete mediation with an agreement. (Kelly [1989]: 275)
- Of those who reached agreement in mediation, two-thirds of both men and women agreed that spousal support was fair, and more than two-thirds of both men and women were satisfied with the division of property. (Kelly [1989]: 279)
- In divorced families, when mothers used negative dispute resolution styles, both mother-child and father-child relationships were poorer compared to families in which mothers used cooperative strategies. (Kelly [1991]: 1, citing Camera and Resnick)

- Women report that the mediation process helped them assume more responsibility in managing their personal affairs than did men, and women had greater confidence in their ability to stand up for themselves as a result of the process. (Kelly [1989]: 279)
- Fathers were much more satisfied with mediation than with litigation, whereas mothers were equally satisfied with both. (Emery, R.E. et al. (2001), Child custody mediation and litigation: Custody, contact and co-parenting 12 years after initial dispute resolution. *Journal of Consulting and Clinical Psychology*, 69(2), 323-332.)
- Men and women have similar satisfaction rates concerning the division of property, child support and willingness to recommend mediation. (Pearson, J. & Thoennes, N., 1989, Divorce mediation: Reflections on a decade of research. In K. Kressel, D.G. Pruitt & Associates (Eds.), Mediation Research: The process and effectiveness of third-party intervention (pp. 9-30).
- Immediately after divorce, rates of satisfaction with mediation are high. Satisfaction rates drop during the ensuing years both for mediation and for litigation. (Emery, R.E. et al. (2001), Child custody mediation and litigation: Custody, contact and co-parenting 12 years after initial dispute resolution. *Journal of Consulting and Clinical Psychology*, 69(2), 323-332.)
- The mediator's gender was unrelated to settlement and did not consistently affect outcome or the parties' assessments of the process. (Wissler, R.L. (1999) *Trapping the Data: An Assessment of Domestic Relations Mediation in Maine and Ohio Courts*. State Justice Institute, Washington.)
- Parties were more likely to experience the process as fair when mediators encouraged them to express feelings or summarized what they said. (Wissler, R.L. (1999) *Trapping the Data: An Assessment of Domestic Relations Mediation in Maine and Ohio Courts*. State Justice Institute, Washington.)
- Parties were more likely to reach a full settlement if neither or only one had an attorney present. When both parties had counsel present, a partial settlement was more likely. (Wissler, R.L. (1999) *Trapping the Data: An Assessment of Domestic Relations Mediation in Maine and Ohio Courts*. State Justice Institute, Washington.)
- Mediation can: (1) settle a large percentage of cases otherwise headed for court; (2) possibly speed settlement, save money, and increase compliance with agreements; (3) clearly increase party satisfaction; and (4) most importantly, lead to remarkably improved relationships between nonresidential parents and children, as well as between divorced parents—even 12 years after dispute settlement. (Emery, R.E., Sbarra, D. and Grover, T. (2005) Divorce Mediation: Research and Reflections, Family Court Review, Volume 43, Issue 1, pages 22–37).
- "Active ingredients" of mediation are likely to include: (1) the call for parental cooperation over the long run of co-parenting beyond the crisis of separation, (2) the opportunity to address underlying emotional issues (albeit briefly), (3) helping parents

to establish a businesslike relationship, and (4) the avoidance of divisive negotiations at a critical time for family relationships. (Emery, R.E., Sbarra, D. and Grover, T. (2005) Divorce Mediation: Research and Reflections, Family Court Review, Volume 43, Issue 1, pages 22–37).

Effect of Intimate Partner Violence

Families with and without a history of intimate partner violence did not make significantly different legal or physical custody or parenting-time arrangements, nor did these groups differ in (1) specifying the details of how to handle issues that could lead to future conflict or (2) the likelihood of agreeing to supervised visitation or exchanges of children in public places. However, mediated agreements of families with a history of IPV were more likely to include safety restrictions (e.g., restrictions on interparental fighting, physical discipline of children, substance use) and counseling referrals. "Comparing the Mediation Agreements of Families With and Without a History of Intimate Partner Violence," John W. Putz, Robin H. Ballard, Julia Gruber Arany, Amy G. Applegate, and Amy Holtzworth-Munroe, FAMILY COURT REVIEW, Vol. 50 No.3, July 2012 413–428 © 2012 Association of Family and Conciliation Courts.

Impact of the Timing of Mediation

When cases are diverted to mediation has enormous consequences in terms of costs. (Fix, M. and Harter, P. (1992), Hard Cases, vulnerable people: An analysis of mediation programs at the multi-door courthouse of the Superior Court of the District of Columbia, Washington, DC: State Justice Institute, Urban Institute.

Impact of a Limited Number of Mediation Sessions

Mediation programs that severely limit the number of sessions (i.e., one or two) do not produce particularly satisfied clients. (Pearson, J. (1994) Family Mediation. In S. Keilitz (Ed.), *A report on current research findings—implications for courts and future research needs* (pp. 53–75). Washington, DC: State Justice Institute.)

Use of Directive Strategies in Session or Outside

Argumentative strategies are easier for divorce attorneys to use on the phone or in documents than when they are in face-to-face meetings with clients present. (McEwen, C.A., Rogers, N.H. & Maiman, R.J. (1995). Bring in the lawyers: Challenging the dominant approaches to ensuring fairness in divorce mediation. *Minnesota Law Review, 79*, 1317–1411.)

Assumptions About Goals of Divorce Lawyers

Nationally, the objective of most divorce lawyers is a "reasonable divorce."(Mather, L., McEwen, C.A. & Maiman, R.J. (2001), *Divorce lawyers at work: Varieties of professionalism in practice*, New York: Oxford University Press.)

Long-Range Impact of Mediation and Process Used

Whether a couple uses mediation or litigation to resolve a divorce dispute, divorce continues to have an impact on parents and children for many years (Laumann-Billings, L. & Emery, R. E. (2000). Distress among young adults from divorced families. *Journal of Family Psychology, 14*(4), 671–687).

Pattern of Couple Interaction After Divorce

Most couples likely continue the same or similar pattern of interaction developed during the marriage during their divorce (Beck, C.J.A. & Sales, B.D. (2001). *Family mediation: Facts, myths and future prospects*. Washington, DC. American Psychological Association.)

Impact on Fee Based Mediation on Relationships of Divorced Spouses

Private, voluntary, fee-for-service mediation programs improve relationships between former spouses (Irving, H.H. & Benjamin, M. (1995). *Family mediation: Contemporary issues*. Thousand Oaks, CA: Sage.

Use of Therapeutic Mediation Model and Couple Relationships

Mediation programs likely to create changes in couple relationship patterns are those which use a therapeutic model of mediation; allow as many sessions as needed; and require follow up contact with the mediator to resolve problems arising shortly after the divorce. (Beck, C.J.A. & Sales, B.D. (2001). Washington, DC. American Psychological Association.)

Relationship Between Informality and Supportive Nature of Mediators and Views of Neutrality

If mediators present themselves to litigants in an informal, intimate and supportive way, the expectation of mediator neutrality is likely enhanced. (Kelly, J.B. (1993). Current research on children's post-divorce adjustment: No simple answers. *Family and Conciliation Courts Review,* 31(1), 29–49.)

Disparity of Attachment Between Spouses and Problem-Solving Behavior

Greater disparity in attachment between family law parties was related to disparity in problem-solving behavior during the mediation and in turn lower settlement rates. (Bickerdike, A.J. & Littlefield, L. (2000) Divorce adjustment and mediation: theoretically grounded process research. *Mediation Quarterly* 18, 181–201.)

Helpful surveys of academic research on mediation. (Putting the peaces together: A situated model of mediation. Coleman, P.T. [PENDING PUBLICATION]; P. T. Coleman, and E. Marcus (Eds.), *The Handbook of Conflict Resolution: Theory and Practice*, 3rd Edition, Jossey-Bass, San Francisco, CA; Moore, C.W. (2003), *The Mediation Process: Practical Strategies for Resolving Conflict*, Jossey-Bass, San Francisco, CA; Wall, J.A. and Dunne, T.C. (2012), "Mediation research: a current review," *Negotiation Journal*, Vol. 28, No. 2, pp. 217–244.)

Sources

David Greatbach and Robert Dingwall, *The Interactive Construction of Interventions by Divorce Mediators,* in New Directions in Mediation: Communication Research and Perspectives 84-109 (Joseph P. Folger and Tricia S. Jones eds.,1994)

Joan B. Kelly, *Conflict and Post-Divorce Adjustment: A Closer took,* STATE BAR OF CALIFORNIA FAMILY LAW NEWS, Fall,1991, at 1

Joan B. Kelly and Lynn 1. Gigy, *Divorce Mediation: Characteristics of Clients and Outcomes,* in Mediation Research 263-84 (Kenneth Kressel and Dean G. Pruitt eds.,1989)

Jessica Pearson and Nancy Thoennes, *Divorce Mediation: Reflections on a Decade of Research,* in Mediation Research 9-30 (Kenneth Kressel and Dean G. Pruitt eds., 1989)

Jessica Pearson and Nancy Thoennes, *Divorce Mediation Research Results,* In Divorce Mediation: Theory and Practice 429, 435-41, Jay Folberg and Ann Milne eds., 1988)

Karen Tracy and Anna Spadlin, *Talking tike a Mediator: Conversational Moves of Experienced Divorce Mediators,* in New Directions in Mediation: Communication Research and Perspectives 110-34 (Joseph P. Folger and Tricia S. Jones eds., 1994)

Appendix C

Key California Mediation Confidentiality Cases

Case Name	Holding
Foxgate Homeowners' Assn. v. Bramalea California, Inc. (2001) 26 Cal.4th 1	California Supreme Court holds that statutory scheme of Evidence Code 1115-1127 is controlling and all communications within mediation are confidential. There are no exceptions for "bad faith" conduct or failure to participate in mediation.
Eisendrath v. Sup. Ct. (2003) 109 Cal. App. 4th 351	In a family law matter, court bars (1) communications of parties outside the presence of the mediator while mediation was ongoing and (2) testimony of the mediator.
In re Marriage of Kieturakis (2006) 138 Cal.App.4th 56	The court affirmed the Judgment and the Trial Court's finding that wife was not prejudiced by the failure to make the requisite disclosures on Judicial Council forms. Court held that mediation confidentiality trumps claims of undue influence due to parties' recitation of voluntary agreement and the policy to support mediation to resolve family law disputes.
Rojas v. Superior Court (2007) 33 Cal. 4th 407	Any document prepared for mediation is confidential, protected from discovery, and inadmissible. However, facts in these documents that are otherwise subject to discovery or admissible remain discoverable and admissible.
Fair v. Bakhtiari (2006) 40 Cal.4th 189	There are no exceptions to strict mediation confidentiality, even where the result seems unjust.
Wimsatt v. Superior Court (2007)152 Cal. App.4th 137	Mediation confidentiality protects mediation communication in the context of a legal malpractice action arising from the handling of the underlying settlement process.
Simmons v. Ghaderi (2008) 44 Cal.4th 570	California Supreme Court holds that mediator's declaration of a settlement reached in mediation but not reduced to writing after a party withdrew consent should be inadmissible and the Court of Appeal cannot create judicial exception of estoppel to the statutory scheme of confidentiality.

Case Name	Holding
Radford v. Shehorn (2010) 187 Cal. App.4th 852	Admitting the mediator's declaration into evidence is held to have been error (albeit harmless error) even though the testimony was limited to stating the number of pages in the settlement agreement reached in mediation.
Estate of Thottam (2008) 165 Cal. App. 4th 1331	Court of Appeal permits admissibility of a chart initialed by the parties showing how a probate estate would be divided among siblings. California Evidence Code §1123(c) requires neither that the express agreement in writing permitting disclosure be contained in the settlement agreement itself nor that it even be made at or after the time the settlement agreement is entered into.
Benesch v. Green (N.D.Cal. 2009) 2009 WL 4885215	Federal district court supports mediation confidentiality even when communication is just between client and lawyer. "Communications between counsel and client that are materially related to the mediation, even if they are not made to another party or the mediator, are "for the purpose of" or "pursuant to mediation." Indeed, if protected communications did not include those *outside* the mediation proceedings, it would be unnecessary for Evid. Code 1122 (a)(2) to provide that communications between fewer than all participants in a mediation may be disclosed if all such participants agree and " the communication . . . does not disclose anything said or done . . . in the course of mediation."
Cassell v .Superior Court (2011) 51 Cal.4th 113	California Supreme Court rules that lawyer-client communication during mediation outside of presence of the mediator is inadmissible in malpractice actions or fee disputes due to the policy of complete mediation confidentiality.
Blix Records v. Cassidy (2010) 91 Cal App. 4th 39	When CCP 664.6 is contained in a mediated settlement agreement and the parties represent to a court that the matter is fully settled, party is estopped from claiming unenforceability despite vagueness or absence of essential terms in the agreement.
Doe 1 v. Superior Court (Roman Catholic Archbishop of Los Angeles, et al., Real Parties in Interest) (2005)132 Cal. App.4th 1160	The church sought to make public written summaries of personnel files of priests who were alleged to have perpetrated childhood sexual molestation. The summaries had been prepared for submission to a settlement and mediation judge in civil litigation based upon the alleged allegations. The accused priests sought a protective order to bar public disclosure of the written summaries. When the trial court denied the motion, priest filed a petition for mandate. The appellate court, citing Section 1119(c), issues writ directing trial court to grant protective order.
Facebook, Inc. v. Pacific Northwest Software, Inc. (2011) 640 F. 3d 1034	Ninth Circuit affirms strict confidentiality by barring mediation communications to support a motion to set aside a settlement reached during court-ordered mediation. (In the Settlement Agreement, certain boilerplate was left to the parties and objections to the boilerplate prepared by Facebook were overruled.)
Marriage of Davenport (2011) 194 Cal App 4th 1507	Court affirms sanctions of $100,000 and attorney fees in the amount of $304,387 in part due to a lawyer's violation of Evidence Code 1119 (by submitting declaration which attached mediation-related documents setting forth what was done and purportedly said in mediation and referring to agreements reached in mediation.)

Case Name	Holding
Marriage of Woolsey (2013) 220 Cal.App.4th 881	Private mediation offers an alternate approach to resolve disputed issues arising from a marital dissolution. Requiring technical compliance with disclosure rules designed for adversarial litigation would undermine the strong public policy of allowing parties to choose speedy and less costly avenues for resolving disputes. Parties who agree to settle their dispute by private mediation may also agree to make financial disclosures that do not meet the technical procedural requirements of sections 2104 and 2105. Thus, strict compliance with sections 2104 and 2105 is not required for private mediations that address issues arising out of a marital dissolution.
Sony v. Hannstar No. M 07-1827 SI (U.S.D.C. N.D. Cal., December 3, 2013)	Federal court holds that despite "inequitable" result, where the parties settled by accepting in writing a mediator's proposal and the mediator stated in writing that the case was settled, because parties failed to include an affirmative statement to the effect that they intended their settlement to be enforceable or binding the e-mails from mediator to parties were inadmissible as evidence of settlement.
Millhouse v. Travelers, SACV 10-10730(November 5, 2013)	US District Court Judge, Cormac Carney permitted evidence of bad faith adduced during a mediation. Evidence was a $7m demand plus $1m for attorney fees. Court indicated plaintiffs waived objection and to exclude mediation evidence would deprive Travelers the right of due process to defend against bad faith
Daly v. Oyster, 14 DJDAR 9961 July 29, 2014. Cal. Ct of Appeals, 2nd District	Court admitted a marital settlement agreement reached in mediation during a prior dismissed case.
Lappe v. Super. Ct. 14 DJDAR (12-19-14)	Parties may be compelled to produce declarations of disclosure exchanged in mediation.
Amis f. Greenberg Traurig Cal. Ct. of Appeals, 2nd District, No. B248227 (3-18-15)	Court directly follows *Cassel* and precludes all mediation communications from being admitted in an attorney malpractice action. Plaintiff admits that all attorney communications for which action is based occurred during mediation.

Appendix D

Phrases for Active Listening and to Prevent Miscommunication

Phrases for Miscommunication

Ordering	"You must." "You have to." "You will."
Threatening	"If you don't, then . . . " "You'd better or else."
Preaching	"You should." "You ought." "It's your duty."
Lecturing	"Here is why you're wrong." "Do you realize . . ."
Giving Answers	"What I would do is . . . " "It would be best if you . . ."
Judging	"You are argumentative . . . lazy . . ." "You'll never change."
Excusing	"It's not so bad." "You'll feel better . . ."
Diagnosing	"You're just trying to get attention." "What you need is . . ."
Prying	"When?" "How?" "What?" "Where?" "Who?"
Labeling	"You're being unrealistic . . . emotional . . . angry . . ."
Manipulating	"Don't you think you should . . ."

Phrases for Active Listening

Encouraging	"Can you tell me more?"
Clarifying	"What did this happen?"
Summarizing	"Let me see if I understand what you just said."
Acknowledging	"I can see you are feeling very angry right now."
Open Questioning	"Why? What would you like to see happen?"

Responding	"I see it this way. How do you see it?"
Soliciting	"I would like your advice about how we can resolve this."
Normalizing	"Many people feel the way you do."
Empathizing	"I can appreciate why you feel that way."
Reframing	"I understand that you feel ___ when he/she ___."
Validating	"I appreciate your willingness to be here."

Reprinted with permission from Ken Cloke, *Mediation: Revenge and the Magic of Forgiveness*

Appendix E

Divorce Mission Statement

LAW AND MEDIATION OFFICE OF
Forrest S. Mosten*

*CERTIFIED FAMILY LAW SPECIALIST
CALIFORNIA BOARD OF LEGAL SPECIALIZATION
+ ADVANCED PRACTITIONER
ASSOCIATION FOR CONFLICT RESOLUTION
++ MEMBER, INTERNATIONAL ACADEMY OF
COLLABORATIVE PROFESSIONALS

9401 WILSHIRE BOULEVARD, 9TH FLOOR
BEVERLY HILLS, CALIFORNIA 90212
TELEPHONE (310) 473-7611
FACSIMILE (310) 473-7422
E-Mail: MOSTEN@MEDIATE.COM
WWW.MOSTENMEDIATION.COM

LOUIS M. BROWN CLIENT LIBRARY

Divorce Mission Statement *

A mission statement for your divorce is your compass guiding you away from conflict and toward peace. There will be many tempting distractions during your divorce. Your mission statement will keep you on track.

You can use the following ideas to craft your divorce mission statement. Select the ideas that resonate most with your core values. Click on as many as you'd like to create your mission statement and then print it below:

At the end of my divorce, I want the following to be true:

- ☐ I was kind and honest throughout the entire process.
- ☐ My children have two supportive parents committed to co-parenting.
- ☐ We did not have to go to court to settle our divorce.
- ☐ We spent as little money as possible on our divorce, preserving assets to be split between us versus paying lawyers.
- ☐ Our financial responsibility was divided fairly.
- ☐ I still respect my former spouse and our relationship is friendly, cordial and civil.
- ☐ I realize my marriage was not a complete mistake and value the years I was with my spouse.
- ☐ Our children understand and are reminded that our divorce is not their fault.
- ☐ I am committed to being cooperative and respectful when my spouse engages with the world as a single person (dating, working, making new friends, etc.).

- [ ] I took responsibility for any feelings of abandonment, rejection, fear, anger, grief and guilt I had, without blaming or shaming my spouse.

I will make sure that the above statements are realized by doing the following:

- [ ] I will ask for advice from people who are a positive influence, and then follow that advice.
- [ ] I will put my children's best interests above my own.
- [ ] I will take care of myself physically and emotionally.
- [ ] I will forgive myself and my spouse for getting divorced.
- [ ] I will focus on moving forward rather than getting bogged down in the past.
- [ ] I will accept situations rather than manipulating outcomes.
- [ ] I will focus on what is important, both short term and long term.
- [ ] I will use written goals and journaling to track my progress.
- [ ] I will not use my divorce to be punish toward myself or my spouse.
- [ ] I will not consider divorce as something that I need to recover from; rather something I can heal through.

Your divorce mission statement will serve as a reminder of who you want to be at the end of your divorce. Keep it handy. You will need these reminders when things get tough. The hard work of staying in touch with your mission, and realigning your behaviors to fit with your mission, will be worth it.

*Diana Mercer and Katie Jane Wennechuk, *Making Divorce Work* (2010)

Appendix F

Sample Agreement for Consulting Attorney Services

AGREEMENT REGARDING MEDIATION CONSULTING ATTORNEY SERVICES

You have retained me to advise you, Agreement for Consulting prepare documents, and negotiate on your behalf as mutually agreed in connection with your mediation. This retention is premised on your stated desire to avoid litigation.

Scope and Duties

My representation of you as a consulting lawyer in mediation differs in some important respects from conventional representation by a litigation lawyer. *Please read particularly carefully* the following section describing my responsibilities, and yours, in my mediation consultation representation under this agreement.

Some of the duties that I shall perform as your mediation consulting attorney include:

1. Legal advice: office visits, telephone calls, fax, mail, e-mail;
2. Advice about availability of alternative means to resolve the dispute, including mediation, collaborative law, various forms of negotiation and arbitration;
3. Legal research and analysis;
4. Guidance and procedural information for filing or serving court documents;
5. Help select mediator;
6. Help you prepare and plan for mediation sessions and develop negotiation strategy and approaches;
7. Review of correspondence and court documents prepared by my office, the mediator, your spouse's lawyer, or others;
8. Prepare and/or suggest documents to be prepared by my office, the mediator, your spouse's lawyer, or others;

9. Communicate with the mediator, your spouse's lawyer, or other persons by phone, email, or in person;
10. Attend mediation sessions and negotiate on your behalf as requested;
11. Refer you to other counsel, expert, or professionals as needed and authorized; and
12. Other duties as we may agree.

Your retention of me as your lawyer is a "limited scope retention." You are retaining me specifically to assist you in reaching a comprehensive agreement with your spouse or partner, and for no other purpose. You retain the right to terminate the mediation process at any time and go to court, *but doing so ends my representation of you.* If your spouse should elect to go to court, this also may terminate the process, however, mediation can continue while court proceedings are in progress. If any request for a court hearing is made, you would need to retain litigation counsel to assist you in court. Accordingly, my representation of you and your retainer agreement are subject to the following:

- I will not be your lawyer of record, except for purposes of filing the Judgment and other necessary non-adversary court documents. I will be filing a Notice of Limited Scope Representation with the court indicating that I will handle all issues in your divorce through negotiation or mediation and that all court notices will be sent to me. The notice will indicate that you are solely responsible for representing yourself in court unless you retain litigation counsel
- I will not represent you or assist in any litigation against YOUR SPOUSE should the mediation process end before a settlement is reached. However, I will cooperate with you in transferring your file to new counsel.
- I will not be called by you to give evidence in any family law litigation against YOUR SPOUSE, nor will I testify if called as a witness.
- I will not negotiate a settlement of any issue without your participation and consent. I will promptly respond to your inquiries.
- You may terminate the mediation process at any time if you wish to seek remedies from the Court.
- You agree to make full disclosure of the nature, extent, value of—and all developments affecting—your income, assets, and liabilities. You authorize me to fully disclose all such information which in my discretion must be provided to your spouse and his or her lawyer. *If you should decline to make disclosures I regard as necessary, I am bound by the lawyer-client privilege to keep such information confidential. However, I will, in my discretion, withdraw as your lawyer.*

The mediation process depends upon good faith participation by both parties. *A dishonest or unscrupulous party could take advantage of the mediation process for delay or advantage in litigation.* Neither I nor any lawyer can guarantee that their client will in fact adhere to the good faith undertakings that are made formally in writing at the start of the process. Remedies against your spouse or partner for bad faith might possibly be available subsequently in court under relevant family law provisions, but might or might not actually remedy the consequences of bad faith behavior in the mediation process. My commitment to you is that I will alert you to any suspicion of bad faith and recommend termination of the process if I suspect bad faith. Similarly, I will withdraw as your counsel if it appears to me that you are unwilling or unable to meet your good faith commitments in the mediation process. In signing this agreement, you are authorizing me to withdraw if, in my judgment, I feel you are failing to participate in good faith.

- I may recommend that you and your spouse work with mental health professionals, and/or a financial consultant or other professionals. Where emotion runs high or where there are minor children, the involvement of therapists may be essential for the mediation process to work effectively. In signing this Agreement you acknowledge your understanding that if such additional professional resources are in my professional judgment necessary, you have the right to decline to retain additional professionals. You also acknowledge and agree that should you so decline, it may not be appropriate to continue the mediation process or for me to remain as your lawyer.
- No lawyer can guarantee that mediation process will be effective in resolving your issues. Success in mediation is possible only if you and your spouse share a commitment to respectful, honest, efficient, and direct consensual resolution of all issues.
- While most couples who elect the mediation process arrive at a full resolution of all issues, some do not. If overall resources (yours and your spouse's) are strained, you should consider carefully whether to allocate limited resources to the mediation process if doing so would impair your ability to retain conventional legal counsel in the event you and your spouse were not able to reach full agreement.
- Candid communication and cooperation among professionals and the mediator is essential for effective process management which is an important component of the service I am able to provide. It is not possible for me to provide representation at the standard I consider appropriate without an understanding that I will communicate confidentially with other professionals, in my discretion, for the sole purpose of helping you to reach a satisfactory and appropriate agreement using the mediation process. These communications are made solely for the purpose of facilitating effective negotiations by improving communications at the mediation table. The content of such professional communications will not necessarily be shared with you. *I will not communicate any matter that you have directed me to keep private.* References and notes concerning confidential process management communications among professionals if any, will not be maintained as part of your file, and *as a condition of our*

representation of you, you agree that they are not part of your file and that you will not request disclosure of or access to any such confidential team process communications or summaries of such communications (if any) from me or from any third party or institution. You agree that you will make no effort to introduce any such confidential process communications into any proceedings, whether in court or otherwise.

I often engage in continuing education, writing, and training to improve the quality of my professional services, including discussions of experiences in actual cases. You agree that I may discuss your case for such educational purposes provided no identifying information about you or your family is disclosed.

I HAVE READ THE ABOVE PROVISIONS AND AGREE TO THEM. I UNDERSTAND THAT I HAVE THE RIGHT TO HAVE THIS AGREEMENT REVIEWED BY ANOTHER ATTORNEY OF MY CHOICE BEFORE I SIGN BELOW.

Date_____ Client_____

Date_____ Attorney_____

Appendix G

Sample Estimate of Consulting Lawyer Fees

ESTIMATE OF MEDIATION CONSULTING ATTORNEY FEES

Every client has a right to understand and manage the costs of their attorney fees. Even though the costs of my services as your consulting attorney in mediation should be far less than if you engaged a lawyer for litigation purposes, the expenses can add up.

Some mediations can be concluded in one session and others may require ten sessions or more. The factors that will impact the cost of your attorney fees are:

- Willingness and ability of the parties to negotiate fairly and efficiently with each other;
- The Level of conflict and communication problems;
- Complexity and Emotionality of Parenting Issues
- Size and Sophistication of the Financial Estate and ability and willingness to disclose assets and liabilities
- Collaboration and Expertise of Lawyers and Other Professionals
- Ease of Scheduling and Willingness to Follow My Recommendations

The following estimate of attorney costs is based on averages in my over 35 years of law and mediation practice. The estimate should give you an overview of the cost structure. Remember: These are only ranges and your situation may be very different.

Initial Consultation	1-2 Hours
Review of Parenting and Financial Situation	1-4 Hours
Attendance at Private Preliminary Planning Sessions	0-3 Hours
Attending Working Sessions	0-20 Hours
3-4 Hours Each Session	

Average 3-5 Sessions

Email and Phone Communication with Mediator, Client, Other Lawyer, Experts, and Other Persons Between Sessions	0-10 Hours
Review Mediator Summary Letters	1-5 Hours
Draft Petition and Initial Court Documents	0-2 Hours
Draft Judgment and Final Court Documents	0-7 Hours
Revise Documents, Facilitate Drafting Issues, and Closing	1-6 Hours
Total Estimated Range of Consulting Attorney Time (Based on 3-5 sessions	4-59 Hours
Additional Professional Time:	To Be Determined

Appendix H

Notice of Limited Scope Representation

		FL-950
ATTORNEY OR PARTY WITHOUT ATTORNEY (Name, state bar number, and address): Forrest S. Mosten Forrest S. Mosten Limited Scope Attorney 11661 San Vicente Blvd., Suite 414 Los Angeles, California 90049 　TELEPHONE NO.: (310) 473-7611　FAX NO. (Optional): E-MAIL ADDRESS (Optional): 　ATTORNEY FOR (Name): Forrest S. Mosten, Limited Scope Attorney		FOR COURT USE ONLY

SUPERIOR COURT OF CALIFORNIA, COUNTY OF
　STREET ADDRESS:
　MAILING ADDRESS:
　CITY AND ZIP CODE:
　BRANCH NAME:

PETITIONER/PLAINTIFF:

RESPONDENT/DEFENDANT:

OTHER PARENT/CLAIMANT:

NOTICE OF LIMITED SCOPE REPRESENTATION ☐ Amended	CASE NUMBER:

1. Attorney *(name)*: Forrest S. Mosten
   and party *(name)*: Unbundled/Limited Scope/Discrete Task/Legal Coaching Client
   have a written agreement that attorney will provide limited scope representation to the party.

2. Attorney will represent the party
   ☐ at the hearing on:　　　　　　　　　☐ and for any continuance of that hearing
   ☐ until submission of the order after hearing
   ☒ until resolution of the issues checked on page 1 by trial or settlement
   ☐ other *(specify duration of representation)*:

3. Attorney will serve as "attorney of record" for the party <u>only</u> for the following issues in this case:
   a. ☒ Child support: (1) ☐ Establish (2) ☐ Enforce (3) ☐ Modify *(describe in detail)*:

   b. ☒ Spousal support: (1) ☐ Establish (2) ☐ Enforce (3) ☐ Modify *(describe in detail)*:

   c. ☐ Restraining order: (1) ☐ Establish (2) ☐ Enforce (3) ☐ Modify *(describe in detail)*:

   d. ☒ Child custody and visitation: (1) ☐ Establish (2) ☐ Enforce (3) ☐ Modify *(describe in detail)*:

   e. ☒ Division of property *(describe in detail)*:

   f. ☒ Pension issues *(describe in detail)*:

Form Adopted for Mandatory Use
Judicial Council of California
FL-950 [New July 1, 2003]

NOTICE OF LIMITED SCOPE REPRESENTATION

Legal Solutions Plus

PETITIONER/PLAINTIFF:	CASE NUMBER:
RESPONDENT/DEFENDANT:	
OTHER PARENT/CLAIMANT:	

g. ☐ Contempt *(describe in detail)*:

h. ☒ Other *(describe in detail)*: Limited Scope Attorney represents client in all services related to negotiation, mediation, and other processes of settlement. Party will represent himself/herself or associate litigation counsel of record for all court hearings and adversarial proceedings, including depositions.

i. ☐ See attachment 3i.

4. By signing this form, the party agrees to sign form MC-050, *Substitution of Attorney - Civil* at the completion of the representation as set forth above.

5. The attorney named above is "attorney of record" and available for service of documents only for those issues specifically checked on pages 1 and 2. For all other matters, the party must be served directly. The party's name, address, and phone number are listed below for that purpose.

Name: Unbundled/Limited Scope/Discrete Task/Legal Coaching Client

Address *(for the purpose of service)*:

Phone: Fax:

This notice accurately sets forth all current matters on which the attorney has agreed to serve as "attorney of record" for the party in this case. The information provided herein is not intended to set forth all of the terms and conditions of the agreement between the party and the attorney for limited scope representation.

Date:

_____   ▶ _____
(TYPE OR PRINT NAME)   (SIGNATURE OF PARTY)

Date:

_____   ▶ _____
(TYPE OR PRINT NAME)   (SIGNATURE OF ATTORNEY)

FL-950 [New July 1, 2003]   **NOTICE OF LIMITED SCOPE REPRESENTATION**

Appendix I

Factors Affecting Appropriateness of Mediation, Collaborative Law, and Cooperative Law Procedures

Factors	Unassisted Negotiation Is Appropriate if	Mediation* Is Appropriate if	Collaborative Law Is Appropriate if	Traditional Litigation Is Appropriate if
Ability of parties to assert their interests	parties are able to assert their interests well	(a) parties are able to assert their interests well and/or (b) lawyers can participate in mediation	one or more parties need or want a lawyer to advocate their interests	one or more parties need or want a lawyer to advocate their interests
Parties' resources and willingness to pay for substantial professional services	parties cannot afford and/or desire professional service, possibly because they want to maximize their own decision making	parties can afford and/or desire a limited level of professional service, possibly because they want to maximize their own decision making	parties are willing and able to pay for substantial professional services and willing to pay cost of hiring new litigation lawyers if there is no agreement in collaborative law	parties are willing and able to pay for substantial professional services
Parties desire for neutral third party to manage the process	Parties do not want neutral third party to manage the process	Parties want neutral third party to manage the process	(a) parties do not want neutral third party to manage the process or (b) are willing to hire mediator in addition to lawyers	(a) parties do not want neutral third party to manage the process or (b) are willing to hire mediator in addition to lawyers

Factors	Unassisted Negotiation Is Appropriate if	Mediation* Is Appropriate if	Collaborative Law Is Appropriate if	Traditional Litigation Is Appropriate if
Parties willingness to hire lawyers	parties are reluctant or unwilling to hire lawyers at all or to take the lead in negotiation	parties are reluctant or unwilling to hire lawyers at all or to take the lead in negotiation	both parties are willing to hire lawyers	at least one party is willing to hire a lawyer
Parties desire to keep their lawyer if the case involves contested litigation	not applicable	parties want to be able to keep their lawyers in contested litigation	parties are willing to risk losing their collaborative lawyers if the parties litigate	parties want to be able to keep their lawyers in contested litigation
Parties desire for well-established dispute resolution procedure and practice	parties are not concerned about using a well-established dispute resolution procedure and practice	parties want a procedure that has been studied extensively and that is the subject of well-developed norms and practices	parties are willing to use an innovative procedure that has not been studied extensively and that is not the subject of well-developed norms and practices	parties want a procedure that is the subject of well-developed norms and practices
Risk that a party would take advantage of another	(a) there is a low risk of parties will try to take advantage of each other, and/or (b) parties are capable of representing themselves effectively, and/or (c) parties may hire professionals if needed	(a) there is a low risk of parties will try to take advantage of each other, and/or (b) parties are capable of representing themselves effectively, and/or (c) parties use mediator skilled in managing conflict, and/or (d) lawyers participate in mediation	(a) there is a low risk of parties will try to take advantage of each other or (b) there is a significant risk of parties trying to take advantage and they are willing to risk that the other party would terminate collaborative law as an adversarial tactic	there may be a significant risk that one party would take advantage of another
Risk that a party may want to use litigation	parties are unwilling to make an investment to reduce risk of contested litigation	parties are willing to make a limited investment to reduce risk of contested litigation	there is a low risk that a party will want to use contested litigation	there may be a significant risk that a party will want to use contested litigation

Appendix I: Factors Affecting Appropriateness of Mediation

Factors	Unassisted Negotiation Is Appropriate if	Mediation* Is Appropriate if	Collaborative Law Is Appropriate if	Traditional Litigation Is Appropriate if
Need for threat of litigation to motivate a party to act reasonably	a party does not need threat of litigation to motivate another party to act reasonably	a party may need threat of litigation to motivate another party to act reasonably	a party does not need threat of litigation to motivate another party to act reasonably	a party may need threat of litigation to motivate another party to act reasonably
Parties desire to avoid contested litigation	parties prefer to avoid litigation but are willing to use it if needed to protect their interests	parties prefer to avoid litigation but are willing to use it if needed to protect their interests	parties strongly prefer to avoid litigation and are willing to use it only as a last resort	parties prefer to avoid litigation but are willing to use it if needed to protect their interests
Relative preference of settlement pressure and litigation pressure	parties are wary of settlement and litigation pressure but willing to risk litigation pressure	parties are wary of settlement pressure and willing to risk greater litigation pressure	parties are wary of litigation pressure and willing to risk greater settlement pressure	parties are wary of settlement pressure and willing to risk greater litigation pressure

*This table assumes that any lawyers for mediation participants do not attend mediation sessions except as noted.

Adapted from John Lande & Gregg Herman, Fitting the Forum to the Family Fuss: Choosing Mediation, Collaborative Law, or Cooperative Law for Negotiating Divorce Cases, 42 *Family Court Review* 280, 286-87 (2004).

Appendix J

Client Information About Collaborative Representation

Elements of Collaborative Representation	Benefits	Risks
Collaborative Guidelines and Principles The collaborative process involves treating each other respectfully and satisfying the interests of all family members rather than trying to gain individual advantage.	• The collaborative process sets a positive tone so that you and your spouse can work to satisfy your interests. • The process can reduce unnecessary and destructive conflict and avoid litigation.	• This process may not produce a constructive agreement if your spouse will respond only to threats, litigation, or a decision by a judge. • The collaborative process may not be appropriate if you or your spouse do not have the ability to participate effectively. • Domestic violence, substance abuse, or mental illness may make the process inappropriate. • You may feel unprotected if you want your attorney to advocate strongly to protect your interests (including your concerns about your children).

Elements of Collaborative Representation	Benefits	Risks
Participation Agreement Requiring Disqualification of Attorneys in Litigation Clients and attorneys sign a Participation Agreement that includes a court disqualification clause, which states that if the parties do not resolve the matter in the collaborative process, neither attorney will represent the parties in any contested litigation between you. If you would want to hire an attorney to represent you in court, you would need to hire another attorney.	• The process can increase the motivation of all parties and attorneys to reach a settlement. If negotiations break down and a law suit is filed, both parties need to hire new attorneys and the collaborative attorneys are out of a job. As a result, everyone in the collaborative process focuses exclusively on reaching agreement. • All parties and Attorneys focus on negotiation from the very beginning of the process. • Collaborative attorneys work to negotiate constructively and avoid attacking the other side.	• If the collaborative representation ends, you and your spouse will need to spend additional time and money to hire new attorneys and may lose some information or momentum during a transition of attorneys. After developing a relationship of trust and confidence with your collaborative attorney, you might feel abandoned emotionally and/or strategically at a time of contentious conflict. • You may feel a lot of pressure if your spouse is willing to terminate the process and you want to stay in it. • You should be cautious about using a collaborative process If you do not trust that your spouse will negotiate honestly and sincerely.
Trained Collaborative Professionals The collaborative process may involve a team of collaborative professionals who have specialized training in collaborative divorce skills. Separate divorce coaches help each party to deal with emotional, relationship, and parenting issues. Child development specialists and financial professionals may be hired jointly to provide unbiased information and advice.	• You and your spouse may benefit from using a team of collaborative professionals with different skills. • Collaborative professionals usually have had special training to help promote constructive settlements. • By investing the time and money for professional training, collaborative professionals demonstrate a commitment to constructive negotiation.	• You or your spouse may feel some pressure to use more professionals that you want or feel that you can afford.

Elements of Collaborative Representation	Benefits	Risks
Direct Communication and Decision Making by the Parties Parties are the key decision makers and you communicate directly with each other and the attorneys.	• You and your spouse control the decisions that affect your lives and families. • You and your spouse can discuss both nonlegal and legal issues. • You and your spouse can develop communication skills and learn how to communicate more effectively in the future.	• You and your spouse might increase conflict without making any progress if your communication styles are disrespectful or harmful to each other and you cannot work together constructively.
Voluntary Disclosure of Assets, Obligations, and Important Information You and your spouse make a binding commitment that you will fully disclose assets and will not to hide important relevant information.	• You and your spouse agree to provide each other with full information of marital and separate assets so that you can make informed decisions. • The collaborative process can include a protection against parties' failure to disclose fully. If either party does not make the required disclosures, the agreement can be set aside. • The collaborative process does not use formal court "discovery" processes to investigate the facts of your case. This can save money and avoid conflicts. Discovery does not necessarily produce full information.	• Your spouse may hide assets and other critical information unless you use a formal discovery process.
Confidentiality of Collaborative Process Communications in the Collaborative process are generally confidential and inadmissible in court.	• Confidentiality can encourage you and your spouse to talk openly and reach creative solutions. • Confidentiality permits your family business to remain private by avoiding public testimony in court and keeping sensitive documents out of the public records.	•

Elements of Collaborative Representation	Benefits	Risks
Divorce Process May Save Time and Money The collaborative process may save you and your spouse time and money in handling your divorce. Some courts give collaborative cases priority within their court system and cases may not have to follow strict court schedules.	• The collaborative process can help you reduce the length of negotiations and the cost of your divorce. • You may save money by avoiding litigation procedures. Specialized collaborative professionals can help resolve disputes that might otherwise go to court. • Settlements can be processed quickly in court so that you can move on with your life.	• Collaborative cases can take a long time if there are no court deadlines to keep the process moving. • The use of a team of professionals can increase the cost of your divorce.

I have read this chart and I understand Collaborative representation and its benefits and risks.

I have had an opportunity to discuss any concerns and questions I may have with my attorney before signing an Attorney-Client Engagement Agreement and before signing a Collaborative Participation Agreement with my spouse.

I also understand that if I have additional questions or concerns about the Collaborative representation after it begins, I am encouraged to discuss them with my attorney.

Date_____   _____
                                                           CLIENT

Source: Forrest S. Mosten, Collaborative Law Practice: An Unbundled Approach to Informed Client Decision-Making, *Journal of Dispute Resolution* 163, 190-93.

Appendix K

Sample Letter to Client Discussing Risks of Going into Mediation

LAW AND MEDIATION OFFICE OF

Forrest S. Mosten*

*CERTIFIED FAMILY LAW SPECIALIST
CALIFORNIA BOARD OF LEGAL SPECIALIZATION
+ ADVANCED PRACTITIONER
ASSOCIATION FOR CONFLICT RESOLUTION
++ MEMBER, INTERNATIONAL ACADEMY OF
COLLABORATIVE PROFESSIONALS

9401 WILSHIRE BLVD, 9TH FLOOR
BEVERLY HILLS, CALIFORNIA 90212
TELEPHONE (310) 473-7611
FACSIMILE (310) 470-2625
E-Mail: MOSTEN@MEDIATE.COM
WWW.MOSTENMEDIATION.COM

LOUIS M. BROWN CLIENT LIBRARY

Dear Client:

As you know, I am supportive of our attempt to settle your matter in mediation for the many reasons we have discussed, including without limitation reduced cost, increased privacy, greater control over the process, less stress on your ongoing family relationships, and your increased ability to fashion your own agreement. There are processes in place within the mediation which are intended to ensure that settlements are reached knowingly and voluntarily and that everyone feels comfortable with the ultimate resolution.

Before we start mediation, I want to review some key considerations:

1. If you agree to a settlement in mediation, it will be binding and enforceable—just as if we had gone to court and the judge had made orders in your case. The binding nature of a mediated settlement is an advantage, in that it gives you the certainty and finality of a court judgment without having to litigate. However, the binding nature of a mediated settlement also means that it will be extraordinarily difficult and expensive to try and get out of it, even if you later feel that you signed due to duress, fraud of your spouse, or a lack of disclosure. California courts almost always affirm mediated agreements.
2. If your spouse prepares and signs his/her Final Declaration of Disclosure during mediation and you later find omitted or understated assets or obligations, you may not be able to get court relief because mediation confidentiality will preclude introduction of the financial disclosure statement into evidence. We can discuss carving out an exception to this confidentiality, but I cannot guarantee that a court would honor that carve-out later.
3. Mediation confidentiality also limits clients' claims against their own attorneys. For example, if an attorney gives a client negligent advice during a mediation that causes the client to settle on terms that he or she later believes to have been unfair or harmful to your case, the client may not be able to use that advice against the attorney in a malpractice action due to mediation confidentiality.

Feel free to discuss with me any questions you may have as to how proceeding with mediation could impact your later rights.

Yours very truly,

| Client Initial ___ |
| Client Initial ___ |

Appendix L

Sample Mediator's Contract

LAW AND MEDIATION OFFICE OF
Forrest S. Mosten*

*CERTIFIED FAMILY LAW SPECIALIST
CALIFORNIA BOARD OF LEGAL SPECIALIZATION
+ ADVANCED PRACTITIONER
ASSOCIATION FOR CONFLICT RESOLUTION
++ MEMBER, INTERNATIONAL ACADEMY OF
COLLABORATIVE PROFESSIONALS

9401 WILSHIRE BLVD, 9TH FLOOR
BEVERLY HILLS, CALIFORNIA 90212
TELEPHONE (310) 473-7611
FACSIMILE (310) 470-2625
E-Mail: MOSTEN@MEDIATE.COM
WWW.MOSTENMEDIATION.COM

LOUIS M. BROWN CLIENT LIBRARY

MEDIATION AGREEMENT (Abridged)

I.

ESTABLISHMENT OF MEDIATION RELATIONSHIP

The undersigned wish to retain the services of FORREST S. MOSTEN to mediate disputed issues. The Mediator is an attorney licensed to practice in the State of California working as a sole Mediator or working conjointly with a professional from another discipline (e.g. a therapist, clergy and/or accountant). All references to "Mediator" apply both to the lawyer Mediator and any other professional serving as Mediator, consultant, assisting the mediator or communicating with the parties in respect to the mediation.

The parties acknowledge that the Mediator has discussed the advantages and disadvantages of the Mediation process and compared that process with being represented by separate attorneys or having the issues resolved through negotiation between lawyers or by a judge in the court.

II.

RIGHT OF INDEPENDENT COUNSEL

During the Mediation, the parties are each encouraged to consult independent counsel at any time. Each party is entitled to the confidentiality of the attorney/client relationship in respect to any communication with an independent attorney. In particular, the parties should consult independent counsel prior to signing any final settlement agreement.

III.

MEDIATOR REPRESENTS NEITHER PARTY

The parties acknowledge that the Mediator does not represent the interests of either party and is acting at all times as a neutral facilitator, not as an attorney for either party. The parties acknowledge that the purpose of Mediation is to facilitate the ultimate resolution and agreement between the parties regarding the issues, problems, and disputes presented in Mediation and that the Mediator does not act as an advocate, representative, fiduciary, or counsel for either party.

IV.

IMPARTIALITY OF MEDIATOR

The parties acknowledge that, although the Mediator will be impartial and that the Mediator does not favor either party, there may be issues in which

| Client Initial ___ |
| Client Initial ___ |

Attorney Fee Agreement
Page 2 of 8

one party may be reasonable and the other may not be reasonable. The Mediator has a duty to assure a balanced dialogue and to diffuse any manipulative or intimidating tactics.

V.

CONFIDENTIALITY

The Mediator agrees to keep all communication from either of the parties confidential in respect to any third persons, unless express verbal consent is given by both parties. For the purpose of facilitating communication and resolving differences between the parties, each party specifically authorizes the Mediator to meet individually with either party, and each party understands that such meetings are confidential and that the mediator <u>has no duty to disclose</u> the contents of those meetings to the other party. Therefore, the Mediator may meet with one party without the presence of the other, and any communication received in such individual sessions shall be confidential to the non-present party at the Mediator's discretion. Such disclosure of communications is to preserve the neutrality of the Mediator.

The parties agree that Sections 1119, 1121, 1122, 1123, 1125, 1126, 1128 are affirmed as the rules of our mediation and the sections are set forth here.

> The parties are aware that the provisions of Section 1119 of the *California Evidence Code* make all communications during the course of a mediation confidential and inadmissible in evidence in any civil proceeding as a matter of public policy. Section 1119 provides as follows:
>
> (a) No evidence of anything said or any admission made for the purpose of, in the course of, or pursuant to, a mediation or mediation consultation is admissible or subject to discovery, and disclosure of the evidence shall not be compelled, in any arbitration, administrative adjudication, civil action, or other noncriminal proceeding in which, pursuant to law, testimony can be compelled to be given.
>
> (b) No writing, as defined in Section 250, that is prepared for the purpose of, in the course of, or pursuant to, a mediation or a mediation consultation, is admissible or subject to discovery, and disclosure of the writing shall not be compelled, in any arbitration, administrative adjudication, civil action, or other noncriminal proceeding in which, pursuant to law, testimony can be compelled to be given.
>
> (c) All communications, negotiations, or settlement discussions by and between participants in the course of a mediation or a mediation consultation shall remain confidential.
>
> The parties are further aware that Section 703.5 of the *California Evidence Code* provides as follows: "No . . . mediator shall be competent to testify, in any subsequent civil proceeding, as to any

| Client Initial ___ |
| Client Initial ___ |

Attorney Fee Agreement
Page 3 of 8

statement, conduct, decision, or ruling, occurring at or in conjunction with the prior proceeding [*i.e.*, the mediation]."

The parties are further aware that the California Supreme Court has held in *Cassell v Superior Court* (2011) 51 Cal. 4th 113 and *Foxgate Homeowners' Assn. v. Bramalea California, Inc.* (2001) 26 Cal.4th 1, that there are no exceptions to this public policy. "To carry out the purpose of encouraging mediation by ensuring confidentiality, the statutory scheme, which includes sections 703.5, 1119, and 1121, unqualifiedly bars disclosure of communications made during mediation absent an express statutory exception."

Admissibility

The parties' agree that any agreement signed by both parties shall be admissible in any legal proceeding, and not otherwise be protected from disclosure, pursuant to the provisions of Section 1119(b) of the *California Evidence Code*. This document is expressly deemed admissible in any legal proceeding and otherwise subject to disclosure pursuant to the provisions of Section 1123 of the *California Evidence Code*. The parties further agree that neither party nor the mediator shall be required to testify in any legal proceeding as to mediation communications in respect to any issues, including communications related to the disclosure documents, and no documents prepared solely for the purpose of mediation shall be admissible in any legal proceeding.

Disclosure of Physical and/or Sex Abuse

The mediator shall not maintain confidential from the other party or to appropriate third parties any communication from the parties that indicates to the mediator any of the following:

1) Ongoing physical abuse of one party;
2) Ongoing or past physical violence or sexual abuse of a minor child;
3) The intention of one party to commit a criminal act endangering the other party or any third party. The parties acknowledge that although the mediator is an attorney licensed in the State of California, communications made in mediation are not protected by the attorney-client statutory privilege and confidentiality if the mediator were acting in the role of attorney and they release and hold mediator from any civil liability or professional ethical violations for disclosing such communication as a mediator which would be privileged of confidentiality.

Mediator reports and communications – Evidence Code Section 1121

Neither a mediator nor anyone else may submit to a court or other adjudicative body, and a court or other adjudicative body may not consider, any report, assessment, evaluation, recommendation, or finding of any kind by the mediator concerning a mediation conducted by the mediator, other than a report that is mandated by court rule or other law and that states only whether an agreement was reached, unless all parties to the mediation expressly agree otherwise in writing.

Client Initial ___
Client Initial ___

Attorney Fee Agreement
Page 4 of 8

Disclosure by Agreement – Evidence Code Section 1122

A communication or a writing that is made or prepared for the purpose of, or in the course of, or pursuant to, a mediation or a mediation consultation, is not made inadmissible, or protected from disclosure if either of the following conditions is satisfied:

(1) All persons who conduct or otherwise participate in the mediation expressly agree in writing, to disclosure of the communication, document, or writing.
(2) The communication, document, or writing was prepared by or on behalf of fewer than all the mediation participants, those participants expressly agree in writing, to its disclosure, and the communication, document, or writing does not disclose anything said or done or any admission made in the course of the mediation.
(3) If the neutral person who conducts a mediation expressly agrees to disclosure, that agreement also binds any other person designated by the mediator to assist in the mediation or to communicate with the participants in preparation for a mediation.

Written settlement agreements reached through mediation – Evidence Code Section 1123

A written settlement agreement prepared in the course of, or pursuant to, a mediation, is not made inadmissible, or protected from disclosure, by provisions of this chapter if the agreement is signed by the settling parties and any of the following conditions are satisfied:

(a) The agreement provides that it is admissible or subject to disclosure, or words to that effect.
(b) The agreement provides that it is enforceable or binding or words to that effect.
(c) All parties to the agreement expressly agree in writing.
(d) The agreement is used to show fraud, duress, or illegality that is relevant to an issue in dispute.

I. When mediation ends – Evidence Code Section 1125

(a) A mediation ends when any one of the following conditions is satisfied:

(1) The parties execute a written settlement agreement that fully resolves the dispute.
(2) The mediator provides the mediation participants with a writing signed by the mediator that states that the mediation is terminated, or words to that effect.
(3) A party provides the mediator and the other mediation participants with a writing stating that the mediation is terminated, or words to that effect. In a mediation involving more than two parties, the mediation may continue as to the remaining parties or be terminated in accordance with this section.

(b) For purposes of confidentiality, if a mediation partially resolves a dispute, mediation ends when either of the following conditions is satisfied:

| Client Initial ___ |
| Client Initial ___ |

Attorney Fee Agreement
Page 5 of 8

(1) The parties execute a written settlement agreement that partially resolves the dispute.

This section does not preclude a party from ending a mediation without reaching an agreement. This section does not otherwise affect the extent to which a party may terminate a mediation.

II. **Effect of end of mediation – Evidence Code Section 1126**

Anything said, any admission made, or any writing that is inadmissible, protected from disclosure, and confidential before a mediation ends, shall remain inadmissible, protected from disclosure, and confidential to the same extent after the mediation ends.

III. **Irregularity in proceedings – Evidence Code Section 1128**

Any reference to a mediation during any subsequent trial is an irregularity in the proceedings of the trial. Any reference to a mediation during any other subsequent noncriminal proceeding is grounds for vacating or modifying the decision in that proceeding, in whole or in party, and granting a new or further hearing on all or part of the issues, if the reference materially affected the substantial rights of the party requesting relief.

VI.

RIGHT OF MEDIATOR TO WITHDRAW

The Mediator will attempt to resolve any outstanding disputes as long as both parties make a good faith effort to reach an agreement based on fairness to both parties. Both parties must be willing and able to participate in the process. A mediated agreement requires compromise, and both parties agree to attempt to be flexible and open to new possibilities for a resolution of the dispute. If the Mediator, in his professional judgment, concludes that agreement is not possible or that continuation of the mediation process would harm or prejudice one or both of the participants or that a conflict exists between either or both parties and the mediator (ie failure to follow Mediator instructions or failure to timely pay in full for Mediator's services), the Mediator shall withdraw and the mediation shall conclude.

VII.

FOLLOWING THE INSTRUCTION(S) OF THE MEDIATOR

The parties agree to follow the instructions of the Mediator throughout the Mediation process. Such instructions are designed to insure that both parties receive full disclosure and development of factual information and that each party has an equal understanding of such information prior to reaching an agreement. Such instructions may include, but are not limited to: seeking advice from independent counsel; making available children, family members or other persons available for participation in Mediation; providing financial information, such as pay-stubs, bank statements, tax returns or other records; contacting and/or retaining independent experts or third parties (e.g. appraiser, therapist, doctor, employer, escrow, banks and/or stock brokers);

Client Initial ___
Client Initial ___

Attorney Fee Agreement
Page 6 of 8

or, anything else reasonably calculated by the Mediator that is to insure fairness in the Mediation process.

If either of the parties fail to follow the Mediator's instructions, each party agrees that Mediator may withdraw forthwith and both parties agree to release, hold harmless and indemnify the Mediator from any claim or liability for refusal to continue the Mediation.

VIII.

TERMINATION OF MEDIATION WITHOUT CAUSE

The Mediation may be terminated without cause by either party at any time. No reason needs to be given, either to the other party or to the Mediator. A decision to terminate Mediation must be made in writing. Mediation may not resume following said notification, unless expressly authorized by both parties.

Upon termination of mediation for any reason, the Mediator agrees not to represent either party against the other, in any court proceeding, adversary negotiation, or for any other reason involving a dispute between the parties.

IX.

VOLUNTARY DISCLOSURE OF POSSIBLE PREJUDICIAL INFORMATION

The parties agree that, while Mediation is in progress, full disclosure of all information is essential to a success full resolution of the issues. Since the court process is not being used to compel information, any agreement made through Mediation may be rescinded in whole or in part if one party fails to disclose relevant information during the Mediation process. Since the voluntary disclosure of this information may give one party an advantage that may not have been obtained through the traditional adversarial process, the parties agree to release and hold harmless the Mediator from any liability or damages caused by voluntary disclosure of prejudicial information in the Mediation process that may be used in subsequent negotiations or court proceedings. The Mediator has no power to bind third parties not to disclose information furnished during Mediation.

X.

THE MEDIATOR SHALL NOT TESTIFY

Pursuant to Evidence Code Section 1127, the parties agree not to call or subpoena the Mediator to testify at any court proceeding nor to produce any document obtained or prepared from any Mediation session without the prior written authorization of both parties. If either party issues a subpoena regarding the Mediator or his or her documents, that party shall pay the Mediator his or her current hourly rate for all hours expended and shall pay all reasonable attorney fees of the other party in respect to the response, compliance, or resistance of said subpoena.

Client Initial ___
Client Initial ___

Attorney Fee Agreement
Page 7 of 8

XI.

THE MEDIATOR DOES NOT PROMISE RESULTS

Each party acknowledges that, since Mediation is a process of compromise, it is possible that either party might agree to settle on terms that might be considered to be less favorable in comparison to what the party <u>might</u> have received from a Judge after a contested court hearing, or through negotiation in which one or both of the parties have retained legal counsel. The Mediator makes no representations that the ultimate result would be the same in kind or degree as might be concluded through negotiation or a contested trial on one or all of the issues. Any questions concerning fairness should be addressed to the Mediator as they occur. In addition, the spouses should consult with independent legal counsel to review compromises made during the course of Mediation, and all provisions of a final agreement prior to executing the Marital Settlement Agreement and other court documents.

XII

REIMBURSEMENT OF COSTS

The parties agree to reimburse the Mediator for any and all costs expended on behalf of the parties that are authorized in advance by the parties.

XIII.

BOTH PARTIES ARE RESPONSIBLE FOR FEES

The parties hereby agree to be jointly and severally responsible for the fees of mediators and staff of Forrest S. Mosten. If, for any reason, the fee of the Mediator is not paid within fifteen (15) days of billing, the Mediator reserves the right to unilaterally refuse to render any further professional services for the parties. The parties agree that, in addition to the payment of any agreed upon fees, each of the parties shall be liable for any costs of collecting the total amount of the fee, including reasonable attorney fees for collecting said fees.

XIV.

FEES AND SERVICES

The services of the Mediator include, but is not limited to: Mediation sessions with either party; telephone or office conferences with either party or with third parties; coordination and referral with other resource persons; drafting of letters or court documents; other services performed by the mediator or behalf of the mediation.

XV

REPLENISHABLE DEPOSIT

If the parties choose not to proceed by credit card or at any time during the mediation, the parties each agree to pay an initial deposit. Parties shall deposit with Mediator an advance deposit to be credited against client's final bill. Parties will pay Mediator monthly in full for services rendered during that month within 15 days of billing. At completion of Mediator's work with Parties

Client Initial ___
Client Initial ___

Attorney Fee Agreement
Page 8 of 8

the retainer will be credited towards Parties' final bill and the remainder will be refunded to the Parties.

XVI

EXECUTION OF MEDIATION AGREEMENT

By signing this Mediation Agreement, each party agrees that he or she has carefully read and considered each and every provision of this Agreement and agrees to each provision of this agreement without reservation. Before signing this agreement, each party has the right and is encouraged to have this agreement reviewed by an attorney.

_____   _____
Date   Name of Party

_____   _____
Date   Name of Party

_____   _____
Date   Mediator

Client Initial ___
Client Initial ___

Appendix M

Sample Estimate of Mediation Expenses

LAW AND MEDIATION OFFICE OF
Forrest S. Mosten*

9401 WILSHIRE BOULEVARD, 9TH FLOOR
BEVERLY HILLS, CALIFORNIA 90212
TELEPHONE (310) 473-7611
FACSIMILE (310) 473-7422
E-Mail: MOSTEN@MEDIATE.COM
WWW.MOSTENMEDIATION.COM

*CERTIFIED FAMILY LAW SPECIALIST
CALIFORNIA BOARD OF LEGAL SPECIALIZATION
+ ADVANCED PRACTITIONER
ASSOCIATION FOR CONFLICT RESOLUTION
++ MEMBER, INTERNATIONAL ACADEMY OF
COLLABORATIVE PROFESSIONALS

LOUIS M. BROWN CLIENT LIBRARY

ESTIMATE OF MEDIATION EXPENSES

Every client has a right to understand and manage the costs of their mediation.

Some mediations can be concluded in one session and others may require 10 sessions or more.

The factors that will impact the cost of your mediation are:

- Willingness and ability of the parties to negotiate fairly and efficiently with each other;
- The level of conflict and communication problems;
- Complexity and emotionality of parenting issues
- Size and sophistication of the financial estate and ability and willingness to disclose assets and liabilities
- Collaboration and expertise of lawyers and other professionals
- Ease of scheduling and willingness to follow my recommendations

The following estimate of mediation costs is based on averages in my over 35 years of mediation practice. The estimate should give you an overview of the mediation cost structure. Remember: These are only ranges and your situation may be very different.

Orientation Session	30 minutes: No Charge
Private Preliminary Planning Sessions 1-2 hours with each Party	2-4 Hours
Working Sessions 3-4 Hours Each Session Average 3-5 Sessions	9-20 Hours

Email and Phone Communication with Parties, Lawyers, Experts, and Other Persons Between Sessions 1 Hour for Each Session	3-5 Hours
Draft Petition and Initial Court Documents	.5-2 Hours
Draft Judgment and Final Court Documents	4-7 Hours
Revise Documents, Facilitate Drafting Issues and Closing	1-6 Hours
Total Estimated Range of Mediator Time	19.5-44 Hours
Additional Professional Time: Lawyers, CPA, Appraisers, Therapist, Others	To Be Determined
Estimated Minimum Cost Filing Fees for Both Parties	$870

Appendix N

Sample Agenda for Divorce Mediation

LAW AND MEDIATION OFFICE OF
Forrest S. Mosten*

*CERTIFIED FAMILY LAW SPECIALIST
CALIFORNIA BOARD OF LEGAL SPECIALIZATION
+ ADVANCED PRACTITIONER
ASSOCIATION FOR CONFLICT RESOLUTION
++ MEMBER, INTERNATIONAL ACADEMY OF
COLLABORATIVE PROFESSIONALS

11661 SAN VICENTE BOULEVARD, SUITE 414
LOS ANGELES, CALIFORNIA 90049-5118
TELEPHONE (310) 473-7611
FACSIMILE (310) 473-7422
E-Mail: MOSTEN@MEDIATE.COM
WWW.MOSTENMEDIATION.COM

LOUIS M. BROWN CLIENT LIBRARY

REBECCA LYN KORINEK
Conflict Resolution Assistant
M.A. in Dispute Resolution

Sample Divorce Mediation Agenda

Two types of issues are the subject of agreements in mediation and collaborative divorce: ***how*** the process of mediation/collaborative divorce and party interaction will work until an agreement is reached and ***what*** the points of the settlement will be. Here is a typical agenda outline (with sub-issues for each agenda topic) of the more than 250 possible issues of a divorce and how they can be handled:

1. Mediation process
   - *Lawyers and Other Divorce Professionals:* Which professionals will participate? What roles they will play? How will they be paid?
   - *Meeting protocol:* How often will parties meet? For how long, and when? Where will the meetings take place?

2. Personal conduct of the parties outside sessions
   - *Telephone calls between parties:* What are the ground rules as to time, length, and subject; the return-call policy; access during travel; and phones for children?
   - *Privacy of residences:* Does a party have a key or the right to enter the residence of the other? Are there areas of residence that are off-limits? Do both parties have the right to the home office, garage workshop, or other areas of the family residence?

3. Separation of the parties
   - *Physical separation:* What are the date and manner of physical separation from the joint residence? How will the children be told and be involved? How will parties handle dating and overnights with new romantic partners?
   - *Separation of finances:* How will income be allocated and deposited? Who pays for expenses and credit card bills? Who has rights to new business contracts and opportunities?

4. Temporary parenting issues
    - *Decision making:* How will parenting decisions be made? What is the balance between privacy and protection of children (for example, may children engage in sky diving, have tattoos, or smoke cigarettes or be subjected to parental second-hand smoke)?
    - *Time sharing:* How will parenting be handled during the regular school schedule, vacations, and special days such as grandparents' birthdays? How can schedules and plans be easily modified in the future?
5. Temporary financial issues
    - *Child and spousal support:* What is the amount and method of payment for expenses such as child care, sports or music lessons, or purchase of clothes? How will the marital standard of living and amount of available income be determined?
    - *Valuing and management of joint assets:* Who operates the family business or arranges for a real estate broker to sell the residence? How will appraisals and accountings be conducted?
6. Permanent property division
    - *Dividing assets and debts:* How will information and financial disclosures with final values and determine equalization and terms (if any) be handled?;
    - *Long-term deferred assets:* When and how will retirement plans and investments will be handled?
7. Other financial issues
    - How will taxes, medical and life insurance, payment of college expenses, trust arrangements for the children, and other issues be handled?
8. Permanent child and spousal support
    - *Income and need:* Will passive income from investment properties and marital lifestyle be used to determine final support amounts?
    - *Conditions for modification and termination:* How will cohabitation with new romantic partners, changes of income, and other factors influence agreed-on arrangements?;
9. Determination of the permanent parenting plan
    - *Revisit temporary plan:* How are the temporary arrangements working for the children? How will temporary agreements be confirmed? How will parents handle issues that were deferred during determination of the temporary plan?

10. Future dispute resolution process
    - *Future meetings:* Will parents arrange for regularly scheduled parenting meetings? How will parties collaboratively reevaluate changing income and needs?
    - *Anticipate future disagreements:* Will there be agreements for notice of disputes, mandatory mediation sessions, and possible use of parenting evaluations as buffers future against court litigation?
11. Draft settlement agreement and other documents
    - *Drafting process:* Who will draft the settlement agreement, and when? What other court, real estate, and business documents need to be drafted, and by whom? How will technical problems such as qualified domestic relations orders for retirement plans be handled?
12. *Review and signing process:* Who will be involved, and when will the ceremony for signing and closure take place? Will there be a formal closure process?

Appendix O

Sample Client Handout: My Role as Your Consulting Lawyer in Mediation

LAW AND MEDIATION OFFICE OF
Forrest S. Mosten*

*CERTIFIED FAMILY LAW SPECIALIST
CALIFORNIA BOARD OF LEGAL SPECIALIZATION
+ ADVANCED PRACTITIONER
ASSOCIATION FOR CONFLICT RESOLUTION
++ MEMBER, INTERNATIONAL ACADEMY OF
COLLABORATIVE PROFESSIONALS

9401 WILSHIRE BLVD, 9TH FLOOR
BEVERLY HILLS, CALIFORNIA 90212
TELEPHONE (310) 473-7611
FACSIMILE (310) 470-2625
E-Mail: MOSTEN@MEDIATE.COM
WWW.MOSTENMEDIATION.COM

LOUIS M. BROWN CLIENT LIBRARY

MY ROLE AS YOUR CONSULTING LAWYER DURING MEDIATION

As your consulting lawyer, I am committed to offering you all the professional obligations of competence and loyalty that you would have in any other lawyer engagement. In concrete terms, this means that I have a duty to pursue your objectives, protect you from financial harm and legal exposure, inform you of your legal rights, produce competent work, keep all attorney-client communications confidential, avoid conflicts of interest, and insure that my fees are understood and are fair.

Although my approach may differ from the traditional lawyer model with which you are familiar, I am still your lawyer. I pledge to give you the advice and professional support as lawyer while at the same time give you the benefit from my "meditative" non-adversarial approach values and perspective. I am constantly walking the tightrope between conciliatory facilitator with your spouse and your advocate.

My Different Roles as Your Collaborative Lawyer

Representative: I am your agent and I will convey your needs and concerns to the mediator, other party, and professionals.

Advocate: I will "advocate" for your interests throughout the mediation process.

Ally: I am your ally in helping you navigate through the mediation process.

Adapted from Forrest S. Mosten, *Collaborative Divorce Handbook,* Wiley (2009).

Coach: As you will often be talking for yourself in mediation sessions and with your spouse, I will coach you with legal, parenting, and financial issues, to help your communication, and to address your emotional needs.

What Do I Do as Your Consulting Lawyer Does During the Process

Educator: My job is to teach you about the various issues to be covered and the key stages of the mediation process. I will often assign you homework such as asking you to contact the children's school for vacation dates, finish your budget, or contact life insurance companies for insurability and rates. As the process develops, I will explain and prepare you for each stage. For example, prior to the first mediation session, I will go over the possible agenda, review the Mediator's Contract Agreement, and help you be ready for unexpected twists and turns.

Manager of the Process: I will work with you and the mediator in scheduling meetings, making sure legal and tax deadlines are met, and work out assignments for fact gathering and drafting. If outside experts are needed, I might raise the need for the expert, help find the expert, and coach you to arrange for the engagement. In essence, I will make sure that the train runs on time and gets to the station. I will also help choreograph communication and negotiation moves for you to be used with the other party and the mediator.

Counselor at Law: I will listen to your concerns and help frame the decisions that you need to make. Such decisions may be about particular issues (how spring break should be divided, who lives in the residence) or about the mediation process (how often should we meet, who should be at the next mediation session). I will present objective criteria (legal principles, financial viability, effect on the parenting relationship) and

Client Initial ___

options for you to make sound decisions. Once decisions are reached, I will help carry out the plan and monitor the situation to see if decisions need to be revisited or revised.

<u>Fact Gatherer:</u> With over 250 issues in a comprehensive divorce, I will make sure that you have sufficient information to make informed decisions. This information comes in many forms: legal and financial documents, emails, websites, conversations with experts and salespeople, and just looking around. For example, to determine where you might live after moving out of the house, someone will need to find out availability and pricing of appropriate apartments and houses for rent. It is my job to determine with you and the mediator what information is needed, how it will be obtained, how it will be analyzed, and how it is to be utilized in decision making. I will also work with you to prepare financial disclosures and review the disclosures from the other party.

<u>Legal Researcher:</u> I am responsible for making sure you have up-to-date legal information from which to evaluate decisions and plan proposals. I will also use relevant statutes, cases, and reports for you to provide to the mediator to help the other party gain reality in assessing possible bargaining range. I will be candid about the strengths and weaknesses of legal positions. However, I will never take advantage of possible ignorance of your spouse or attorney or the mediator in any way, including in the use of legal authority.

<u>Negotiator and Negotiation Coach</u>: Since you and I will work as a team, we will discuss and resolve issues, both small and large. If you choose, I can be your agent in negotiations with the other party's attorney and the mediator. I will also prepare you to present your own proposals both in mediation sessions when I am not present. I may even have simulated role playing practice sessions with you in which I could play the other

Client Initial ___

party and give you a rehearsal. Or you might play the role of your spouse so you can feel what it is like to have her perspective that might alter or refine your negotiation strategy.

Drafter/Ghost Writer: It will be my responsibility to review summary letters, interim or partial agreements, the full settlement agreement and/or court judgment/decree, other court documents, real estate, business, and other documents that may be required. If the mediator does not have the competence/expertise to draft a particular document or it is agreed that the lawyers should do so, it may be necessary to have me or the other lawyer or expert do that work. In addition to drafting documents, I can be "on-call" for you to review and edit letters, emails, and other documents that you might wish to send to your spouse or third person. If there is such as a qualified retirement plan that will be divided, I will want a highly technical document such as a Qualified Domestic Relations Order to be drafted by an outside expert rather than by either lawyer.

Preventive Legal Health Provider: Divorce can be one of life's most upsetting events. During the negotiation of the settlement agreement and afterward, my role may shift from dispute resolution to conflict prevention. In this preventive function, I can help you in several ways. I may recommend an expert to draft wills, trusts, durable powers of attorney, or living wills, recommend and draft future dispute resolution clauses, calendar and monitor future events provided in the agreement (e.g., buy-out of house, change of school in the 7th grade), or arrange for parenting or support update meetings.

There may be other roles that I can play based on our discussion or tasks that you will do yourself rather than have me do. The basis of our relationship is up-to-date communication and I shall be available to address your questions and concerns.

Client Initial ___

Appendix P

Sample Agreement for Attorney Disqualification in Mediation

LAW AND MEDIATION OFFICE OF
Forrest S. Mosten*

*CERTIFIED FAMILY LAW SPECIALIST
CALIFORNIA BOARD OF LEGAL SPECIALIZATION
+ ADVANCED PRACTITIONER
ASSOCIATION FOR CONFLICT RESOLUTION
++ MEMBER, INTERNATIONAL ACADEMY OF
COLLABORATIVE PROFESSIONALS

9401 WILSHIRE BLVD, 9TH FLOOR
BEVERLY HILLS, CALIFORNIA 90212
TELEPHONE (310) 473-7611
FACSIMILE (310) 470-2625
E-Mail: MOSTEN@MEDIATE.COM
WWW.MOSTENMEDIATION.COM

LOUIS M. BROWN CLIENT LIBRARY

Attorney Disqualification Agreement for Parties in Mediation

Wife and Husband are participants in mediation with Forrest S. Mosten, Mediator.

The parties agree that the engagement of consulting attorneys by each party will facilitate the mediation process by providing legal advice and support to each party.

The parties further agree that the below disqualification of attorneys upon any termination of mediation will permit the attorneys to support the parties' commitment to resolve all matters within the safe confidential container of mediation without threats of court action or court action itself.

Both parties agree that should mediation terminate and the attorneys are disqualified, there will be additional expense and time necessary to engage substitute legal counsel.

The parties agree that all communications by either the party or the mediator with their respective attorney swill remain confidential. The mediator may speak with the either or both attorneys outside the presence of the parties

The parties shall mutually agree whether the mediator shall send summary agreements directly to the attorneys.

If either party wants his/her attorney to attend a mediation session, this may occur without the agreement of the other party. However, the party intending to have his/her lawyer attend a mediation session must give at least 3 days notice to the other party and to the mediator so that the other party may bring her/his lawyer.

If a set time for a mediation is not convenient for either lawyer, it is agreed that the date of the mediation will be changed to accommodate both parties and both lawyers.

_____ has been retained by Wife to advise her during the course of this mediation and _____ has been retained by Husband to advise him during the course of this mediation. Each attorney named above has agreed to be bound by the terms of this agreement. Should the mediation terminate due to request for termination by either party or the mediator, each attorney named above, and any attorney in association with such attorney, shall immediately withdraw and terminate legal services and is forever disqualified from appearing as an attorney of record in contested matters for either party named above in this proceeding or in any other family law or civil matter involving both parties. An attorney shall be deemed "in association" if, at any time during the pendency of these proceedings or future family law proceedings between these parties, such attorney is the employer or employee of, or co-employee with, or shares a relationship of partnership or independent contractor status with any attorney named above.

Client Initial ___
Client Initial ___

Appendix Q

Sample Dispute Resolution Protocol and Mediation Clause

Mediation Clause

This clause may be used in any family law agreement or court order. As in any clause, this model provides a structure from which innovative modifications may be made.

In *Mediation: Law Policy and Practice*, Nancy Rogers and Craig McEwen cite a Connecticut statute dealing with enforcement of a physician's mediation clause: "In order to merit enforcement, the clause must be clear enough for persons with a sixth grade level of education to understand and on a form no longer than one page in length."

Is there a different standard in family law in which the clause is a product of a negotiated agreement, and would this model mediation clause be enforceable under the Connecticut standard?

Mediation Clause (Short)

Prior to filing any court action (absent emergency), the parties agree to participate in meaningful mediation with a mediator mutually selected or appointed by the court. The parties shall equally pay for the costs of mediation.

Mediation Clause (Long)

Absent emergency (which shall be narrowly construed by the court), neither party shall be permitted to file in superior court for any type of relief without filing a written stipulation of the parties' mutually requesting relief or without demonstrating to the court that the following have preceded the court filing:

1. Written notice to the other party detailing the following:

A. The specific relief requested and the facts supporting the re-quested relief. Such notice is encouraged (but not required) to include a statement indicating why the children and/or the parties would benefit from the relief requested or would be harmed if such relief is not be granted.

B. The names, addresses, and telephones numbers of three mediators acceptable to the requesting party who have been contacted by the requesting party and have available dates within 30 days of the notice.

C. The date and times of least one four-hour time block for each mediator.

2. A declaration under penalty of perjury that the requesting party has meaningfully participated in good faith in mediation for a minimum of four hours with the other party or that the other party has refused to participate meaningfully in mediation for a minimum of four hours.

If the matter is not resolved after four hours of mediation, the parties are encouraged to continue to mediate until final resolution.

All costs for mediation shall be advanced equally by the parties in a manner reasonably requested by the mediator. The final allocation of these costs may be an issue in mediation or determined by the court.

Appendix R

Personal Legal Wellness Checkup and Protocol

The following legal wellness checkup was approved in May 1996 by the American Bar Association Section of Law Practice Management to be given to lawyers in that section to diagnose their legal health. The results will be assessed by the section's Law Task Force, chaired by Thomas Gonser, former ABA executive director, to recommend an ABA agenda for preventive law and use of the legal checkup by American lawyers for themselves and, most important, for their clients.

Take the legal checkup yourself to monitor your own legal health. Does it stimulate any thinking or concerns about decisions or actions you wish to consider in your own life? How can you use it with your own clients in its present or modified form? Can you see ways of using it as a marketing tool to attract new clients or generate additional revenue for your law office?

CLIENT LEGAL CHECK-UP

All of our lawyers and support staff are dedicated to not only solving your immediate legal problems but also insuring your on-going legal health and wellness. Like a legal thermometer, this check-up helps us assess your current legal health so that we can work as a team to prevent or minimize legal troubles in your life. Please take a few minutes to complete this confidential check-up.

Date: _____

Name: _____

Do you have a will which has been revised within the past three years?	Yes ❑ No ❑
Do you currently have any concerns about your job or business?	Yes ❑ No ❑
Do you have adequate life insurance protection?	Yes ❑ No ❑
Do you have adequate medical insurance?	Yes ❑ No ❑
Do you presently have a written and current listing of all important future dates concerning your legal and financial matters?	Yes ❑ No ❑
Do you have a file, stored in a secure and fireproof location, containing all important documents (wills, titles, securities, contracts, marriage, divorce papers, deeds, pension plans, profit sharing plans, etc.)?	Yes ❑ No ❑
Within the last three years have you reviewed the beneficiary designations on insurance policies, pension plans, bank accounts and other important documents?	Yes ❑ No ❑
Do you have a complete and current personal financial statement which lists in detail all of your personal assets and liabilities?	Yes ❑ No ❑
Do you currently have a monthly budget which details your current income and all expenses?	Yes ❑ No ❑
Do you have any concerns about your debts?	Yes ❑ No ❑
Do you have a complete and current inventory of all your physical possessions sufficient to support a claim in the event of a loss?	Yes ❑ No ❑
Do you have concerns about the academic, emotional, or social development of your child(ren)?	Yes ❑ No ❑
Are there currently extraordinary emotional pressures and stresses on your life?	Yes ❑ No ❑
If you and your spouse have been separated for less than two years, is the current support and economic arrangement between the two of you satisfactory?	Yes ❑ No ❑
If you and your spouse have been separated for more than two years, has the support and economic arrangement been reviewed in the last two years?	Yes ❑ No ❑

After reviewing these questions, are there any matters or issues which you believe   Yes ❏ No ❏
should be updated, reconsidered or brought to the attention of your attorney? Please explain below.

Have any of these questions caused you to consider taking some action or making   Yes ❏ No ❏
some further review? Please explain below.

Is there any other legal, financial, or personal concern which you believe should be   Yes ❏ No ❏
brought to the attention of your attorney? Please explain below.

On the lines below, please expand on any of your answers which you believe would give your attorney a better picture of your current legal health.

_____
_____
_____
_____
_____
_____
_____
_____

ATTORNEY NOTES:

Sample Personal Legal Checkup Protocol

Developed Jointly by the National Center for Preventive Law and the American Association of Retired Persons (AARP) for Model Program in Pennsylvania (Reprinted with Permission)

Every client and any type of contact provides an opportunity for the mediation- and prevention-friendly lawyers to educate and probe for asymptotic legal disease. Once diagnosed, it is the client's responsibility to decide whether to take action and, if so, whether professional help is needed.

The legal checkup provides an illustration of diagnostic tools that are available to the family lawyer to prevent future conflict and maximize legal health.

General Steps Individuals Can Take to Help Keep Their Legal Health in Order

When making agreements or transactions, or when dealing with important documents:

- Read documents carefully before signing.
- Ask for an explanation of anything you do not understand before signing.
- Consider writing the explanation you receive on the document you are signing.
- Keep copies of anything you sign.
- Put any agreement you consider important in writing.
- Use certified mail when sending important documents to verify transmittal.
- Keep documents, like wills, up to date by reviewing them after major events like births, death, marriage, or divorce.
- Keep notes of conversations you have that you consider to be important, especially if the conversation concerns money or property.

Keep the following documents for at least six years:

- Agreements, loan papers, and similar documents
- Bank statements and canceled checks
- Copies of income tax returns
- Real estate bills
- Child-care payments

Consider keeping the following documents in a safe deposit box for safekeeping (someone else should be made aware of the safe deposit box so that it can be accessed if you are somehow incapacitated):

- Adoption papers
- Automobile ownership certificate (pink slip)
- Birth certificate
- Marriage license
- Will
- Deed to your home and title insurance policy for your home
- Life insurance policies
- Stock certificates and bonds
- Passport
- A current list of personal property, including descriptions of major items along with identification numbers, purchase receipts for the items, and photographs of the items. This may help verify your loss to the police and your insurance company in case of theft or fire.

Keep your canceled checks or get and keep receipts when paying cash for the following:

- Mortgage or rent payment
- Insurance payments
- Automobile payments
- Credit card payments
- Consumer loan payments

General Steps

Consider making a chart of significant dates and keeping it in a handy place where you can refer to it as a reminder of when you need to take action. You may wish to include the following, and any additional dates of personal significance that you wish to remember:

EVENT	TRIGGER DATE
Federal income tax return and payment	
Estimated tax and payment	
Pennsylvania income tax return and payment	
Estimated tax and payment	
Auto insurance premium due	
Auto insurance policy expiration date	
Auto loan maturity date	
Auto loan monthly payment due	
Home insurance premium due	
Home insurance expiration date	
Life insurance premium due	
Life insurance option date	
Lease or rental agreement termination date	
Mortgage payment due date	
Real estate tax due	
Rent payment due date	
Automobile registration expiration date	
Drivers license expiration date	
Passport expiration date	
Convertible securities—conversion date	
Bank loan maturity date	
Bank loan monthly payment due	
Credit union loan maturity date	
Credit union loan payment due	

Checklists

We're Getting Married

We must arrange for a:
- ❏ blood test
- ❏ marriage license

If one of us makes a last name change, we should notify:
- ❏ credit card companies
- ❏ charge accounts
- ❏ banks and other financial institutions
- ❏ other organizations where we have investments
- ❏ insurance companies
- ❏ Social Security Administration (need to get new Social Security card)
- ❏ employers
- ❏ Pennsylvania Department of Transportation (need to change name on drivers license & automobile registration)

We should review the beneficiaries listed in our:
- ❏ wills
- ❏ life insurance policies
- ❏ bank accounts
- ❏ annuities
- ❏ pension plans
- ❏ testamentary or living trusts

We should review the funds and possessions that will be considered to be our:
- ❏ joint property (things we own together)
- ❏ separate property (things we own apart from one another)

We should determine the best way (separately or together) to:
- ❏ sign income tax returns (for tax savings)
- ❏ sign leases (in terms of liability)
- ❏ own property (real and personal)

I'm Buying a Home

I may need to budget these costs:
- ❏ appraisal
- ❏ inspection
- ❏ down payment

- ❑ monthly mortgage payments
- ❑ escrow service
- ❑ loan application fee
- ❑ title insurance
- ❑ mortgage insurance
- ❑ monthly utility bills
- ❑ property taxes
- ❑ maintenance costs
- ❑ "fixer-upper" improvements
- ❑ insurance costs
- ❑ homeowner assoc. fees (in some cases)
- ❑ possible assessments (e.g., streetlights, sewers)

I should consider these inspections:
- ❑ general structural inspection
- ❑ pest control (termites and dry rot)
- ❑ asbestos
- ❑ soil stability (of, for example, hillside property)
- ❑ radon gas

My offer on the house should cover all important terms:
- ❑ complete description of the property (full street address and legal description, if available)
- ❑ description of anything else included in the sale (appliances, etc.)
- ❑ exact purchase price
- ❑ purchase price broken down into deposit, down payment, amount of loan
- ❑ my rights if inspections uncover a problem
- ❑ whether my deposit will be returned if I cancel

I can shop for a loan at:
- ❑ banks
- ❑ savings and loan associations
- ❑ insurance companies
- ❑ credit unions
- ❑ mortgage brokers
- ❑ mortgage bankers

Among other things, my loan may:
- ❑ have a fixed or adjustable interest rate

- [ ] be seller financed
- [ ] be assumed (taken over from seller)
- [ ] be due in full if I sell the house

I should consider the advantages/disadvantages of a:
- [ ] standard down payment
- [ ] larger down payment and smaller monthly payments

My taxes and heirs are affected by whether I own the house:
- [ ] by myself
- [ ] as tenants by the entirety with my spouse
- [ ] as a joint tenant with one or more people
- [ ] as a tenant-in-common with one or more people

If I fail to pay the mortgage, the lender can foreclose and:
- [ ] must notify me that my property will be sold
- [ ] must give me a chance to make the missed payments
- [ ] collect late fees and costs of foreclosure from me

Appendix S

Required Statutory Forms for Financial Disclosure (California)

```
                                                                              FL-140
ATTORNEY OR PARTY WITHOUT ATTORNEY (Name, State Bar number, and address):
   2: FILING ATTORNEY'S NAME     75: SBN
   4: NAME OF LAW FIRM FILING ACTION
   5: STREET ADDRESS OF FIRM FILING ACTION
   6: CITY STATE AND ZIP CODE OF FIRM
 TELEPHONE NO.: 3: FIRM PHONE #    FAX NO.: 76: FIRM FAX #
 E-MAIL ADDRESS: 169: E-MAIL ADDRESS
 ATTORNEY FOR (Name): 7: ATTORNEY FOR NAME
SUPERIOR COURT OF CALIFORNIA, COUNTY OF  101: COUNTY FILED
    STREET ADDRESS: 9: STREET ADDRESS OF COURT
    MAILING ADDRESS: 10: POST OFFICE ADDRESS OF COURT
    CITY AND ZIP CODE: 11: CITY STATE AND ZIP OF COURT
    BRANCH NAME: 12: BRANCH OF COURT
         PETITIONER: 13: PLAINTIFF/PETITIONER LINE ONE
         RESPONDENT: 15: DEFENDANT/RESPONDENT LINE ONE
OTHER PARENT/PARTY: 21: OTHER PARENT

              DECLARATION OF DISCLOSURE                    CASE NUMBER:
    ☐ Petitioner's      ☐ Preliminary                      17: CASE NUMBER
    ☐ Respondent's      ☐ Final
```

DO NOT FILE DECLARATIONS OF DISCLOSURE OR FINANCIAL ATTACHMENTS WITH THE COURT

In a dissolution, legal separation, or nullity action, both a preliminary and a final declaration of disclosure must be served on the other party with certain exceptions. Neither disclosure is filed with the court. Instead, a declaration stating that service of disclosure documents was completed or waived must be filed with the court (see form FL-141).

- In summary dissolution cases, each spouse or domestic partner must exchange preliminary disclosures as described in Summary Dissolution Information (form FL-810). Final disclosures are not required (see Family Code section 2109).
- In a default judgment case that is not a stipulated judgment or a judgment based on a marital settlement agreement, only the petitioner is required to complete and serve a preliminary declaration of disclosure. A final disclosure is not required of either party (see Family Code section 2110).
- Service of preliminary declarations of disclosure may not be waived by an agreement between the parties.
- Parties who agree to waive final declarations of disclosure must file their written agreement with the court (see form FL-144).

The petitioner must serve a preliminary declaration of disclosure at the same time as the Petition or within 60 days of filing the Petition. The respondent must serve a preliminary declaration of disclosure at the same time as the Response or within 60 days of filing the Response. The time periods may be extended by written agreement of the parties or by court order (see Family Code section 2104(f)).

Attached are the following:

1. ☐ A completed *Schedule of Assets and Debts* (form FL-142) or ☐ A *Property Declaration* (form FL-160) for *(specify)*:
   ☐ Community and Quasi-Community Property ☐ Separate Property.
2. ☐ A completed *Income and Expense Declaration* (form FL-150).
3. ☐ All tax returns filed by the party in the two years before the date that the party served the disclosure documents.
4. ☐ A statement of all material facts and information regarding valuation of all assets that are community property or in which the community has an interest *(not a form)*.
5. ☐ A statement of all material facts and information regarding obligations for which the community is liable *(not a form)*.
6. ☐ An accurate and complete written disclosure of any investment opportunity, business opportunity, or other income-producing opportunity presented since the date of separation that results from any investment, significant business, or other income-producing opportunity from the date of marriage to the date of separation *(not a form)*.

I declare under penalty of perjury under the laws of the State of California that the foregoing is true and correct.

Date:

_____   ▶ _____
         (TYPE OR PRINT NAME)   SIGNATURE

Form Adopted for Mandatory Use   **DECLARATION OF DISCLOSURE**   Family Code, §§ 2102, 2104,
Judicial Council of California   (Family Law)   2105, 2106, 2112
FL-140 [Rev. July 1, 2013]   www.courts.ca.gov

                                                              1: SAMPLE CLIENT

APPENDIX S: REQUIRED STATUTORY FORMS FOR FINANCIAL DISCLOSURE (CALIFORNIA) 287

FL-141

ATTORNEY OR PARTY WITHOUT ATTORNEY (Name, State Bar number, and address):
2: FILING ATTORNEY'S NAME 75: SBN
4: NAME OF LAW FIRM FILING ACTION
5: STREET ADDRESS OF FIRM FILING ACTION
6: CITY STATE AND ZIP CODE OF FIRM
TELEPHONE NO.: 3: FIRM PHONE #   FAX NO.: 76: FIRM FAX #
E-MAIL ADDRESS: 169: E-MAIL ADDRESS
ATTORNEY FOR (Name): 7: ATTORNEY FOR NAME

SUPERIOR COURT OF CALIFORNIA, COUNTY OF 101: COUNTY FILED
STREET ADDRESS: 9: STREET ADDRESS OF COURT
MAILING ADDRESS: 10: POST OFFICE ADDRESS OF COURT
CITY AND ZIP CODE: 11: CITY STATE AND ZIP OF COURT
BRANCH NAME: 12: BRANCH OF COURT

PETITIONER: 13: PLAINTIFF/PETITIONER LINE ONE
RESPONDENT: 15: DEFENDANT/RESPONDENT LINE ONE
OTHER PARENT/PARTY: 21: OTHER PARENT

DECLARATION REGARDING SERVICE OF DECLARATION OF DISCLOSURE AND INCOME AND EXPENSE DECLARATION
☐ Petitioner's   ☐ Preliminary
☐ Respondent's   ☐ Final

CASE NUMBER:
17: CASE NUMBER

1. I am the ☐ attorney for ☐ petitioner ☐ respondent in this matter.

2. ☐ Petitioner's ☐ Respondent's *Preliminary Declaration of Disclosure* (form FL-140), current* *Income and Expense Declaration* (form FL-150), completed *Schedule of Assets and Debts* (form FL-142) or *Community and Separate Property Declarations* (form FL-160) with appropriate attachments, all tax returns filed by the party in the two years before service of the preliminary disclosures, and all other required information under Family Code section 2104 were served on:
☐ the other party   ☐ the other party's attorney by   ☐ personal service   ☐ mail
☐ Other (specify):
on (date):

3. ☐ Petitioner's ☐ Respondent's *Final Declaration of Disclosure* (form FL-140), current* *Income and Expense Declaration* (form FL-150), completed *Schedule of Assets and Debts* (form FL-142) or *Community or Separate Property Declarations* (form FL-160) with attachments, and the material facts and information required by Family Code section 2105 were served on:
☐ the other party   ☐ other party's attorney   by   ☐ personal service   ☐ mail
☐ Other (specify):
on (date):

4. ☐ Service of ☐ Petitioner's ☐ Respondent's ☐ preliminary ☐ final declaration of disclosure ☐ current income and expense declaration has been waived as follows:
   a. ☐ The parties agreed to waive final declaration of disclosure requirements under Family Code section 2105(d). (Form FL-144 may be used for this purpose.) The waiver ☐ was filed on (date):
   ☐ is being filed at the same time as this form.
   b. ☐ The party has failed to comply with disclosure requirements, and the court has granted the request for voluntary waiver of receipt under Family Code section 2107 on (date):
   c. ☐ This is a default proceeding that does not include a stipulated judgment or settlement agreement. Petitioner waives final disclosure requirements under Family Code section 2110.

*Current is defined as completed within the past three months providing no facts have changed. (Cal. Rules of Court, rule 5.260.)

I declare under penalty of perjury under the laws of the State of California that the foregoing is true and correct.

Date:
▶
(TYPE OR PRINT NAME)   SIGNATURE

NOTE: File this document with the court.
Do not file a copy of the Preliminary or Final Declaration of Disclosure or
any attachments to either declaration of disclosure with this document.

Page 1 of 1

Form Adopted for Mandatory Use
Judicial Council of California
FL-141 [Rev. July 1, 2013]

DECLARATION REGARDING SERVICE OF DECLARATION OF DISCLOSURE AND INCOME AND EXPENSE DECLARATION
(Family Law)

Family Code, §§ 2102, 2104, 2105, 2106, 2112
www.courts.ca.gov

Martin Dean's
ESSENTIAL FORMS™

1: SAMPLE CLIENT

THIS FORM SHOULD NOT BE FILED WITH THE COURT FL-142

ATTORNEY OR PARTY WITHOUT ATTORNEY (Name and Address):	TELEPHONE NO.:
2: FILING ATTORNEY'S NAME 4: NAME OF LAW FIRM FILING ACTION 5: STREET ADDRESS OF FIRM FILING ACTION 6: CITY STATE AND ZIP CODE OF FIRM	3: FIRM PHONE #
ATTORNEY FOR (Name): 7: ATTORNEY FOR NAME	

SUPERIOR COURT OF CALIFORNIA, COUNTY OF
101: COUNTY FILED

PETITIONER: 13: PLAINTIFF/PETITIONER LINE ONE

RESPONDENT: 15: DEFENDANT/RESPONDENT LINE ONE

SCHEDULE OF ASSETS AND DEBTS ☐ Petitioner's ☐ Respondent's	CASE NUMBER: 17: CASE NUMBER

- INSTRUCTIONS -

List all your known community and separate assets or debts. Include assets even if they are in the possession of another person, including your spouse. If you contend an asset or debt is separate, put P (for Petitioner) or R (for Respondent) in the first column (separate property) to indicate to whom you contend it belongs.

All values should be as of the date of signing the declaration unless you specify a different valuation date with the description. For additional space, use a continuation sheet numbered to show which item is being continued.

ITEM NO.	ASSETS DESCRIPTION	SEP. PROP	DATE ACQUIRED	CURRENT GROSS FAIR MARKET VALUE	AMOUNT OF MONEY OWED OR ENCUMBRANCE
1.	REAL ESTATE (Give street addresses and attach copies of deeds with legal descriptions and latest lender's statement.)			$	$
2.	HOUSEHOLD FURNITURE, FURNISHINGS, APPLIANCES (Identify.)				
3.	JEWELRY, ANTIQUES, ART, COIN COLLECTIONS, etc. (Identify.)				

Form Approved for Optional Use
Judicial Council of California
FL-142 [Rev. January 1, 2005]

SCHEDULE OF ASSETS AND DEBTS
(Family Law)

Code of Civil Procedure, §§ 2030(c), 2033.5
www.courtinfo.ca.gov

Page 1 of 4

1: SAMPLE CLIENT

ITEM NO.	ASSETS DESCRIPTION	SEP. PROP	DATE ACQUIRED	CURRENT GROSS FAIR MARKET VALUE	AMOUNT OF MONEY OWED OR ENCUMBRANCE
4.	VEHICLES, BOATS, TRAILERS *(Describe and attach copy of title document.)*			$	$
5.	SAVINGS ACCOUNTS *(Account name, account number, bank, and branch. Attach copy of latest statement.)*				
6.	CHECKING ACCOUNTS *(Account name and number, bank, and branch. Attach copy of latest statement.)*				
7.	CREDIT UNION, OTHER DEPOSIT ACCOUNTS *(Account name and number, bank, and branch. Attach copy of latest statement.)*				
8.	CASH *(Give location.)*				
9.	TAX REFUND				
10.	LIFE INSURANCE WITH CASH SURRENDER OR LOAN VALUE *(Attach copy of declaration page for each policy.)*				

SCHEDULE OF ASSETS AND DEBTS
(Family Law)

1: SAMPLE CLIENT

ITEM NO.	ASSETS DESCRIPTION	SEP. PROP	DATE ACQUIRED	CURRENT GROSS FAIR MARKET VALUE	AMOUNT OF MONEY OWED OR ENCUMBRANCE
11.	STOCKS, BONDS, SECURED NOTES, MUTUAL FUNDS *(Give certificate number and attach copy of the certificate or copy of latest statement.)*			$	$
12.	RETIREMENT AND PENSIONS *(Attach copy of latest summary plan documents and latest benefit statement.)*				
13.	PROFIT-SHARING, ANNUITIES, IRAS, DEFERRED COMPENSATION *(Attach copy of latest statement.)*				
14.	ACCOUNTS RECEIVABLE AND UNSECURED NOTES *(Attach copy of each.)*				
15.	PARTNERSHIPS AND OTHER BUSINESS INTERESTS *(Attach copy of most current K-1 form and Schedule C.)*				
16.	OTHER ASSETS				
17.	TOTAL ASSETS FROM CONTINUATION SHEET				
18.	TOTAL ASSETS			$ 0	$ 0

SCHEDULE OF ASSETS AND DEBTS
(Family Law)

1: SAMPLE CLIENT

ITEM NO.	DEBTS-SHOW TO WHOM OWED	SEP. PROP	TOTAL OWING	DATE INCURRED
			$	
19.	STUDENT LOANS *(Give details.)*			
20.	TAXES *(Give details.)*			
21.	SUPPORT ARREARAGES *(Attach copies of orders and statements.)*			
22.	LOANS - UNSECURED *(Give bank name and loan number and attach copy of latest statement.)*			
23.	CREDIT CARDS *(Give creditor's name and address and the account number. Attach copy of latest statement.)*			
24.	OTHER DEBTS *(Specify.):*			
25.	TOTAL DEBTS FROM CONTINUATION SHEET			
26.	TOTAL DEBTS		$ 0	

27. ☐ *(Specify number)* : _____ pages are attached as continuation sheets.

I declare under penalty of perjury under the laws of the State of California that the foregoing is true and correct.

Date:

_____ ▶ _____
(TYPE OR PRINT NAME)   (SIGNATURE OF DECLARANT)

FL-142 [Rev. January 1, 2005]
Martin Dean's
ESSENTIAL FORMS™

SCHEDULE OF ASSETS AND DEBTS
(Family Law)

1: SAMPLE CLIENT

```
                                                                              FL-150
ATTORNEY OR PARTY WITHOUT ATTORNEY (Name, State Bar number, and address):   FOR COURT USE ONLY
 2: FILING ATTORNEY'S NAME              75: SBN
 4: NAME OF LAW FIRM FILING ACTION
 5: STREET ADDRESS OF FIRM FILING ACTION
 6: CITY STATE AND ZIP CODE OF FIRM
TELEPHONE NO.: 3: FIRM PHONE #    76: FIRM FAX #
E-MAIL ADDRESS (Optional):  169: E-MAIL ADDRESS
ATTORNEY FOR (Name):  7: ATTORNEY FOR NAME
SUPERIOR COURT OF CALIFORNIA, COUNTY OF  101: COUNTY FILED
   STREET ADDRESS: 9: STREET ADDRESS OF COURT
   MAILING ADDRESS: 10: POST OFFICE ADDRESS OF COURT
   CITY AND ZIP CODE: 11: CITY STATE AND ZIP OF COURT
   BRANCH NAME: 12: BRANCH OF COURT
PETITIONER/PLAINTIFF: 13: PLAINTIFF/PETITIONER LINE ONE
RESPONDENT/DEFENDANT: 15: DEFENDANT/RESPONDENT LINE ONE
OTHER PARENT/CLAIMANT: 21: OTHER PARENT
         INCOME AND EXPENSE DECLARATION                CASE NUMBER:
                                                        17: CASE NUMBER
```

1. **Employment** *(Give information on your current job or, if you're unemployed, your most recent job.)*

   Attach copies of your pay stubs for last two months (black out social security numbers).

   a. Employer:
   b. Employer's address: 30: OUR CLIENT'S BUSINESS ADDRESS
   c. Employer's phone number: 32: OUR CLIENT'S BUSINESS
   d. Occupation: 33: OUR CLIENT'S OCCUPATION
   e. Date job started:
   f. If unemployed, date job ended:
   g. I work about ____ hours per week.
   h. I get paid $ ____ gross (before taxes) ☐ per month ☐ per week ☐ per hour.

   (If you have more than one job, attach an 8 1/2-by-11-inch sheet of paper and list the same information as above for your other jobs. Write "Question 1 - Other Jobs" at the top.)

2. **Age and education**
   a. My age is *(specify):* 23:
   b. I have completed high school or the equivalent: ☐ Yes ☐ No If no, highest grade completed *(specify):*
   c. Number of years of college completed *(specify):* ☐ Degree(s) obtained *(specify):*
   d. Number of years of graduate school completed *(specify):* ☐ Degree(s) obtained *(specify):*
   e. I have: ☐ professional/occupational license(s) *(specify):*
             ☐ vocational training *(specify):*

3. **Tax information**
   a. ☐ I last filed taxes for tax year *(specify year):*
   b. My tax filing status is ☐ single ☐ head of household ☐ married, filing separately
      ☐ married, filing jointly with *(specify name):*
   c. I file state tax returns in ☐ California ☐ other *(specify state):*
   d. I claim the following number of exemptions (including myself) on my taxes *(specify):*

4. **Other party's income.** I estimate the gross monthly income (before taxes) of the other party in this case at *(specify):* $
   This estimate is based on *(explain):*

(If you need more space to answer any questions on this form, attach an 8 1/2-by-11-inch sheet of paper and write the question number before your answer.)   Number of pages attached: _____

I declare under penalty of perjury under the laws of the State of California that the information contained on all pages of this form and any attachments is true and correct.

Date:

_____ ▶ _____
(TYPE OR PRINT NAME)   (SIGNATURE OF DECLARANT)

                                                                  Page 1 of 4
Form Adopted for Mandatory Use   INCOME AND EXPENSE DECLARATION   Family Code, §§ 2030-2032,
Judicial Council of California   2100-2113, 3552, 3620-3634,
FL-150 [Rev. January 1, 2007]   *Martin Dean's*   4050-4076, 4300-4339
                                  ESSENTIAL FORMS   www.courtinfo.ca.gov

                                                             1: SAMPLE CLIENT

APPENDIX S: REQUIRED STATUTORY FORMS FOR FINANCIAL DISCLOSURE (CALIFORNIA)   293

FL-150

PETITIONER/PLAINTIFF: 13: PLAINTIFF/PETITIONER LINE ONE	CASE NUMBER:
RESPONDENT/DEFENDANT: 15: DEFENDANT/RESPONDENT LINE ONE	17: CASE NUMBER
OTHER PARENT/CLAIMANT: 21: OTHER PARENT	

Attach copies of your pay stubs for the last two months and proof of any other income. Take a copy of your latest federal tax return to the court hearing. *(Black out your social security number on the pay stub and tax return.)*

5. **Income** *(For average monthly, add up all the income you received in each category in the last 12 months and divide the total by 12.)* — Last month / Average monthly
   a. Salary or wages (gross, before taxes) .... $_____ _____
   b. Overtime (gross, before taxes) .... $_____ _____
   c. Commissions or bonuses .... $_____ _____
   d. Public assistance (for example: TANF, SSI, GA/GR) ☐ currently receiving .... $_____ _____
   e. Spousal support ☐ from this marriage ☐ from a different marriage .... $_____ _____
   f. Partner support ☐ from this domestic partnership ☐ from a different domestic partnership $_____ _____
   g. Pension/retirement fund payments .... $_____ _____
   h. Social security retirement (not SSI) .... $_____ _____
   i. Disability: ☐ Social security (not SSI) ☐ State disability (SDI) ☐ Private insurance. $_____ _____
   j. Unemployment compensation .... $_____ _____
   k. Workers' compensation .... $_____ _____
   l. Other (military BAQ, royalty payments, etc.) *(specify)*: _____ $_____ _____

6. **Investment income** *(Attach a schedule showing gross receipts less cash expenses for each piece of property.)*
   a. Dividends/interest .... $_____ _____
   b. Rental property income .... $_____ _____
   c. Trust income .... $_____ _____
   d. Other *(specify)*: _____ $_____ _____

7. **Income from self-employment, after business expenses for all businesses** .... $_____ _____
   I am the ☐ owner/sole proprietor ☐ business partner ☐ other *(specify)*:
   Number of years in this business *(specify)*:
   Name of business *(specify)*:
   Type of business *(specify)*:
   Attach a profit and loss statement for the last two years or a Schedule C from your last federal tax return. Black out your social security number. If you have more than one business, provide the information above for each of your businesses.

8. ☐ **Additional income.** I received one-time money (lottery winnings, inheritance, etc.) in the last 12 months *(specify source and amount)*:

9. ☐ **Change in income.** My financial situation has changed significantly over the last 12 months because *(specify)*:

10. **Deductions** — Last month
    a. Required union dues .... $_____
    b. Required retirement payments (not social security, FICA, 401(k), or IRA) .... $_____
    c. Medical, hospital, dental, and other health insurance premiums *(total monthly amount)* .... $_____
    d. Child support that I pay for children from other relationships .... $_____
    e. Spousal support that I pay by court order from a different marriage .... $_____
    f. Partner support that I pay by court order from a different domestic partnership .... $_____
    g. Necessary job-related expenses not reimbursed by my employer *(attach explanation labeled "Question 10g")* ... $_____

11. **Assets** — Total
    a. Cash and checking accounts, savings, credit union, money market, and other deposit accounts .... $_____
    b. Stocks, bonds, and other assets I could easily sell .... $_____
    c. All other property, ☐ real and ☐ personal *(estimate fair market value minus the debts you owe)* $_____

FL-150 [Rev. January 1, 2007]   **INCOME AND EXPENSE DECLARATION**   Page 2 of 4
Martin Dean's ESSENTIAL FORMS™

1: SAMPLE CLIENT

		FL-150
PETITIONER/PLAINTIFF: 13: PLAINTIFF/PETITIONER LINE ONE	CASE NUMBER:	
RESPONDENT/DEFENDANT: 15: DEFENDANT/RESPONDENT LINE ONE	17: CASE NUMBER	
OTHER PARENT/CLAIMANT: 21: OTHER PARENT		

12. **The following people live with me:**

Name	Age	How the person is related to me? *(ex: son)*	That person's gross monthly income	Pays some of the household expenses?
a.				☐ Yes ☐ No
b.				☐ Yes ☐ No
c.				☐ Yes ☐ No
d.				☐ Yes ☐ No
e.				☐ Yes ☐ No

13. **Average monthly expenses** ☐ Estimated expenses ☐ Actual expenses ☐ Proposed needs
   a. Home:
      (1) ☐ Rent or ☐ mortgage .... $_____
      If mortgage:
         (a) average principal: $_____
         (b) average interest: $_____
      (2) Real property taxes .... $_____
      (3) Homeowner's or renter's insurance
         (if not included above) .... $_____
      (4) Maintenance and repair .... $_____
   b. Health-care costs not paid by insurance ... $_____
   c. Child care .... $_____
   d. Groceries and household supplies .... $_____
   e. Eating out .... $_____
   f. Utilities (gas, electric, water, trash) .... $_____
   g. Telephone, cell phone, and e-mail .... $_____
   h. Laundry and cleaning .... $_____
   i. Clothes .... $_____
   j. Education .... $_____
   k. Entertainment, gifts, and vacation .... $_____
   l. Auto expenses and transportation
      (insurance, gas, repairs, bus, etc.) .... $_____
   m. Insurance (life, accident, etc.; do not
      include auto, home, or health insurance) $_____
   n. Savings and investments .... $_____
   o. Charitable contributions .... $_____
   p. Monthly payments listed in item 14
      (itemize below in 14 and insert total here) $_____ 0
   q. Other *(specify)*: .... $_____
   r. **TOTAL EXPENSES** (a-q) *(do not add in* $_____ 0
      the amounts in a(1)(a) and (b))
   s. Amount of expenses paid by others $_____

14. **Installment payments and debts not listed above**

Paid to	For	Amount	Balance	Date of last payment
		$	$	
		$	$	
		$	$	
		$	$	
		$	$	
		$	$	

15. **Attorney fees** *(This is required if either party is requesting attorney fees.):*
   a. To date, I have paid my attorney this amount for fees and costs *(specify)*: $
   b. The source of this money was *(specify)*:
   c. I still owe the following fees and costs to my attorney *(specify total owed)*: $
   d. My attorney's hourly rate is *(specify)*: $

I confirm this fee arrangement.

Date:

2: FILING ATTORNEY'S NAME ▶ _____
(TYPE OR PRINT NAME OF ATTORNEY) (SIGNATURE OF ATTORNEY)

FL-150 [Rev. January 1, 2007]   **INCOME AND EXPENSE DECLARATION**   Page 3 of 4

1: SAMPLE CLIENT

APPENDIX S: REQUIRED STATUTORY FORMS FOR FINANCIAL DISCLOSURE (CALIFORNIA) 295

FL-150

PETITIONER/PLAINTIFF: 13: PLAINTIFF/PETITIONER LINE ONE	CASE NUMBER:
RESPONDENT/DEFENDANT: 15: DEFENDANT/RESPONDENT LINE ONE	17: CASE NUMBER
OTHER PARENT/CLAIMANT: 21: OTHER PARENT	

CHILD SUPPORT INFORMATION
(NOTE: Fill out this page only if your case involves child support.)

16. **Number of children**
    a. I have *(specify number)*:   children under the age of 18 with the other parent in this case.
    b. The children spend   percent of their time with me and   percent of their time with the other parent.
    (If you're not sure about percentage or it has not been agreed on, please describe your parenting schedule here.)

17. **Children's health-care expenses**
    a. ☐ I do ☐ I do not   have health insurance available to me for the children through my job.
    b. Name of insurance company:
    c. Address of insurance company:

    d. The monthly cost for the **children's** health insurance is or would be *(specify)*: $
       (Do not include the amount your employer pays.)

18. **Additional expenses for the children in this case**   Amount per month
    a. Child care so I can work or get job training .... $
    b. Children's health care not covered by insurance .... $
    c. Travel expenses for visitation .... $
    d. Children's educational or other special needs *(specify below)*: $

19. **Special hardships.** I ask the court to consider the following special financial circumstances
    (attach documentation of any item listed here, including court orders):
                                                                                    Amount per month   For how many months?
    a. Extraordinary health expenses not included in 18b .... $

    b. Major losses not covered by insurance (examples: fire, theft, other
       insured loss) .... $

    c. (1) Expenses for my minor children who are from other relationships and
           are living with me .... $
       (2) Names and ages of those children *(specify)*:

       (3) Child support I receive for those children .... $

    The expenses listed in a, b and c create an extreme financial hardship because *(explain)*:

20. **Other information I want the court to know concerning support in my case** *(specify)*:

FL-150 [Rev. January 1, 2007]   **INCOME AND EXPENSE DECLARATION**   Page 4 of 4
Martin Dean's
ESSENTIAL FORMS™
                                                                              1: SAMPLE CLIENT

Appendix T

Court Endorsement of ADR (San Mateo County)

ATTORNEY OR PARTY WITHOUT ATTORNEY (Name and Address)	TELEPHONE NO.:	FOR COURT USE ONLY
ATTORNEY FOR (Name):		

SUPERIOR COURT OF CALIFORNIA, COUNTY OF SAN MATEO

STREET ADDRESS:
MAILING ADDRESS:
CITY AND ZIP CODE:
BRANCH NAME:

PLAINTIFF/PETITIONER:	CASE NUMBER:
DEFENDANT/RESPONDENT:	

The San Mateo County Superior Court recommends Alternative Dispute Resolution options in lieu of formal court litigation.

"Alternative" or "Appropriate" Dispute Resolution (ADR) is a general term for methods of resolving a dispute without going through the formal court process. ADR can save you time, money, and increase your overall satisfaction with the outcome of your case.

ADR can be used at any point in your case to resolve disputes regarding property division, child support, spousal support, paternity, child custody, parenting plans, and many other family law issues.

Did you know that the vast majority of cases filed in court (95-98%) do not go to trial? Most cases are settled or decided in some other way. But in many cases, the settlement comes only after considerable resources have been expended. This is why the San Mateo County Superior Court supports the use of dispute resolution alternatives at the earliest possible time. Local Rule 5.5(A) states:

> California Rules of Court and the Family Law Act strongly encourage alternative dispute resolution (ADR) of family matters. The Family Law Department recognizes that formal litigation of legal claims and disputes is expensive and time consuming. The goals of this Court are: to reduce hostilities between the parties; facilitate the early resolution of issues; and provide parties with an opportunity to maximize their satisfaction with the resolution of their case. It is therefore the policy of this Court to promote and encourage the parties to settle their disputes by the use of appropriate dispute resolution options which include mediation, arbitration, collaborative practice, court supervised settlement conferences and/or judicial case management.

The court strongly encourages the use of ADR but does not favor any particular form of ADR, endorse any particular attorney, nor guarantee the outcome in any particular case.

Instructions: All parties and counsel shall read the Notice, sign on page three, and have this Notice served on the other party with any Petition or Response under the Family Law Act, Uniform Parentage Act, Order to Show Cause, Response to Order to Show Cause, Notice of Motion, Response to Notice of Motion, or any other family law pleading which will result in a court hearing or trial. A proof of service shall be filed with the Court. *(Local Rule 5.5)(B)*

PLAINTIFF/PETITIONER:	CASE NUMBER:
DEFENDANT/RESPONDENT:	

DESCRIPTION OF SERVICES AND COST:

The Court manages a panel of attorneys with special training in mediation and arbitration and a commitment to finding alternatives to formal litigation. The attorneys who serve on the ADR panel have agreed to offer participants a 90-minute session for $100 ($50 per party). Additional sessions are available at the attorney's market rate. For more information call the ADR office at: (650) 261-5076 or (650) 261-5075, or visit the website at: www.sanmateocourt.org/court_divisions/adr/family_law/.

- **Mediation**

  Mediation through the ADR program is voluntary. A neutral attorney called a "mediator" meets with parties and/or their attorneys to assist them in reaching an agreement. The mediator facilitates communication between the participants, clarifies issues, explores each party's needs and interests, and helps the participants to consider options for settlement.

  The parties may resolve a single issue or the entire case. The agreements reached in mediation are not limited by the results available under the law so mediated solutions can more easily accommodate the circumstances of individual cases. An agreement reached in mediation is binding once it is turned into a court order and signed by the Judge. You cannot be forced to accept a decision in mediation and participating in mediation does not impact your right to a court hearing. If an agreement is not reached you may continue through the court system.

  Mediation is private and confidential. The sessions are conducted in the mediator's office. Anything spoken or written during mediation by any of the participants is confidential and may not be disclosed to the Court or any other person without the consent of the participants.

- **Arbitration**

  Arbitration is private and less formal than a court trial. In arbitration a neutral attorney called the "arbitrator" makes a decision based on the information presented by both sides. The arbitrator then prepares a written decision and sends it to both parties and the Court. This court's ADR program offers binding arbitration with a neutral serving as a temporary judge. "Binding" means there is no right to appeal and you will accept the arbitrator's decision as final.

- **Collaborative Law**

  In the collaborative law process, you and the other party each have a private attorney and make a commitment to resolve your disputes without going to court. Similar to mediation, collaborative law operates in the spirit of honesty and cooperation. In the collaborative process, both parties together with professionals (attorneys, mental health and financial experts) work as a team to resolve disputes respectfully with an emphasis on financial responsibility and cooperative co-parenting. Collaborative Practice San Mateo County is a private organization of professionals specially trained in collaborative practice. For more information, fees, or for a list of professionals, please see their web site at: http://www.collaborative-law.com/ or call (650) 590-2228.

Instructions: All parties and counsel shall read the Notice, sign on page three, and have this Notice served on the other party with any Petition or Response under the Family Law Act, Uniform Parentage Act, Order to Show Cause, Response to Order to Show Cause, Notice of Motion, Response to Notice of Motion, or any other family law pleading which will result in a court hearing or trial. A proof of service shall be filed with the Court. *(Local Rule 5.5)(B)*

PLAINTIFF/PETITIONER:	CASE NUMBER:
DEFENDANT/RESPONDENT:	

FAMILY COURT SERVICES MEDIATION:

The Court encourages the use of the ADR options described above to resolve custody and parenting plan disputes. However, if you do not reach an agreement on these issues, California law requires you to meet with Family Court Services (FCS) before submitting these issues to a Judge. FCS will first attempt to settle the issues through mediation, however, if no agreement is reached then the FCS counselor will prepare a written recommendation to the Court based upon the best interests of the child(ren). FCS mediation is not confidential and does not address your property or financial disputes. There is no fee for mediation with FCS.

DOMESTIC VIOLENCE AND ADR:

ADR is most effective when parties are able to communicate and solve problems without fear or intimidation. For this reason when there is a history of domestic violence in a relationship, ADR may not be appropriate.

The undersigned certifies that s/he has read this Notice in compliance with San Mateo County Local Rule 5.5.

Date: Date:

_____   _____
Signature of Petitioner   Signature or Respondent

Attorney certification of compliance with San Mateo County Local Rule 5.5:

Date: Date:

_____   _____
Signature of Attorney for Petitioner   Signature of Attorney for Respondent

---

Instructions: All parties and counsel shall read the Notice, sign on page three, and have this Notice served on the other party with any Petition or Response under the Family Law Act, Uniform Parentage Act, Order to Show Cause, Response to Order to Show Cause, Notice of Motion, Response to Notice of Motion, or any other family law pleading which will result in a court hearing or trial. A proof of service shall be filed with the Court. *(Local Rule 5.5)(B)*

Appendix U

Letter from Presiding Judge of Family Law Division Endorsing Mediation (English and Spanish)

CHAMBERS OF
FAMILY LAW DEPARTMENTS
LOS ANGELES, CALIFORNIA 90012

TELEPHONE
(213) 974-1234

MARJORIE S. STEINBERG
SUPERVISING JUDGE

Dear Petitioner or Respondent:

You have a Family Law case in our court. During this time in your life, you have a number of decisions to make about your future and perhaps the future of your children. I would like you to know that our court would like to help make this process as easy as possible for you and your family.

You may have a dispute with your spouse regarding where your children will live, what support will be provided and how you will divide your property. You have the right to have a court hearing and have a judicial officer decide these matters for you, which may be the most appropriate way to proceed, especially if you feel threatened by or fearful of your spouse.

However, going to court is not the only way to resolve family law disputes. Some other ways include having attorneys negotiate directly, having a neutral third party help both sides negotiate a solution (mediation) or using a method such as collaborative law. These other ways may help people find solutions that are mutually acceptable and may be preferable for several reasons: 1) You will directly participate in finding solutions; 2) You probably will be able to resolve your dispute sooner; 3) It may be much less expensive; 4) You may end the process with a better relationship with your former spouse; and 5) You will likely find it less stressful than court hearings. You can speak with your attorney, if you have one, about all of these methods of resolving your case so the two of you can decide which method may be best for you.

It is to your benefit to consider opportunities to reduce conflict and reduce expenses incurred in the Family Law process. I recommend that you focus on what is most important. Many people spend time, effort and money attempting to obtain satisfaction by prolonging the dispute with the other party, but this does not guarantee either party will be fully satisfied with the outcome.

If you have children, you must be particularly careful in choosing how to proceed. Everything you can do to avoid involving them in the dispute or engaging in conflict concerning them will benefit them and you. Your agreement does not need to be perfect. It does need to be acceptable to both of you. For the mediation of disputes regarding your child(ren) and how they will spend time with each parent after the divorce, the court offers a free mediation service through Family Court Services. To make an appointment, call (213) 974-5524.

Please save this letter. Please read it several times during the dissolution process.

Sincerely,

MARJORIE S. STEINBERG, Supervising Judge
Family Law Departments

CHAMBERS OF
The Superior Court
FAMILY LAW DEPARTMENTS
LOS ANGELES, CALIFORNIA 90012

TELEPHONE
(213) 974-1234

MARJORIE S. STEINBERG
SUPERVISING JUDGE

Estimado(a) demandante o demandado(a):

Usted tiene un caso relacionado con el Derecho de Familia en nuestro tribunal. Durante este momento de su vida tendrá que tomar una serie de decisiones acerca de su futuro y quizás también el futuro de sus hijos. Quiero que sepa que nuestro tribunal procurará que este proceso sea lo más llevadero posible para usted y su familia.

Es posible que tenga una disputa con su cónyuge referente a dónde vivirán sus hijos, la manutención que recibirán y cómo se dividirán los bienes que le pertenecen. Usted tiene el derecho de tener una audiencia ante un oficial judicial para decidir estos asuntos, lo cual podría ser la manera más apropiada de proceder, especialmente si teme o se siente amenazado(a) por su cónyuge.

Sin embargo, acudir al tribunal no es la única manera de resolver disputas relacionadas con el derecho de familia. También es posible que los abogados negocien directamente, que una tercera parte neutral ayude a los interesados a negociar una solución (mediación) o que se utilice un método tal como el derecho de colaboración. Estos modos alternativos de resolver disputas podrían ayudar a los interesados a encontrar soluciones mutuamente aceptables y podrían ser preferibles por diversas razones: (1) Usted participará directamente para encontrar soluciones; (2) Es probable que pueda resolver la disputa más rápidamente; (3) Podría resultar mucho menos costoso; (4) Al término del proceso, su relación con su ex-cónyuge podría ser más cordial; y (5) Es probable que la experiencia le cause menos estrés que las audiencias en el tribunal. Si tiene abogado, hable con él acerca de todos estos métodos para resolver el caso, de modo que los dos puedan decidir qué método es el que más le conviene.

Resulta ventajoso para usted considerar las oportunidades para reducir el conflicto y los gastos contraídos en el proceso del Derecho de Familia. Le recomiendo que se centre en lo que es más importante. Muchas personas invierten tiempo, esfuerzo y dinero tratando de obtener satisfacción mediante la prolongación de la disputa con la otra parte, pero esto no significa que ninguna de las partes vaya a quedar completamente satisfecha con el resultado.

Si tiene hijos, deberá actuar aún con mayor cautela al decidir cómo proceder. Hacer todo lo posible por evitar implicarlos en la disputa o por evitar enzarzarse en un conflicto referente a ellos será beneficioso tanto para usted como para ellos. El acuerdo al que lleguen no tiene por qué ser perfecto. Simplemente, debe ser aceptable para ambas partes. El tribunal ofrece un servicio gratuito de mediación, a través de los Servicios del Tribunal de Familia, para la mediación de disputas referentes a sus hijos y al modo en que pasarán tiempo con el padre y la madre después del divorcio. Para solicitar una cita, llame al (213) 974-5524.

Por favor, conserve esta carta. Léala varias veces durante el proceso de disolución del matrimonio.

Atentamente,

MARJORIE S. STEINBERG, Juez Supervisoro
Departamentos de Derecho de Familia

Appendix V

Making Your Office a Classroom for Client Education

Give yourself a mediation-friendly office quiz:	Yes	No
1. Does my waiting room have educational materials for clients?	___	___
2. Do I have a dedicated space for a client library?	___	___
3. Have I prepared written instructions and checklists to help clients?	___	___
4. Do I have a staff training program geared to educate and assist clients in mediation?	___	___
5. Will my clients feel welcomed and that their comfort and empowerment is the #1 priority of my practice?	___	___

Establish a Client Library in Your Office

If informed client consent is the bedrock of mediation, clients must have access to sufficient

Try walking in your client's shoes. How does it feel to be in your office? What tools, resources, and space are available to your clients to help them solve improve their experience as a client?

A client library can be the client's home and learning center within your office.

The concept of a client library is is a collection of consumer-friendly books, video DVDs, audio tapes, brochures, or other client resources. The client library's materials should be easy to read and to access. Ideally, the client library should have chairs and tables (or even just a writing ledge) so that clients can comfortably do their own work there rather than in your office or in the public waiting room.

You might provide computers so clients can draft their own letters, court documents, or their opening statement for a mediation.. In child support matters, clients can run the numbers using a guideline child support program in order to educate themselves and realistically prepare for an upcoming negotiation the mediation session. Cutting edge client libraries also provide internet access so that your clients can access helpful programs such as www.uptoparents.org or www.ourfamilywizard.com .

When clients aren't visiting, the client library can serve as a breakout room for caucuses or an extra consultation room or inspirational setting for your mediation intern. Even if you do not have an extra office or fancy computer gadgets, you can still set up a client library in your waiting room. All you need to get started are a few books, a couple of videos, a DVD player and a monitor. Earphones are a nice added feature if the video is in the waiting room.

The very existence of the client library symbolizes that clients rank very high in the priorities of your office and that you highly value client empowerment. The client library demonstrates to clients that you are willing to devote expensive office space and purchase significant books and DVDs to provide for their education. Qne, If you were shopping for a family lawyer, would you choose one who has a client library or one who has no place to sit and no resources to use?

The client library also serves as another waiting room—a learning room. New clients get a sense of the firm and necessary information on their presenting problem. Just by leafing through books on your shelf, returning clients deepen their understanding and perspectives—and may uncover unmet needs and concerns that you can address.

It costs so much in hard dollars to acquire new clients that being able to serve their needs beyond the presenting problem helps amortize the high marketing and management costs to operate your practice. Your current client base is your highest profit center; tools such as the client library that help you maximize your current client base cannot be overvalued.

Another use of the client library is to serve as a child-care center. It is ideally better for your clients with dependent children to make arrangements for them outside the office. But we don't live in an ideal world, and sometimes due to cost or logistics, the kids come along in tow. If you have age appropriate videotapes, books, toys, and games in your client libraries, pop them in. Most kids can be happily amused while their parent(s) do their business with you.

Show Videos to Clients

Sometimes, parties may watch a video together and are able to work out a full settlement on their own before the session ever starts.

Lending Books to Clients

There are two basic ways that your clients can use the client library: self-selected or prescribed by you. Once parked in the client library, many clients browse and self-select material that they want to use. The library's collection can be in a notebook or accessible by computer. At our office, most clients use the library without much staff help at all. That's the point. You should have clear written or video client instructions so that you do not need to spend additional monies in staff time to explain the library to clients.

Mosten Mediation Centers doesn't lend books to clients—they must be read on premises. In nine years of operation, we have never had a book or video stolen But mediators such as Academy of Family Mediators President Nina Meirding, who do lend books from their client libraries, report about a 100% return rate as well.

The client library can also be a preventive classroom. Before every mediation, each client can be given a conflict-wellness checkup. The checkup is a thermometer for legal health and the client library is a perfect place for your clients to self-administer the written checkup questionnaire or read material on preventing future disputes in their lives. Maryland Legal Services Corporation is developing a legal checkup for the web and I already have one on my website (http://www.MostenMediation.com). As these technological developments increase, your clients will be able to improve their legal health from their seats in your client library or from home.

Appendix W

Books and Articles

This book is the foundation and beginning of your reading and training as a peacemaking family lawyer. You need to study and learn much more.

The following resource section is not a bibliography as found in scholarly articles and books. Since you are using this book to improve your practice, we have chosen not to flood you with most of the 2500 titles on conflict resolution currently in print. Rather, we have limited the reading list to key categories:

Representing Clients in Mediation
Mediator Concepts and Strategies
Mediation Confidentiality
Negotiation Concepts and Strategies
Limited Scope Representation
Collaborative Law
Preventive Law
Peacemaking
Expanding Your Practice With A Client-Centered Consumer Approach
Divorce Books for Clients
Divorce Books for Children

Representing Clients in Mediation

Abramson, Harold, *Mediation Representation: Advocating as a Problem Solver in any Country or Culture*, 2nd Edition (2010)
Galton, Eric R. *Representing Clients in Mediation* (1994)
Golann, Dwight, *Sharing a Mediator's Powers, Effective Advocacy in Settlement* (2014)

Mediator Concepts and Strategies

Deutsch, Morton and Coleman, Peter, *The Handbook of Conflict Resolution: Theory and Practice.* (2nd Ed.) (2006)

Folberg, Jay, Ann Milne, and Salem, Peter. Salem (eds.). *Divorce and Family Mediation: Models, Techniques, and Applications* (2004)

Frenkel, Douglas N. and Stark, James H., *The Practice of Mediation* 2nd Edition (2012)

Galton, Eric and Love, Lela, *Stories That Mediators Tell* (2013)

Goldberg, S., and Shaw, M. *The Secrets of Successful (and Unsuccessful) Mediators Continued: Studies Two and Three*, Negotiation Journal (2007)

Haynes, John M.. *The Fundamentals of Family Mediation.* Albany, N.Y.: State University of New York Press (1994)

Kolb, Deborah M. *When Talk Works: Profiles of Mediators.* San Francisco: Jossey-Bass (2001)

Land, Michael and Taylor, Allison, *The Making of a Mediator* (2000)

Saposnek, D. *Mediating Child Custody Disputes.* (Rev.ed.). San Francisco: Jossey-Bass (1998)

Moore, Christopher, *The Mediation Process: Practical Strategies for Resolving Conflict.* (3rd Ed.) (2003)

Mediation Confidentiality

Cassel v. Superior Court (Wasserman, et al.) (2011) 51 Cal.4th 113

Coben, James, Hamline Mediation Case Law Project: Examining Lessons from Failed Mediations http://www.hamline.edu/law/dri/mediation-case-law-project/. See also: James Coben and Peter N. Thompson, *Disputing Irony: A Systematic Look at Litigation About Mediation* (2006) 11 HARV. NEG. L. REV. 43

Waldman, Ellen, *Mediation Ethics* (2011)

Negotiation Concepts and Strategies

Chialdini, Robert B., *Influence: The Psychology of Persuasion* (1993)

Coleman, Peter T., *The Five Percent Solution: Finding Solutions for Seemingly Impossible Conflicts* (2011)

Eddy, William A., *High Conflict People in Legal Disputes* (2006)

Fisher, Roger and Ury, William and Patton, Bruce, *Getting to Yes: Negotiating Agreement Without Giving In* (1983)

Folberg, Jay and Golann, Dwight, *Lawyer Negotiation: Theory, Practice, and Law* (2006)

Korobkin, Russell, *Negotiation Theory and Strategy* (2002)

Krivis, Jeffrey, *Improvisational Negotiation* (2006)

Lande, John, *Early Planned Negotiation* (2012)

Lewicki, R. J., Barry, B., and Saunders, D. M., *Essentials of Negotiation* (4th ed.) New York: McGraw-Hill/Irwin, 2007.

Mayer, Bernard, *The Dynamics of Conflict Resolution* (2000)

Mnookin, Robert H et al, *Beyond Winning: Negotiating to Create Value in Deals and Disputes* (2000)

Mnookin, Robert H. & Kornhausert, Lewis, *Bargaining in the Shadow of the Law*, 88 YALE L.J. 950, 968 (1979)

Mnookin, Robert H., *Bargaining with the Devil* (2011)

Limited Scope Representation

Beck, Connie, Sales, Bruce, & Hahn, Richard K., *Self-Representation in Divorce Cases* (1993)

Bergman, P. And Berman-Barrett, S.J. *Represent Yourself in Court: How to Prepare and Try a Winning Case.* Berkeley: Nolo Press (1993)

Kimbro, Stephanie L., *Limited Scope Legal Services: Unbundling and the Self-Help Client* (2012)

Macfarlane, J., *Identifying and Meeting the Needs of Self-Represented Litigants* (May 2013)

Mosten, Forrest S., *Unbundling Legal Services* (2000)

Rhode, Deborah L., *Access to Justice* (2004)

Talia, Sue M. *Unbundling Your Divorce: How to Find a Lawyer to Help You Help Yourself.* (Rev. Ed.) Nexus Publishing Company, 2006.

Collaborative Law

Cameron, Susan, *Deepening the Dialogue* (2004)

Mosten, Forrest S., *Collaborative Divorce Handbook* (2009)

Tesler, Pauline H. and Thompson, Peggy, *Collaborative Divorce* (2007)

Preventive Law

Barton, Thomas D., *Preventive Law and Problem Solving: Lawyering for the Future* (2009)
Brown, Louis M., *Manual for Periodic Legal Checkup* (1983)
Brown, Louis M., *Lawyering Through Life: The Origin of Preventive Law* (1986)
Israel, Laurie, http: www.MaritalMediation.com
Rosenbloom, S. M., and Nesburn, J., Isn't It Unromantic: Collaboratively Negotiating Pre and Post Nuptial Agreements, COLLABORATIVE REVIEW, 2008, 10(1), 18–19

Peacemaking

Bowling, Daniel and Hoffman, David, *Bringing Peace into the Room* (2003)
Burnett, Nan Waller, *Calm in the Face of the Storm* (2007)
Daicoff, Susan, *Law as a Healing Profession: The "Comprehensive Law Movement,"* 6 PEPP. DISP. RESOL. L.J. 1, 50–51 (2006)
Galton, Eric R., *Ripples from Peace Lake: Essays for Mediators and Peacemakers* (2004)
LeBaron, Michelle., *Bridging Troubled Waters: Conflict Resolution from the Heart* (2002) Lederach, John Paul, *The Little Book of Conflict Transformation* (2003)
Mosten, Forrest S., *Lawyer as Peacemaker: Building a Successful Law Practice Without Ever Going to Court,* 43 FAMILY LAW QUARTERLY, Fall 2009.
Nolan-Haley, Jacqueline, Finding Interior Peace in the Ordinary Practice of Law: Wisdom from the Spiritual Tradition of St. Teresa of Avila, 44 J. Catholic Legal Stud. 29, 39 (2007)
Noll, Douglas. *Peacemaking: Practicing at the Intersection of Law and Human Conflict* (2003)
Wright, Kim J. Lawyers as Peacemakers: Practicing Holistic, Problem-Solving Law (2010)

Expanding Your Practice with a Client-Centered Consumer Approach

Binder, David A. and Bergman, Paul, et al., *Lawyers As Counselors: A Client-Centered Approach* (2nd Ed.) (2004)
Foonberg, J., *How to Start and Build a Law Practice.* (5th ed.) (2004)
Herrera, Luz, *Reinventing the Practice of Law* (2014)
Lovenheim. Peter, *Becoming a Mediator: An Insider's Guide to Exploring Careers in Mediation* (2002)
Mather, L., McEwen, C.A. & Maiman, R.J., *Divorce Lawyers at Work: Varieties of Professionalism in Practice* (2001)

McFarlane, Julie, *The New Lawyer: How Settlement Is Transforming the Practice of Law* (2008)

Mosten, Forrest S., *Mediation Career Guide: A Strategic Approach to Building a Successful Practice* (2001)

Sarat, A., and Felstiner, W., *Divorce Lawyers and Their Clients* (1995)

Divorce Books for Clients

Ahrons, Constance R.. *The Good Divorce* (1994)

Ahrons, Constance R.. *We Are Still Family* (2007)

Bienenfeld, Florence. *Helping Your Child Succeed after Divorce* (1987)

Brazelton, Berry T.. *Touch Points: The Essential Reference—Your Child's Emotional and Behavioral Development* (1992)

Clapp, Genevieve, *Divorce and New Beginnings: An Authoritative Guide to Recovery and Growth, Solo Parenting, and Stepfamilies* (1992)

Curry, Kayden, Denis Clfford, Frederick Hertz & Robin Leonard,. *A Legal Guide for Lesbian and Gay Couples* (1991)

Diamond, Louise, *The Peace Book* (2001)

Ellias, Stephen R. and Susan Levinkind, *Legal Research* (1998)

Friedman, James T., *The Divorce Handbook: Your Basic Guide to Divorce* (1984)

Gardner, Richard, *The Parents Book About Divorce* (1977)

Gold, Lois, M.S.W., *Between Love and Hate: A Guide to Civilized Divorce* (1995)

Hetherington, E. Mavis and Kelly, John, *For Better or For Worse: Surprising Results from the Most Comprehensive Study of Divorce in America* (2002)

Grollman, Earl A., *Explaining Divorce to Children* (1972)

Krantzler, Mel, *Creative Divorce* (1973)

Lansky, Vicki, *Divorce Book for Parents* (1989)

LaViolette, Alyce D. and Barnett, Olga W., *It Could Happen to Anyone: Why Battered Women Stay*, 4th Edition (2014)

Ricci, Isolina, *Mom's House, Dad's House: Making Shared Custody Work: How Parents Can Make Two Homes for Their Children After Divorce*. 1980.

Robertson, Christina, *A Woman's Guide to Divorce and Decision Making: A Supportive Workbook for Women Facing the Process of Divorce* (1989)

Ross, Julie A. and Judy Corcoran, *Joint Custody with a Jerk* (2011)

Wallerstein, Judith S. and Sandra Blakeslee, *Second Chances: Men, Women and Children A Decade After Divorce. Who Wins, Who Loses—and Why* (1989)

Woodhouse, Violet and Victoria F. Collins, *Divorce and Money* (1998)

Divorce Books for Children

Brown, Laurene Kransy and Brown, Marc, *Dinosaur's Divorce* (1986)
Drescher, Joan, *My Mother's Getting Married* (1989)
Gardner, Richard A., *The Boys and Girls Book About Divorce* (1970)
Lewis, Helen Coale. *All About Families: The Second Time Around (For Boys and Girls, Their Parents and Stepparents)* (1980)
Ricci, Isolina, *Mom's House, Dad's House for Kids* (2006)
Udry, Janice May, *What Mary Jo Shared* (1966)

Index

A

AARP (American Association of Retired Persons), 279
ABA Model Code of Professional Responsibility, 26
ABA Model Standards for Mediators, 38
Academy of Family Mediators (AML), 307
acknowledging, 221
active listening, 189
adoptions, preventive mediations in, xvii
ADR pledge. *See* alternative dispute resolution (ADR)
adviser, lawyer as, 116–117
agenda setting, 189
agreements, 40–41
    disqualification, 83–84
    finalizing, 50–51
    participation, 83
    premarital, xvii
    readiness of, 130–131
    salvaging, 140
    settlement, 40–41
agreements, building, 120
    caucus, 122
    compiling client's financial information, 117–118
    educating/advising on legal position of, 117
    lawyers at mediation table, 123
    lawyers' role, 123–124
    practice tips, 127
    review of documents, 121–122
    sample notebook contents, 120
    use of experts, 125–126
agreements, reaching, 138–139
    at mediation table, 137–138
    bifurcate divorce issues and, 140
    divorce agenda, 129–130
    emotional reframing and, 140
    experimenting and testing solutions, 138–139
    ground rules, 132–133
    identifying and acknowledging initial positions of parties, 131
    interest-based negotiations, 134–135
    involvement of children in, 138–139
    mediator proposals, 141
    negotiating with mediator, 140–141
    new approach to solving problem, 131
    normalcy, 137
    red flag rule, 133
    solvability, 137
    starter toolbox for, 139–140
    suggesting alternatives in, 132
    use of articles and research, 138
agreements, reviewing and drafting
    aspirations, 155
    boilerplate, 155
    drafting the agreement, 153–154
    lawyer mediators and, 150–151
    memorandum, 147–148
    practice tips, 158
    review level, 151–152

agreements (*continued*)
    signatures, 156–157
    summary letters, 147–148
Ahrons, Constance, 16, 173
alternative dispute resolution (ADR), 12, 19. *See also* mediation
    court endorsement of (San Mateo County), 297
    definition of, 189
    duty to advise about, 20
    options, 29–30
    practice tips, 33
    rules of professional responsibility, 20–21
    settlement agreements and, 40–41
    voluntary ADR pledges, 24–25
American Association of Retired Persons (AARP), 279
American Bar Association, 6
    Commission on Nonlawyer Practice, 7
    Family Law Section, 197
appellate courts, 13
arbitration, 168–169
    definition of, 189
Association of Family and Conciliation Courts (AFCC), 197
attorneys. *See* lawyers
Aviel, Rebecca, 148
Avvo, 3

B
bad faith, 39
bargaining range, 189
Bartee, Brenda, 1
Barton, Thomas D., 163
BATNA (Best Alternative to Negotiated Agreement), 134, 189
Bergman, Paul, 28, 189
Best Alternative to Negotiated Agreement (BATNA), 189
Best Lawyers, 3
Beverly Hills Bar Association, 24, 33
Binder, David, 28, 189
binding adjudication, 168–169
Blankley, Kristen M., 61
boilerplate, 155
Boulle, Laurence, 112
Bowen, Murray, 90
brainstorming, 190
breakout room, 190
briefs, 108–109
Brown, Louis M., 175
Burnett, Nan Waller, 181
Burns, Daniel, 108
Bush, Robert, 173, 195
Business and Professions Code, 22–23

C
California
    key confidentiality cases in, 217
    statutory forms for financial disclosure in, 285
California ADR Practice Guide, 21
California Association of Realtors, 24
California Civil Procedure, 23
California Family Code, 23
California Judicial Council, 73, 74, 119
Calm in the Peace of the Storm (Burnett), 181
Cameron, Nancy J., 81
Cassel v. Superior Court, 35
catering, 112
caucus, 122, 190
Center for Dispute Resolution Code of Professional Conduct (Moore), 192

Certified Divorce Financial Analyst (CDFA), 117
Certified Financial Divorce Practitioner (CFDP), 117
Certified Financial Divorce Specialist (CFDS), 117
Chang, Wendy Wen Yun, 66
child abuse, 91
child custody evaluators, 89
children
    divorce books for, 314
    involvement in reaching agreements, 138–139
child specialist, 91–92
Church, Terrence, 21
Circuit Court of Cook County, 47
civil immunity. *See* immunity
clarifying, 221
client-centered approach, books and articles, 312
client coach, 190
clients
    as judge, 136
    discontented, 7–8
    divorce books for, 313
    educating/advising on legal position of, 117
    financial information, 117–118
    goal, expectations and needs of, 28
    information in collaborative representation, 241
    lending books to, 306–307
    library for, 305
    sample handouts for, 265
    sample letter discussing risk of mediation, 245
    showing videos to, 306–307
    types of, 66
    with cognition issues, 66

coaching
    conflict management, 67
    court, 72
    negotiation, 69–70
    rich and vulnerable clients, 69
    simulated, 194
    vs. full-service representation, 68
coach, lawyers as, 64–65
collaborative lawyering, 22
    books and articles, 311–312
    child specialist/co-parenting coach and, 91–92
    client information, 241
    description of, 81–82
    disqualification agreement, 83–84
    divorce coach/process facilitator/communications coach and, 90
    factors affecting appropriateness of, 237
    financial professionals and, 93
    mediator, 82
    participation agreement in, 83
    practice of, 83
    practice tips, 94
    sample client handout, 265
    training in, 184–185
    use of other collaborative professionals in, 89–90
Collaborative Practice: Deepening the Dialogue (Cameron), 81
collection rates, 13–14
Colorado Bar Association, 24
Colorado Rules of Professional Conduct, 20
co-mediation, xix, 169, 190, 191
commonly asked questions
    dual representation, xvii–xviii
    reasons for hiring mediator, xvii
communications coach, 90

compassion, 184
Complementary Dispute Resolution (CDR), 53
Comprehensive Legal Needs Study, 9
comprehensive mediation, 190
conciliation, 190
conciliation court, 52
confidentiality, 191
    as core principle in mediation, 35
    benefit of, 36–37
    books and articles, 310
    conflicting public policies and, 39–40
    exceptions to, 40
    of court-annexed mediation, 48–49
    practice tips, 41–42
    settlement agreements and, 40–41
    sources of rules, 38
confidential mini-evaluation (CME), 166–167, 191
conflict management coaching, 67
conflict prevention
    arbitration, 168–169
    binding adjudication, 168–169
    confidential mini-evaluation, 166–167
    drafting future dispute resolution clauses, 163–164
    formal evaluation report, 168
    in-person meeting, 164–165
    non-litigation calendar, 176
    practice tips, 176–177
    preventive legal wellness checkups, 173–174
    preventive mediation, 171–172
    private judges in, 169–170
    required mediation, 164
    written notice of dispute, 164
conjoint sessions, 191
consensus building, 191
consumerism, 2–3
control freak, 66
convening organizations, 197
Coogler, O.J., 4
Cook County Circuit Court, 47
Cooper), 163
cooperation, 181, 182
cooperative law procedures, factors affecting appropriateness of, 237
Cooper, James M., 163
co-parenting coach, 91–92
costs
    of divorce, 8
    of mediation, 109–110
    sample estimate of, 257
countertransference, 191
court-annexed mediation, 48–49
    confidentiality, 48–49
    finalizing agreements, 50–51
    individual vs. conjoint sessions, 50–51
    issues covered by, 52–53
    mandatory settlement conferences, 55–56
    participants, 49
    practice tips, 58–59
    refusal to participate, 51
    role of lawyers in, 54
    timing of, 49
court coach, lawyers as, 72
court pleadings, 1, 23, 72, 73, 84
court-referred mediation, 52–53
    complementary dispute resolution, 53
    malpractice protection for court mediators, 53–54
    mandatory settlement conferences, 55–56
    outside mediator, 53
    practice tips, 58–59
    role of lawyers in, 54
courtroom clerks, 5

coy communicator, 66
CPAs, 93, 117
creativity, 181, 183
cultural competence, 97

D
date of mediation, 102–103
Davidovich, Nathan, 4
decrees, 55, 149, 149–150, 164
deposition, 63, 64, 66, 110–111, 118, 127, 152
deposits, 8, 9, 110–111
diagnosing, phrase for miscommunication, 221
discrete task representation. *See* unbundling
Dispute Resolution
    Negotiation, Mediation, and other Processes(Goldberg, Sander & Rogers), 189, 191, 193
Dispute Resolution and Lawyers (Riskin & Westbrook), 145
dispute resolution manager
    advising clients about alternatives to litigation, 27–28
    as lawyer of record, 20
    definition of, 191
    ethical duty to advise about ADR, 20
    malpractice exposure, 25
    voluntary ADR pledges, 24–25
disqualification agreement, 83–84
    sample agreement, 271
divorce, 6
    agenda, 129–130
    books and articles, 313
    market share, 11–12
    teaching dynamics of, 70
    transaction costs of, 8
    types of, 66

divorce coach, 90
Divorce Corp. (movie), 7
divorce mediation
    couple interaction after, 214–215
    directive strategies in session or outside, 214
    disparity of spousal attachment, 215–216
    effect of intimate partner violence, 213
    fee-based, 214–215
    goals of divorce lawyers, 214
    impact of limited number of sessions, 213–214
    impact of mediation and process used, 214
    impact of timing of, 213–214
    informality and neutrality of, 215
    mediation process, 210–211
    outcome and satisfaction, 211
    sample agenda for, 261
    sources, 215–216
    standards for practice for, 197
    therapeutic mediation model, 215
    who chooses to mediate, 209–210
Doherty, William J., 149
domestic violence, 91
drafting
    agreements, 153–154
    aspirations, 155
    boilerplate, 155
    electronic drafts, 155
    future dispute resolution clauses, 163–164
dry erase board, 195
dual representation, xvii–xviii
duty to advise, 20

E
Early Neutral Evaluation (ENE), 191

economic divorce, 66
education, of clients, 305
electronic drafts, 155
e-mail, 155
emergency client, 66
emotional reframing, 140
empathizing, 222
empowerment, 181, 182
encouraging, 221
endorsement letter, 301
enforceable private separation agreement, 149
ethics, 15, 20, 21, 39, 72, 73. *See also* malpractice
excusing, phrase for miscommunication, 221
expenses, sample estimate of, 257
experts, 125–126

F
fairness, 181, 182
family businesses, preventive mediations in, xvii
family law organizations, 186
family law practice, 1–2
   economic pressures of operating, 9–10
family mediation
   standards for practice for, 197
   state regulation of, 206–207
family records, 36
favor client, 66
fees
   of mediators, xix–xx
   profitability and, 12
Feinberg, Rhonda, 191, 195
financial disclosure
   compiling client's financial information, 117–118

   confidentiality and, 36, 39
   required statutory forms in California, 285
financial planners, 89, 93, 117
financial professionals, 89, 93, 117
First Amendment, 36
first case, handling, xx
First Judicial Circuit of Florida, 47
Fisher, Roger, 189, 192, 195
flip chart, 192
Floied, Adam, 1
Folberg, H. Jay, 191
Folger, Joseph P., 173, 195
food and drink, 112
format, hybrid, 106–107
format of mediation, 104–105
   multisession, 105–106
   single-session, 104–106
framing, 192
fraud, 36
Frenkel, Douglas N., 129
Freshman, Clark, 180
Friedman, Gary J., 173
full-service representation, 62

G
Garfield, Franklin, 117
Garris v. Severson, 25
Georgia Ethical Consideration 7-5, 21
Getting to Yes (Fisher & Ury), 189, 192
Getting to Yes: Negotiating Agreements Without Giving In (Fisher, Ury, & Patton), 134, 136
giving answers, phrase for miscommunication, 221
Glassman, Frederick, 117
Golann, Dwight, 107
Goldberg, Steven, 189, 191, 193

Good Divorce, The (Ahrons), 16
Google, 3
Gornbein, Henry, 115
great expectations client, 66
Greene, James, 191, 195
Gregorio Haldeman Piazza, 110
Grillo, Trin, 193
ground rules, 132–133
Gyatso, Tenzin, 179

H
handouts, sample, 265
Hazard, Geoffrey, 152
high-net-worth clients, 37
high-profile clients, 37
hope, 181, 183
horizontal unbundling, 74
hotels, as site of mediation, 111
Howard v. Drapkin, 53
hybrid format, 106–107
Hyman, Michael B., 61

I
identity theft, 36
immunity, 7, 53, 145. *See also* malpractice
impartiality, 192
impasse, 192
income, xviii–xix
incompetent advice, 39
interest-based bargaining, 192
interest-based negotiations, 134–135
International Academy if Collaborative Professionals, 82
International Bar Association, 28
International Mediation (Fisher), 195
Internet, 2, 36, 99, 111, 305
intervention, 192
intimate partner violence, 213

J
judges
    in mandatory settlement conferences, 56–57
    private, 169–170
judging, phrase for miscommunication, 221
judgments, 20, 21, 25, 62–63
    confidential mini-evaluation and, 166, 168, 169
    financial disclosure and, 117, 119
    informed consent and, 115
    in-person meeting and, 164
    marital dissolution, 149–150, 157
    signing, 156
    stipulated, 148
judicial case management, 192
Judicial Council, 22–23

K
Kansas Bar Association, 21
Kichaven, Jeffrey G., 97
Kovach, Kimberlee, 191, 192, 193, 194
Kuroda, David, 90

L
labeling, phrase for miscommunication, 221
Lake Utopia Paper Ltd. v. Connelly Containers, Inc, 36
law office
    as classroom for client education, 305
    as site of mediation, 111
    set-up, xx
Lawyer as Counselor, The (Binder & Bergman), 28
lawyers. *See also* mediators
    as adviser, 116–117
    as coach, 64–65

lawyers (*continued*)
   as conflict management coach, 67
   as court coach, 72
   as negotiation coach, 69–70, 126–127
   at mediation table, 123
   benefits of mediation, 11
   betters lives for, 15–16
   control, 13–14
   dual representation by, xvii–xviii
   full-service representation, 62
   role at mediation session, 123–124
   role in court mediation, 54
   share of divorce market, 11–12
Lawyers as Counselors (Binder, Bergman & Price), 189
"leaning in" spouse, 149
"leaning out" spouse, 149
lecturing, phrase for miscommunication, 221
Legal Aid Foundation, 66
legal divorce, 66
legal wellness checkups, 173–174
LegalZoom, 5
library, for clients, 305
limited scope representation. *See* unbundling
LinkedIn, 3
litigation, 28–29
long-term separation, 149–150
Los Angeles Superior Court Letter, 23
Louis M. Brown and Forrest S. Mosten International Client Consultation Competition, 28
Lund, Mary, 173
Lurie, Paul, 25

M
malpractice, 25
   coverage, 8
   exposure, xviii, 13–14
   fear of, 72–73
   protection for court mediators, 53–54
mandatory mediation, 192
mandatory settlement conference (MSC), 193
mandatory settlement conferences, 55–56
   judge, 56–57
   vs. mediation, 57
manipulating, phrase for miscommunication, 221
Maricopa County, Arizona, 5
marital dissolution, court decree/judgment of, 150, 157
marital settlement agreements, 148, 149–150
McEwen, Craig, 275
med-arb, 193
mediation. *See also* alternative dispute resolution (ADR)
   agreement, 101–102
   commonly asked questions, xvii
   confidentiality. *See* confidentiality
   court-annexed, 48–49
   court-referred, 52–53
   definition of, 193
   factors affecting appropriateness of, 237
   format, 104–105
   getting started, xx
   key confidentiality cases in California, 217
   lawyer benefits of, 11
   letter from presiding judge endorsing, 301
   notes, 143
   preventive, 171–172, 194
   profit increase in, 12–13
   questions about, xx

sample estimate of expenses, 257
sample letter discussing risk of, 245
single-session, 194
training in, 184–185
transformative, 195
vs. mandatory settlement conferences, 57
Mediation Alternative (Grillo), 193
mediation brief, 193
mediation clause, 275
Mediation: Law Policy and Practice (Rogers & McEwen), 275
Mediation: Principles and Practice (Kovach), 191, 192, 193, 194
Mediation: Principles, Process, and Practice (Boulle), 112
Mediation Process, The (Moore), 189, 190, 192
mediation, setting up
   approving the mediation agreement, 101–102
   briefs, 108–109
   costs, 109–110
   designing the process, 101–102
   food and drink, 112
   orientation with mediator, 102–103
   practice tips, 113
   preliminary private sessions, 106–108
   selecting the mediator, 97–98
   setting the date, 102–103
   site of mediation, 111–112
   telephone conference call, 102–103
mediation work bill, 53
mediators. *See also* lawyers
   as third-party neutral, xviii
   books and articles, 310
   family law litigation veterans as, 98
   fees, xix–xx
   letting other spouse/counsel nominate, 99–100
   malpractice protection for, 53–54
   negotiating with, 140–141
   nominating process, 99–100
   orientation with, 102–103
   payment of, 109–110
   proposals, 141
   reasons for hiring, xvii–xviii
   retired judicial officers as, 98
   sample contract, 247
   selecting, 97–98
   unqualified, xviii
Meirding, Nina, 307
memorandum, 147–148, 153
Menkel-Meadow, Carrie, 126, 195
mindfulness, 180–181
Model Standards of Practice for Family and Divorce Mediation, 197
Moore, Christopher, 189, 190, 192
Mosten Mediation Centers, 307
multisession format, 105–106, 112
multisession mediation, 193

N

National Center for State Courts, 38
National Conference of Commissioners on Uniform State Laws, 35
National Council of Dispute Resolution Organizations (NCDRO), 197
National Standards for Court Connected Dispute Resolution Programs, 206–207
National Standards of Court Connected Mediation Programs, 47, 51, 52
negligence, xviii, 7, 8–9, 25, 43, 152
negotiation
   books and articles, 310–311
   interest-based, 134–135

with mediators, 140–141
negotiation coach, 69–70, 126–127
New Zealand, 54
Nolo, 5
non-enforceable private separation agreement, 149
nonenforceable terms, 155
nonlawyer providers, 7–8
non-litigation calendar, 176
nonpayment, 12
normalcy, 137
normalizing, 222
notebook contents, 120
Notice of Limited Scope Appearance (FL-950), 73

O
O'Donnell v. Pennsylvania Department of Corrections, 51
office
    as classroom for client education, 305
    as site of mediation, 111
    set-up, xx
one issue mediation, 193
online attorney evaluation sites, 3
open questioning, 221
options, 181, 183
ordering, phrase for miscommunication, 221
outfamilywizard.com (website), 66
overcharging, xix–xx

P
paralawyer client, 66
paralegal, 3, 5, 7
parental divorce, 66
payment methods, 110–111
peacemaker
    collaboration with other professionals, 185
    core values, 181
    definition of, 179
    family law organizations and, 186
    honoring colleagues, 185–186
    improving and expanding practice, 186–187
    mindfulness, 180–181
    peacemaking in daily lawyering work, 184–185
    prevention of future conflict, 184–185
    training in mediation and collaborative law, 184–185
peacemaking, 179, 181, 182, 184–185
    books and articles, 312
PEACE Program, 52
pension specialists, 93
personal information, disclosure of, 36
Petit and Martin, 8
Philips, John R., 116
positional bargaining, 193
post-marital agreement, 149
power imbalance, 193
Practice of Mediation, The: A Video-Integrated Text (Frenkel & Stark), 129
preaching, phrase for miscommunication, 221
preliminary joint session, 194
preliminary private sessions, 106–108
premarital agreements, preventive mediations in, xvii
Press, Sharon, 25
preventive law, books and articles, 312
preventive legal wellness checkups, 173–174
preventive mediation, 171–172, 194
Price, Susan, 189

primary dispute resolution (PDR), 19
principled client, 66
private judges, 169–170
private sessions, preliminary, 106–108
process facilitator, 90
professional articles and research, 138
profits, increasing, 12–13
Promise of Mediation, The (Bush & Folger), 195
pro se movement, 5–6
prying, phrase for miscommunication, 221

Q

questions, commonly asked, xvii, xviii
    dual representation, xvii–xviii
    fees, xix–xx
    first case, handling, xx
    income effect, xviii–xix
    legal advice, xx
    malpractice exposure, xviii
    negligent referral, xviii
    office set-up, xx
    reasons for hiring mediator, xvii–xviii
    settlement of cases, xix–xx
    training, xix

R

rational problem solving, 181, 183
reality testing, 194
reconciliation, 149, 179, 181, 183
reconciliation agreement, 149
red flag rule, 133
reframing, 194, 222
repeat business, 12
research, in divorce mediation, 138
responding, 222
retainers, 12
Riskin, Leonard L., 145, 180

Rogers, Nancy, 189, 191, 193, 275
Rosenberg, Joshua, 191
Rothchild, Toby, 66
Rules of Professional Liability, 20–21
Russell, Newton, 22

S

Sander, Frank, 189, 191, 193
San Mateo County, court endorsement of ADR in, 297
satisfaction, 181, 183
Schepard, Andrew, 52
scripting, 73
self-help centers, 6
settlement agreements. *See* agreements
settlement weeks, 194
Sharing a Mediator's Power: Effective Advocacy in Settlement (Golann), 107, 124
Shephard, Andrew, 21
signatures, 156–157
simulated coaching, 194
single-session format, 104–106, 112
single-session mediation, 194
site of mediation, 111–112
social media, 3
Social Security numbers, 36
soliciting, 222
solvability, 137
Split (video), 91
spousal divorce, 66
Stark, James H., 129
stipulated judgments, 148
Stone, Vicki, 97
stress, 9
Structured Mediation in Divorce Settlement (Coogler), 4
summarizing, 221
summary letter of mediation sessions, 194

summary letters, 147–148
Super Lawyers, 3

T

Taberer v. Armstrong World Industries, 51
Tao of Negotiations, The (Edelman), 106–108
tax lawyers, 93
telephone conference call, 102–103
temporary physical separation, 149
Theobald, Robert, 170
threatening, phrase for miscommunication, 221
training, xix
transference, 195
transformation, 181, 183
transformative mediation, 195
trust, 184
trust building, 195

U

unbundling
　and lawyer fear of malpractice, 72–73
　barriers to, 72–73
　books and articles, 311
　client types and, 66
　defined, 63
　definition of, 195
　divorce and, 11
　horizontal, 74
　lawyer as, 66
　lawyer as coach, 64–65
　lawyer as conflict management coach, 67
　lawyer as negotiation coach, 69–70
　notice of limited scope representation, 233
　notice of limited scope role and, 73–74
　practice tips, 78
　use in mediation room, 76
　use outside mediation room, 74–75
　vertical, 74
　vs. full-service representation, 68
Uniform Collaborative Act (2010), 21
Uniform Mediation Act (UMA), 35–36, 38, 40–41
unqualified mediator, xviii
uptoparents.org (website), 66, 91, 305
Ury, William, 189, 192

V

validating, 222
vertical unbundling, 74
voluntary ADR pledges, 24–25

W

Walsh, Patrick, 25
Westbrook, James E., 145
white board, 195
written notice of dispute, 164

Y

Yeend, Nancy Neal, 21
Your Divorce Deposition (video), 66

Z

zero-sum game, 195